THE ICE

THE ICE

A Journey to Antarctica

Stephen J. Pyne

Arlington Books
King Street, St. James's
London S.W.1.

THE ICE

First published in the United States of America
this edition published 1987 by
Arlington Books (Publishers) Ltd
15-17 King Street, St. James's
London SW1

© *University of Iowa 1986*

Printed and bound by
Biddles Ltd, Guildford

'The End of the World' by Archibald MacLeish,
New and Collected Poems 1917–1976
© *Archibald MacLeish 1976*
Reproduced by permission of
Houghton Miffin Co.

British Library Cataloguing in Publication Data

Pyne, Stephen J.
The ice : a journey to Antarctica.
1. Geology — Antarctic
I. Title
559.8'9   QE350

ISBN 0–85140–709–9

To Sonja,
who saw the future where I
saw only the past

Contents

Prologue   The Berg / 1

Chapter 1   The Pack / 25

Chapter 2   No Middle Way:
The Exploration of Antarctica / 65

Chapter 3   The Shelf / 117

Chapter 4   Heart of Whiteness:
The Literature and Art of Antarctica / 149

Chapter 5   The Glacier / 207

Chapter 6   Earth and Ice:
The Earth Sciences in Antarctica / 241

Chapter 7   The Sheet / 289

Chapter 8   The Cold Peace:
The Geopolitics of Antarctica / 323

Epilogue   The Source / 379

Afterword / 389

Notes / 393

Sources / 403

Index / 413

. . . *there was another thought, or rather vague, nameless horror concerning him, which at times by its intensity completely overpowered all the rest; and yet so mystical and well nigh ineffable was it, that I almost despair of putting it in a comprehensible form. It was the whiteness of the whale that above all things appalled me. But how can I hope to explain myself here; and yet, in some dim, random way, explain myself I must, else all these chapters might be naught. . . .*

Is it by its indefiniteness it shadows forth the heartless voids and immensities of the universe, and thus stabs us from behind with the thought of annihilation, when beholding the white depths of the milky way? Or is it, that as in essence whiteness is not so much a color as the visible absence of color, and at the same time the concrete of all colors; is it for these reasons that there is such a dumb blankness, full of meaning, in a wide landscape of snows—a colorless, all-color of atheism from which we shrink? . . . and when we proceed further, and consider that the mystical cosmetic which produces every one of her hues, the great principle of light, for ever remains white or colorless in itself, and if operating without medium upon matter, would touch all objects . . . with its own blank tinge—pondering all this, the palsied universe lies before us a leper; and like wilful travellers in Lapland, who refuse to wear colored and coloring glasses upon their eyes, so the wretched infidel gazes himself blind at the monumental white shroud that wraps all the prospect around him. And of all these things the Albino whale was the symbol. Wonder ye then at the fiery hunt?

—Herman Melville, *Moby-Dick* (1851)

Prologue. The Berg

And now there came both mist and snow,
And it grew wondrous cold:
And ice, mast-high, came floating by,
As green as emerald.

The ice was here, the ice was there,
The ice was all around:
It cracked and growled, and roared and
howled,
Like noises in a swound!

> —Samuel T. Coleridge,
> *The Rime of the Ancient Mariner* (1798)

. . . the Southern half of the horizon was en-
lightened by the reflected rays of the Ice to
considerable height. The Clouds near the
horizon were of a perfect Snow whiteness and
were difficult to be distinguished from the Ice
hills whose lofty summits reached the Clouds.
The Northern edge of this immense Ice field
was composed of loose or broken ice so close
packed together that nothing could enter it
. . . we counted Ninety Seven Ice Hills or
Mountains, many of them vastly large. . . . It
was indeed my opinion as well as the opinion
of most on board, that this Ice extended quite
to the Pole or perhaps joins some land, to
which it had been fixed from the
creation. . . .

> —Capt. James Cook, *Journals, Voyage of the*
> *Resolution and Adventure* (1774)

It appears out of the fog and low clouds, like a white comet in the twilight.

To enter Greater Antarctica is to be drawn into a slow maelstrom of ice. Ice is the beginning of Antarctica and ice is its end. As one moves from perimeter to interior, the proportion of ice relentlessly increases. Ice creates more ice, and ice defines ice. Everything else is suppressed. This is a world derived from a single substance, water, in a single crystalline state, snow, transformed into a lithosphere composed of a single mineral, ice. This is earthscape transfigured into icescape. Here is a world informed by ice: ice that welds together a continent: ice on such a scale that it shapes and defines itself: ice that is both substance and style: ice that is both landscape and allegory. The berg is a microcosm of this world. It is the first and, paradoxically, the most complex materialization of The Ice. It is a fragment torn loose from the bottom of the globe, the icy underworld of the Earth; from the ends of the world, its past and future; from the Earth's polar source, the end that makes possible the means. The berg is both substance and symbol. "Everything is in it," as Conrad wrote of the human mind, "all the past as well as all the future." The journey of the ice from core to margin, from polar plateau to open sea, narrates an allegory of mind and matter.

The great berg spins in a slow, counterclockwise gyre.

It is only another of a series of rotations that have characterized the berg's fantastic journey. The continental plates that comprise the land form a lithospheric mosaic and spin with the infinitesimal patience of geologic time; the Southern Ocean courses around them, the gyre of the circumpolar current; storm cells swirl over the ocean, epicycles of the polar vortex; sea ice floes, like a belt of asteroids, circle endlessly, a life cycle of freezing and melting; icebergs, large and small, circle like comets around their peculiar icy sun. Superimposed over all these motions, the Earth itself rotates around its pole and revolves around the Sun. The ice terranes ring the core like concentric crystalline spheres. The ice mass that became the berg has passed from ice dome to sheet ice to glacier ice to shelf ice to pack ice to the diminutions of the bergs, cycle by cycle, like the gears of an ice orrery. The large bergs fragment into smaller bergs, the small bergs into bergy bits, the bits into growlers, the growlers into brash ice, the brash into chips and meltwater. With each outward frontier the pace of activity quickens.

Ice informs the geophysics and geography of Antarctica. It connects land to land, land to sea, sea to air, air to land, ice to ice. The Antarctic atmosphere consists of ice clouds and ice vapor. The hydrosphere exists as ice rivers and ice seas. The lithosphere is composed of ice plateaus and ice mountains. Even those features not completely saturated with ice are vastly reduced. The atmosphere is much thinner at the poles than elsewhere, in part because of the great height of the polar ice sheet. The hydrosphere is charged with bergs and coated with ice floes; during the polar night, its cover of sea ice effectively doubles the total ice field of Antarctica. The lithosphere is little more than a matrix for ice. Less than 3 percent of Antarctica consists of exposed rock, and the rock is profoundly influenced by periglacial processes, an indirect manifestation of ice.

Out of simple ice crystals is constructed a vast hierarchy of ice masses, ice terranes, and ice structures. These higher-order ice forms collectively compose the entire continent: *the icebergs*: tabular bergs, glacier bergs, ice islands, bergy bits, growlers, brash ice, white ice, blue ice, green ice, dirty ice; *the sea ices*: pack ice, ice floes, ice rinds, ice hummocks, ice ridges, ice flowers, ice stalactites, pancake ice, frazil ice, grease ice, congelation ice, infiltration ice, undersea ice, vuggy ice, new ice, old ice, brown ice, rotten ice; *the coastal ices*: fast ice, shore ice, glacial-ice tongues, ice piedmonts, ice fringes, ice cakes, ice foots, ice fronts, ice walls, floating ice, grounded ice, anchor ice, rime ice, ice ports, ice shelves, ice rises, ice bastions, ice haycocks, ice lobes, ice streams; *the mountain ices*: glacial ice, valley glaciers, cirque glaciers, piedmont glaciers, ice fjords, ice layers, ice pipes, ice falls, ice folds, ice faults, ice pinnacles, ice lenses, ice aprons, ice falls, ice fronts, ice slush; *the ground ices*: ice wedges, ice veins, permafrost; *the polar plateau ices*: ice sheets, ice caps, ice domes, ice streams, ice divides, ice saddles, ice rumples; *the atmospheric ices*: ice grains, ice crystals, ice dust, pencil ice, plate ice, bullet ice. The ice field is organized into a series of roughly concentric ice terranes, like the ordered rings comprising the hierarchy of Dante's cosmology.

It is not merely the variety of ice that is overwhelming: the magnitude of ice is no less staggering. The Earth, the fabled water planet, is also an ice planet. More than 10 percent of the

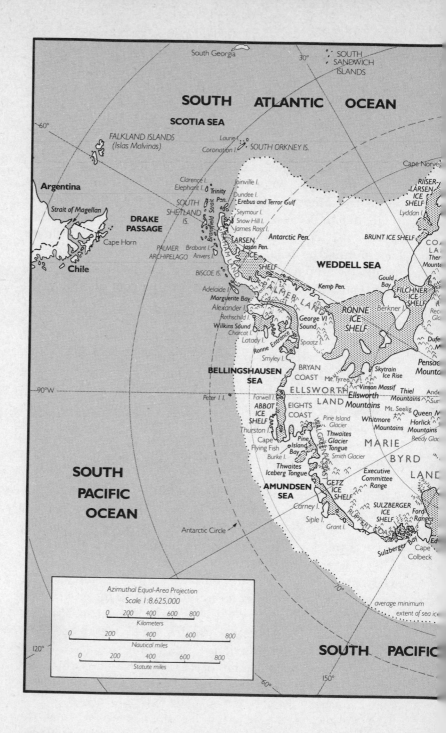

Antarctica, showing major physiographic provinces. Redrawn, original
courtesy National Science Foundation.

INDIAN
OCEAN

FIMBUL ICE SHELF

Antarctic Circle

PRINCESS RAGNHILD COAST
Riiser-Larsen Pen.
Lützow-Holm Bay
Cape Ann
PRINCE OLAV COAST
ENDERBY LAND
Cape Boothby

Mühlig-Hofmann Mountains
Wohlthat Mountains
Isachsen Mt.
Sør Rondane Mountains
Kirwan Escarpment
Belgica Mountains
Queen Fabiola Mountains
Shirase Glacier

QUEEN MAUD LAND

MAC. ROBERTSON LAND
Prince Charles Mountains
Mt. Menzies
Cape Darnley
MacKenzie Bay
AMERY ICE SHELF
Prydz Bay
WEST ICE SHELF

Lambert Glacier
American Highland
INGRID CHRISTENSEN COAST
Gaussberg

South Pole
DAVIS SEA
Drygalski I.
SHACKLETON ICE SHELF

Transantarctic Mountains

QUEEN MARY COAST
Mill I.
Bowman I.
Bunger Hills
KNOX COAST

South Geomagnetic Pole

Nilsen Plateau
Dominion Range
Beardmore Glacier
Queen Elizabeth Range
Churchill Mountains
Mt. Marshall
Byrd Glacier

ROSS ICE SHELF

Cook Mountains
Mulock Glacier
Mt. Lister
Dry Valleys

Dome C

WILKES LAND

Totten Glacier
Cape Poinsett
SABRINA COAST
VOYEYKOV ICE SHELF

Prince Albert Mountains
David Glacier
McMurdo Sound
Drygalski Ice Tongue
Coulman I.

ROSS SEA

Porpoise Bay

Admiralty Mountains
Rennick Glacier
Mertz Glacier
GEORGE V COAST
ADÉLIE COAST
Dibble Iceberg Tongue
South Magnetic Pole (1980)

Cape Adare
OATES COAST
COOK ICE SHELF

INDIAN OCEAN

OCEAN

average minimum extent of sea ice

BALLENY IS.
Sturge I.
Buckle I.
Young I.
Scott I.

INDIAN OCEAN

terrestrial Earth now lies under ice, with another 14 percent affected by periglacial environments and permafrost. Some 7 percent of the world ocean is covered by sea ice, and at any minute nearly 25 percent of the world ocean is affected by ice, especially icebergs. The vast proportion of the bergs inhabit the Southern Ocean, corralled by the Antarctic convergence. Of the Earth's cryosphere, 99 percent is glacial ice, and 96 percent of that—over 60 percent of the world's freshwater reserves—is in Antarctica. Within past geologic eras, the proportion of ice on the Earth has grown enormously. During the last glaciation in the Pleistocene, ice extended over 30 percent of the planet's land surface and affected 50 percent of the world ocean. The immensity of the ice sheet even today is sufficient to deform the entire planet, so depressing the south polar region as to make the globe slightly pear-shaped.

The Ice is, in turn, a constituent of an ice regime broadcast throughout the solar system. Pluto is an entire ice planet; the satellites of the outer planets are ice moons. On Mars and Earth, there are polar ice sheets; on some asteroids and amid the rings of Saturn, ice debris; and in the form of comets, interplanetary icebergs from the Oort cloud. The Earth's cryosphere joins it to other worlds and other times—to the outer solar system and to vanished geologic pasts. It is a white warp in space and time. That the Earth's ice consists not of ammonia or carbon dioxide or methane but of water, that it is crystalline rather than amorphous, and that the planet's temperature range falls within the triple point of water account for the Earth's uniqueness, and dynamism, as a member of the ice cosmos.

The berg contains a record of all this. Its travels have a mythic quality, a retrograde journey out of an underworld. It is a voyage that joins microcosm to macrocosm, that builds from a single substance—ice crystals—a vast, almost unbounded continent. Yet a descent to this underworld—from the ice-induced fog that shrouds the continent to the unblinking emptiness that commands its center—does not lead to more splendid scenes, as a trip through the gorge of the Grand Canyon does, or to richer displays of life, as a voyage to the interior of the Amazon does, or to more opulent civilizations, living or dead, as the excavation of Egypt's Valley of the Kings or the cities of Troy does, or to greater knowledge, as the ultimately moral journeys of Odysseus, Aeneas, Dante, even Marlowe do. It leads only to more ice. Almost everything is there because almost nothing is there.

Antarctica is the Earth's great sink, not only for water and
heat but for information. Between core and margin there exist
powerful gradients of energy and information. These gradients
measure the alienness of The Ice as a geographic and cultural
entity. The Ice is profoundly passive: it does not give, it takes.
The Ice is a study in reductionism. Toward the interior everything is simplifed. The Ice absorbs and, an imperfect mirror, its
ineffable whiteness reflects back what remains. Toward the perimeter, ice becomes more complex, its shapes multiply, and its
motions accelerate. The ephemeral sample, the berg, is more interesting than the invariant whole, the plateau. The extraordinary isolation of Antarctica is not merely geophysical but metaphysical. Cultural understanding and assimilation demand
more than the power to overcome the energy gradient that surrounds The Ice: they demand the capacity and desire to overcome the information gradient. Of all the ice masses in Greater
Antarctica the berg is the most varied, the most informative,
and the most accessible. The assimilation of The Ice begins
with the assimilation of the iceberg.

The great berg hesitates.
A cloud passes before the sun. The berg glows blue amid a tar-
black sea. Then almost imperceptibly it retreats, drawn back
into the fog and pack ice, back into the first of the great veils of
The Ice.

Glaciology of the Berg

The berg synopsizes the natural history of Antarctic ice. The
whole ice field derives from the recrystallization and rearrangement of a single substance, water, in a single state, the solid,
under the influence of a single force, gravity. Its geology contains virtually an entire rock cycle based on a solitary mineral,
ice. Its larger geography is organized into roughly concentric
ice terranes: the berg, the pack, the shelf, the glacier, the sheet,
and the source domes. Within its ice the berg contains a frozen
record of these terranes and a history of movement through
them. Thus the berg is by far the most complex ice mass, and its
dazzling whiteness masks a dense fabric of acquired ices and
shapes—of old materials, now reworked into new stuff; of old
shapes, now subjected to new internal stresses and external

sculpturings; of old motions, now propelled into new movements; of inherited appearances, now brilliantly illuminated by
the contrasts of the berg's new surroundings. Like the world-
encompassing summas of medieval philosophy, in which a
single principle of logic could endlessly ramify a limited body
of texts, the berg evolves out of ice a grand synthesis of structure upon structure.

The process begins with the simple fall of ice crystals. In the
interior of the continent, this involves little more than the settling of ice dust consisting of tiny prisms. Outward, along the
coast, aggregates of prisms form snowflakes. The piling of crystal upon crystal leads to a process of ice lithification and metamorphosis. A stratigraphy of snow develops. Loose debris is
transformed into structured layers. As snow builds up, compression and sintering round off individual crystals and reorganize
the strata into a texture of toughened ice grains saturated with
irregularly shaped bubbles of trapped air. Under further heat
and pressure, the ice recrystallizes into ice slates, ice schists, and
ice gneisses. Some air is squeezed out, other bubbles reshape
into tiny globes, and swaths of bubbles form flow bands of white
ice. Relentlessly, the density increases and firn becomes glacial
ice—blue, hard, translucent. The speed of this metamorphosis
varies with temperature and the thickness of the superimposed
snow, both of which increase toward the perimeter of the ice
field. With a density about one-third that of average rock and
about 90 percent that of seawater, glacial ice floats. The heavy
snowfall along the coast increases the proportion of snow and
firn to glacial ice, with the result that Antarctic bergs can be
relatively buoyant.

But there is more to the berg than its source ice. Chemically,
Antarctic ice is the purest form of water on the planet. Yet from
the beginning the ice fabric incorporates air, and glacial ice
will typically show bands of blue ice and milky white bubbles.
Other snows and other impurities will be acquired by the ice
during its journey to the sea. Additional terrestrial dusts, nitrates, radioactive fallout, and extraterrestrial particulates all
become embedded into the ice, often as nuclei for precipitants.
Coastal glaciers may acquire rocky debris from adjacent mountains and eroding beds, while mountain glaciers may experience strong deformations that reconstitute their inherited ices,
perhaps purging them of trapped air. Ice shelves pick up saline
ice, which is frozen into bottom crevasses. The freezing of this

saline ice can, in turn, capture organic material for the general
ice matrix. Brine infiltrates firn and snow—blown as sea spray,
insinuating along the permeability boundaries that segregate
firn from glacial ice, and rising through vertical fissures in the
glacial ice. Blue ice and white ice may be splotched with black
(dirty) ice from morainal debris, or with green ice embedded
within the ice fabric. The origin of the jade-green ice is uncertain. Green ice includes a mixture of contaminants, especially particulate protein-nitrogen, but its peculiar appearance
seems to derive from a pure, bubble-free ice fabric that apparently originates in the vigorous shear zones found in mountain
glaciers. This odd ice—like bottles wrapped in snow—may represent the optical effect of light on a highly oriented, clear ice.

The formation of the berg profoundly alters the composition
of the ice. Liberated, the berg adds new materials, loses old
ones, and rearranges its inherited constituents. More sea spray
is absorbed and more brine infiltrates along the firn boundary.
Additional saline ice may be acquired when the berg pauses in
its journey, frozen amidst shore and fast ice. While the berg is at
sea additional snow is added to the top, although more is also
melted. This surface melting—the result of greater sunlight and
higher ambient temperatures away from the ice field—perco-
lates into the substratum and, in some cases, collects into snow
swamps that drain off the sides of the berg. Meltwater percolation profoundly alters the internal ice structure, and seepage
passes through the porous firn until it reaches a low enough
temperature to refreeze. This change of state releases heat to the
surrounding ice, with the result that the internal temperature of
the iceberg rises to 6 degrees C. or higher. The recrystallized ice
rearranges the stratigraphy of the inherited ice and adds new ice
inclusions. This process of heat transfer by percolating meltwater—much more effective than heat conduction through
ice—leads to rapid decay, a thermal rot. The disintegration
of glacial ice releases the nitrates bound within the ice. The
resulting nutrient bloom around the berg attracts algae and
plankton. Other organisms are drawn to these primary producers, and a small marine biosphere encircles the berg, just as,
for similar reasons, a marine biosphere encircles Antarctica.

Icebergs are fundamental to the energy budget and hydrologic cycle of the ice field—and of the Earth. Only a minuscule
portion of Antarctic snow melts, and that is restricted to intermittent streams of glacial meltwater confined to rocky oases. A

much greater proportion of snow sublimates, vaporized by katabatic winds warming as they pour down from the polar plateau.
Some snow is blown to sea by powerful offshore winds. But virtually all the ice on the continent ablates in the form of icebergs, calved from vast ice shelves and isolated outlet glaciers
—the Amazons and Mississippis of Antarctica. The discharge of
nutrients, water, and eroded earth from Antarctica is thus dissi-
pated around the Southern Ocean by wandering icebergs. In
places the deposition of debris by icebergs, "drift," is considerable. Off the coast of South Africa more than a meter of glacial
till has accumulated, evidently the product of iceberg rafting
from Antarctica during the past glaciation. Similarly, icebergs
affect the distribution of fresh waters around the Southern
Ocean. Instead of entering the sea in relatively concentrated
streams, there is a slow leaching of fresh water from a wandering mosaic of thaw-points. Since major melting does not occur
until the berg leaves the near-shore environment, and usually
not until the pack ice is breached, discharge by icebergs is diffuse and far-flung. This, in turn, affects the salinity, density
profile, and thermodynamics of the outer Southern Ocean. It
requires almost as much energy to melt ice as to raise the temperature of the resulting water to its boiling point. This energy
must come from the sea.

Similarly, the amount of water and heat drained into the Antarctic sink has global consequences. The Ice is the cold core of
the planet. The amount of precipitation that falls on Antarctica
is small by tropical standards, and only in selected areas does it
approach the rates typical of temperate zones. The interior is a
cold desert, the most total desert on Earth. But the continent is
so huge and its storage capacity so enormous that the quantity
of fresh water it contains dominates the global water budget.
Over 60 percent of the world's fresh water resides in the ice of
Antarctica, an amount equivalent to sixty years of global precipitation or forty-six thousand years of flow by the Mississippi
River. Its fresh water is the largest and most accessible of Antarctica's mineral resources, and it is all discharged in quantum
bits, as bergs.

Annually, Antarctica produces some five thousand bergs,
about 6.5 times the production of the Arctic. The average size of
Antarctic bergs is much greater than that of Arctic bergs, each
Antarctic berg averaging about one million tons of pure fresh
water. Total production equals nearly 690 cubic kilometers of

ice. Unlike Greenland bergs, calving off fast-moving glaciers, Antarctic bergs tend to calve from ice shelves or from the tongues of outlet glaciers protruding into the sea. The Greenland bergs, accordingly, resemble small peaks, while the Antarctic bergs resemble great tabular plateaus. On the average, Antarctic bergs are 100–400 meters long, with 12–40 meters of exposed freeboard. The ratio of length to width varies between 1:1 and 4:1, with an average of 1.6:1. Similarly, the ratio of sail to keel, or the exposed freeboard to the submerged stratum, varies widely. For freshly calved tabular bergs, the ratio is 1:10. The actual value will depend on the source and the character of the ablation process—in particular, the thickness of the firn layer and the vitality of fresh snowfalls, and the relative vigor of bottom melting compared to surface erosion. For domed bergs, the ratio is closer to 1:6; for blocky bergs, 1:4; for drydock bergs, with their much-eroded spindly pinnacles, 1:2.5. Both ratios—of sail to keel and length to width—are influential in determining how responsive the berg is to wind and wave, how it erodes, and how likely it is to overturn.

Antarctic bergs may reach immense sizes. One sighted in 1927 was reported as 160 kilometers long, with a freeboard height of 35 meters. Others have been measured at 140 x 60 kilometers, 100 x 70 kilometers, and 100 x 43 kilometers. The greatest, tracked in 1965, was 140 kilometers long and featured a surface area of 7,000 square kilometers. One colossal berg, the Trolltunga, began as a severed ice tongue roughly the size of Belgium. The larger bergs cluster near the shore, where they contribute to a chilling of air and sea and to the production of an insulating fog, but once beyond the pack they risk rapid disintegration. In fact, some sort of fragmentation may be necessary to move a berg through the pack. Most bergs will not survive two months, or less than a single summer season, in the open sea.

The berg is a record of Antarctic ice shapes no less than of ice substances. Its structural cryology chronicles ice deformation, much as its stratigraphy chronicles ice deposition. Berg structure is internal as well as external: it records ice deformations and ice movements experienced while the ice mass existed within the confines of the ice field, and it documents the free-floating behavior of the ice mass in its reincarnation as a berg. Together these two forms of movement—internal flow and external displacement—generate a hierarchy of shapes, extending from the microcosm of ice crystals to the macrocosm of ice sheets. As ice masses respond to new stress fields, their shapes reform. The shape of the berg itself is only a fleeting phase in this history.

The berg, nonetheless, displays by far the greatest variety of structures. On the microscopic level, there are ice fabrics—mosaics of ice crystals and inclusions like air—that hark back to the origin of the ice mass and that all glacial ices exhibit. As more snow accumulates and as the entire ice matrix flows, the fabrics constantly reform, recrystallize, and reorganize. On a larger scale, other structures become visible—ice fissures and ice faults, crevasses torn by moving ice and icequake; ice strata, the product of the inexorable compression that transforms snow into firn, firn into ice, and glacial ice into metamorphic ice schists and ice gneisses; ice folds, the buckling of ice as it meets earth or more ice; long-wave flexures of ice, undulations of large-scale ice bodies. On the macroscopic level, structures are defined as the ice mass encounters distinct boundaries to its spread—sea, land, other ice. Ice masses become ice terranes. Some of these structures will vanish as new stresses reshape the ice mass. Some will persist for a time, surviving as ghostly sutures or relic fabrics. Some—those that lead to the rupture which finally releases the ice mass from its ice field—will shape the iceberg.

The berg takes its gross shape from the properties of the ice shelf or ice tongue from which it derived and the deformations that liberated it as a distinct ice mass from those terranes. The floating ice sheets come under the influence of waves, tides, and the internal flow that results from thinning as land-based ice spreads out across the sea. Infinitesimal cracks preserved in the ice fabric propagate, and large inherited fissures persist. New stresses, particularly near the exposed terminus, develop into new fractures. Seawater etches along crystal boundaries, and brine infiltration along cracks and within the firn lowers the strength of the ice dramatically. The processes involved may be complex and competitive, but the composite mechanical effects of wind, tide, and wave cause exposed ice to bend and fracture, fatigue and fail. The calved ice mass becomes an iceberg.

The iceberg accelerates the motions, and the shaping, of its ice terrane. The ice mass is subjected to a new range of external stresses from wind and wave, as well as new internal stresses resulting from its recent liberation from a confining ice field. Its

inherited structures are quickly reworked. Previously, the ice
mass slowly accumulated or, at the least, it was conserved.
Changes in form resulted from the rearrangement of ice. Now
the ice is shed. Processes other than those characteristic of confining ice begin to operate, and the berg breaks up and melts.
The entire mass, not only its internal fabric, is restructured.
The shapes become more visible and vastly more exotic, the rate
of change accelerates, and the ice reverts to water. The most interesting period in the ice shaping is also the most transient. In
Antarctica, ice begets ice. The ice—its composition, shape,
movements—exists because of its informing ice field. When the
ice field breaks up, the ice mass loses its identity as ice.

The process of disintegration is both mechanical and thermal.
Each aids the other. Melting begins while the ice mass remains
within an ice shelf or glacial tongue. Some melting scours the
exposed ice front, some scours the top, and some scours the
floating bottom. Along the bottom there will be both melting
and freezing. But if the freezing predominates before the ice
mass calves, it will soon be superseded by melting once the berg
takes to sea. Top melting will result in the percolation of meltwater through the porous firn. Side melting, especially active
when accompanied by waves, carves out the flanks, and the
berg acquires a scalloped texture. Small convective cells eat
away at the sides; the released fresh water and air bubbles form
a turbulent boundary layer along both ice and seawater and rise
through a series of thermal terraces. These carved subsurface
facets expose yet more ice surfaces and encourage still faster
melting. If sufficient meltwaters accumulate on the top, they
may flow down the sides to give the berg a fluted appearance.
But the roughened bottom, gouged by large crevasses, disintegrates most rapidly. The fissures widen and rise; the berg thins,
making it more susceptible to wave-induced flexing; and the
berg itself calves.

Of the two processes, melting ultimately triumphs over mechanical disintegration. Melting prepares the ice mass for ruptures, large and small, and unlike breakage it reduces the volume of the ice. Melting is the final solution: ice is no longer
reformed into ice but transformed into water, a change of state
that will remove it from the ice field completely. Yet the mechanical processes assist melting by increasing the proportion
of the total ice that is exposed to thermal activity. Some ice
spalls off the sides. Some is mechanically eroded by waves—

melting into exposed pinnacles that quickly rot and into terraces that, as overhanging cliffs, soon fail and drop. The thinning of the berg encourages rupture by allowing the ice mass to flex amidst long ocean swells. Some disintegration follows from simple collision, especially where a grounded berg is struck by a free-floating one. Grounded bergs, in fact, are a prominent source of brash ice. Differential heating—the sharp contrast between cold ice and warmer sea—can lead to thermal spalling, with chunks and slabs of ice breaking free like exfoliating granite and sandstone. The permeability boundary between firn and glacial ice, a zone of potential penetration by brine, may lead to the large-scale slumping of firn, a process of mass wasting.

The marks of the strain that produced calving will persist for a time, although fissures will slowly heal shut, and some of the fractures may become zones of weakness for further mechanical disintegration as the berg experiences a new set of stresses. The intensity of this activity will vary with the size of the berg, and it will be reflected in the berg's shape. Gigantic bergs—with dimensions measured by tens of kilometers—will not undergo much internal change. Only the edges of the berg will be affected. Smaller bergs, with higher proportions of newly exposed edges, will show proportionately greater change. No longer subjected to a high confining pressure and no longer protected by an enveloping shield of ice, the sides of the ice mass will ablate rapidly.

The berg's motions, too, are a curious amalgamation of its history and its present state. All the movements that have characterized the ice mass on its journey are present. Past motions are preserved in the internal ice fabric. Current motions are revealed by the gross movement of the berg, as many former stresses vanish and new stresses appear. Its free-floating motions give the berg many of its distinctive characteristics. Unlike other ice masses, the berg will not merely flow internally, within the confines of the rigid ice field, but will respond more or less freely to its new environment of fluids, the sea and the air. The berg will drift in ocean currents and wind fields. It will bob, rock, and spin. It will tilt or even overturn as erosion modifies its density profile. From the simplest of motions, that which governs the settling and compression of snow, the iceberg has acquired an almost limitless mobility. The price paid for this mobility is disintegration. Time itself accelerates; events crowd one upon the other; the more rapidly the berg moves, the more swiftly it decays. The ice began in a nearly timeless state, prolonged over centuries, even millennia, because the extreme cold of the source region slowed movement to a vanishing point. But as the ice acquires composition, shape, movement, variety on its journey outward, it correspondingly wastes away. The smaller the berg, the greater its mobility and the faster its disintegration.

Very large tabular bergs are the least mobile and show the greatest persistence. They cling to the shore, grounded or entrapped in pack ice. The heavy concentration of large bergs near the coast contributes to the preservation of a wide belt of fast ice and shore ice even during the summer. Only when they break up into smaller units and proceed through the pack do bergs respond freely to wind and wave. In broad terms, their drift is set by ocean currents. Because of its large draught, its keel, the berg behaves as a current integrator, sailing roughly eastward with the nearshore flow of the Antarctic circumpolar current and ultimately breaking free of shore influences to enter the broad west wind drift out to the Antarctic convergence. There are considerable variations, however.

The act of breaking loose from the coast is typically not a single event. Several years may pass before the berg actually becomes a free-floating vessel. Frequently, the berg grounds as it attempts to sail from the continental shelf or to pass around peninsulas of ice or land, or as it encounters eddies within the current that trap it temporarily in a frozen gyre of bergs and pack ice. From its first calving the berg may be recaptured several times by the ice field—to be refrozen, reincorporated, then liberated again. The vast majority of large bergs hug the coast, and most of the bergs that survive many years do so because they move ponderously out from the ice shore. The average longevity of an Antarctic iceberg is four to six years. The colossal Trolltunga berg, however, was tracked for over eleven years, slowly creeping along the frozen shoreline of Queen Maud Land before it was absorbed within the Weddell gyre, where it spent more than two years before being catapulted into the South Atlantic. Once it enters more or less open ocean, a berg advances an average of 8–13 kilometers a day.

Other influences shape the actual drift track of the berg. The Coriolis force, pronounced at high latitudes, gives a small northward component to the berg's circumpolar drift. Tides work to lift grounded bergs and to move others, while winds shape considerably the local pattern of drift. How influential winds become depends on the strength of the wind, the size of the berg, and the proportion of sail to keel. High winds (over 50 kilometers per hour), small bergs, and large sails make for responsive ice. Even large bergs will be sensitive to very high winds and the waves they generate. But the storm cells that orbit the continent follow the general trend of the Antarctic circumpolar current. While, in the short term, wind and current may compete, in the larger scale of things they complement each other. The bergs circle the continent like ice debris in the rings of Saturn.

The perimeter of ice varies with the ebb and flow of the circumpolar current and the general climate. The pack ice remains frozen much of the year, retarding the movement of trapped bergs. At other times, the perimeter of the circumpolar current swells outward and icebergs range widely over the Southern Ocean. Occasionally, very large bergs encounter favorable circumstances that fling them outward well beyond the Antarctic convergence altogether. Bergs have been sighted from South Africa after being hurled out of the Weddell Sea gyre, as well as off the coast of Peru, embedded in the cold Humboldt current.

Ocean swells cause the berg to oscillate (if the ice is rigid) or vibrate (if the ice is elastic). Some of the movement is linear, making the berg bob up and down like a glacial cork. Some is angular, encouraging the berg to rock back and forth. Both oscillations and vibrations, however, set up stress fields within the ice. How the berg responds depends on the wavelength of the swell, the thickness of the berg, and the presence of internal fissures. Very large, thick bergs absorb the vibrations with little effect; the entire berg may slowly bob or rock but there will be little internal deformation. Thinner bergs or ice shelves may simply bend elastically without rupture. But under the proper circumstances—if the wavelength of the swell and the ratio of thickness to width in the berg are in the right proportion—rupture may occur. Should the berg vibrate near its natural frequency, it will shake into large pieces. Flexure and fatigue failure seem to be important processes in the calving of bergs from shelves. For large bergs, especially those with residual cracks that may propagate under the proper stresses, the process of stress failure continues to operate.

The berg even rotates. One rotation is slight but constant, the product of a sheath of meltwater that surrounds the berg as it ablates. This liberated freshwater has a lower density than the surrounding seawater and accordingly it rises. At lower levels, the pressure differential is sufficient to have an impact. Seawater enters the sheath, but under the impress of the Coriolis force, the flow deflects to the left; the berg spins. More dramatic are those rotations from top to bottom of the berg. The density profile of an Antarctic iceberg shows a lighter top of snow and firn riding above a much denser ice substratum. But as the top erodes, as side disintegration results from thermal ablation and the mechanical response to the new stress field, and as the bottom reshapes from crevasse erosion and thermal convection along the sides, the berg can become unstable. The top may roll over. The critical variable seems to be the ratio of berg length to width. For a berg 200 meters thick, the minimum width should be 220 meters to prevent roll instability.

Only occasionally does the process get this far. More common is an adjustment of shape to density that causes the berg to tilt perpetually one way and then another. The berg will list more often than it will capsize. The lighter snow and firn are particularly susceptible to wave erosion, brine infiltration, meltwater percolation. A drifting berg will experience a wave-cut underwater terrace to its rear, and the removal of this material causes the rear to rise and the front to lower. This tilting affects the way the berg intercepts current and wind, and the berg rotates. The newly exposed top will, in turn, be subjected to more vigorous wave erosion. In theory the process can continue indefinitely. But before an ice peneplain can result, the berg will most likely dissolve into a kaleidoscope of exotic forms, a happy entropy of particles and motions.

A Plastic Art: The Esthetics of Icebergs

Ice is a plastic art. No other object more fully challenges the theory and practice of esthetics. The journey of the ice from crystal to berg is not simply a story of matter and motion: it is an esthetic journey of the first magnitude. And of all Antarctic ices the berg is the most artful. It contains all the stuff, the shapes, and the motions of other Antarctic ice, yet it combines them uniquely and it mounts them, like a set jewel, in an environment that enhances their effects. To James Eights, first naturalist to land on the continent, the icebergs were "in a peculiar manner, adapted to create feelings of awe and admiration in the bosom of the beholder, not alone from the majesty of their size, but likewise, by the variety of the forms and ever changing hues that they assume."[1] To veteran Antarctic explorer and scholar Frank Debenham, the bergs were "of all the natural features of the Antarctic the most strange and impressive."[2]

No other ice mass displays such a range of sculptural forms. Though the largest bergs are impressive by virtue of their sheer monotonous size, the smaller bergs take the shapes of white earthscapes. Erosion weathers them and instabilities tilt them into exotic spires, castellated facades, and ice sphinxes. Others assume the lumpish mass and abstract blocky forms of modernist sculpture. The ice terrane as a whole presents a sculpture garden of kinetic art.

No other ice mass plays with light so effectively. The berg's appearance changes constantly, with the orientation of berg to sun and to the surrounding environs of sea ice, fog, and cloud. The berg's translucent blue and green ices, its dull luminous firn, and its brilliant reflective snow make the berg into a virtual prism. In purest forms, glacial ice glows with a bluish tint. Occasionally absorbing impurities or acquiring glasslike properties of sheared ice, it takes on a greenish lustre, like dull jade. In still other circumstances, its bottom strata are charged with rocky, brownish debris which may rise to the surface should the berg overturn. With bands of whitish bubbles swirling through it and fresh snow lacing its fabric of fractures, the blue ice resembles a patch of sky streaked with ice clouds—a bizarre reification of its source in the polar plateau.

Immersed in direct sunlight, the snowy berg hurls the light back with dazzling intensity. The berg sparkles amid its surroundings, an undifferentiated, unearthly presence. Nothing of the berg itself is revealed. Better understanding requires more subtle lights. In oblique sunlight the berg appears like ivory, dull and opaque. In fog the berg is highlighted by shadow, a grey outline amidst a whitish mist. In stronger sunlight, it emits a ghostly translucence, becoming a kind of ice opal. Under an overcast sky, white light cannot penetrate. But other wavelengths act on the ice and snow to produce an eerie, bluish-white phosphorescence, a luminous glow that accents the internal structure of the berg and contrasts weirdly with the ivory-colored sea ice and the navy-blue sea.

The berg synopsizes the esthetics as much as the glaciology

and geography of Antarctica. Yet it does so by virtue of a paradox. The simplicity of The Ice is staggering, and embedded within the ice field an ice mass is flat, opaque, almost featureless. It only reflects those perceptions brought to it, or refracts that information extracted from it. The ice field from which the berg emerges is an esthetic sink. The character of The Ice is derived and its brilliance secondary. The Ice adds by removing, transforms without creating, informs by obscuring. Its meaning does not reside within Antarctica, awaiting revelation, but derives from the illumination brought to it from outside. Ice does not merely reflect mind: it absorbs it. The more it absorbs, the larger it becomes; the more light brought to it, the more powerful its reflection.

The special properties and meaning of the berg both as a natural phenomenon and as an esthetic object derive instead from its surroundings, from the fact that this ice mass has been removed from its confining ice field. There are contrasts—ice and ocean, ice and the esthetic canons brought to bear on it. The berg is the most revealing, and most pleasing, of Antarctic ices because it is the least typical. It is the most intellectually and emotionally accessible of Antarctic ices because it is the most complex. In this, too, the berg symbolizes Antarctica— the least known and least knowable of continents, not because it is the most complex but because it is the most simple. This is a looking-glass landscape where things may be less, not more, than they seem.

Its simplicity is stupefying. Contrasts, comparisons, analogies, metaphors—all vanish before the pure immensity of the ice monolith. Antarctica mocks the belief that the essence of art—or of life or of civilization—is simplicity. This is a minimalist landscape that requires a high order of esthetics to be appreciated. Where the ice is ensconced within ice within more ice, art finds itself without information; the senses are stripped; perception vanishes into a white nirvana. At its source, The Ice is a world in a state that approximates frozen invariance. The Ice is nature as modernist.

But the iceberg escapes this condition. The berg was accessible to traditions of representational art and, almost alone among Antarctic ices, it was painted and photographed by premodernists. It is easy to value the berg because one can contrast its ice mass to non-ice surroundings. Broken out of the ice field, the berg acquires new properties, new motions, new structures.

It offers contrasts, often brilliant, with its new environs. It does not match ice with ice but ice with sky, sea, earth. Were the ice still embedded in the polar plateau or the ice shelf, the appearance of the berg would be far less dramatic; it would not even have an identity in any meaningful sense. But amidst the Southern Ocean—surrounded with chunks of glacial ice, pack-ice floes, ocean waves, storms, mixed clouds, changing skies, aquatic life—the berg acquires immediate esthetic appeal. There is even sound: the cries of birds, the slap of waves and whitecaps, the hissing of air bubbles rupturing from glacial ice. The berg breaks, at last, the enormous silence of The Ice.

So it is with the ice field of Antarctica. Were the Earth truly an ice planet, the Antarctic would hold little interest. It is the contrast of ice to Earth, and of Ice to Idea, that makes it fascinating. The whiteness of the berg would be oppressive—meaningless—without its surrounding environment of sea and civilization. The berg is the most revealing of Antarctic ices because, in departing the ice field, it is the least typical. It is the most accessible of Antarctic ices because, in its many contrasts, it is the most complex. The berg is rich in information and knowable; its appearance can be quickly appreciated and assimilated. In Antarctica, the complicated is easy, the simple baffling.

VANISHING POINT

The iceberg, much reduced, drifts and disintegrates.

As it nears the boundary of the convergence, it breaks and ablates rapidly. It spins ponderously in its sheath of meltwater. Those waters vanish into the bottom circulation of the world ocean and the ambient humidity of the global atmosphere. They are part of the hydrologic cycle, the final cycle The Ice will know. The berg has lived within a great series of vortices, a geophysical field shaped by ice. At their source is a profound stillness, as close as the Earth can get to a condition of absolute zero, a cold so intense as to seemingly halt all motion. Outward from this origin the ice accelerates, the cycles multiply. The Antarctic convergence is the final perimeter. Once the berg crosses that frontier it is outside the ice field and soon expires. Its disintegration is rapid and inevitable. Slowly it spins its final rotations. Its bobbing causes a patch of green ice within it to flash like a semaphore from a field of white, a bottle in a message. The berg blinks like a dying pulsar, then disappears.

For a while its particles fly free from the ice, like the tedious outward burst of a frozen big bang. But none will ever escape that influence entirely. And over geologic time some will return. Once again they will be reduced from complexity to simplicity, reshaped to unearthly minima, and drawn back into the great polar vortex—back to the ends of the world, back to the spiraling nebula of Ice that is Antarctica, sweeping everything within its field into the heart of an immense whiteness.

The Ice

The Pack

*[The ship] came to the limits of the world, to
  the deep flowing
Oceanus . . . shrouded in mist and cloud. . . .*

 —Homer, *The Odyssey*, Book XI

*I will not say it was impossible anywhere to
get in among this Ice, but I will assert that
the bare attempting of it would be a very dangerous enterprise and what I believe no man
in my situation would have thought of. I
whose ambition leads me not only farther
than any other man has been before me, but
as far as I think it possible for man to go, was
not sorry at meeting with this interruption, as
it in some measure relieved us from the dangers and hardships, inseparable with the Navigation of the Southern Polar regions.*

 —Capt. James Cook, *Journals, Voyage of
  the Resolution and Adventure* (1774)

They raft across a wine-dark sea, sometimes isolated, sometimes strung together, circling the continent like gears within a
vast orrery of floating ice.

A veil of low cloud and grey fog, a stygian current of black
sea, a mobile breakwater of white ice: these define the terrane
of the pack and the oscillating perimeter of The Ice. The boundary is multiple. The cold core of the global atmosphere and the
tangled vortex of the world ocean roughly coincide with the ice
field of Greater Antarctica, creating a complex zone of mixing.
The Ice is surrounded by a circumference of swirling storms,
where Antarctic and subantarctic air masses mingle; by braided
currents and fronts that mix Antarctic and subantarctic waters;
by a shadow line that separates the varied calendar of temperate
time from the two seasons of the polar day. That all of these
zones approximately overlap accounts for the intensity of Antarctica's isolation. Of these processes, sea ice is both a product
and a producer. As the zones wax and wane with the seasons,
the ice field grows and decays on a grand scale, and the pack
becomes the effective boundary of the continent.

While the iceberg is the most interesting ice mass in Antarctica, the pack ice is the most interesting ice terrane. Its rapid
life cycle, its explosive winter growth and catastrophic summer
collapse, the infinite movements of its numberless floes, with
their constant rupturing and resuturing, the volatility of its
position as a solid-phase boundary between two fluid regimes,
air and sea—all give the pack a collective dynamism and variety unparalleled among Antarctic ices. This is the most complex and active of Antarctic systems. In part, the pack reflects
this vigor and reduces it. The floes form an ice membrane between air and sea, atmosphere and hydrosphere; between land
and the air-sea matrix, Antarctica and the fluids that bind it to
the Earth; between biosphere and cryosphere, life and an in-
organic lithosphere. In this twilight zone between Earth and
Ice are mixed sea and sky, sea and ice, sky and ice, sea ice and
land ice, life and lithosphere. Even in their colors and geometry
the black sea and white ice recapitulate the two polar seasons:
the summer day and the winter night.

This intermingling, so characteristic of the pack and so different from what goes on in the rest of the ice field, leads not to
more complexity but to less. As the pack matures, it reduces

dramatically the interactions among its component systems,
and the reductionism and solipsism of The Ice are boldly extended outward. The mingling of sea, sky, and ice makes this
region among the cloudiest on Earth: a perennial fog hangs
cloyingly over the pack; the scene is shrouded in a stormy grey
twilight. The ragged front of the pack creates a geographic
warp, an icescape where space expands and dissolves, where
time slows and distorts. Around the ice field the floes orbit,
waxing and waning with the seasonal tides: at times loose
and free-floating in the circumpolar current, like ice fragments
trapped within the rings of Saturn, and at times frozen more or
less solid, slowly creaking around, their gyres like Aristotelian
spheres of quintessential crystal. Only the power of the outside
world reverses the trend to greater and greater simplicity and
uniformity. For millennia, the pack was the commanding barrier not only to human travel but to human mind. One could
reach The Ice only by passing through the pack.

Glaciology of the Pack

The progradation of the pack begins with the coming of the austral twilight. The sun circles low on the horizon, a cold white
globe. As ambient temperatures fall below the freezing point of
seawater, sea ice begins to form. Ice forms first in protected embayments along the coast, most rapidly in the protected seas
that ring the continent. Some takes the form of congelation ice,
which organizes surface crystals into a scaffolding; some takes
the form of frazil ice, slushy clumps of ice crystals suspended
within supercooled seawater. From their structured mixing the
floe evolves, by a series of stages. More ice and snow are added.
Metamorphism restructures the ice breccias that comprise the
floe. What happens on the microscopic level is then repeated on
a macroscopic level. Individual floes interact, form a matrix,
accept more ices, move around and away from the coast, and
acquire a collective identity as the Antarctic pack. The expansion of the pack measures the outward march of subfreezing
temperatures that accompanies the encroaching polar night.

The Southern Ocean is never far from freezing. Much of the
surface water is perennially supercooled. As less sunlight heats
open waters and as cold air streams off the continent, water
turns to ice. The fundamental crystal is a hexagon, but it can

aggregate in two habits: sometimes hexagon stacks on hexagon to make long filaments and needles of ice, and sometimes hexagons are annexed side-by-side to make plates and disks. Initially, both habits are apparent. But the crystals exist in two states, and two kinds of ice result. Along the sea surface, needles give way preferentially to plates. The heat of fusion released during crystallization locally warms a site, and platy crystals appear between needles. As the platy structure expands, it coats the surface with a filmy grey sheen known as grease ice. Away from the surface, however, no such preference occurs. Ice crystals proliferate into an unstructured slush called frazil ice. The two kinds of ice evolve in different ways and contribute differently to the mass of the pack.

Which ice predominates apparently depends on the role of snow, the formation of polynyas, and the local hydrometeorology. Congelation ice requires a stable environment, which it progressively sheets over. Frazil ice requires open, turbulent waters. It is assisted by winds that break apart the embryonic ice sheeting, by the convective mixing that results from the liberation of brine during surface-ice freezing, and by the persistence of open water like leads and polynyas. Snowfall assists both ice masses, contributing directly to the surface of congelation ice sheets, and it may be vital to the formation of frazil ice by providing suitable nuclei. Depending on the turbulence of the local seas, ice crystals may coat the surface in the form of congelation ice or they may ride like turbid sediment, frazil ice, within subsurface waters. Congelation and frazil ice frequently combine. Where frazil ice forms a dense sludge, congelation ice may grow along the exposed frozen surface; and where congelation ice evolves a well-developed structure, frazil ice may collect in clumps. Yet the two ices are also competitive. The sealing of the surface by congelation ice, for example, prevents snowfall from furnishing new nuclei for frazil ice.

While some pack expansion is attributable to a simple process of freezing along the perimeter, most seems to occur by a process of interstitial freezing between floes. Storms, offshore winds, and ocean currents break up the ice veneer, the protofloes rift outward, and interstitial leads between them freeze. Where open water persists, sea ice—frazil ice in particular—can form in abundance. Polynyas thus coincide, not accidentally, with major centers of ice production. Some polynyas are semipermanent features of the Southern Ocean—in part the

product of warm water upwelling and persistent winds. The
pack expands not by a process of simple accretion along its margin but by a more complex interaction of winds, water, and ice.

In many places, the pack will consist of about equal portions
of congelation ice and frazil ice. In the Ross Sea, however, congelation ice predominates; and particularly in the protected,
polynya-free region of McMurdo Sound, where fast ice is abundant, congelation ice is the norm. But in the Weddell Sea, where
polynyas persist, between 50 and 90 percent of sea ice consists of
frazil ice. Since nearly one-third of the entire Antarctic pack
belongs within the Weddell gyre, frazil ice is a significant constituent of the ice field. Frazil ice tends to be more common
near the coast (within 30–40 kilometers), where windblown
snowfall is more abundant. Whatever the mixture, however,
frazil ice will be supplemented by snow and other ices that become incorporated within the general sea ice matrix.

Congelation ice brings structure to pack ice. Initially, the
mingling of ice needles and ice plates creates a porous crystalline scaffolding called skeletal ice. Filamentlike crystals
branch outward toward patches of water that are characterized
by reduced salinity and higher freezing points. This framework
thickens and spreads laterally across the sea surface into a sheen
of grease ice. The evolution of congelation ice, if unbroken, in-
terferes with the production of subsurface frazil ice and fundamentally redefines the boundary between air and sea. When
this evolution is complete, the exchange of mass and energy between atmosphere and ocean ends. In its place, the pack initi-
ates fluxes of salt, water, and heat between the ice and the ocean.
Some of these processes involve positive feedback mechanisms,
such that the presence of sea ice encourages the further production of sea ice. Snow insulates the ice floes, the ice floes insulate
the sea, the chilled boundary of air and sea promotes fog,
which further reduces insolation. Storm tracks and ice edge become interdependent. A dense pack increases albedo and reduces mixing. Ice leads to ice.

The salt flux is especially important. When seawater freezes,
it liberates salt and releases the latent heat of fusion. The vent-
ing of this heat by and large replaces the direct exchange of heat
between ocean and atmosphere. The ice crystals themselves
hold little salt. Instead salt is extruded into interstitial pores
around which further ice crystals form. Its increased salt content lowers the freezing point of the brine, so that the brine

pocket does not immediately freeze but becomes mechanically encased by the rapidly emerging ice lattice. As the lattice freezes inward, the brine pocket eventually shrinks. The more rapid the freezing, the more brine is entrapped within the structure and the less homogeneous is the resulting ice lattice. Where frazil ice is abundant, it brings a high proportion of brine to the over-all matrix. The more brine, the weaker the ice structure. Mean-while, the extrusion of brine salts through capillaries and inter-granular discharge channels upsets the density profile of the subsurface waters, and a convective cell develops in the waters beneath the pack.

As a lattice evolves, the random orientation of the initial ice crystals is replaced by a stronger, more columnar framework. Grease ice and skeletal ice thicken and spread into ice paddies that resemble grey lily pads. As the overall structure grows by the erection of more congelation ice, other ices are captured. Frazil ice attaches in globs to the sides and bottom. Snow falls on the surface. When melted and refrozen, it forms lenses of in-filtration ice. Other infiltration ice results from the capture of seawater on the surface by spray and wave. Underwater ice may develop in the form of ice stalactites, growing along brine ex-trusion channels. Anchor ice—frazil ice that collects on the shallow sea floor—may break loose and rise upward into the ice matrix on the surface. Ice flowers may form on the surface as feathery growths of crystals nucleate on salts excreted along freezing ice columns. Other ices—bergy bits, brash ice, the me-chanical debris left by colliding floes—become incorporated into the matrix. The structure may even contain an ice biota, a product of the sudden entrapment of brine impregnated with al-gae and plankton. From all these sources, out of all these pro-cesses, emerges a complex ice fabric, a partially stratified ice breccia that is frequently spongy and malleable.

This concatenation of ices eventually elaborates the ice paddy into a tabular slab called pancake ice. As pancake ice butts and jostles, its edges curl upward. Snow and seawater collect inside to produce infiltration ice. Further thickening, freezing, and de-formation convert spongy slabs of pancake ice into a hardened floe. The floes multiply into an ice terrane, the pack.

In its shape a floe crudely resembles the platy ice crystals that constitute its microstructure. Floes are roughly equidimen-sional, 10–100 meters across. Because of constant collisions, their top edges curl up. The thickness of a floe varies with the

relative effectiveness of ice production and ice ablation. The
floe can ablate from the bottom by melting and from the top by
evaporation, sublimation, melting, and wind scour. The resulting equilibrium thickness varies from 2.75 to 3.35 meters. The
actual composition and structure of the floe will depend on its
unique history.

This internal history will reflect thermal and mechanical
metamorphisms. The collision of floe with floe, driven by wind
and wave, can mechanically deform a floe. Ice masses can
shear, crumple, and override one another to form pressure
ridges and ice massifs. While in the Arctic pack such features
are common, in the Antarctic they are restricted to local sites
where high stress can accumulate. Some mechanical metamorphism occurs in fast ice, where at least one side of the ice
mass is rigidly frozen to the shore, and in the oceanic gyres, like
the Weddell, where floes are drawn into a crushing spiral. But
more commonly the effect of wind and wave is to shove the pack
outward rather than in on itself. This tendency accelerates the
overall process of pack formation by pushing floes from sites
where ice is readily made into more marginal sites and by ex-
posing, under favorable conditions, new seawater for freezing.
The ice terrane becomes larger rather than more complex.

Thermal metamorphism takes several forms. If the insulating
snow cover is removed, the exposed surface may contract, leading to thermal cracks. It may also melt, allowing meltwater to
percolate into the ice lattice, refreeze as infiltration ice, and release more heat that can induce further local melting. Such
melting can occur over and over. The permeation of fresh meltwater through the floe flushes salts out of the interior and
strengthens the lattice. In the Antarctic, the presence of brine,
algae, and plankton within floes sometimes causes insolation to
warm the interior of the floe, not merely the surface. This encourages brine migration and expulsion which, in turn, may
lead to the formation of undersea ice—ice stalactites—that
protrudes downward from the floe. In ideal systems ice accretes
on the bottom of the floe and ablates from the top, and a floe
will experience several cycles of metamorphism. Multi-year ice
preserves not only more mechanical deformation than single-
year ice, but more thermal cycling. There is some multi-year
fast ice in protected embayments, and sea ice in the Weddell
gyre survives perhaps two seasons. But unlike the Arctic, where
sea ice is constantly reworked and converted into fresh ice, the

Antarctic experiences an annual renewal of virtually the entire pack. Nearly all sea ice dates from the onset of the austral autumn and expires during the austral summer. The awesomeness of the pack derives from its enormous geographic extent, not its history or internal intricacy.

Once embedded within the pack, a floe enjoys a collective identity. Floe interacts with floe, and the pack with the sea, the air, and other ice terranes. The pack has a collective geography and a collective history. Geographically, it is organized by two boundaries, one rigid and one dynamic. Near the continent, where it originates, the pack is bounded by land, ice shelves, and fast ice. As the season matures, free-floating floes move north as an ensemble of diverging shards. Later in the season the ice near the continent freezes solid or moves by means of the slow shearing of floe past floe. On its outer margin, the ice is not so rigidly confined. The dynamics of air and sea demarcate this outer fringe, and these processes vary by season and year. The outermost boundary of the pack lies somewhat inside the Antarctic convergence, which defines the perimeter of the Southern Ocean. The actual shape of the pack depends on storms that roughly follow, but do not precisely mimic, the contours of the ocean. Near-shore currents and winds drive coastal floes eastward, most spectacularly around the gigantic gyre that forms in the Weddell Sea. More distant floes spin within the larger, westward drift of the Antarctic circumpolar current.

The constant pulverization of floes yields ice fragments. Some of these shards are swept under floes, causing them to thicken; some are carried out to sea in clusters and streamers; some are reabsorbed, in the proper season, to make new floes. To this ensemble land ices also contribute. Grounded bergs keep their surrounding near-shore environs cold, divert winds, damp out approaching waves, and ward off warmer water from entering shelves and bays. The presence of land ice thus encourages the formation of sea ice. Some bergs will be frozen in among the pack during the winter. Others, when wind and current urge them, plow through the pack like icebreakers. Their debris— bergy bits and brash ice—may be incorporated into the churning breccia that constitutes the pack.

The pack experiences a life cycle. The rate of progradation varies considerably by year, but on the average the advancing edge of the sea ice moves 4.2 kilometers per day, and the total ice terrane increases by about 100,000 square kilometers per day.

In September the pack reaches a maximum extent of 20 million square kilometers. Retrogradation ends when the last of the shore-fast ice breaks out in late January or early February. Sea ice then has a minimum extent of 4 million square kilometers, virtually all in the Weddell Sea. In an average annual cycle nearly 16 million square kilometers of sea ice freeze and melt. But the process fluctuates enormously by year and place. The annual variation is as much as 75 percent of maximum, and individual seas show more variability than does the whole. Each sea features regionally distinctive meteorological and oceanographic processes and, hence, sea ice production. At the same time, there apparently exist some compensatory mechanisms by which the different sectors of the Southern Ocean adjust to one another. In any calculation, however, the Weddell Sea enjoys a commanding role.

Convergence: The Southern Ocean

It is the great vortex and heat sink of the world ocean, and it girdles The Ice like the River Styx. The Southern Ocean works like a slow centrifugal pump that mixes the major oceans of the globe and supplies out of its peculiar ices the bottom waters which layer the abyssal plains of the Pacific, Atlantic, and Indian oceans. Its geography is defined on one side by the ice coastline of Antarctica, with its multiple seas, and on the other by the Antarctic convergence, the mobile interface the Southern Ocean shares with other oceans. Its dynamics are driven by stark contrasts of heat and cold, both oceanographic and atmospheric. Warm bodies move toward the continent and cold bodies away from it. Within these gradients, mixing occurs by means of anastomosing currents that circle the continent, one to the east and one to the west.

Its interior seas are all arrayed along the crenulated coastline of West Antarctica, a mountainous archipelago welded by land ice into a unified subcontinent. The largest, the Weddell and Ross seas, mark the boundary between West Antarctica and East, a true continent. Smaller seas—the Amundsen and the Bellingshausen—trace the rocky outline of the Antarctic Peninsula. The Scotia Sea, a cold Caribbean, extends the peninsula outward to the South Atlantic along an island arc system. Only where it joins West Antarctica does East Antarctica exhibit

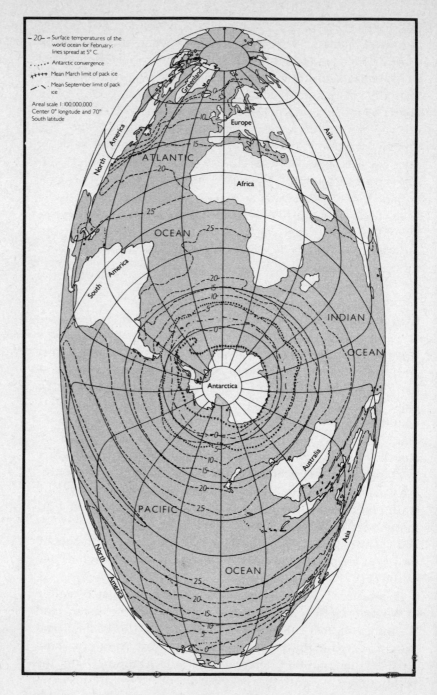

Antarctica in relation to the world ocean, Hammer transverse elliptical equal-area projection. Note position of the Antarctic convergence. Redrawn, original courtesy American Geographical Society.

anything but a uniform coastline of ice, the flange of a great ice
dome, varied only by the proportions of land, sea, and fast ice
that compose it. The seas show some local currents, but apart
from the gigantic gyre of the Weddell Sea, the dynamics of the
Southern Ocean are dominated by its circumpolar currents.

Between them the two circumpolar currents integrate the
protected seas that indent West Antarctica, mix and give new
identities to the water masses brought across the convergence,
and shape the ice terranes of the berg and the pack. The two
currents are countervailing: a nearshore current flows east,
while an offshore current flows west. Overall, the dynamics of
the Southern Ocean are dominated by the clockwise Antarctic
circumpolar current (ACC), driven by the prevailing west wind
drift. Nearshore flow, however, is controlled by the Antarctic
coastal current. Under the impress of easterly winds (east wind
drift) the coastal current is rapid and thorough, extending
throughout the water column. When this coastal flow encounters deep embayments, like those containing the lesser seas,
gyres of varying sizes and intensities are formed. Where the
coastal current is shielded from the outer Antarctic circumpolar current the effect is powerful: the Weddell Sea becomes an
extraordinary gyre of ices, chilled air, and unprecedentedly
cold water.

The two currents inscribe two important oceanographic
boundaries. The Antarctic divergence defines the interface between the coastal current and the circumpolar current. The
Antarctic convergence segregates the Antarctic circumpolar
current from other oceans. Between the counterclockwise Antarctic coastal current and the clockwise Antarctic circumpolar
current is a dynamic boundary that is simultaneously oceanographic and meteorological. It demarks not only two opposing
oceanic flows but a zone of atmospheric mixing—of semipermanent cyclones—where the prevailing winds shift from
easterlies to westerlies. Its subsurface influence extends downward as the Antarctic front.

The Antarctic convergence is a major feature of the world
ocean. Here the waters of Antarctica shear against the waters of
the neighboring oceans. The effect is both deep and broad. The
surface zone, marked by the convergence, corresponds to a subsurface zone, the polar front. The transition is immediately apparent, marked by discontinuities in the properties of adjacent
water masses, especially their temperature and density, their

flow regimes, and their biology. In fact, the convergence denotes a biotic no less than a hydrographic and atmospheric front. Species rarely cross from one side to the other; even for a given genus, like krill, species occupy one side or the other. The actual boundary is always apparent but never exact. To cross it perpendicularly gives the sense that the convergence is rigidly drawn, but to cross it obliquely reveals a quantum lumpiness to the boundary, a patchiness full of small eddies and clumps of isolated water masses. At least in the Scotia Sea it appears that the boundary encourages the formation of cyclones that break free to be sent north as enclosed rings of cold Antarctic waters. In general, the actual convergence occupies a 100-kilometer belt around a mean position. The polar front, too, is a broken, fluid plane of exchange, full of interweaving cold and warm waters.

The flow of waters into and out of the Southern Ocean occurs on several levels. Some inflow occurs as fresh water discharged from the continent in the form of icebergs. The greatest inflow —known as circumpolar deep water (or warm deep water)— proceeds at intermediate levels of the water column. It is this water mass that the Southern Ocean mixes, transforms, and ejects. As this water mass approaches the continent, it becomes more homogeneous, weakening in the final 100 kilometers and allowing for fuller, deeper convection. The Antarctic front marks its horizontal limit, and in the process the water loses its original identity. Some of the circumpolar deep water combines with fresher surface waters, from melting icebergs and an excess of precipitation over evaporation, to create the Antarctic surface waters, whose boundary coincides with the Antarctic divergence. Some contributes, primarily by mixing with surface waters, to Antarctic intermediate water, which moves north across the polar front. And some contributes, in complex ways, to the formation of Antarctic bottom water, destined for the abyssal plains of the world ocean. Mixing is deep and continuous because the water masses never achieve equilibriums of density or temperature. The salt flux from surface-ice formation, the temperature differences between intermediate and surface waters, turbulence along the boundaries of the strata, and circumpolar flow all result in constant stirring. A stable surface layer never forms.

But not only does Antarctica transform the circumpolar deep waters: they also transform Antarctica. The release of heat brought by the circumpolar deep waters to the region alters circumpolar air masses and helps direct storm tracks. The mixing of Antarctic surface water with circumpolar deep water results in a net loss of heat to the Antarctic atmosphere and a net loss of salt through dilution with fresh water. The upwelled waters bring to the surface high concentrations of nutrients that are in good measure responsible for the phenomenal biotic richness of the Southern Ocean.

This inflow is balanced by an outflow. Most, by volume, takes the form of Antarctic intermediate waters, the product of mixing deep and surface waters. But two water masses above and below these intermediate strata are distinctive to the Southern Ocean, and both are profoundly influenced by the ice terranes with which they interact. Antarctic surface water—lighter, fresher than Antarctic intermediate waters—reflects the presence of icebergs, relatively poor evaporation, and the seasonally important plating of sea ice. Eventually, most of the surface water is reconstituted with deep water to make the Antarctic intermediate waters that are drafted north across the polar front. The mechanism of Antarctic bottom water formation is less well understood but appears to be intimately connected to the presence of persistent ice, both ice shelves and pack ice.

Specifically, the vast proportion of Antarctic bottom water seems to come from the Weddell Sea. Here circumpolar deep water is modified first with surface water, cooled and freshened by the winter waters that result from the intense production of sea ice during the polar night. This altered circumpolar deep water then mixes with shelf water from the western Weddell Sea region—a site almost constantly under the influence of shelf ice and pack ice. This new mixture interacts again with circumpolar deep water as it flows out of the Weddell Sea. Deep-water circumpolar currents and the topography of the deep ocean basins carry the Antarctic bottom water clockwise around the continent. The final composition of Antarctic bottom water is one-eighth winter waters, one-fourth western shelf waters, and five-eighths circumpolar deep water. Other bottom waters, notably from the Ross Sea, add to the volume as the mass circulates around the Southern Ocean. But the Weddell Sea is clearly the primary source, and the properties of the mass blur as it distances itself from the Weddell Sea and as portions are siphoned off to fill the abyssal plains of the Atlantic, Indian, and Pacific basins.

Because of its ice regimes, the continental shelf harbors another zone of distinctive water masses. The continental shelf of Antarctica is not extensive. The weight of the land-based ice sheets so depresses the continent that its shelves are the deepest in the world, and the flooding of the larger embayments with land ice to form enormous ice shelves further reduces their areal dimensions. In effect, ice shelves replace continental shelves. The ice shelves are extensions of terrestrial ice sheets that at some point float. These floating shelves redefine the contour of the continent and influence the flow regimes and characteristics of waters in the Southern Ocean. There is little encroachment, for example, by circumpolar deep waters onto the continental shelves. Other areas, like the Weddell Sea, are subjected to almost perennial sea ice that also greatly influences the character of the subsurface waters.

Land ice affects subsurface waters in somewhat different ways than does sea ice. Beneath the pack, winter water collects in large quantities, vertical mixing is good, and a deep layer of surface water develops. By contrast, the ice shelves encourage the production of lesser quantities of very cold water. Water beneath the floating shelves is subjected to higher hydrostatic pressures than water at an equivalent depth in the open sea. This increase in pressure lowers the freezing temperature of the water, allowing for subshelf waters to reach much lower temperatures than they otherwise could. The liberation of this very cold water onto continental shelves may be responsible for some of the peculiarities of Antarctic bottom water. Thus, again, land ice affects sea ice, which in turn influences the weather patterns that sustain the continental source regions.

The Antarctic ice field becomes one vast self-reinforcing system in which air, water, and land are integrated through the medium of ice, a system in which The Ice transforms everything into more ice. The pack contributes directly to such parameters of the Southern Ocean as its salinity and temperature profiles, its vertical turbulence, its density structure and momentum, and its production of shelf, surface, and bottom waters. Other contributions are more indirect, a consequence of the pack's role as a thermal insulator and reflector. The geography of the pack affects weather patterns, the distribution of warm and cold waters, and the relative proportions of sea to ice, with their differential abilities to absorb and reflect sunlight. Yet despite an annual balance, the processes are at any one time out

of synchronization. Salt flux is at a maximum during winter
freezing, heat flux during summer, when there is abundant open water; fresh water flux requires the melting of icebergs. The Southern Ocean is constantly imbalanced. The integrating medium, ice, lags. What ultimately unifies these processes is a shared geophysical core: the great ice continent itself.

This whole cryospheric cycle has to begin somehow, and the establishment of the Antarctic circumpolar current is the most likely source. The Southern Ocean has evolved piecemeal over the course of 120 million years. The Drake Passage—formed by the complex displacement of the mountain chain binding the Andes to the Antarctic Peninsula, an island arc system—appeared only in late Eocene times, 38 million years ago. The establishment of a proto-ice sheet dates from this event. The ancestral Antarctic circumpolar current developed within a few million years afterward; for the last 30 million years or so, although the Southern Ocean basin has continued to expand outward, the current has been stable. There has been a change of size, a migration northward, but not a fundamental reconstitution of the flow regime. The present-day characteristics of the Southern Ocean apparently date from the early Pliocene, 3–4 million years ago. That this date coincides with the onset of the most recent planetary glacial epoch is no accident. Currently, the circumpolar deep waters circulate between Antarctica and the world ocean on a cycle of about one thousand years.

The Antarctic, then, makes an almost perfect antipode to the Arctic. The Arctic is a true ocean surrounded by continents; the Antarctic, a continent surrounded by oceans. Their climates, ocean currents, ices—all differ. And from these geographic differences derive the distinctive human histories of the two regions, which are antithetical in nearly every aspect.

In the world ocean the anastomosing Antarctic is a central vortex, a primary zone of mixing. The Arctic Ocean, connected only by narrow straits, is a virtual eddy. Its waters, air masses, and ices circulate in the polar gyre, occasionally discharging in streams southward. Its fundamentally maritime climate is comparatively mild, with a mean temperature at the pole of −18 degrees C. Its sea ice persists for years, acquiring structure; fast ice and shore effects are common along the coastline; and glacial ice is rare, confined to isolated ice caps like those on Baffin Island and to the Greenland ice sheet, along the margin of the Arctic. Its biota is splendidly varied, with a strong terrestrial component. And the circum-Arctic, including the fringes of the Greenland ice sheet, has long been integrated into the biotic and human history of the planet. There are economic resources to exploit. Geopolitical considerations have superimposed anthropogenic boundaries over Arctic geography and directed much of its contemporary history. There has even evolved an indigenous art of Eskimos, Indians, Siberians, and Lapplanders.

None of this is true of the Antarctic. Its climate is continental. Nearly all of its land mass is submerged beneath crushing ice sheets. Its pack ice ebbs and flows with the seasons. It mixes the world ocean and serves as a depository for the world's surplus heat and moisture. The mean temperature at the pole is a numbing −50 degrees C. Its ice terranes far exceed those of the Arctic. Its pack ice is larger and thicker than that of the Arctic, and it is reproduced annually. Its land ice comprises 90 percent of the world's total. It produces nearly all of the world mass of icebergs. The effect of its ice field is correspondingly more pronounced. Ice is only one component of Arctic geography: in the Antarctic it becomes increasingly the only component.

Although it stands at the central vortex of the world ocean— in fact, partly *because* of that—Antarctica as a continent exists in almost extraterrestrial isolation. There is a circumpolar uniformity imposed by The Ice, but it is a shared emptiness. Glaciology replaces geology, biology, meteorology. Like the bottom waters of Antarctica, the geophysical sinews that bind Antarctica to the Earth are remote, unobvious, and abstract. An ecosystem exists, directly or indirectly, only on the ocean and the pack. There is no human history in a traditional sense. Explorers did not sight the continent until the mid-nineteenth century, did not make true landfall until the twentieth, and did not establish quasi-permanent colonies until the post–World War II era. The geopolitics of the region belong with that of the deep oceans and the Moon.

Cold Core: The Antarctic Atmosphere

Antarctica is the cold core of the atmosphere, a region so intensely frigid that it deflects the meteorological equator of the

Storm rings around Antarctica. The actual pattern is a spiral, with cyclones veering inward to the Ross and Weddell seas. West Antarctica is frequently crossed, East Antarctica almost never. Courtesy NOAA.

globe northward nearly 10 degrees latitude. The solar radiation balance of Antarctica is negative all year round. In the winter night, no radiation enters; in the summer, the snow and ice reflect virtually all of the incoming radiation back into space, with little interference from the dry clear atmosphere over the continent. Even the Arctic enjoys a positive radiation balance for at least a portion of the year. Not so the Antarctic. It is the great refrigerator of the planetary atmosphere. Its unremitting cold is the supreme reality of Antarctic meteorology. The ice terranes of the Antarctic are both an outcome and a contributor to that fact.

The Antarctic climate consists of three terranes, each with its own subclimate: the continent, the ice-free sea, and the pack ice. The continent is a heat sink; the ocean, a heat source; and the pack, a great filter that regulates the exchange of heat and moisture between ocean and atmosphere, sea and land. Each of the three regions has its own zone of mixing, and the pattern of atmospheric circulation closely conforms to the cycle of atmospheric heat loss. As the polar night deepens, the temperature gradient between perimeter and core increases, storms acquire more vigor, and the polar winds rush more ferociously. Compared to the Northern Hemisphere, the Southern has a high proportion of ocean to land; and a good chunk of its terra firma, Antarctica, is a high-albedo ice field, not a heat-exchanging land mass. Continental warming is meager. The coupling of ocean and atmosphere is only feebly interrupted by lands, and the kinetic energy of air movement (as east-west flow) is nearly double that of the Northern Hemisphere. The perimeter of the pack is among the stormiest sites on the planet.

The south polar atmosphere mirrors, by inversion, the dynamics and structure of the Southern Ocean. There is a similar stratification (in this case of air masses), a similar gradient flow into and out of the region, and a similar continental circulation, dominated by a circumpolar vortex. A vertical profile shows three prominent strata: a layer of surface air, powerfully influenced by ice; an intermediate stratum of warm air, flowing from the temperate regions to the polar interior where it is chilled, transformed, and returned outward; and a remote upper layer, the high-latitude stratosphere, only tenuously bound to the others. The upper and lower strata transport cold air away from the continent, while the intermediate layer brings heat and moisture from more temperate regions inward to the pole by means of a circumflex vortex. The heat of this intermediate stratum is exchanged by simple advection to the interior, by adiabatic sinking, and by turbulent mixing along the boundary it shares with the surface inversion. Its ambient humidity and clouds trap heat reradiated from the surface. Return flow outward from the continent develops from both the bottom and the top of the Antarctic air mass, with a variety of surface winds off the ice dome and, during the austral summer, a circumpolar anticyclone in the stratosphere. The linkages between these strata are uncertain. But the intensity and magnitude of the surface outflow demand a major inflow, and much of this converging air is transferred to the surface stratum.

The spatial distribution of Antarctic air masses mimics that of the ocean masses to which they are intimately coupled. Subpolar, polar, and Antarctic fronts segregate polar from temperate air masses and define the general zones of mixing. Two patterns of storms are typical. Around the coastline, within the Antarctic front, storms occupy a narrow belt and involve relatively shallow air masses. Here the surface winds that prevail over the continent intermingle with air ultimately derived from marine systems. This type of storm rings the continent with a veil of cloud and snow drizzle. Sea fog forms as warm air is advected over the ice; sea smoke collects as cold offshore winds interact with exposed leads; ice fog and snow haze drape across the horizon from fine crystal precipitates in the air; whiteouts result from various combinations of clouds and snow which so scatter incoming light that all shadow is lost; and blizzards add violence to the opaque curtains of cloud that commonly envelop the continental fringe.

Further outward, along or beyond the perimeter of the pack, the polar front generates deeper storms. It is here that the major mixing of polar and temperate air occurs, that storms are most vigorous. These storms, too, tend to revolve around the continent, but being better developed, they also spiral inward, like eddies caught in a slow, larger vortex. This storm belt oscillates in rough synchroneity with the pack. Sea ice retards that exchange of energy between ocean and atmosphere which helps sustain major cyclones. At the same time, winter storms are capable of penetrating more deeply into the interior than summer storms because winter cooling encourages a much more intense temperature gradient between the Antarctic and temperate regions. But for the most part, Antarctic cyclones require heat released from the ocean, and they tend to follow areas of open water. Frequently, however, storms cross the West Antarctic ice sheet, and occasionally they make inroads into the colossal East Antarctic ice dome. Precipitation—always as snow—is important for local glaciation, for ice shelves, and for floes.

The polar and Antarctic fronts, then, are not fixed by continental boundaries. They fluctuate and are fragmented, much like the pack with which they are associated. Occluded fronts can regenerate over exposed waters along the coast, especially in the Bellingshausen and Ross seas. Once rejuvenated, they may settle for days. Air masses that attempt to cross the continent must confront the topography of the ice sheets and the two great chains of mountains—the Antarctic Andes (Antarcandes) of the peninsula and the Transantarctics that extend between East and West Antarctica. The ice dome itself is a formidable barrier. Considering the thinness of the polar atmosphere (at the equator the atmosphere is twice as dense), the elevation of the ice sheets removes them from most storms. The mountains deflect surface winds in characteristic patterns.

Overall circulation is vortical. A belt of low pressure, populated by a chain of major cyclones, spirals around the continent with the westerlies, roughly between latitudes 60 and 70 degrees South. This is the polar front, the atmospheric equivalent to the convergence. Closer to the coastline, there is a narrower belt of cyclones where the polar easterlies shear against the westerlies. This is equivalent to the Antarctic front. It is from this zone, not from Antarctica proper, that cold outbreaks of Antarctic air seem to emanate. The atmospheric mechanics thus differ from those typical of the Northern Hemisphere. The great ice sheets create a continual sheath of cold air, which they shed by surface-wind flow and occasional cyclonic mixing to the zone of coastal convergence. From here—once mixed—the cold air participates in outbreaks to the north. The bulk of warmer air drafted above the surface—the atmospheric equivalent to the circumpolar deep water—spirals into the interior in what is known as the Antarctic circumpolar vortex. In the winter, when temperature gradients are greatest, the circumpolar vortex intensifies as it reaches upward well into the stratosphere.

The Antarctic atmosphere most differs from the Southern Ocean in that air extends over the continent itself. The atmosphere must interact with all the ice terranes, not merely with the pack. Contact with these ices creates an intense layer of

dense, frigid air. The surface weather of Antarctica is dominated by the permanent presence of this sheath. The inversion
forms because the ice sheet is cold and elevated, the extraordinary albedo of snow reflects most of the incident sunlight, and
the clear dry skies allow reradiated heat to escape. Air near the
surface becomes chilled and dense, and during the polar night
the inversion deepens. Normally, a temperature inversion of
this sort makes for a stable atmosphere, with little vertical
mixing. The cold air collects quietly in topographic basins. Not
in Antarctica. The elevation and topography of the ice dome
shape an abrupt plateau of enormous dimensions; more than
half of the ice surface exceeds elevations of 2,000 meters, and
nearly everywhere the 1,000-meter contour line can be found
within 200 kilometers of the coast, often less. Instead of pooling
tranquilly in local basins, the dense air is shed outward and
down the ice dome to form the surface winds—and the perceived weather—of Antarctica. Much as pack ice simplifies the
atmosphere and ocean, so terrestrial ice simplifies weather into
a meteorology of surface-air dynamics, for which simple rules
of synoptic meteorology, which relate winds to pressure gradients, are not adequate to explain the consequences.[1]

Instead the atmosphere is seemingly reduced to the interaction of air and ice. Ice not only creates the sheath of inversion
air but directs it. The dense air sloughs off the ice dome like
sheet runoff on a desert slope. There is some accommodation to
geostrophic effects; the Coriolis force, strong at the poles, deflects the flow to the left, thus forming the polar easterlies. Special flow regimes result from the interaction of inversion winds
with topographic features. In some places the surface air diverges, weakening as it splays outward from the dome, while in
other places it converges through valleys or mountain passes
and intensifies. In still other places major mountains act as barriers that redirect airflow or that, when air occasionally spills
over them, establish foehn winds. And there is some association
with cyclonic storms along the coast, as they alternately dam
up and release outflows of surface air.

The surface weather is by and large the weather of the inversion. It is most intense where the inversion is deepest, most vigorous where the terrain is steepest. In the short term, the surface weather is almost completely uncoupled from that of the
intermediate stratum of Antarctic air. In the interior, to know
the depth of the inversion and the topography of site is usually

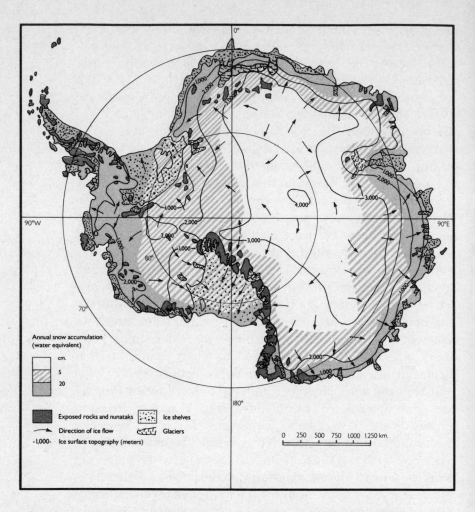

Snow accumulation and ice flow regimes. Accumulation and rates of flow increase toward the perimeter. In general, katabatic wind flow conforms to ice flow patterns. Redrawn, original courtesy Encyclopedia Britannica.

adequate for predicting the surface wind-regime. On the coast,
the process becomes more complicated. Topography steepens
and becomes irregular; surface winds must mingle with air
masses from the pack and beyond; the properties of the air
masses in three dimensions and their complex exchanges of
heat and mass with sea and broken ice fields become significant.
Antarctica has the simplest meteorology of any continent. That
simplicity increases with the increase of ice toward the interior.
Weather patterns may be fierce and huge, but they show nothing
of the complexity of weather elsewhere. Weather seems to be
reduced to surface winds and the numbing constancy of the
inversion.

A special wind mediates between the interior and the coast.
Between inversion winds and cyclonal winds, there exists a
transitional regime of powerful, gravity-driven winds known as
katabatics. Irregular in outflow, yet often dominant locally, katabatics have a much stronger inertial energy than do simple inversion winds. A large drainage area, intense surface cooling,
and a convergent flow pattern are all among preconditions for
katabatic flow. These furnish an adequate air mass. The dynamics of katabatic winds seem to depend, in part, upon the synoptic weather around the coast, especially the movement of
cyclones. Ordinary katabatic winds erupt for periods of hours,
perhaps days, then give way to periods of simple inversion winds
or even calm. Extraordinary katabatic winds, however, can persist for days or even weeks, completely overriding the otherwise
prevalent synoptic weather. For much of Antarctica, outbursts
of katabatic winds—blizzards—constitute the local "storms."
Katabatics are the winds of The Ice.

Typically, katabatic flow begins rapidly, reaches a plateau of
gustiness, then abruptly subsides. As the air avalanche rushes
downslope, it warms adiabatically, and turbulence with the
overlying, warmer air stratum results in further warming. In
some cases, the prevailing lapse rate means that this temperature increase still leaves the katabatic wind colder than the
coastal air it displaces, but often the katabatic air is actually
warmer, although denser. An explanation is that in the process
of descending, the wind scours the surface snowfield, entraining
a considerable volume of snow, and this increases its overall
density such that the warming it experiences is not adequate to
slow its gravitationally driven momentum. Where the drop between plateau and coast is steepest, the winds can reach stag-

gering velocities. Where the source region is also vast and air convergence is the norm—for example, near Adelie Land—extraordinary katabatics may be commonplace for months.

The strength of the katabatics can vary according to their interaction with migrating cyclones. As a storm approaches, relatively warm, moist air is advected inland. As this air mass rides over and against the ice or the cold air of the inversion, it leads to cloudiness and snow drizzles. More importantly, the advected air and unfavorable pressure gradient may dam up the normal outflow of inversion winds or katabatics. As the storm passes, however, a new pressure gradient encourages outflow from the continent. The katabatics rush down the ice, first violently, then steadily, until another cyclone approaches. The blizzards for which Antarctica is so celebrated generally develop when gravity winds (katabatics) and gradient winds (cyclones) act in concert. They are most intense where conditions favor vigorous, extraordinary katabatics—steep slopes, sharp temperature contrasts, developed storm tracks. The winds tumble down the ice dome, sublimating some snow and entraining more, creating a white dust storm from the polar desert. Curiously, the winds in Antarctica know little moderation: they tend to blow either fiercely or mutedly.

Katabatics are best developed over East Antarctica. Here the polar plateau is so massive and elevated that storms from the thin Antarctic atmosphere can barely penetrate anywhere into the interior. By contrast, the smaller, lower West Antarctic ice sheet is crossed so frequently by storms that katabatic flow may be considered secondary. The topography of the Antarctic Peninsula is nonetheless important for local weather. When shallow winds crossing the Weddell Sea reach the Antarcandes, most are dammed and deflected to the right (north) as barrier winds. A small proportion crosses the summit to form foehn winds. Of the winds greater than 10 meters per second in the region, 79 percent are cold barrier-winds from the south and 20 percent are foehn winds from the west. The climate on the east side of the mountains, which is consequently severe, helps account for the prevalence of the pack in the Weddell Sea and the otherwise anomalous presence of the Larsen Ice Shelf.

The barrier winds sustain a geophysical "conveyor belt" to transport ice, cold air, and cold water north within the Weddell gyre. The great outward swelling of the convergence, the string of bergs and broken pack that flare north from the peninsula,

the persistent pack ice and shelf ice so influential in the formation of Antarctic bottom water—all depend on this peculiar
wind regime. In no other sector of the Antarctic has a similar
pattern so fully developed, and only the Ross Sea offers even a
mild analogue. The interruption of the polar easterlies exposes
the upper portions of the west side of the peninsula to marine
influences that make it a distinctive climatic region of the Antarctic. It alone is spared a wind regime connected directly to
the polar plateau. In this balmier state rain rather than snow is
a frequent occurrence, and some influence from South America
is manifest across the Drake Passage.

The katabatic winds have many effects. They scour some
snow off the surface, sublimate other snows, and redeposit still
more. This erosion helps to maintain the steep topographic gradients that, in turn, encourage katabatic flow. Where the cold
katabatic wind slides over warmer seas, snowspouts—whirls of
entrained snow—may dance along the coast, the product of
violent mixing. On a larger scale, the interaction of katabatic
outflow and marine air helps account for the belt of shallow
cyclones that encircles the continent. The effects are limited to
a few kilometers beyond the coast, but they can be dramatic—a
nearly perpetual veil of clouds and blowing snow, torn only by
occasional outbreaks of wind associated with frontal passages.
Unstable lapse rates, associated with katabatics, promote the
transfer of heat and moisture from the ocean to the atmosphere.
Offshore winds interact with the pack ice in important ways,
too. They sublimate and redeposit snow, remove surface meltwater, and drive floes outward. During pack progradation, floe
separation is an important mechanism for promoting interstitial freezing and frazil-ice formation. During storms, when
pack coverage is not total, floe separation exposes seawater,
whose released heat and moisture may intensify the storm. The
katabatics extend the influence of the interior ice outward.

Everywhere the presence of ice is felt. Sea ice is a filter, intervening between air and sea, land and ocean; a lever, amplifying
small changes in environmental conditions into larger effects;
and a matrix, for a mixture of ice masses and for life. The explosive growth of pack ice—in effect, an extension of the Antarctic land mass—is one of the fundamental facts of Antarctic
and Earth weather. The pack severs the connection between
ocean and atmosphere around the continent, expanding and intensifying the polar heat sink. It reflects incident radiation,

cools air and water in contact with it, and breaks the exchange of heat from ocean to atmosphere. Compared to the atmosphere, the oceans have higher heat capacity (1,600:1), greater mass (400:1), and larger momentum (4:1). The atmosphere drives ocean currents, mainly by an exchange of momentum from wind to wave; the ocean, in turn, drives atmospheric processes, primarily by a transfer to heat. Open water transmits nearly one hundred times as much heat to the atmosphere as ice does. Regionally, ice amplifies the conditions that generate the ice; several mechanisms unite ice cover, temperature, and albedo in positive feedback. Globally, The Ice can amplify small changes of atmospheric conditions into larger effects, perhaps even full-blown ice ages.

Biotic Barrier

The pack ice is one of the great biotic boundaries on the planet. It divides the biotic from the abiotic environments of Antarctica, and it marks the limits of life on Earth. Except along the pack, Antarctica constitutes an enormous abiotic oasis segregated from the planetary biosphere. The pack is both a matrix for indigenous life and a biological filter against migration—the only ice terrane with indigenous life. Its biota contributes immensely to the complexity and attractiveness of the terrane.

The biology of Antarctica is almost wholly a marine biology. There are several hundred species of mosses and lichens at selected land sites, a few insects and a spider, a handful of higher plants, but these are confined to subantarctic islands, the milder west coast of the peninsula, and far-flung deglaciated oases. Other than a few cryoalgae, who colonize melting snowfields, no organisms live on land ice exclusively; there is no terrestrial cryo-ecosphere. The biota of Antarctica—proverbially productive and exotic—is confined to the Southern Ocean. A much impoverished terrestrial biota thrives best in areas subject to maritime influences. For geologic eons, the continent has been isolated from any land connection, and its ice sheets have been unable to support an indigenous biota. For a while in the Tertiary Period, a land bridge joined the peninsula to South America, much as the Panamanian isthmus now joins the Americas; but this was severed. Unlike Australia, which was also isolated, Antarctica could not sustain terrestrial life on its own. Unlike

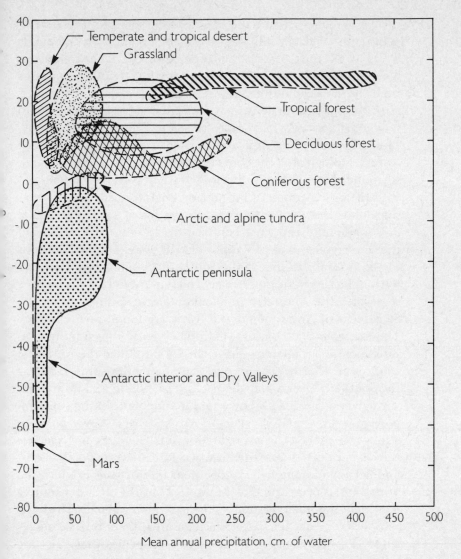

Milieu of terrestrial and Martian biomes. Note the intermediary status of Antarctic biomes, especially away from the peninsula. Redrawn, original courtesy Smithsonian Institution.

the Arctic, where seasonally exposed land supports a terrestrial population that can inhabit sea ice or amphibious mammals who can occupy sea and land, the Antarctic lacks organisms who can live off the icescape or who can occupy the interior from the sea. And unlike the Arctic pack, the Antarctic pack is not continuous enough in space and time to weld land mass to land mass. Its biological connections are wholly maritime, sustained by upwelling from the nutrient-rich circumpolar deep waters. Biologically, the continent is a vast, cold, desert island, surrounded by a formidable moat of frigid surface waters.

With the exception of far-ranging migratory species, such as some birds and whales, the great proportion of Antarctic species are unique and endemic, confined to the continent or within the convergence. The geography of krill, for example, conforms to the frontal systems of the Southern Ocean. Most krill live within the Antarctic divergence, and the Antarctic convergence segregates the Antarctic from subantarctic species. Similarly, 86 percent of Antarctic coastal fishes are found nowhere else. The isolation and cold of Antarctica—both long-standing environmental parameters—have greatly simplified the Antarctic ecosystem. Marine life in The Ice shows the same traits as the Southern Ocean and the pack. It is mobile and migratory, strongly seasonal, with powerful circumpolar mixing superimposed over regional diversity. Terrestrial life shows an even stronger tendency toward reductionism. There are few species; they experience simple life histories, form discrete populations, and occupy circumscribed sites; their interactions are few and direct. It has been said that Antarctica has the most diminutive continental flora and fauna on the planet. For all this The Ice is responsible. Once ice has claimed an area, there is little opportunity for organisms to recolonize. The species that exist are survivors from the last glaciations.

The pack, however, does provide a matrix for life. It exerts an indirect influence through its effects on the Antarctic atmosphere and the Southern Ocean. But its biotic services are direct, too, and seasonal productivity closely parallels the annual cycle of sea ice. The pack furnishes a necessary platform for many marine mammals and birds. The heaviest concentrations of krill, squid, and fish are somewhat away from the ice-abraded shoreline; the pack furnishes rafts to carry seals and penguins to primary feeding grounds, small islands upon which they may rest, sleep, and even mate. Paradoxically, unlike the Arctic, where the continuous pack provides a platform for humans, the Antarctic pack has been a primary barrier for human movement into and around the Antarctic. In this respect, the sea ice again functions as an insulator, a filter, not between air and sea but between civilization and *terra nunquam cognita*.

Perhaps most spectacularly, the pack features a special biota of microorganisms. Unlike land ice, sea ice is not a desert. Two communities of organisms actually exist within it. A snow community forms from sea wash collected on the snowy surface of floes. More productive by several orders of magnitude is an epontic community of microorganisms that thrives on the bottom and interior of floes. The sudden freezing of congelation ice traps algae, diatoms, ciliates, and flagellates within a crystalline scaffolding. Other organisms are caught up in brash-ice slush and frazil-ice clumps that are incorporated into the larger floe. Thus there is a surface snow-biota and a subsurface ice-biota. There are ample nutrients for each. Nitrates and phosphates gravitate to the lower strata of floes, where biological productivity is greatest, and microalgae migrate along capillaries and through brine channels within the floe—weakening the structural strength of the floe and tinging the floe with a brownish stain. Incredibly, the density of microalgae populations and the productivity of the ice biota are perhaps greater than in seawater. An ice fauna, in turn, grazes on this ice flora. Ice biotas contribute as much as 20 percent of the total primary production of Southern Ocean biomass. Whether or not the nutrients and biota released by the recession of the pack actually "seed" the phytoplankton bloom that occurs at the same time is undetermined, but this bloom contributes significantly to the seasonal cycle of life.

The trophic hierarchy of Antarctica is comparatively simple. The food chain is characterized by large numbers of a few species, an enormous biomass within a less diverse ecosystem than those typical of temperate or tropic lands. Virtually all of its bird biomass (99 percent) consists of penguins, and they are dominated by one species, the Adelie. Nearly three-fourths of all Antarctic fishes belong to one group, the nototheniformes. The crabeater seal is the most abundant seal in the world; this single species accounts for 85 percent of Antarctic pinnipeds. The baleen whale dominates the Antarctic whale population, the greatest herd in the world ocean. The impressive yields are best explained by an abbreviated food chain. Even compared to

the Arctic—with its biotic connections to the land masses of
Asia, Europe, and North America—the Antarctic is almost
artlessly uncomplicated. The marine ecosystem thus mimics
The Ice: great bulk in an equally awesome simplicity. Among
the advantages enjoyed by this marine ecosystem, it should be
noted that sea temperatures remain relatively constant and that
the main seasonal change is restricted to the oscillation of the
pack. The tremendous seasonal fluctuations in sunlight and ice
cover, however, are vital for controlling the variable productivity of the system. Continental influences act indirectly on the
biota through their control over pack ice production.

Phytoplankton consist principally of diatoms and dinoflagel-
lates. Their abundance is legendary. The figures may be exaggerated, but the primary productivity of the system is often
estimated to be the richest in the world ocean, perhaps four
times greater than anywhere else. Primary production is greatest
along the coastal areas, excluding the nearshore environments
that are scoured or coated by ice, and amid the coastal seas, the
deep embayments that surround West Antarctica. The nutrient-
rich cold broth that upwells from the circumpolar deep water,
along with possible contributions of phosphate or other minerals from discharged icebergs, accounts for much of this abundance. Accordingly, productivity is most prominent just below
the cold surface waters that veneer the nearshore drift, and it
shows pronounced geographic and seasonal variations.

But it is the next trophic layer that provides a universal link
in the food chain. The euphausiid shrimp known as krill is the
only significant connection between the primary producers and
all the higher trophic feeders. Like the phytoplankton on which
it grazes, krill converges around the Antarctic Peninsula; the
Scotia Sea, nourished by the cold waters of the Weddell Sea, is
especially favored. But the importance of krill to the circumpolar ecosystem depends also on its mobility. It is found everywhere around the continent, though the heaviest concentrations of *Euphasia superba* are embedded within the east wind
drift of the Antarctic circumpolar current. Krill feeds by migrating in a daily rhythm vertically through the water column,
exploiting the upward leaching of nutrients, and it migrates
around the continent in vast surface or near-surface swarms,
with tons of krill to a swarm. Because of its universal importance, directly or indirectly, to all subsequent trophic levels,

krill establishes the basic geography and dynamics of biology in the Antarctic. Life is pelagic, migratory, seasonal, abundant in mass and scanty in variety.

On the krill swarms feed squid and fish; on them feed other fish, birds, and mammals. Although relatively constant in its temperature, the Southern Ocean is bitterly cold. Cold-blooded species, such as fish, adapt by several means to temperatures that would otherwise freeze internal fluids, including the production of several chemical antifreezes that swirl through their body fluids. Warm-blooded species acquire insulating layers, such as blubber or down, by which to retain heat. Virtually all Antarctic birds are pelagic. Some, like the albatross, live and breed outside the pack; others, like penguins, live on the pack; a few, like skuas and penguins, reside at least seasonally along the coastline. But, apart from its penguins—eleven of the eighteen species are present—Antarctica is best known for its marine mammals. There is a fur seal that inhabits subpolar islands and there are true seals—the leopard, crabeater, Weddell, Ross, and elephant—that thrive on the pack. There is a porpoise, the killer whale. And, of course, there are the famed true whales. Whales migrate to the Antarctic during the austral summer, but their abundance is (or was) astonishing. The presence of fur seals and whales first drew humans to the south polar regions.

Humans, of course, are the great anomaly in the Antarctic ecosystem. In some respects—notably their migratory and seasonal habits—they resemble typical Antarctic organisms. But in other ways they are ill-adapted aliens who find the Antarctic as disruptive as the Antarctic biota finds them. They arrived on the continent only in the twentieth century, and they have never become an integral part of the marine ecosystem. They extract from the system, removing organisms to take back to civilization, but they never contribute to the ecosystem's productivity. Their best adaptations are simply to limit the amount they take from the system, or to substitute for the higher trophic feeders, such as whales, whose numbers they have reduced. It is not that humans cannot cope with polar environments; they have adapted famously to the Arctic. Rather, the peculiar isolation and reductionism of The Ice render its occupation problematical for humans. In coping with The Ice, humans must overcome not only the energy gradient, with its abstraction of accessible food and water, but the information gradient, which

strips the region of meaning. By its nature the polar vortex re-
pulses rather than beckons. It drains rather than contributes. By
its awesome simplicity The Ice becomes exclusive.

Yet humans have one singular achievement: they have bound
the marine ecosystem to those terrestrial ecosystems which humans inhabit elsewhere and, through them, have begun the biotic occupation of the Antarctic continent. No other organism
systematically lives on the interior ice sheets. It is precisely because humans need not live off the ice, however, that they can
live on it, that they alone have crossed the biotic boundary
shielding the lifeless Ice from the living Earth. For the most
part, inland from the coastline biological complexity in the
Antarctic ceases. It is the peculiar burden and desire of humans—those from certain civilizations—to extend that complexity inward. It is a complexity of information, not merely of
ecology. It is not what they find in Antarctica that sustains these
humans but what they bring to it and surrender to The Ice.

A Kinetic Art:
The Esthetics of the Pack

The pack marks an esthetic no less than a geographic border. In
its light, colors, shapes, and motions, the pack defines the
ragged transition from landscape to icescape, from Earth art to
Ice art. Because it is a vast zone of mixing, the pack is the most
active and variously populated ice terrane; the site of the most
striking contrasts of sky, sea, light, shape, motion, and ice; the
region richest in sensory data, information, and perspectives.
Of all the terranes within the Antarctic ice field, the pack is the
most complex. It is no accident that so many artists who come
to Antarctica confine themselves to the pack, where access is
easiest, where life is abundant and exotic, where light effects
are varied and subtle, where (if near the coast) mountainous
backdrops offer traditional perspective and a reassuring allu-
sion to alpine esthetics.

Much of the variety results from seasonal changes. During
midsummer, after the pack has rapidly disintegrated and the fog
that normally shadows it has vanished, something resembling a
modified seascape is possible. Sunlight plays with storm cloud
to illuminate a silver-grey sea, dappled with ripples and swells,
ice flakes and floes. The sky is colored with subdued pastels of

yellow, grey, and blue, mixed with grey and white cloud. In the distance, bounded by the pack, the horizon is obliterated by a grey fogbank, flaked by white scuds of cloud. Sea and sky— roughly in equal proportion, with a minimum of ice—mirror one another.

With the progradation of the pack, with the deepening of winter, with proximity to the continent, the proportion of ice effects increases. On the seaward fringe of the pack there is not enough ice, while along the shore there is too much. Between these extremes, however, the pack is at its most attractive. There are variations in the objects that populate the scene, in the mixtures of sea, light, cloud, air, and ice, in the choice of perspective. In particular, the appearance of the pack changes dramatically with changes in the character and the distribution of incident light. For much of the year, a veil of snow drizzle, sea smoke, and ice fog envelops the terrane and blocks, distorts, and reflects incoming sunlight. But breaks in the clouds, new orientations of the object to sunlight, and movement of the ice can swiftly recompose and color the same collection of objects.

During the austral summer, sunlight is rarely blocked completely. The cloud deck is low, often consisting of sea smoke or ice fog. Yet there are breaks from time to time, and the dense haze is partially translucent. With or without openings light diffuses through the veil, reduced in intensity and sometimes scattered to bluish hues. Often light is so altered that apparent shadows replace true shadows. It is possible to look to one side of a scene, immersed in diffused sunlight, to discover a virtual whiteout, with heavy pack ice, ghostly icebergs, and finely sprayed fog merged into a single pale luminescence. To the other side, the shadow zone, objects are distinct. Ice floes and bergs gleam iridescently, as if from some inner radiance; the sea glowers in dull black; and the clouds thicken gloomily. In the same way, an iceberg may present a greyish or dull ivory color at one locale, then after passing out of the shadow zone glow a brilliant white.

The surface texture and composition of the ice masses also vary the character of the reflected light. Fresh snow on a floe or berg radiates a dazzling white; meltwater, dull yellow; exposed sea ice, a yellow grey, often lightly stained brown; and exposed glacial ice, blue and white. Just beneath the sea surface, washed free of snow, ice appears green and turquoise. At times, in vigorous sunlight, the ice gleams like whalebone; and in light more strongly filtered and scattered, it is a pale blue. Apertures of blue and turquoise sky may momentarily open in the cloud deck to immerse the surface in brilliant, if localized, lighting effects. Sunlight on ice clouds and ice surfaces induces optical spectacles—haloes, parhelia, arcs—and the surface inversion above the pack promotes mirages. Where clouds reflect open leads, a dark water-sky results. Where the pack is reflected, the yellow-white flush of iceblink brightens the cloying haze.

Seawater, too, exhibits a range of colors as a function of how much incident light is scattered and absorbed. The waters of the Southern Ocean are famously pure, adding little coloration through light scatter from contaminants. When the sun shines directly on open water, the sea appears a dull green-grey. When viewed in thin shadow, the sea seems darkly blue-grey. In deep shadow, with maximum absorption and minimum scatter, the sea is as black as tar. Thus, a composite scene of bergs, floes, and sea may be swallowed up into whitish obscurity when viewed in strong light and low fog; or reveal muted contrasts of shape and design when observed in a shadow zone; or starkly counterpoint black sea and white ice, bluish berg and turquoise streaks of open sky, when seen under a deep or fractured overcast.

The pack may be profusely populated with scenic objects. Small chunks of ice litter the sea like frozen foam. Sea ice floes endlessly change shape, color, and motions, both individually and collectively. Bergs, like prisms, may capture and refract light differently as they raft across the scene. No other ice terrane possesses so many kinds of ices or such a welter of ice masses of different dimensions. Even more, there is life. Penguins and seals adorn floes with color, shape, and movement. Sea ice biotas stain floes. The combinations are endless.

Seen from beneath, the translucent ice suffuses the interacting blue, white, and green light with a subfloe topography punctuated by spires and hummocks. The view is arresting, but too strongly filtered by the ice to hold interest for long. Viewed from above, the pack presents a wonderfully abstract geometry. Its pattern of ruptures and sutures makes an ice embroidery of floes. Their different ages, as they congeal or dissolve, make floes differentially translucent and colored. A melange of dark sea and white ice, of serpentine polynyas and rigid ice polygons, combines the genres of action painting, collage, and abstract expressionism. Where the pack is dense and snow-covered, the white of the ice overpowers the white of the clouds; clouds glide over the icescape like disembodied grey shadows. All these perspectives of the pack, moreover, have in common that they are pictures of surfaces, patterns of colors on a flat canvas of sea and ice. They lack depth, borders. Yet this variety of perspectives is nowhere else approached by the ice terranes of Antarctica.

The pack is most interesting when it exhibits, within a single scene, a good mixture of all its potential effects. Such an ensemble is rare. More typical is the modulation of a given scene by variations in the intensity and the distribution of light. The result is a subtle permutation of color or of apparent composition. There is a darkening or lightening of hues or a reconstitution of ice and sea amid a somber twilight. The scene simplifies into a vast duotone of grey, dull ivory, or pale blue. In dense, overcast pack, sky and sea take on the same color, sheen, and texture. In the absence of motion and color the horizon vanishes into a common smudge of grey. The sparseness of strong light blurs shape as well as color into an immense spectral monotone. Gneisslike bands of slightly lighter or darker greys differentiate the elements of the scene—if anything can. This oppressive uniformity is broken only by the irregular arrangement of ice. White on white, grey on grey, opaque cloud on opaque floe, flat ice on a flat horizon of floe and fog, a collage of white particles on a white surface. Only icebergs, mountainous white shadows, manage to interrupt the scene. Occasionally, a berg of blue ice, still enveloped in mist, captures a shaft of sunlight and gleams like sapphire, an effect both stunning and enchanting—the setting of a blue sun amid a grey twilight.

As autumn deepens and the pack stiffens near the coast, the terrane sheds the variability of light, motion, and objects that makes it attractive. Instead, by a process of subtraction, the scene simplifies and intensifies. More and more is removed. The scene is compressed, like the Antarctic sea and atmosphere, into a shallow surface—a linearity of banded low clouds, floes, and tabular bergs. Perspective lapses into indeterminacy. Composition blurs as borders proceed to infinity and objects lose their mass and structure. Color is erased into whiteout and greyout. Even motion slows. The pack, welding into a continuous sheet, dampens ocean swells. The only movement is the slow freezing of open leads, the grappling of frazil ice to floe, the muted impact of floe upon floe, the stately, imperceptible tread of the bergs—luminous shadows, ice sphinxes, full of grey inscrutability. The pack as a whole may move under the impress of tides and deep ocean swells, but it does so with ponderous undulations, like an earthquake in slow motion. Near the shore, as winter approaches, motion ceases. Ice fragments weld into a rigid mosaic of inertness, a still life painted in white and grey. Then, amidst the polar night, all discriminations are lost in a frozen entropic darkness.

These are the common esthetics of all The Ice. What makes the pack special among the icescapes of Antarctica is its relative abundance and variability, its dramatic mixing of Earth and Ice. Compared to normal landscapes, the pack is esthetically impoverished. What dramatic spectacles it contains appear episodically and mechanically. Compared, however, to the interior icescape—monolithic and seasonally invariant—the pack offers a bewildering ensemble of effects and scenery. Its matrix of fluids—the air and the sea—brings far more mobility and uncertainty to the scenery of the pack than is possible where an ice mass is wholly embedded in solids. There is an element of randomness. Surprise is possible. Accordingly, the pack is most spectacular where it mixes floes, sea, bergs, and broken sky; when the ice grows and moves and storms reshuffle; when the ice is not complete, the fog not total, the sky neither wholly obscured nor utterly open; when there is a certain proportion of light and dark in vivid contrast, not homogenized into a uniform twilight; when some ice surfaces reflect incident light and some ice prisms refract them. White ice abuts black sea, with no gradation between them other than the muted light that diffuses through mixed clouds.

It is an ensemble that mimics the ebb and flow of the polar day, that instantly encapsulates the seasonal progradation and retrogradation of the pack. The contrast—the proportions—accounts for the effectiveness of the scene. No single process or esthetic dominates completely. In the scene's finest expressions, all are mixed and in motion. Each, by its contrast, heightens the other.

RETROGRADATION

The floes hesitate, suspended in an instantaneous equilibrium of seasons, like the globular clusters of an expanding universe caught at their maximum extent before gravity induces a slow collapse.

Then the retrogradation of the pack begins. Maximum progradation is reached sometime in October, just after the vernal equinox. Now comes the recession. It is not an implosion so much as an erosion of the ragged perimeter, a steady exposure of sea at the expense of ice. The processes that directed the progradation of the pack now guide its retrogradation. The same principles of positive feedback accelerate the trend. What has changed is the general climate under which these processes operate. The polar night favors ice production; the polar day, ice erosion. What makes the recession possible is not simply the removal of old ice but the failure to regenerate new ice. The net balance between ice growth and ice decay tilts toward loss. The areal extent of the Antarctic ice field is halved as the pack retreats inward, drawing back the veil, a disintegrating vortex of ice floes and bergs.

The individual floes ablate in several ways, but surface meltwater, so integral to the destruction of sea ice in the Arctic, has little role in the Antarctic. Winds from the interior polar desert sublimate the surface snow off floes and evaporate any standing meltwater. The katabatics of Antarctica are much drier and 60–100 percent stronger than Arctic winds. Only thin films of water develop over the surface, although melting does occur internally, concentrated around the black bodies of inclusions like microorganisms trapped within the rapidly assembled skeleton of the floe. Instead, open leads between floes take the place of surface meltponds. Winds drive apart those floes along the outer edge, but instead of refreezing, the interstitial leads remain open. The growth of open water reduces the albedo of the pack, encouraging solar heating of open water; warmer water upwells into the pools, promoting further melting of floes; waves penetrate the pack, leading to more thermal decay and mechanical disintegration; icebergs, increasingly mobile in the more fluid matrix of the collapsing pack, plow through floes, widening leads and crushing smaller ice masses. Since storms tend to hover over the circumpolar ring of maximum thermal upwelling, which generally coincides with the perimeter of the pack, the seasonal temperature change brought on by the waxing polar day can initiate the process of retrogradation. The storm belt, in turn, moves inward with the receding pack. Curiously, the pace of the recession outstrips that of the progression.

By February sea ice is at a minimum. Over half the total decay occurs from mid-November to mid-January. For the most part, the pack contracts steadily southward toward the coast. The Weddell Sea is again an exception. Here the pack persists, although it retreats along an axis from east to west. But the collapse is never complete. Some floes linger, mingling with bergs and other ice breccia. Some are trapped in the Weddell Sea gyre, adding another year to their life cycle. Some are caught as fast ice in protected areas of the shore, part of a coastal ice terrane that, unlike the pack, rings the continent with a nearly immobile, quasi-permanent shield. A hybrid of sea ice, snow, and firn, fast ice connects the ice terrane of the pack to the ice terrane of the continent. It is itself a partial metamorphosis of sea ice into land ice, floe to glacial tongue, pack ice to ice shelf.

The processes that shape sea ice and land ice are also responsible for fast ice, with the addition that both sets of processes here interact and their ices intercalate into a unique stratigraphy. The ice begins under the same conditions that generate sea ice. A protected embayment, perhaps sprinkled with grounded bergs; light winds, currents, and tides; and open water (a polynya is ideal) to generate fresh crystals—all lead to an ice matrix and the creation of a sheet of sea ice frozen to coastal ice or land. Anchor ice and frazil ice add to the expansion of the lower stratum. Crystal growth by congelation ice and the incorporation of other ice fragments expands the floe along its margins. Snow, recrystallizing meltwater, and (when the snow weights the floe so that the ice layer falls beneath sea level) percolating seawater all add ice strata to the surface. The saturation of surface snow (and sometimes firn) by seawater, which then freezes, can account for 25–90 percent of the total ice mass. Some seawater represents simple wash, trapped on the surface; but some enters the floe interior from beneath, along fissures that then freeze to form lenses and veins of infiltration ice. Grounded bergs promote fast ice by creating a breakwater that dampens sea and wind, traps snow, cools the adjacent seawaters. Fast ice, in turn, helps shield the bergs from erosion.

But fast ice also erodes, and the resulting terrane represents a new outcome between the addition of new snows and ices and their subtraction. Open water seasonally erodes the sides and bottoms of the ice, winds and tides contribute to its mechanical disintegration, and winds ablate some surface snows. Solar heating melts other snows, particularly when they are contami-

nated with dark organic and abiotic debris. The uneven topography of the resulting ice surface leads to differential filling
and emptying, an alternating relief of scourings and deposits.
This asymmetric erosion is even more intense in the presence of
dirty ice. By absorbing more radiation than pure ice does, dirty
ice surfaces can erode into fantastic sculpturings, the most exotic shapes in Antarctica. Shore ice that is only seasonally fast
breaks out in sudden surges.

In general more ice is formed than removed, and the special
circumstances that favor the formation of fast ice also favor its
preservation. Protected from ocean swells and chilled by a matrix of land ice—glaciers and bergs both—fast ice persists. It
experiences some disintegration, some ablation and breakage.
But new ice replaces the old; ices of different composition, origins, and structure combine into a unique amalgamation. Snow
cover and frozen sea-slush are underlain by strata of congelation ice and veins of infiltration ice, which are in turn underlain by loosely consolidated frazil ice, congelation ice, anchor
ice, and ice stalactites. In place of the annual ontogeny of
growth and decay that characterizes individual floes in the open
sea or the seasonal waxing and waning that accompany the life
cycle of the pack, fast ice acquires an internal structure and a
history.

This fragment of sea ice, now firmly fastened to the coast, is
all that remains of the mighty pack. Part of an inner, less mobile perimeter, the spotty terrane of fast ice traces a new zone of
cold mixing, one that mingles solids rather than fluids. The particle of fast ice thus has symbolic as well as geographic importance. It marks a ragged cryospheric boundary, the first one that
is internal to The Ice. Elsewhere land ice is sloughed off into sea
ice, to join the phylogeny of the pack. But here land ice replaces
or metamorphoses sea ice, and sea ice is transformed into an approximation of land ice. Land replaces sea, land ice displaces
sea ice, Ice supersedes Earth.

2 No Middle Way
The Exploration of Antarctica

> *Come, my friends,*
> *Tis not too late to seek a newer world.*
> *Push off, and sitting well in order smite*
> *The sounding furrows; for my purpose holds*
> *To sail beyond the sunset, and the baths*
> *Of all the western stars, until I die.*
>
> —Alfred, Lord Tennyson, "Ulysses" (1842)

> *The Pole lay in the center of a limitless*
> *plain. . . . One gets there, and that is about*
> *all there is for the telling. It is the effort to*
> *get there that counts.*
>
> —Richard E. Byrd, *Little America* (1930)

This simplest of the world's environments harbors the simplest of the world's civilizations, one based almost exclusively on exploration. The pack ice and the veil of fog that perpetually shrouds the pack warded off human inquiry until renewed speculation about a tropical *terra australis* situated near the South Pole, a concept whose ancestry traces back to Greek geographers, inspired Great Britain to send Capt. James Cook to discover the facts. Antarctica thus began as an idea, and its discovery would be intimately connected to intellectuals and intellectual history. Its extraordinary isolation was not merely geophysical but metaphysical. The transition to Antarctic exploration demanded more than the power to overcome the energy gradients that surrounded The Ice: it demanded the capacity and the desire to overcome Antarctica's information gradient. The penetration of Antarctica thus required not only the development of special ships and steam power or aircraft, but suitable syndromes of thought. Antarctic exploration would be deliberate, not accidental. "No one comes here casually," observed J. Tuzo Wilson, presiding over the International Geophysical Year. "It is a continent of extremes and of contrasts where there is no middle way."[1]

The Ice stripped civilization (and exploration) to its most elemental forms. Exploration often became a matter of simple survival. Antarctic outposts evolved into information colonies, importing energy and ideas and exporting raw data. Discovery proceeded inland without the alliances and associations of former epochs—without trade, conquest, missionizing, pilgrimage, travel; without a community of life from which explorers could derive sustenance and inspiration; without indigenous human societies which could supply guides, native technologies, companionship, and alternate moral universes. Discovery had a remote, abstract, surficial quality. Expeditions traveled to such intangible geographic sites as the pole of rotation, the geomagnetic pole, and the pole of inaccessibility, or sought against the stark Antarctic icescape to recapitulate such traditional exploration gestures as a circumnavigation of the seas or a cross-continental traverse. In some respects, Antarctica is best understood by what it is not, and Antarctic discovery is perhaps best revealed by the things it lacked. It is appropriate that Captain Cook—the exponent of negative discovery, as Daniel Boorstin describes him—should inaugurate the exploration of Antarctica by setting out to disprove its existence.[2] In the end, explorers and the civilization that sent them did not discover The Ice so much as The Ice allowed them to discover themselves. The ineffable whiteness of the polar plateau became a vast, imperfect mirror that reflected back the character of the person and civilization that gazed upon it.

Not even the Arctic offered a comparable degree of alienness. During the great explosion of Renaissance exploration, the search for a Northwest Passage around the Americas and a Northeast Passage around the top of Europe led to a quick assessment of the Arctic. The density of its pack ice made maritime exploration impossible for any distance. But the circumpolar Arctic was occupied by native peoples, the technology existed by which to travel over the pack at least seasonally, and the lands themselves provided a ready point of access. Eventually European and American explorers learned to live off the pack and its shores, to exploit the drift of the pack—the Arctic gyre—to advantage. Although the Arctic pack decayed annually along its perimeter and its summer surface was almost impenetrable because of meltponds and pressure ridges, the pack retained its identity throughout the year. Arctic sea ice was a surrogate land surface. Antarctic sea ice was not. The Antarctic pack was a formidable barrier, and it defined the rhythms of Antarctic discovery.

Unlike the Arctic, too, there were no ecosystems or permanent human societies on the Antarctic ice terranes. Humans confronted an entirely physical universe one-to-one—without intervening biological communities or indigenous cultures. Much of what passed for discovery prior to Antarctica was in reality a process of translation from one culture to another. Native guides and native collectors, interpreters, and scholars who immersed themselves in the lore of other peoples were fundamental to the acquisition of geographic knowledge by Western civilization. Europe reworked these assorted systems of learning into a grand synthesis, much as it connected disparate maritime (and later land-based) civilizations into a world network. The success of Arctic explorers, for example, was predicated on adapting native technology to new purposes. Robert Peary, Fritjof Nansen, and Vilhjalmur Stefansson—these great Arctic explorers became in effect white Eskimos. None of this was possible on The Ice. Wally Herbert recorded the astonishment of a group of Greenland Eskimos who were shown a film about Antarctica:

What my audience in Greenland had seen of the Antarctic projected on the screen was as strange to them as the expression I had seen on their eyes. . . . They had seen only a cold desert, beautiful but barren. There was no vegetation there; no gnats, mosquitoes, mice or hares; no musk-oxen, reindeer, caribou or polar bears. It was a weird world they had seen in these pictures, desolate and pure—quite unlike their living, breathing, hunting territory.[3]

The isolation of Antarctica was almost total. The Ice was sui generis; it was solipsistic, self-reflexive. The other continents had been information sources; the quintessential experience of the explorer had been one of novelty, of an abundance of specimens, artifacts, data, scenery, and experiences. Western civilization had evolved systems of knowledge and procedures for learning which assumed just such expectations. The Ice, by contrast, was an information sink. The explorer was compelled to look not out, but inward. The power of discovery depended on what was brought to the scene more than on what could be generated out of it. Like other discovered worlds, Antarctica posed immense problems of assimilation—political, economic, intellectual. But unlike with the seas or the other continents, traditional means of institutional absorption and understanding broke down on The Ice. Paradoxically, what began as a richly imagined continent not unlike others became, when finally explored, a white spot on the globe.

Not until the mid-twentieth century was Antarctica prepared to become a point of departure for an epoch of exploration rather than a terminus. Antarctica would join the deep oceans and interplanetary space as an arena for exploration, but the transition would come at a cost. The human perspective—best symbolized by the relationship between an explorer and his interpreter or guide, or by the explorer submerged in native lore—would be replaced by a more abstract flow of information from distant prosthetic devices interrogating a geography relentlessly hostile to human presence and alien to traditional human understanding. On The Ice there were no native peoples or prior civilizations with whom explorers or the other Western institutions could interact. The exploration of Antarctica would not be encumbered by the spectacle of clashing cultures, but neither would it be enriched by their interchange. No Bartolomé de Las Casas would publicize a Black Myth, but no George Catlin would record the simple splendor of the Plains Indians, no Vilhjalmur Stefansson would write about the vitality of the Inuit, no Franz Boas, enthralled by the Eskimos of Baffin Island, would argue for the cultural relativity of moral worlds. There would be no anthropology in Antarctica, no myths of primitivism—no Noble Savage, no Virgin Forest—by which to contrast and criticize the artificialities of Western civilization. The Ice is utterly inhuman. Two centuries after Captain Cook's vessels, the *Resolution* and the *Adventure*, maneuvered through the pack, two decades after the International Geophysical Year inaugurated the full-scale exploration and occupation of Antarctica, Vikings 1 and 2 landed on Mars. The ethnocentricity of Western exploration was gone, but so was its anthropocentricity.

"In further search of the said continent"

The discovery of Antarctica pivoted on two events which were fundamental to the larger history of Western exploration and for which Antarctic discovery was a principal objective: the voyages of Captain James Cook and the International Geophysical Year. Until then the Southern Ocean, pack ice, and icebergs represented the outermost of seas and islands discovered through Western exploration since the Renaissance. The Southern Ocean became the last of the world's oceans to be explored, Antarctica the last of the continents. The discovery of Antarctica, however, did not introduce dramatically novel modes of exploration or produce unassimilable information. Although the 1920s introduced a transitional phase in the purposes and techniques of exploration, only with the advent of the International Geophysical Year (IGY) in the mid-1950s did Antarctica become really fundamental. For the first time it became integral rather than marginal to a new era of discovery. It found conceptual ties with other uninhabited (or uninhabitable) regions in the solar system, witnessed the invention of new techniques for penetrating The Ice, and posed immense, often unprecedented legal and geopolitical questions.

The first empirical work of discovery around Antarctica, the second of Cook's celebrated voyages (1772–1775), put the hypothetical southern continent center stage in exploration. Curiously, already the abstract and intellectual attributes of Antarctica were apparent, for Cook's objective was to prove or disprove the existence of the continent. "You are to proceed upon farther Discoveries . . . keeping in as high a Latitude as you can, & prosecuting your discoveries as near to the South Pole as possible," his "secret instructions" read, "in further Search of the said Continent. . . ."[4] But Cook's voyages were themselves a transitional event in the evolution of the exploring tradition of the West, and it is worth examining the nature of this metamorphosis for what it reveals about the relationship of Antarctica to Western civilization.

Captain James Cook was the most prominent of a swarm of eighteenth-century circumnavigators who brought to a culmination an era of predominantly maritime exploration which had its origins in Renaissance Europe. More than their mere fact or the data they shipped back to an awestruck Europe, those voyages set in motion a social dynamic: exploration became an institution, the explorer a role. There are many ways by which one culture can learn about other lands and peoples. But exploration—as an institution, a concept, and a tradition—is apparently an invention of Western civilization, and it appeared, not accidentally, with that other Western invention, modern science. By themselves, the voyages of the fifteenth and sixteenth centuries were logical successors to centuries of European travel, trade, conquest, and seafaring. The exploits of Alexander the Great, for example, may be thought of as a kind of exploration by conquest; the sudden acquisition of lands, wealth, exotic peoples, and knowledge created problems in intellectual and geopolitical assimilation identical to those posed by the voyages of the Renaissance. The Hellenistic synthesis achieved by the Alexandrian school, symbolized by the school's magnificent library, is an archetype for the information explosions that would typically follow future eras of discovery.

Yet the pattern in the fifteenth century was different, too. Other times and other peoples had experienced challenges similar to that posed by Alexander in the ancient world without becoming the basis for a world system. By contrast, the process set in motion by the European voyages of discovery was a process of world discovery, and it would result in a single world geography. It established a unique activity, exploration, and it created a unique if syncretic role, that of the explorer. A composite of old activities and preexisting technologies, the result was, like modern science, peculiarly new. Geographic discovery, the

articulation of a scientific philosophy, a religious reformation,
a rebirth of trade, art, and maritime city-states—all reinforced
each other to make the nation-states of modern Europe different
from the tribal entities and empires of antiquity, the scientific
outlook distinct from earlier natural philosophies, and the process of discovery something curiously different from travel, adventure, pilgrimage, and trade.

In a sense, there was one world to be discovered, and Europe
would discover it. Other periods of travel and exploration had
had a self-arresting, ethnocentric quality. But this new era had
a self-reinforcing mechanism that continually thrust outward
and would, sooner rather than later, absorb European civilization as it did other societies. It would challenge the explorer as
much as the explored. The events surrounding the first great
voyages set in motion a dynamic of exploration—tied on one
hand to the geopolitics of European expansion and on the other
to the equally aggressive principles of modern science—that
would prove irreversible. Although in some ways a model for
the new empirical sciences, especially in its challenge to au-
thoritative texts of the ancients and to Holy Scripture, geographic discovery was a beneficiary of the new philosophy.
Experimental science was limited only by the ingenuity and
technology of its practitioners; the limitations on the growth of
knowledge lay in society, not in nature. Unlike geographic exploration on the traditional model, the experimental philosophy did not depend on the availability of new lands and new
peoples.

The great vehicle for European discovery was the ship. Exploration was predominantly maritime, intimately bound to the
founding of coastal cities, the development of oceanic empires,
and the mapping of the world's coastlines. Its outstanding revelation was the unity of the world's oceans; its grand expression,
a voyage of circumnavigation; and its intellectual achievement,
a *mappa mundi* of the Earth's coastlines. The process began
with the interior seas of Europe, then spread into the Atlantic
and beyond. The Mediterranean and the Baltic were themselves
composites of smaller seas, seas dotted with islands large and
small and joined by straits of greater and lesser significance. No
continent has a higher ratio of coastline to land mass than Europe, although North America has an analogous system of interior seas with the Caribbean, the Gulf of Mexico, and Hudson

Bay. Not surprisingly, Europe's outward expansion came by water, beginning with the hybridization of Europe's northern (Baltic) and southern (Mediterranean) seafaring traditions.

Seafaring and the establishment of maritime empires were not unique to Europe. As J. H. Parry has observed, there were many maritime cultures around the globe, and the problem of European "discovery" was really a process of connecting these various maritime states.[5] Marco Polo, after all, returned from Cathay to Venice by sea, hopping from one maritime network to another. The essence of the European achievement was to recognize that these various enclaves of maritime prowess collectively formed a single world ocean, to join these various civilizations into a general geopolitical economy, and to organize the geographic and technological knowledge of these peoples into a larger intellectual construct. The process was often one of adaptation and translation; interpreters were fundamental to the success of the enterprise. Vasco da Gama made the Indian Ocean crossing after seizing an Arab pilot along the coast of Africa. Magellan's crew, after the massacre of its leaders on Luzon, wandered aimlessly in the South China Sea until they captured a local pilot who took them to the Moluccas. And Columbus relied on indigenous peoples to find his way around the islands of the Caribbean.

Nor was the exchange limited to geographic lore. Other bodies of information found their way into European consciousness. Although Western civilization would be the vehicle for discovery, the intellectual universe of the West would be as profoundly altered by the revelation of this information as were the cultures and lands it visited. Europe's inherited systems of thought gradually crumbled—not merely expanded by the infusion of data, but utterly redesigned from new, sometimes alien points of view. The effects would ramify throughout that entire intellectual universe of art, science, natural philosophy, political theory, natural history, jurisprudence, literature.

To the voyages of discovery the continents—other than Asia, the objective—were impediments. Instead seaborne explorers searched eagerly, even maniacally, for passages around or straits through the land masses. The conviction slowly grew, some of it based on inherited speculation from the sages of antiquity, that the various oceans were united, and the European experience in the Mediterranean and the Baltic-Atlantic had suggested that connections would be found by probing coastlines, bays, and inlets. The search for a Northwest Passage around North America and a Northeast Passage around Scandinavia; the quest for saltwater straits, such as that discovered by Magellan and those, such as the Anian or Buenaventura, which existed only in the imagination; the hunt for an isthmus, like that at Panama, which would connect two seas by a brief overland passage—all amplified prior European experience. Ultimately, the successful circumnavigation of the globe by Magellan demonstrated that the world's oceans were one, and throughout the era European exploration remained true to its maritime origins. Outposts for trade in the Far East, Africa, and the New World required a maritime nexus sustained by a succession of maritime empires. Portuguese, Dutch, and English mercantile and political ambitions began with the establishment of port cities; before New World conquistadores ventured inland to topple Precolumbian empires they first constructed seaports; new colonies were coastal, never venturing far from their maritime lifeline. Expeditions into the interior proceeded along waterways, by river or lake, if not by saltwater inlet.

During this process of discovery, the techniques used to explore new regions and the interpretive systems within which information about them was incorporated broke down. The world ocean could not be assimilated by a simple elaboration of piloting skills and portolan charts developed for the Mediterranean and the Baltic-North seas. There were problems of scale that could not be solved through a simple enlargement but that demanded new principles of organization. Because of the voyages, the *Geographia* of Claudius Ptolemy, the summa of ancient geographic wisdom, would be superseded instead of merely revised, much as the *De Revolutionibus* of Nicolaus Copernicus would replace, not merely redesign, the inherited lore contained in Ptolemy's companion cosmology, the *Almagest*.

In many ways, Antarctica conformed to this pattern. The myth of a great southern land and sea, the fabled *terra australis*—an inheritance from Hellenistic lore—was among the last of the Cíbolas, El Dorados, and Brasils to dissolve beneath the harsh gaze of exploration. The Greek passion for symmetry demanded that the globe contain an immense land mass south of the torrid zone (the equator) to balance the vast known lands to the north. For centuries, while cartographers invented new techniques of projection and radically redrew the known outline of the world's coastlines, incorporating a New World unimagined by the ancients, *mappae mundi* contained the hypothetical Southern Continent. The discovery of the Straits of Magellan and even the Drake Passage did not destroy this tradition. Magellan saw land to both sides, and his strait could be envisioned as a New World equivalent to the Dardanelles. Drake did not see land to the south, but that fact, when accepted, only shrank the dimensions of the imagined continent. Meanwhile, intermittent landfalls on large masses in the Pacific announced what might be peninsulas from the *terra australis*.

Here the voyages of Cook assume their importance. Systematically, Cook investigated the remaining coastlines of the Pacific. The reputed outliers from the Southern Continent were, in reality, the islands of New Zealand and Australia—whose great size earned it the old name. The Northwest Passage did not exist. The Southern Continent, if it existed, was in a forbidding region of polar ice, wholly uninhabitable. During Cook's second voyage (1772–1775), on which he enjoyed favorable pack-ice conditions, he circumnavigated the Southern Ocean, crossed the Antarctic Circle, and penetrated to latitude 71 degrees 10 minutes South, near the Amundsen Sea. Though he found abundant marine riches—his popular account, *A Voyage towards the South Pole* (1777), started a veritable rush of whalers and fur sealers to the subpolar area—he fatally wounded the vision of a flourishing civilization near the pole. Cook did not make landfall or even see the coast, though he "firmly believed" that some land existed farther south which was responsible for the ice. Instead he had to content himself with threading his two ships through the decaying perimeter of the pack and around enormous "ice islands." In exploration, as in other dimensions of natural history, the pack ice defined the effective perimeter—the littoral—of the continent. Interestingly, Cook's greatest geographic discoveries did not reveal new lands so much as they defined the dimensions of known coastlines and erased whole continents of a hypothetical geography. Cook summarized:

> I have now made the circuit of the Southern Ocean in a high Latitude, and traversed it in such a manner as to leave not the least room for the Possibility of there being a continent, unless near the Pole and out of the reach of Navigation. . . . Thus I flatter myself that the intention of the Voyage has in every respect been fully Answered, the Southern

Hemisphere sufficiently explored and a final end put to the searching after a Southern Continent, which has at times ingrossed the attention of some of the Maritime Powers for near two Centuries past and the Geographers of all ages. [6]

Cook thus became the great practitioner of "negative discovery," and it is appropriate that the scene of his grandest triumph should be the Antarctic—the "country of Refusal," as poet Katha Pollitt describes it, where "No was final." [7]

Even the indomitable Cook, however, backed away, sensibly enough, from deeper penetrations into The Ice. "The risk one runs in exploreing a coast in these unknown and Icy Seas, is so very great, that I can be bold to say, that no man will ever venture farther than I have done and that the lands which may lie to the South will never be explored." [8] Should anyone have "the resolution and perseverance to find . . . beyond where I have been," he concluded, "I shall not envy him the honour of the discovery, but I will be bold to say, that the world will not be benefited by it." [9] The challenge was not merely technological but intellectual. There were no means to enter The Ice and no purpose to justify the attempt.

It was recognized even in the eighteenth century that Cook's remarkable voyages were special, that they combined new skills with new purposes of exploration. Yet they were not isolated phenomena. Cook was only the highest expression of the era; other circumnavigators sailed the unknown seas, and scientific inquiry had begun to move inland from the coast. New lands were discovered and old ones resurveyed in the spirit and with the intellectual apparatus of the Enlightenment. Especially in the Antarctic, where the true coastline had not yet been visited, there was ample room for both amateur and professional. Cook's travels became an exemplar and stimulant for further voyages of discovery, and his published reports inspired a good deal of political and economic rivalry for the lands and resources he had observed.

But the North Pacific was more promising than the Southern Ocean; the northwest coast of North America was already an active arena for imperial ambitions, and its sea otters and fur seals were more accessible than the seals and whales of Antarctica. Not until 1819 did interest in Antarctica awaken—promoted in part by the accidental discovery of the South Shetland

Islands by William Smith, a British merchant captain blown off course by a storm, and in part by the systematic voyages of Fabian Gottlieb von Bellingshausen, who had been sent by Czar Alexander I on "an extended voyage of discovery" in the ships *Vostok* and *Mirnyi*. "Every effort will be made to approach as closely as possible to the South Pole," read Bellingshausen's instructions, "searching for as yet unknown land, and only abandoning the undertaking in the face of insurmountable obstacles."[10] The South Shetlands were fecund with fur seals, and after confirmation of the find by Capt. James Sheffield, an American sealer, word of their commercial possibilities spread rapidly. Within a year scores of sealers had swarmed around the islands, and the senior British officer at Valparaiso, Capt. Edward Bransfield, hastily organized an expedition (which included Smith) to the islands in order to claim them for Britain.

The rapid exhaustion of seals led to a search for other rookeries in the region, principally by British and American sealers. Capt. Benjamin Pendleton, overseeing a flotilla of five ships (1820–1821), dispatched Capt. Nathaniel Palmer of the *Hero* on a voyage from the South Shetlands to the Antarctic Peninsula (Palmer Land) across the Bransfield Strait. At one point Palmer visited Bellingshausen aboard his ship. Capts. John Davis and Christopher Burdick (1820–1821) also crossed the strait and made the first documented landing on the mainland. The *Lord Melville* unwillingly spent the first Antarctic winter. The next year, Pendleton and Palmer returned with eight ships, explored King George, Clarence, and Elephant islands, and, in the company of George Powell, a British sealing captain, discovered the South Orkney Islands. Pendleton later brought three ships south for a combination of sealing and scientific exploration (1829–1831); the accounts of the expedition's naturalist, James Eights, inaugurate the scientific assimilation of Antarctica. Palmer's exploits were publicized by his mentor, Edmund Fanning. Although others probably saw land at the same time (the place was swarming with sealers), they lacked the desire or talent for publicity that came to Palmer.

Meanwhile, Capt. Benjamin Morrell (1822–1823) entered the Weddell Sea on the east side of the peninsula. A book he wrote about his voyages, while perhaps inaccurate, roused considerable popular interest in the south polar regions—not the first or last time that literature would prove as powerful an incentive to Antarctic exploration as science. Nonetheless, a scientific expedition under Capt. Henry Foster of the Royal Navy visited the South Shetlands (1828–1831) to take gravity measurements, part of a series of global geodetic experiments, and Capt. James Weddell inaugurated the long involvement of the merchant firm Samuel Enderby and Sons in the economic and exploration history of Antarctica.

Enderby had previously opened up the South Pacific whaling grounds. Discovering the pack at a historic minimum (1822–1824), Weddell entered the sea that now bears his name to latitude 74 degrees, a feat never since duplicated. The Enderbys continued their mixture of business and patronage throughout the 1830s, with voyages under Capt. John Briscoe (1830–1832) that circumnavigated the Southern Ocean and discovered Enderby Land, under Capt. Peter Kemp (1833–1834) that led to the discovery of Kemp Coast, and under Capt. John Balleny (1838–1839) that mapped Balleny Island and may have sighted the mainland around what was later named Wilkes Land. Charles Enderby became a charter member of the Royal Geographical Society (1830), and in defiance of normal sealing and whaling practices, with their fanatical secrecy, he deposited ship's logs with the society.

But the big story was an impressive display of international rivalry: in the late 1830s expeditions were launched more or less simultaneously by France, Great Britain, and the United States. To this group may be added a fourth, Imperial Russia; although it preceded the others by nearly twenty years and led to no further Russian interest in the region for another 130 years, the enigmatic voyages of Bellingshausen share the characteristics of the expeditions of d'Urville, Ross, and Wilkes. All built upon the example and accounts of Cook. Collectively, they confirmed the existence of an Antarctic continent, mapped as much of the coastline as wooden ships operating in fog and pack ice could, and closed out an era of Antarctic discovery.

Bellingshausen explored the region for two austral summers and found it pretty much as Cook described it. He conducted one pass from the South Sandwich Islands, along the pack, to Australia, probably sighting the continent in the vicinity of Queen Maud Land. His second voyage, from Australia to the Antarctic Peninsula, completed a successful circumnavigation of the Southern Ocean. While in the area of the peninsula, Bellingshausen discovered several islands, visited with some of the first sealers to the South Shetland Island area, and possibly spied the mainland. But, as he notes in his journal, "in this climate the sky is seldom unclouded," fog and snow drizzles were endless, the seas were choked with icebergs, and floes from the loose summer pack made navigation treacherous. After "two years' uninterrupted navigation" among the ice, Bellingshausen concluded, in words echoing Cook, that "this ice must extend across the Pole and must be immovable and attached in places to shallows or to such islands as Peter I Island."[11] Isolated from both the international scene and further Russian interest, however, the expedition was forgotten, its findings dormant until the advent of IGY and the revival of Soviet concern with the Antarctic.

Not so the later, competing exploratory voyages sent by France, Britain, and America. All were national exploring expeditions, well integrated into scientific institutions. All of the voyages aspired to advance the domain of useful knowledge no less than the prestige of their sponsoring governments. The French expedition under Capt. Dumont d'Urville and the British expedition under Capt. James Clark Ross had as primary objectives the exact determination of the south magnetic pole. This was a subject with both practical and popular appeal as well as scientific significance. Carl Friedrich Gauss had articulated a theory of terrestrial magnetism that predicted the exact location of the pole, and Alexander von Humboldt had championed the cause, pleading for a global magnetic survey that would lead to a geomagnetic map. In addition, d'Urville had specific instructions to proceed more deeply into the Weddell Sea than Weddell had and thereby claim for France the honors of the farthest voyage south. The United States Exploring Expedition, under the command of Lt. Charles Wilkes, proceeded—after enduring years of political buffoonery during which its existence was several times threatened amid the exuberant turmoil of Jacksonian democracy—under a bizarre mixture of purposes, among them the service of American whaling and sealing interests, the desires of fledgling scientific organizations, the nationalist sentiments of Capt. Benjamin Pendleton and Josiah Reynolds, and the crackpot idea of William Symmes (the popularly styled "Newton of the West") that a subterranean paradise existed in the Antarctic which could be entered through a colossal hole at the pole. The d'Urville and Wilkes expeditions spent two austral seasons in their voyages, the Ross expedition three.

Although d'Urville had two prior voyages of discovery to the
South Pacific behind him, his expedition was something of a
disappointment. Not surprisingly, he failed to penetrate the
pack in the Weddell gyre, and his travels along the coast of East
Antarctica indicated that the magnetic pole lay impossibly distant from him, on the other side of the ice. He did, however,
sight the mainland (Terre Adelie) at nearly the same time as
Wilkes. Sponsored by the British Association for the Advancement of Science and the Royal Society, as well as by the Royal
Navy, Ross had no better luck with the Weddell Sea or the magnetic pole. But the handsome veteran of Arctic voyages (he had
already been to the north magnetic pole) made fundamental
discoveries in the area of the Ross Sea, including Ross Island and
the Ross Ice Shelf. His two ships, *Terror* and *Erebus*, provided the
names for the volcanoes on Ross Island, an area of great significance to subsequent Antarctic exploration.

It was Wilkes, however, whose orders were nebulous, whose
expedition existed in almost constant disarray, and whose ships
were ill-fitted for polar travel; it was Wilkes who first proclaimed an "Antarctic continent" based on his scattered but
consistent observations of the East Antarctic mainland. Predic-
tably, too, it was the prickly Wilkes who generated the most
controversy. While his maps of Antarctica and Pacific islands
proved remarkably sound, and the expedition's collections
helped launch several scientific careers and became an argument for the establishment of a national museum (eventually,
the Smithsonian), Wilkes endured scorn from Ross over conflicting sightings of land, faced a court-martial upon his return
for his recourse to harsh discipline, engendered (because of his
manipulation of the ship's log) a controversy over whether he or
d'Urville had first sighted the mainland, and suffered through a
subsequent naval career in near ostracism until the American
Civil War saw his rank restored. During the war he precipitated
another international crisis by seizing two Confederate envoys
from a British ship and thrusting Britain and America to the
brink of war. Again he was court-martialed. Between 1847 and
1849 his five-volume narrative appeared, and over the next
thirty years scientists wrote eighteen volumes more, but Congress declined to appropriate sufficient money to allow the
full work of the expedition to be published, and only one hundred official copies of Wilkes's narrative were actually printed.
Wilkes so lapsed into obscurity that when he died in 1877, as

William Stanton notes, "many newspapers forgot to mention that he had commanded the First Great National Exploring Expedition."[12] Nonetheless, Mark Twain recalled that during his Missouri childhood Wilkes had been the most famous name in America.[13] As with Wilkes, so with the U.S. Exploring Expedition: it was ever a source of controversy and missed opportunities, well symbolized by the fate of one of its great treasures, the cornucopia of Polynesian artifacts gathered by artist-naturalist Titian Peale. In the mid-1890s the long-missing collection was accidentally unearthed beneath several tons of coal in the basement of the Smithsonian Institution.

There followed a hiatus in Antarctic exploration. The Franklin disaster refocused polar discovery by Britain and the U.S. to the Arctic, and the recession of the fur seal and whaling industries removed economic incentives from the Antarctic. For a while almost the sole advocate of south polar exploration was Matthew Fontaine Maury, superintendent of the U.S. Naval Observatory and Hydrographic Office and author of two seminal works in oceanography: *Wind and Current Charts* (1847) and the celebrated *Physical Geography of the Sea*, first published in 1855. Antarctica—or the absence of solid geographic information about it—increasingly preoccupied Maury. He admonished the naval powers that "one sixth part of the entire landed surface of our planet" is "as unknown to the inhabitants of the earth as is the interior of one of Jupiter's satellites." Elaborating on the contrast with Arctic exploration, he argued that "for the last 200 years the Arctic Ocean has been a theatre for exploration; but as for the antarctic, no expedition has attempted to make any *persistent* exploration or even to winter there." Dismayed over U.S. disinterest in further exploration (the popular interest in polar exploration lay in Elisha Kane's Arctic travels, and the country was otherwise preoccupied with the exploration of its far western territories and with the political crisis that would culminate in the Civil War), Maury in 1860 urged that Antarctic exploration "should be a joint one among the nations that are concerned in maritime pursuits." The development of steam power, he argued, made penetration of the pack ice possible.[14]

Instead, traditional activity in Antarctica continued, although on a vastly reduced scale. Commercial sealers and whalers revisited favorite sites, refining local geographic knowledge. In the 1870s a final burst of activity effectively closed the era and symbolically returned it to its origins. To commemorate

the centennial of Cook's voyages, the British Admiralty and the
Royal Society sponsored a four-year (1872–1876) circumnavigation of the world sea for the purposes of oceanographic research.
A specially outfitted ship, the *Challenger*, brought the latest in
scientific equipment to bear on the problem. But the *Challenger*
expedition in the Antarctic confined itself to the subantarctic
islands, to physical measurements of the sea, and to the collection of specimens of marine life. While its dredgings would help
revive scientific interest in the question of a polar continent
twenty years later, so primitive were its researches in the remote Antarctic that it failed to recognize as gross an oceanographic boundary as the Antarctic convergence. Meanwhile,
another cooperative international undertaking—to measure the
transit of Venus in 1874—recalled the 1769 transit that had under-
written Cook's first voyage to the Pacific. The U.S. established a
base at Kerguelen Island, along the convergence. And finally a
German expedition again combined sealing with exploration,
voyaging under the command of Capt. Eduard Dallman to the
west side of the Antarctic Peninsula, where some minor islands
were discovered.

"To strive, to seek, to find, and not to yield"

In the eighteenth century, scientific exploration on the grand
scale was epitomized by the international effort to survey the
transit of Venus. Not only did it dispatch Cook on his first voyage to the South Seas, but it sent such luminaries as Peter Pallas, then under the direction of the Russian Academy of Sciences, on his expedition to the Urals and the Land of Sibir. The
organizational complexity, the emphasis on natural philosophy,
and the anticipated practical benefits all identified these explorers as savants of the Enlightenment, not intellectual buc-
caneers out of the Renaissance. Yet even as Cook conducted his
circumnavigations the character of exploration was being reconstituted. Maritime discovery was being complemented by an
even more powerful wave of continental exploration; new instruments and technologies refined the purposes and redirected the
goals of discovery; and the intellectual context of the Cook era,
embedded in the Enlightenment, was being superseded by the
sensibilities of Romanticism. Their emphasis on scientific research made explorers something more than foragers of empire.

Out of them would evolve the Romantic explorer, with his fascination for natural history, who would carry discovery into the continental interiors and who would dominate exploration in the nineteenth century. This transformation was part of a vast act of reperception, of intellectual systems-building, and of political and cultural assimilation so fundamental that William Goetzmann has termed it a Second Great Age of Discovery.[15] The effects, in fact, were reciprocal. Western civilization greatly expanded its reach, but it also had to grapple with the political, social, economic, and intellectual consequences of assimilating the new lands it unveiled or the old lands it visited anew.

As with the voyages of the Renaissance, the process began in Europe, this time prepared by an era of internal travels by European intellectuals. The example of Cook's explorations was instrumental in forging the purposes and style of these journeys, although they were no longer restricted to the coasts or to the conceptual context of natural philosophy. In particular, a German ethnographer on Cook's second voyage, Georg Forster, inspired the man who would symbolize the explorer of the new era, Alexander von Humboldt. Quickly, this new mode of exploration was transported from Europe to the other continents. In place of circumnavigation, a traverse across a continent became the grand gesture of the explorer, and in place of a *mappa mundi* of the world ocean, a cross-section of a continent's natural history became the supreme intellectual achievement of an exploring expedition. Previously, travels into the interior had only supplemented sea power. Their purpose had not been to conduct general surveys of geography and natural history but to seek out the treasure and the capitals of unknown civilizations like the Incas and Aztecs, or to establish commercial contact with such ancient peoples as the Chinese and Indians. Explorers, like "the rulers and investors who sent them out," were "practical men," observes Parry. "One cannot imagine fifteenth-century explorers searching for the North Pole."[16] Increasingly, however, the primary purpose of ships was to transport men and equipment to new lands; the great treasures were the artifacts of natural history and those natural resources not yet converted by native civilizations. In the process, the character of exploration metamorphosed, and the natural history of Europe—its rocks, its flora and fauna, its peoples—was systematically compared to that of other lands.

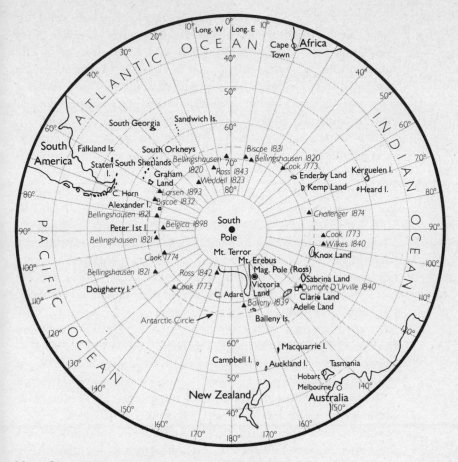

Map of Antarctica as it was known at the onset of the heroic age.
Expeditions and landforms are both indicated. Only the tip of the peninsula
and portions of the Ross Sea were known with any confidence. Redrawn from
Robert Scott, The Voyage of the Discovery.

This contrast was broad and its effects powerful. Not only scientific data but experiences, images, sensations, artifacts, and specimens were all information that had to be processed. The sheer volume as well as the novelty of much of this information demanded new sciences such as geology and new sensibilities such as those expressed in Romantic landscape painting, novels, and travelogues. Natural history, in particular, enjoyed an explosive, popular growth. Geographic discovery asked and answered questions of fundamental significance to this civilization. Moreover, the mode of exploration advertised by Humboldt and his imitators involved not only surveying, mapping, and cataloguing the abundance of material objects in the world; it celebrated that very profusion. The exhaustive collections and encyclopedic tomes of these explorers exemplified a facet of the Romantic syndrome, the Promethean desire to encompass everything. Writing from South America, Humboldt told how he and his companion, Aimé Bonpland, dashed about like madmen picking up one new object after another, how they would go mad "if the wonders don't cease soon."[17] No more than its classification schemas could the sensibilities of the Enlightenment survive such an onslaught of information without profound disruptions.

Within this expanding realm of experience, however, Antarctica was an anomaly, a universe unto itself. It was impenetrable to maritime exploration, except as its inconstant pack ice allowed, and it was even more hostile to overland, cross-continental traverses. Its only rivers were glaciers. But the problem was not solely the formidable physical geography of the ice terranes: The Ice also challenged the philosophical precepts, artistic genres, and scientific systems by which the era had understood the metaphysics (and metahistory) of nature. The abundance of the observed world was stripped away. The novelty, the revelatory message, the inspiration of Nature were all erased. The process became progressive as one advanced to the interior, to the informing source of The Ice. The Promethean desire to embrace everything lost its meaning in a landscape of nothingness. In place of increasing information, there was less. In place of abundant objects, there was only ice; and in place of tangible landmarks, such as mountains or lakes, there were only abstract concepts, such as the poles of rotation, magnetism, or inaccessibility, all invisible to the senses. The only civilization explorers discovered in Antarctica was the one they had brought

there. Inquisitiveness, knowledge, sensibility were simply re-
boldtean explorer had been to cope with an overabundance of
information, but the Antarctic explorer confronted an under-
abundance of information. Finding technological means by
which to penetrate the pack or to proceed inland did not by itself resolve the question of perception and assimilation.

The Antarctic would not—could not—be ignored. There
were several causes for the revival of interest in Antarctica. The
simple fact that the region was unexplored and geographically
unknown was a compelling argument for at least some scientific
reconnaissance. Steam power made travel into the pack possible, and decades of successful Arctic exploration had developed ship designs and materials (and customized ships) that
could withstand the crushing pressures of the pack ice. A desire
to resuscitate the whaling industry brought commercial ships
back to the Southern Ocean, and in 1892 Scottish and Norwegian whalers visited Antarctica. The *Antarctica*, under Capt.
Carl Larsen, investigated new coastline along the eastern side
of the peninsula. Eventually, the Larsen firm became for twentieth-century Antarctic exploration what the Enderby Brothers
had been for the nineteenth century. Its modest success led to
another private expedition under Henrik Bull which, at Cape
Adare in January 1895, made the first landing on the Antarctic
mainland.

Perhaps the most compelling cause for renewed attention was
the dangerous expansion of European colonial rivalry and the
growing realization that Antarctica was the last of the world's
continents not yet explored. In 1893 John Murray, the Canadian
biologist and oceanographer who had collated the fifty volumes
published by the *Challenger* expedition, read a paper to the
Royal Geographic Society in which he argued for the existence
of an Antarctic continent and proposed an outline of its coast.
The idea stirred his rival, Clements Markham, then head of the
society. At the Sixth International Geographical Congress
(1895), held in London and presided over by Markham, it was
resolved that "the exploration of the Antarctic regions is the
greatest piece of geographical exploration still to be undertaken."[18] Although the North Pole had not yet been reached,
the Arctic was generally known with an accuracy acceptable to
the state of geographic knowledge; a race to the pole was a
coup, a monument to ambition and Arctic survival skills. But

Antarctica, not simply the South Pole, was as much a *terra incognita* as it had been during the Renaissance. What Rudyard Kipling wrote in "The Explorer" (1898) seemed especially applicable to the Antarctic:

> Till a voice, as bad as Conscience, rang interminable
>   changes
>   On one everlasting Whisper day and night repeated—so:
>   "Something hidden. Go and find it. Go and look behind the
>   Ranges—
>   "Something lost behind the Ranges. Lost and waiting for
>   you.
>   Go!"

Now that conscience could be answered. Adequate technology, an international consensus on the continent's scientific significance, national competition, and nearly a century of experience with this mode of exploration—everything was present to make Antarctica a centerpiece for Western discovery. The next International Geographical Congress (Berlin, 1899) proclaimed 1901 as "Antarctica Year." Quickly, a score of major expeditions attempted to achieve for the alien Antarctic what Pallas had done for central Asia, Lewis and Clark for North America, and Humboldt for South America. The heroic age of Antarctic exploration was underway.

It began modestly with a Belgian expedition (1897–1899) led by Lt. Adrien de Gerlache. The *Belgica* explored the west coast of the Antarctic Peninsula and wintered, inadvertently, in the Bellingshausen Sea. Among the members of the expedition were Frederick A. Cook, soon to be embroiled in an infamous controversy with Robert Peary over the discovery of the North Pole, and Roald Amundsen, who, frustrated in his desire to reach the North Pole, redirected his efforts to the South Pole instead. Already the genealogical—almost tribal—character of polar exploration was evident. So was the practice of naming expeditions after their ships. And so also were the special challenges of Antarctic discovery. During the *Belgica*'s long winter imprisonment, nearly everyone suffered anemia, lethargy, acute depression, or paranoia; there was one death from a heart attack, and two men went mad. Meanwhile, a member of the Norwegian whaling expedition to Cape Adare, Carsten Borch-

grevink, returned with the *Southern Cross* expedition (1898–
1900), which was sponsored by a British newspaper magnate.
Borchgrevink sailed to Cape Adare, established the first land
base on the continent, made a sledging journey to the Ross Ice
Shelf, wintered over, conducted meteorological and magnetic
investigations, and collected specimens of rocks and marine
fauna.

Borchgrevink was only the point man for the great national
expeditions to follow. At the New York meeting of the International Geographical Congress (1904), Henryk Arctowski of
the *Belgica* expedition revived Maury's plea for an internation-
ally sponsored exploration of the Antarctic. But national rivalry
was a greater motivator than international cooperation. Even
new nations, such as Norway, found in polar exploration a suitable international arena to display their nationalist energies.
Still, there was some attempt at coordinating independent national expeditions. Markham, for example, orchestrated the
earliest wave so that the Germans went to East Antarctica, the
Swedes to the peninsula, and the British to the Ross Sea. But in
its intensity no less than its scale, this was truly the heroic age
of Antarctic discovery.

Its range of participants would not be matched until the
1950s: the National Antarctic Expedition (*Discovery*) under
Capt. Robert Scott (1901–1904), the German Antarctic Expedition (*Gauss*) under Prof. Erich von Drygalski (1901–1903), the
Swedish Antarctic Expedition (*Antarctica*) under Dr. Otto Nordenskjöld (1901–1903), the Scottish National Antarctic Expedition (*Scotia*) led by Dr. William S. Bruce (1902–1904), the
French Antarctic Expedition (*Le Français*) headed by Dr. J.-B.
Charcot (1903–1904), the British Antarctic Expedition (*Nimrod*) under Lt. Ernest Shackleton (1907–1909), the Second
French Antarctic Expedition (*Pourquoi Pas?*), also under Charcot (1908–1910), the Amundsen (*Fram*) expedition led by
Roald Amundsen (1910–1912), the second Scott (*Terra Nova*) expedition (1910–1913), the Japanese (*Kainan Maru*) expedition
under Lt. Choku Shirase (1911–1912), a second German expedition (*Deutschland*) led by Dr. Wilhelm Filchner (1911–1912),
the Australasian Antarctic Expedition (*Aurora*) led by a veteran
of the first Shackleton expedition, Douglas Mawson (1911–
1914), and the British Imperial Trans-Antarctic Expedition (*Endurance*), under Ernest Shackleton (1914–1916).

Nearly all of these expeditions had some assistance from their national governments, although contributions from scientific societies and wealthy industrialists were important. Most tended to include substantial scientific staffs, filled with specialists in various fields. All exhibited at least some transfer of techniques or personnel from north polar exploration. And beginning with Scott's first expedition (*Discovery*), the desire to reach the South Pole (or for some, the south magnetic pole) or to traverse the continent was a fundamental objective to most of the exploring parties. All this—an exotic destination, a traverse that would provide a cross-section of the continent, a preoccupation with geographic inquiry—was in keeping with the tradition of continental exploration that had emerged over the previous century.

Interestingly, two of the earliest nations to engage in Antarctic exploration, Russia and the United States, were absent. Tsarist Russia was preoccupied with wars, revolution, and an Arctic sea-route to Siberia; the United States was preoccupied with the insular empire it had newly acquired from war with Spain, with Alaskan gold, and with an old tradition of Arctic exploration stemming from the Franklin searches of Elisha Kent Kane and Charles Francis Hall and from the tragic sufferings of the Greeley Expedition to Greenland during the First Polar Year. In 1902 the Carnegie Museum in Pittsburgh proposed to collect specimens in the Antarctic Peninsula, and in 1909 the American Philosophical Society authorized a committee to promote an American expedition to Wilkes Land, an idea that received the blessing of President Roosevelt; but nothing came of either suggestion. Instead the race for the North Pole, vividly personified in the demonic Robert Peary, commanded national attention. When Peary later campaigned in 1912 for an American expedition to winter at the South Pole—the logistics for which were "only a matter of detail"—other expeditions were already en route to the pole and there was little enthusiasm within the scientific community.[19]

Yet Antarctica was not Africa or Australia or the Americas or even the Arctic. It was not simply a more forbidding continent but an almost extraterrestrial presence. Once an exploring party passed the coast, there was nothing to stand between it and the purely physical systems that comprised Antarctica. There was no ecosystem, however threatening, that could sustain an explorer. There was no native culture, maritime or terrestrial, that could guide, inform, or assist. No pilots from the

indigenous culture of seafarers would navigate a ship through
the pack ice. No guides would direct overland parties to new
villages, water holes, or trails. No interpreters would intercede
between the emissaries of Western civilization and native populations. No native hunters would translate their indigenous
knowledge of geography or educate these missionaries of Western enthusiasm in survival skills. Exploration did not accompany a folk migration, as it did in North America, Australia,
and Central Asia; popularly acquired lore could not assist formal discovery or be challenged by it. And exploration did not
consort with the state-making of European imperialism, as it
did in South America and Africa. There was no mechanism by
which to systematically transfer knowledge from native lore
into the intellectual systems of the West. The Antarctic landscape was far from rich in the kinds of information to which
natural history had become accustomed. Only along the coast
were there organisms; only in selected oases were there even
rocks; nowhere were there strange peoples or lost civilizations.
There was only ice and more ice. In such an environment the
Antarctic explorer could no longer act as the Romantic hero; he
became an existentialist hero or a modernist antihero. Even as
the great flurry of expeditions sailed south and sledged across
the ice—full of visions of Humboldt, Kipling, and Robert Service—the intellectual explosion that would be called modernism was revolutionizing science, art, and literature. As participants in intellectual history, the explorers of the heroic age
were splendid anachronisms, the last and purest of a breed for
which Antarctica had offered a final refuge.

The exploration of the Arctic offered only a partial equiva-
lence. There was some transfer of equipment, such as sledges
and ships; some transfer of purpose, notably the race to the
poles; and a mixed transfer of explorers, especially as the explorer came to be a professional, an all-purpose figure ready to
go to any number of unvisited regions. Roald Amundsen, Frederick Cook, Erich von Drygalski, John Rymill, Hubert Wilkins,
Richard Byrd, Laurence Gould, Hjalmar Riiser-Larsen, to name
a few, all explored both in the Arctic and Antarctic. Other
Arctic explorers, such as Peary and Nansen, had traversed the
Greenland ice sheet and developed techniques useful on Antarctic shelves and sheets. Borchgrevink brought two Lapps to
assist with his sledging, and Robert Peary strongly recommended
that Eskimos be transported to the Antarctic. Specially de-

signed polar ships, such as the *Fram*, were used in both packs. Along the Antarctic coast, exploring parties could hunt seals (or less desirably, penguins) for food. But the differences between the Arctic and the Antarctic were far more impressive.

They begin with the "very striking antithesis of natural conditions," as Peary referred to it, between the two polar regions. Arctic exploration was physically dominated by the pack—ice and sea, pressure ridge and lead. The scene was ever changing, and the explorer was, in Peary's words, ever confronted with the "choice between the possibility of drowning by going on or starving to death by standing still."[20] In the Antarctic, the pack was a barrier to penetrate by ship before the real business of exploration could begin. The crevasse fields of mountain glaciers offered a hazard analogous to that of leads, but without the vitality and drama. The constant discovery of islands amid the Arctic Sea had extended the range of traditional voyages of maritime exploration. These islands reduced the Arctic basin to a series of smaller seas and served as points of departure and refuge. The Antarctic islands offered much less, although some presented convenient anchorages and less massive coastal ice terranes than the mainland, and most voyages of the heroic age established bases on them. In some cases, such as the Drygalski expedition, the party never successfully left the island.

The critical distinction between the two polar regions was the absence of life and native cultures in Antarctica. The "Peary system"—a distillation of decades of Arctic experience—relied heavily on local foodstuffs and on native technology and lore. Though he brought bread and pemmican and other foods, Peary procured fresh meat by hunting in advance of the journey. Walrus, bear, musk ox, whale, seal, caribou (reindeer), hare, some birds and fish—one could live off the land. In Antarctica, exploring parties hunted seals (and when desperate, penguin), but only along the pack and coast. More fundamentally, the Arctic had the polar Eskimo and his dogs, and the successful Arctic explorer began by learning Eskimo language and Eskimo culture. What the Western explorer brought was a new degree of organization and a new sense of purpose—intellectual products of a larger civilization, like the steamships that poked through the pack. Where the polar Eskimo had a score of words for particular kinds of snow and ice, thanks to institutions like science and exploration Western civilization would soon have hundreds and would constantly add new ones. Similarly, while Amundsen's successful trek to the South Pole relied heavily on Arctic (modified Eskimo) techniques, its purpose was foreign to Eskimo culture.

Once a Western explorer was in the Arctic, his equipment consisted of adaptations of native technology, and as often as not it was easier to recruit native assistants than to train other, inexperienced Europeans. The greatest of Arctic explorers—the Nansens, the Stefanssons, the Pearys—in effect became natives, white Eskimos. Their writings on Eskimo (or Lapp or Siberian) life and the humanitarian spirit of comradeship that they felt with their native associates account for much of the charm of Arctic literature. When Peary reached the North Pole, he arrived in the company of one black American (Matt Henson, his old valet) and four Eskimos. The episode is a vivid reminder both of Leslie Fiedler's observation that the heroes of nineteenth-century American literature were almost always accompanied by dark-skinned companions and of the extent to which Western civilization had absorbed the learning of other cultures into a grand new system.[21]

The encounters with other peoples—an inevitable consequence of exploration—eventually led to the development of anthropology. Explorers had to cope with alien cultural environments as much as with foreign landscapes. Not merely their empirical data on latitudes and temperatures, or their encyclopedic collections of artifacts and specimens, but their experiences within other moral universes formed part of the expanding horizon of information that was the principal intellectual legacy of the era. Franz Boas would revolutionize American anthropology in large part out of his experience with Greenland Eskimos. Vilhjalmur Stefansson would live for years within Eskimo society, and in *Northward the Course of Empire* he improbably proposed that the future world civilization would be Nordic. No one would write an Antarctic equivalent to his *The Friendly Arctic*; on the contrary, Antarctic literature would abound in dystopias. Information requires contrast. The geographic contrast of the Arctic between sea and ice, the deadly dance between lead and floe, was echoed in the contrast between life and death, European and Eskimo. But there was no such contrast in the interior of Antarctica, only the sublime emptiness of the ice sheet, a self-reflexive mirror. The alienness of Antarctica consisted not simply in the continent's physical harshness but in its unrelenting cultural and biological impov-

erishment, a profound deprivation that could be both psycho-
logically and physiologically unsettling.

As Amundsen demonstrated, the Peary system by which
forced marches were used to reach an explicit destination could
be brought to Antarctica. Other Antarctic expeditions exploited such tactics to attain one of the south poles, although
the British stayed with ponies and man-hauling for motive
power. But neither in purpose nor in equipment could this system sustain long-term exploring parties on the scale necessary
to systematically survey the Antarctic interior. This was more
than a question of dogs versus horses versus men as prime mov-
ers of Antarctic sledges; all would soon be displaced by tractors
and aircraft. For all its harshness, the Arctic had been inextricably bound up with human society for millennia and with
Europe for centuries. No one had so much as passed a winter in
Antarctica until Borchgrevink did it on the eve of the twentieth
century. Without a biotic and cultural environment, not only
was exploration more difficult, but discovery lost much of its
charm. The traditional travelogue, with its abundant anecdotes
about native life, was turned inward into a monologue. In Antarctica there was no society except that of the exploring expedition, no contrast between cultures, only the looking-glass Ice
that reflected back, in simplified form, what was brought to it.

The remarkable successes of the heroic age came at a tremendous cost. Exploration, like other activities brought to The Ice,
was stripped to its most elemental forms, and it became almost
pathologically single-minded. The great tales of Antarctic
adventure—the last real sagas in Western exploration—were
stories of survival. In fact, the desire to struggle, to test oneself,
was apparently one of the things Western civilization brought to
The Ice. The celebration of martial discipline, of self-striving,
of exploration, primitivism, and physical adventure was rampant in the West. Shackleton's recruiting advertisement in a London paper said it all: "Men wanted for hazardous journey. Small
wages, bitter cold, long months of complete darkness, constant
danger, safe return doubtful. Honor and recognition in case of
success."[22] The response was overwhelming. Such men accomplished astonishing feats but often endured unnecessary hardships. Cherry-Garrard, for example, lamented that "men were
allowed to do too much," that frequently "we wasted our manpower" through requests for volunteers.[23] Other purposes than

character-testing and other means than man-hauled sledges, he
insisted, would have to justify future expeditions.

Nor was this enthusiasm all a sop to popular whims, all bogus contests dreamed up by yellow journalism to sell its tabloids. The sentiments were strong among intellectuals, and the expedition leaders, supporters, and organizers were by and large intellectuals or men of education. In the United States the appeal took a slightly different form, manifest in the "strenuous life" urged by Teddy Roosevelt, the Klondike verse of Robert Service, the call for a "moral equivalent of war" by philosopher William James, and the literature of naturalism, epitomized by Jack London. "It is a source of satisfaction," affirmed Peary on behalf of an age, "that the two last great physical adventures, the winning of the North Pole and the South Pole . . . should have been won by brute physical soundness and endurance, by the oldest and most perfect of all machines—the animal machine—man and the Eskimo dog."[24] The Antarctic showed in this matter, as in others, an inversion: it was as though the object was not to struggle to advance a goal, but to discover a goal that would justify struggle.

As if there were a psychological obsession among Anglo-Americans to show that they were as hardy as the explorers, pioneers, and soldiers who had first built the European empires, the heroic age was populated with sagas of a number and intensity without parallel in the exploration of other continents. Associated with the age are the various journeys of the *Terra Nova* expedition: the Polar Party, led by Robert Scott, perishing miserably if heroically on the Ross Ice Shelf after reaching the pole; the Crozier Party under Edward Wilson, stumbling horribly around the crevasse-ridden ice shelf off Ross Island in the course of winter journey, enduring temperatures of −75 degrees F. to collect the egg of an emperor penguin; the Northern Party under Raymond Priestley, brought by ship from Cape Adare to Terra Nova Bay, only to be stranded because of pack ice and to winter in a stone hut on Inexpressible Island, living on penguins before making a journey on foot back to Ross Island; Douglas Mawson, his other comrades dead, struggling to pull himself out of a crevasse, then outfitted with crude wooden crampons wrestling a half-sled across 150 miles of "an accursed land," his skin sloughing off from malnutrition; the Nordenskjöld expedition, with one party marooned a second winter at Snow Hill Island, another stuck on Paulet Island, and a third, the crew of the rescue ship *Antarctica* which sank in the pack, meeting by chance on the ice before being removed by the first Argentine vessel to venture to Antarctica; Ernest Shackleton, pioneering a route to the pole during his *Nimrod* expedition, only to be forced to withdraw within 97 miles of his destination; and Shackleton again, during the *Endurance* expedition, trapped in the pressure pack of the Weddell Sea, watching his ship crushed within the ice, riding ice floes and small ships to Elephant Island on the tip of the peninsula, setting out in an open skiff to South Georgia Island, climbing the South Georgian Alps to reach the whaling village of Grytviken and, ultimately, to rescue his entire crew without the loss of a man. The success stories of Antarctic exploration (such as Amundsen's lightning march to the pole) are nearly forgotten or dismissed as too simple. It was not merely what was done but how it was done that was important. The competent but prosaic Roald Amundsen seems to function chiefly as a foil for the tragic Robert Scott. Nowhere in Western literature is there a more compelling, sustained chronicle of life, humanity, and civilization reduced to their minima.

In the end, these were sentiments as much imported to The Ice as extracted from it. The Ice reduces, distorts, reflects, and preserves, but it does not create. The heroic age did not arise solely out of Antarctica but from Western civilization's encounter with Antarctica. The conclusion of the heroic age did not result from a change in The Ice: it came about because of new experiences in the civilization that sent out the explorers. For explorers, the celebration of the life of strenuous endeavor ended on the ice sheets of Antarctica, and for Western civilization as a whole it ended in the trenches of the Great War. It seemed pointless to carry the White Man's Burden across the white nihilism of The Ice. Gradually, the principal actors in the drama—both the explorers and their supporters—passed from the scene or, like Mawson, retooled for a new era. The intellectual and political fervor for imperialism abated, and modernism dissolved many of the scientific and cultural ties that had sustained this mode of geographic exploration. No longer did visits to remote tribes, jungle-covered ruins, or wind-swept deserts answer fundamental questions. Even the major sciences such as geology, which had been invented to accommodate the data of continental discovery, failed to adapt to new ideas and lapsed into a moribund state, becoming tied more to the laboratory and the library than to the field.

Exploration itself suffered a crisis of identity and purpose. On one hand, it was progressively equipped with new, mechanized technology, while on the other it lacked new lands and peoples to discover. The interior of Antarctica was simply too vast and the rewards too meager to justify further expeditions in the mode of the heroic age. The long-sought transcontinental traverse would not occur until the mid-1950s, and by then it had lost much of its meaning, not because the deed itself was different but because its context had changed. Even as the Berlin Congress proclaimed its Antarctic Year, reaffirming the value of Antarctica for geography, Max Planck published his quantum theory of black-body radiation; De Vries, Correns, and von Tschermak simultaneously announced the rediscovery of Mendelian genetics; and Sigmund Freud promised to reconstruct the basis of psychology with *The Interpretation of Dreams*. As Scott's loyal party erected its memorial cross, complete with inscription from Tennyson, Niels Bohr outlined a new theory of the atom. As Shackleton engineered the escape of the *Endurance* expedition from the Weddell Sea, Albert Einstein elaborated the general theory of relativity. The empirical, conceptual, and philosophical foundations of modern science were experiencing their most important transformation since the seventeenth century, and the relationship of science to exploration as a mode of inquiry would, in time, share that revolution. By the 1920s a transition was underway, not only in the character of Western exploration but in its liaison to the earth sciences. An epoch of exploration had survived in the distant wastes of The Ice, but in much the same way that the twilight wedge preserves the refracted rays of the setting sun. The heroic age passed with remarkable suddenness.

The premier Antarctic adventurer, Ernest Shackleton, obtained a private sponsor, a ship christened *Quest*, and his old first mate, Frank Wild, in an attempt to revive Antarctic exploration after World War I with an expedition to Wilkes Land in 1921–1922. Unfortunately, the strain of command and a series of severe storms encountered by the *Quest* as it steered toward the pack from South Georgia aggravated a heart condition, and Shackleton, at age forty-seven, died before reaching The Ice. Dispirited, the crew persisted in a troubled, desultory attempt to find worthy projects before more storms forced them to retire altogether from the Antarctic. It had been the man and the myth more than the place that had attracted the exploring party. The Antarctic had not beckoned, it had been sought out. Chroniclers might well have echoed Starbuck in the final drama of *Moby-Dick*. "Oh! Ahab. . . . See! Moby Dick seeks thee not. It is thou, thou, that madly seekest him!"[25] Melville's Ahab represented the demonic side of the era's restless searching, as Tennyson's Ulysses showed its nobler side. But by the 1920s neither dimension was present. The heroic age drifted away—an aimless *Quest*, a *Pequod* stripped of both its Ahab and its Moby Dick, a Ulysses buried at South Georgia.

Only a decade earlier the scene had been quite different. When Scott's party perished on The Ice, one by one, the tragedy could evoke the full-blown sentiment and rhetoric of an era; Scott's final words, entered painfully in his diary, could be quoted for their lessons on how an English gentleman lived, strived, and died. The heroic age was then at its climax, the last grand expression of an era of Western exploration. It had literally reached the ends of the Earth. Chroniclers like Cherry-Garrard and Scott himself were suitably prepared to explicate the meaning of Antarctic exploration, if not the meaning of The Ice itself. The *Oxford Book of English Verse* and the *Collected Poems of Robert Service* would be carried to The Ice, just as a few years hence they would be buried in Flanders fields. What transpired on Antarctica seemed like a fantasy, an optical trick of the polar desert, a superior mirage that had cast a distant image from another place and time high into the unblinking Antarctic sky.

The survivors of the *Terra Nova* expedition erected a jarrahwood cross atop Observation Hill, near the site of the *Discovery* hut on Ross Island. On it they carved the closing lines from Tennyson's "Ulysses"—words written a few years before Darwin ventured forth on the *Beagle* and Humboldt first dreamed of summarizing the whole realm of physical knowledge through a geographic compilation he called *Cosmos*, sentiments published the same year the Wilkes expedition returned to the United States. Its choice was perhaps more suitable than the *Terra Nova* expedition realized. Tennyson had transformed a wanderer into an explorer, a yearning for home into a passion for knowledge, a struggle against fate into an obsession for struggle and a refusal to accept the limits of geography, time, or experience. Re-

shaping a pagan hero from classical antiquity into a Romantic
explorer, Tennyson symbolized how the neoclassical world of
the Enlightenment, with its rational codifications and attach-
ment to "useful knowledge," had been overwhelmed and expanded into something larger. Perhaps something too large. No
one could romanticize the death of Cook as the survivors could
romanticize the death of Scott. Their selection of the poem as a
testimonial to the South Pole Party signified the intellectual
continuity that the *Terra Nova* expedition shared with the whole
character of discovery that had emerged after Cook. But by the
time the *Quest* reached the pack, leaderless and purposeless,
that succession had been broken. Sailing beyond the sunset had
only brought the survivors to The Ice.

> Death closes all; but something ere the end,
> Some work of noble note, may yet be done,
>
> .   .   .   .
>
> Tho' much is taken, much abides; and tho'
> We are not now that strength which in old days
> Moved earth and heaven; that which we are, we are;
> One equal temper of heroic hearts,
> Made weak by time and fate, but strong in will
> To strive, to seek, to find, and not to yield.

Vital Interlude: Richard E. Byrd

When interest in Antarctica revived, it did so in ways that mod-
ernized traditional expeditions and purposes. Beginning in
1923, Norwegian whalers resuscitated the mixture of commercial activity, exploration, and territorial claim-making that
had typified much of nineteenth-century discovery. They also
attempted to relocate Antarctic whaling from the peninsula to
the Ross Sea, a move made possible by the development of pelagic whaling. Between 1926 and 1937, the firm of Lars Christiansen was preeminent. In 1931 Capt. Riiser-Larsen made the
first circumnavigation of the continent since Wilkes and Ross.
During the same period two major oceanographic surveys entered the Southern Ocean. Germany's *Meteor* expedition (1925–
1927), intent on studying the physical properties of the Atlantic,
introduced a new state of sophistication into research around
the Antarctic, including the use of an echo sounder, the first of

the remote-sensing devices so crucial to later Antarctic exploration. More sustained and productive were the expeditions of the Discovery Committee (1925–1939), organized by Great Britain to conduct oceanographic research in the Falkland Islands Dependencies. Much of the work was biological—a program of whale conservation was an objective—but the study of submarine geography and the definition of the Southern Ocean were also important consequences. For the continent proper, however, the big story was the trilogy of expeditions that ventured to the Antarctic coast and interior—the Wilkins-Hearst expedition, the first Byrd Antarctic Expedition, and the British–Australian–New Zealand Antarctic Research Expedition (BANZARE) under Antarctic veteran Mawson.

In one sense, these activities only reconfirmed the traditional parameters of Antarctic exploration. In another sense, however, they collectively signalled a slow reformation, one that involved new technology, new participants, and a new cultural context. The most visible change was the introduction of aircraft. Virtually every commentator on polar exploration—from Cherry-Garrard to Peary—believed that the airplane was the vehicle of the future. The Wilkins-Hearst expedition (1928–1930), which ventured toward the peninsula for two austral summers, inaugurated the process with a flight in December 1928. Within ten weeks, the first Byrd Antarctic Expedition—the whole strategy of which centered around the use of three aircraft—began its flights from the Bay of Whales, on the west side of the Ross Ice Shelf.

Airplanes were not the first machines in the Antarctic, however; the heroic age, after all, had been predicated on the steamship, which made possible routine navigation through the pack. Shackleton, Mawson, and Scott had all experimented with tractors in lieu of dogs and horses, and Mawson had brought a radio and a propeller-driven air sledge. Scott and Drygalski had used captive balloons. But these devices had all been intended to supplement overland traverses on the Arctic model. It was otherwise with the airplane. Once introduced, it progressively dominated the mechanics, composition, and purposes of Antarctic exploration. The appearance on The Ice of a mechanized society was accelerated by the transfer to civilian pursuits of technologies developed under the impress of World War I. And not merely machines but new perspectives were being brought to bear on the question of Antarctic discovery. It is no accident, for example, that Buckminster Fuller published his dymaxion air chart the same year that Wilkins and Byrd first flew over Antarctica.

The new generation of Antarcticans were aviators in search of exploits—Antarctic Lindberghs—as much as explorers eager to seize upon novel tools for geographic discovery. Hubert Wilkins wanted to realize Shackleton's old ambition to cross the continent, though he proposed to do it by plane. An Australian who had Arctic experience and a veteran of the *Quest* expedition, Wilkins planned to fly from the Antarctic Peninsula to the Ross Sea. Twice he failed—once in 1928 and again in 1930—but he flew over large portions of Graham Land and took many aerial photographs. (Later, Wilkins unsuccessfully tried to complement his flights over the Arctic and Antarctic by passing under both regions in a rickety submarine, the *Nautilus*.) Meanwhile, the British–Australian–New Zealand Antarctic Research Expedition under Mawson remained along the coast of East Antarctica. Although flights were made, high winds prevented extensive aerial photography and the expedition contented itself with biological research and with the subantarctic islands. Even the Norwegian whalers outfitted their factory ships with small seaplanes, and by 1930 no serious expedition to Antarctica failed to rely on aircraft.

The introduction of new machines and new purposes was matched by the introduction of new men. While Britain institutionalized its experience by the creation of the Scott Polar Research Institute at Cambridge, which was endowed with money left from public donations to support the widowed families of the *Terra Nova* expedition, and while there were plentiful published journals and memoirs with which to inspire and instruct aspiring Antarcticans, new players dominated the scene. Among the commanders of the heroic age, only Mawson really survived to lead another expedition. In fact, it may be said that between the heroic age and the advent of the International Geophysical Year (IGY), Antarctic exploration was dominated by one nation, the U.S., and American interest was largely the product of one man, Richard E. Byrd. Byrd took his first expedition south in 1928–1930; his second in 1933–1935; his third, transfigured into a governmental body, the U.S. Antarctic Service, in 1939–1941; his fourth, the Antarctic Developments Project of the U.S. Navy, of which he was cheerleader and titular head, in 1946–1948; and, to complete the transition, the American Antarctic contribution to the International Geophysical Year (1954–1958), of which he was honorary chief. Almost single-handedly he re-established an American presence and created a cadre of explorers who would staff future American expeditions.

That Americans had not participated in the heroic age was a mixed blessing: they had no tradition of Antarctic exploration to rely upon, but neither did they have inherited practices to uphold. While many commentators on Antarctic history gloried in the sagas of the heroic age, survivors of the age were generally keen to reform the system—from its mode of transportation to its rations to its financing. In theory, Americans could do this. At the same time, Americans had not been in Antarctica since Wilkes, and the U.S. had no pool of experienced Antarcticans from which to staff an expedition. Hence, although it was conceived and financed by Americans, the Wilkins-Hearst expedition had to recruit its chief out of the British Empire. Americans trained instead in the Arctic. Byrd, for example, had begun as a naval aviator, and in the course of planning transatlantic and Arctic flights he had learned something about how to organize an expedition. He also had valuable experience in navigation over featureless terrain. After a flight over the North Pole (1926), he jested with Amundsen that his next feat would be to fly over the South Pole. Amundsen urged him to do it. A polar flight became the centerpiece for his first expedition.

That expedition proved enormously successful. It rallied popular enthusiasm among the American public, confirmed the value of aircraft for Antarctic exploration, and unveiled substantial portions of the interior never before seen. Byrd's integration of overland sledging parties with aerial reconnaissances, all operating out of a main base camp, established the modern pattern of polar logistics. Mechanization—with aircraft at the core—became integral to all aspects of Antarctic exploration. Aerial reconnaissance preceded overland traverses. Aerial photography became the basis for cartography, with ground parties dedicated to correlation. Radios provided communication between field parties and between colony and mother country, and tractors (motor toboggans) began to replace dog teams. Extensive meteorological and magnetic observations were conducted, providing data vital to aviation as well as to general science. Seismic profiling was adapted from oil exploration. Later, Byrd experimented with autogyros and with a massive tracked vehicle, the flawed snow-cruiser. In November 1929 he realized his desire to fly over the South Pole. The integration of aircraft with ground parties and the syncretization of such popular spectaculars as the polar flight with comprehensive scientific investigations were not innovations of Byrd's. But he brought a level of intensive mechanization, reconfirmed standards for comprehensive Antarctic research, reestablished an American presence, and injected additional, embarrassingly utopian purposes into Antarctic exploration.

Meanwhile, Britain mounted a prolonged, meticulous survey of the peninsula, the British Graham Land Expedition (1934–1937) under John Rymill, in which aerial and ground surveys complemented each other with prodigious success. And the German Antarctic Expedition (1938–1939), under the leadership of Alfred Ritscher and the sponsorship of Reichsmarschall Göring briefly conducted aerial reconnaissances over what was ominously called New Schwabenland. The Wilkins-Hearst expedition had American sponsors, and Lincoln Ellsworth, a millionaire American sportsman, engaged in aerial feats over the Antarctic in the course of two expeditions. Ellsworth did not establish a scientific base; his simple goal was a transcontinental flight, with whatever aerial photography and ancillary geographic information that could bring. His first series of attempts (1933–1936) brought success in November 1935, when he flew from the tip of the Antarctic Peninsula to Roosevelt Island, near Byrd's abandoned base camp. With no possibility of a return flight and no provision for rescue should the plane crash, Ellsworth's flight was a bravura performance. And it did answer the nagging question of whether the Weddell and Ross seas joined. A second transcontinental flight (across East Antarctica) scheduled for 1938–1939 had to be abandoned. Instead Ellsworth contented himself with aerial reconnaissances around the Amery Ice Shelf and with some land claims.

At the same time, Byrd was an improbable successor to the heroic age. Born into an old Virginia family with roots in seventeenth-century plantations, Byrd envisioned a society in Antarctica and cast himself in the role of colonizer. He was the first man to really consider Antarctica as a site for quasi-permanent settlement, not simply as a *terra incognita* awaiting geographic discovery or an arena for individual exploits. His base at the Bay of Whales, Little America, was not simply an instrument for data collection—the usual "hut" of Antarctic expeditions—but a village, a way of life, a society that was to be purified by The Ice. In more fanciful moments, Byrd imagined that Little America would become a model of sorts, a twentieth-century City on the Ice that would, like some early American settlements, ideally inspire the civilization that had sent it there. Little America was established to address not only the latest scientific questions but the oldest question, how to live. "In a word we are trying to get away from the false standards by which men live under more civilized conditions," Byrd explained. "The Antarctic is a new world for all of us which requires its own standards, and these are materially different from those set up in civilization, whereby we venerate prestige, influence and associated characteristics and ignore the inconspicuous, but equally valid properties." If it were possible, Byrd exhorted, "I wanted to create a single attitude—a single state of mind—unfettered by the trivial considerations of civilization." [26]

Strange words from an Antarctic explorer, one of whose goals was to fly an airplane over the South Pole. Byrd readily admitted that only scientific research could legitimate an undertaking on the scale he envisioned, and he proclaimed of his second expedition that it "achieved, by a fair margin, the most complete program of scientific research in the history of polar exploration." [27] But that same expedition witnessed Byrd's enigmatic decision to winter over alone at Bolling Advance Base, a hut for meteorological readings 100 kilometers south of Little America. There were ample Arctic precedents for solitary winterings, and Courtauld had recently survived several months in an ice cave in central Greenland. Yet the real origins of Byrd's decision apparently lay in his peculiar philosophy and his vision of an Antarctic society, which made the episode less an aberration than a further, nearly fatal distillation of that vision.

What had changed was not so much the character of the men but the character of their society, the cultural context within which they would interpret their experience. It is no accident, perhaps, that Americans—much less scarred by the Great War than Europeans—would lead the return to Antarctica. Byrd brought to the inherited pattern of Antarctic exploration the traits of 1920s America, with its glorification of the businessman, its interest in corporate endeavors, its premium on organizational talent, mass advertising, and the machine. It is not too much to suggest, as Peter Anderson has, that Byrd perhaps reluctantly made a business out of exploration. [28] The Antarctic explorers of the 1920s and 1930s were no less courageous than those in the two prior decades. Byrd's flight to the pole had moments of high drama, as he pushed out bales of emergency food to give the plane enough lift to carry it over the Transantarctics. Laurence Gould executed the longest scientific dog-sledging expedition in Antarctic history during his journey to the Queen Maud Mountains. And there is nothing in the heroic age to compare with Ellsworth's all-or-nothing transcontinental flight; even Shackleton turned back within 97 miles of the pole for fear that he might not be able to return safely. But Byrd also saw beyond adventure to appreciate the essential passivity of Antarctica. The Ice was more—or rather less—than a great white stage for strenuous exertion. Essentially, survival meant surmounting the inactivity and lethargy of the polar night and enduring the introspection and deprivation that were the supreme Antarctic attributes.

A commercial, middle-class audience cheered Byrd on, and wealthy philanthropists helped finance his expeditions as they did new observatories and scientific schools such as the California Institute of Technology. The values Byrd celebrated were different from those of British gentility, and the hero was confused with the celebrity. The genuine explorer had to compete for public adulation with the traveler and the tourist, with movie stars and athletes, the Great White South with the Silver Screen. Lindbergh's transatlantic flight, after all, had not been a voyage of exploration, only a stunt hyped into mass hysteria. The revelation of never-visited icescapes had to compete as spectacles of natural history with such popular travel narratives as Margaret Mead's account of Samoan sexual mores, with its timely implied attack on "Puritanism," and accounts of life in a remote scientific settlement contended with endless satires on small-town morality. The traveler and the tourist were superseding the explorer as vehicles for communicating information about distant lands and peoples. Especially problematic was the fact that interior Antarctica revealed only a colossal whiteness, utterly without "human interest" other than that of the explorer himself.

The ties between Antarctica and middle America, however, were not matched by ties to high culture. A century earlier, an American exploring expedition like Wilkes's might have had difficulty rousing political enthusiasms, but there was little doubt among intellectuals that geographic discovery was important. Art, literature, science, and exploration all shared a similar intellectual universe, and the results of discovery would be worked over in several genres. That was no longer the case by the time of the Byrd Antarctic Expedition. Aside from some science fiction stories, the new era of exploration would not inspire the kind of literary response that earlier epochs of discovery had, and explorers would not see themselves as litterateurs. Literary figures traveled to Paris, not to the pole. The village virus inflamed writers with endless bile toward Main Street at exactly the time that Byrd sought to establish a small-town utopia, Little America, in remote Antarctica. But more was involved than fashion and literary taste. An aggressive modernism was redefining for intellectuals a new range of subject matter and appropriate methods of inquiry. The Museum of Modern Art, for example, opened as Byrd sailed south.

More serious was the relationship of exploration to modern science. As Byrd readily confessed, only scientific investigation could justify expeditions on the scale he contemplated. The new times made possible a reform in Antarctic exploration that would vastly expand the accuracy and extent of geographic discovery. Yet the Antarctic experience lost something of its significance, and the value of geographic discovery was uncertain. In pleading for Antarctic exploration, Maury had declared that "no discoveries have conferred more honor and glory upon the age in which they were made, or been more beneficial to the world, than geographical discoveries."[29] No one could make a similar claim in the 1920s. Byrd recognized the problem, referring to Antarctica as a "frozen asset." Geographical discovery, he continued, "is still, as it always was, the brightest weapon in the explorer's armory," but in the "new philosophy of exploration" it must bring the apparatus of science to bear upon the "*unknown*," not simply the unvisited.[30] More powerful modern sciences than geography had to flesh out the scientific program. Consciously echoing Maury, Byrd wrote after his second expedition that it was a "curious but readily accredited fact" that astronomers had settled the Martian canal question, but geography and geology could not determine "whether Antarctica only 10,000 miles away was one continent or two."[31]

Yet few people were willing to concede to those discoveries the same sense of intellectual importance commanded by the new physics or the American school of genetics. The greatest scientific minds were in other disciplines. While Byrd planned his first expedition, with its flight to the pole, Werner Heisenberg articulated for quantum mechanics the uncertainty principle; while Byrd sat alone at Advance Base, searching for philosophical roots in the eternal verities, Kurt Gödel offered his proof on logical indeterminacy; while the U.S. Antarctic Service established two bases for permanent colonization in Antarctica and Paul Siple developed his concept of wind chill as a doctoral dissertation, Theodosius Dobzhansky helped complete the modern synthesis of genetics and evolution, chance and time. Antarctic exploration seemed to reveal only ice and more ice. This is not to say that the expeditions lacked any serious intellectual content. On the contrary, they were usually justified—correctly—as intellectual enterprises. But a century earlier geographic discovery had been a commanding discipline, integral to the sciences and with wide cultural ramifications. By the 1920s that was no longer true.

In particular, the earth sciences—the great beneficiaries of the continental explorations—failed to experience an intellectual revolution comparable to that in the physical, mathematical, or life sciences. Instead, earth science was poised for an era of massive complacency, the American school of geology being especially affected. The contrast with what happened in the American West, where geology thrived by association with exploration, is revealing. The year Byrd first sailed south, 1928, makes a convenient turning point. Contrast two books, both relevant to Antarctica, which were published that year. The American Geographical Society brought out its *Problems of Polar Research*, an international summary of Arctic and Antarctic knowledge gained during the heroic age. There were chapters by Byrd, Ellsworth, and Wilkins on the use of aircraft in polar exploration. The book admitted that the techniques for south polar discovery were available, and it documented fairly well the domain of existing knowledge. But the other book, *The Theory of Continental Drift*, the published proceedings of an international symposium on the subject sponsored by the American Association of Petroleum Geologists, indirectly challenged the geologic significance of Antarctic discovery. The theory of continental drift made Antarctica central to the reconstruction of Gondwanaland. American geologists, however, not only rejected but ridiculed the idea of large continental displacements, delaying for decades the revolution that would propel the earth sciences into the twentieth century. In the process, they deprived Antarctic earth science of a deeper intellectual significance than that of a gigantic mopping-up operation of traditional geography. Byrd obliquely confessed as much when he defended Antarctic discovery as "one of the great *undone* tasks of the world."[32] The exploration of Antarctica seemed to be an expensive sideshow, a reluctant terminus to an archaic era rather than a point of departure for a new epoch of adventure and learning.

As Byrd planned a third expedition, the U.S. government, with the personal attention of President Franklin Roosevelt, expressed a keen interest in Antarctica. The reasons were several, including the impression made on Roosevelt by Byrd's earlier expeditions and the president's taste for establishing new cities, from the Matanuska Colony in Alaska to suburban Greenbelt City, Maryland. But the specter of a Nazi-sponsored expedition to Antarctica and the invasion of Poland no doubt confirmed the potential strategic significance of Antarctica. As a result, an interagency civilian bureau, the U.S. Antarctic Service (1939–1941), was created; two permanently manned bases were established in Antarctica—one (west base) near Little America and another (east base) on Stonington Island off the Antarctic Peninsula—and a legal foundation for land claims was secured should the United States wish to assert sovereignty at some future time. Byrd directed the program, and the operations were heavily staffed with members of his first two expeditions. Government support, however, had its liabilities. The bureaucratization of Antarctic research haltingly lurched into the future. Eventually, the demands of the war and the removal of Antarctica from U.S. strategic interests terminated the Antarctic Service and the first attempt to permanently colonize The Ice.

Yet an important pattern had been established. The old territorial claims, which had never had more than symbolic importance, acquired a new urgency amid the war emergency and became uncertain amid the postwar assault on colonialism. With Britain preoccupied by the war in Europe, Argentina defied British claims to the peninsula and removed British artifacts from Melchior and Deception islands. Britain sent a naval force (Operation Tabarin) to reclaim the area, then followed in 1944 with the creation of a permanent program of scientific research, the Falkland Islands Dependencies Survey, later renamed the British Antarctic Survey (1956). By then, Chile and Argentina had begun erecting meteorological stations on and around the peninsula, and Australia had created the Australian National Antarctic Research Expedition (ANARE), followed by the establishment of Mawson station in 1954. France revived interest a year later and constructed a station on the Adelie Coast in 1950. The Norwegians stayed with their whalers and—the most important scientific event of the period—the Norwegian-British-Swedish Antarctic Expedition (1949–1952). The establishment of permanent bases as a means of shoring up territorial claims and the use of Antarctica as an arena for military operations became the rage.

The U.S. returned in 1946–1947 with a thirteen-ship armada that included an icebreaker, an aircraft carrier, and even a submarine. Operation Highjump (officially, U.S. Antarctic Developments Project) sought to make use of recent surplus war machinery; to test clothing, men, and equipment under polar conditions; and to apply aerial mapping to Antarctica in a big way. Highjump can be seen as part of the slow scaling-down of the American military machine built up during World War II and the gradual redirection to confront a polar antagonist, the Soviet Union. It was one of a series of cold-weather exercises, most of which were conducted in Alaska and Greenland. Byrd had urged the Navy to consider Antarctica, and when Highjump was authorized, it was nominally placed under his direction. The three task forces flew the perimeter of the continent, putting some 3,900,000 square kilometers under aerial photogrammetry. The second U.S. Antarctic Developments Project (Operation Windmill) returned the following year with a much leaner program in order to collect ground-survey points. And another Byrd veteran, Finne Ronne, supported by a mixture of public and private funds, organized the Ronne Antarctic Research Expedition (1947–1948), which investigated the east side of the peninsula and the Ronne Ice Shelf. A third Antarctic Developments Project expired in a fit of politicking and fiscal restraint. In 1948 the Department of State, pondering what position the U.S. should take in the looming territorial disputes, requested the National Academy of Sciences to review the feasibility of future scientific programs in Antarctica.

Within a few years, however, the whole scene changed. Everything connected with Antarctic exploration and science was dominated by the preparations for the International Geophysical Year (IGY). All the essential precedents were established. Operation Highjump had demonstrated the techniques and power of massive logistical support; the Norwegian-British-Swedish Antarctic Expedition had outlined the terms by which an international science program could be coordinated; the resurgence of rival territorial claimants reasserted the geopolitical importance of Antarctica, and the scientific program of IGY confirmed its geophysical significance. It remained only to consolidate these parts into a whole. IGY did just that. In the process Antarctica became something more than a geographic anomaly, no longer simply the extremity of planet Earth but its nexus to interplanetary space.

IGY: The Third Great Age of Discovery

The International Geophysical Year effectively announced a new phase in the character of exploration by Western civilization. It inaugurated the geophysical inventory of the solar system, beginning with planet Earth. Like other epochs, this one had its special geographic realms: it investigated the outer atmosphere and interplanetary space, both of which had been previously unvisited; mapped the solid floor of the oceans and systematically collected its sediments; and surveyed, for the first time with any comprehensiveness, the interior of Antarctica. Instead of comparing seas or continents, this new phase of discovery compared whole planets. Like other epochs, too, this one posed problems of intellectual and geopolitical assimilation. The newly exposed regions had to be incorporated, on one hand, into political, social, and economic systems and, on the other, into systems of science, literature, and art. There were institutional precedents for IGY, and some research had been done in all the areas it visited. But IGY brought an intellectual synergism, a scale of operations, and an institutional momentum that would make it qualitatively different from earlier modes of discovery. IGY bonded exploration to Big Science, Western discovery shed its ethnocentricity, and this epoch, like its predecessors, accompanied an intellectual revolution, a reformation in metaphysics no less than in geophysics. Exploration and science could be interpreted within the prism of modernism and such new, fundamental concepts of time and process as relativity, information theory, systems theory, and cybernetics.

The IGY idea began modestly at a 1950 dinner party for British geophysicist Sydney Chapman, an authority on the aurora. Lloyd Berkner, a veteran of Byrd's first expedition, suggested that the time had come to organize a new international polar year. The first international polar year had been the brainchild of Lt. Carl Weyprecht, commander of the Austro-Hungarian Arctic expedition (1872–1874). Not unlike Maury's program for the Antarctic, Weyprecht's proposal involved moving beyond simple geographic discovery through the orchestration of multinational expeditions and observations in the polar regions. There were a number of precedents, including the nineteenth-century campaign of Humboldt and others to coordinate meteorological and geomagnetic data-gathering, an undertaking that had helped launch the Ross, d'Urville, and Wilkes expeditions. There had also been, since 1769, a tradition of coordinated international programs to measure the transit of Venus. The Austro-Hungarian Arctic Expedition had been, in part, a contribution to the 1874 transit of Venus, in support of which the U.S. had dispatched a party to Kerguelen Island. Weyprecht's proposed polar program coincided with yet another transit, in 1882–1883.

During the International Polar Year eleven countries participated with promising results, although activities focused on the Arctic and Greenland. Fifty years later, a second polar year was organized (1932–1933). This time there was at least a nominal nod toward the Antarctic when survey parties were sent to a few subantarctic islands. Most of Chapman's colleagues at the dinner party had themselves participated in the second polar year. Berkner, however, observed that the radical advancements in technology stimulated by World War II made possible a far more comprehensive investigation of polar phenomena and promised access to the interior of Antarctica. Land parties could exploit reliable tractors, aircraft, rockets, remote sensors, durable instruments, and advances in wartime logistics; icebreakers and long-range transport aircraft could circumvent the rhythms of the pack. A third polar year, Berkner suggested, ought to be held after twenty-five years instead of fifty and ought to make Antarctica a principal objective.

Berkner and Chapman, then president of the International Union for Geodesy and Geophysics (IUGG), took the idea to the International Council of Scientific Unions (ICSU). Other international scientific societies soon enrolled. In 1952 the World Meteorological Organization recommended that the concept of a polar year be expanded in scope to embrace an international geophysical year. The idea was readily accepted, a Special Committee for the International Geophysical Year (CSAGI) was established, and countries began to organize national committees to secure funding and to direct the programs that they would contribute. A crucial political impediment was overcome when the Soviet Union, recently unburdened by the death of Stalin, agreed to participate. In all, nearly thirty thousand scientists from sixty-six nations took part, and some one thousand scientific stations were established. Among the most spectacular programs planned were the use of rockets to explore the upper atmosphere and a multinational investigation of Antarctica.

In a sense, the geophysical exploration of Antarctica had been the raison d'être for the whole project, and the centrality of Antarctica, although overshadowed by the popular hysteria surrounding Sputnik and the rocket program, would never be lost. The CSAGI observed that Antarctica "by virtue of its unique position and its physical characteristics represents a region of almost unparalleled interest in the fields of geophysics and geography alike." Its geophysics had "many significant unexplored aspects," and the IGY agenda represented "the first really thorough world effort to uncover the geophysical secrets of this continent."[33] At a 1954 meeting the CSAGI elected to concentrate on outer space and Antarctica as the two most novel and powerful geophysical unknowns, and the IGY logo prominently tilted the Earth to reveal the south polar region. A special subcommittee on Antarctica was established in 1955; twelve nations submitted programs and collectively erected over forty stations in the Antarctic. Not the least of its consequences, IGY encouraged and made politically acceptable the Russians' return to Antarctica. Once established, nations with or without territorial ambitions made permanent some of their IGY Antarctic bases. The general good feeling engendered by IGY, the success of international cooperation on scientific research, and the unsettled political environment of Antarctica all led, in turn, to the invention of a special regime for the government of the region.

The relationship between Antarctica and outer space was not lost on IGY participants. The IGY agenda was heavily weighted toward such fields as the upper atmosphere, solar activity, cosmic rays, the aurora and airglow, ionospheric physics, and geomagnetism. Antarctica offered a stable platform ideally situated near the magnetic pole from which to observe all these phenomena. The exploration of Antarctica, that is, would be naturally allied not to that of the other continents but to interplanetary space. In response to the rocket program of IGY, made resoundingly visible by Sputnik, the U.S. created the National Aeronautics and Space Administration (NASA) in 1958. The first post-IGY symposium on Antarctic geosciences was held in 1959, followed a year later by the first international symposium on space science and two years after that by the first international symposium on remote sensing. Such veterans of earlier expeditions as Paul Siple marveled that the residents of South Pole Station "were like men who had been fired off in rockets to take up life on another planet."[34] For their part, the architects of America's manned space program often saw in Antarctica an analogue for the problems and promises of lunar exploration. Ernst Stuhlinger described how he and others from NASA, including Wernher von Braun, went to Antarctica "because this was as close to lunar conditions as we could get here on Earth."[35]

Interplanetary space and Antarctica were soon joined by a third region that in many ways became the most scientifically productive. In the 1940s the deep oceans were as unknown as the dark side of the Moon. They were believed to be the silent, permanent depositories of earth processes, the planetary dumping ground for sediment, as Antarctica was for water and heat.[36] Not until 1956 was the mid-Atlantic ridge recognized as a continuous feature. But the same combination that brought outer space and Antarctica together into a new regime of exploration—technological developments, Big Science, and perceived intellectual value—added the deep ocean basins. World War II had vastly stimulated new oceanographic technologies, including possible manned submersibles, capable of descending to unimagined depths; remote sensing equipment, by which to map the topography of the ocean floor and to take geophysical measurements of gravity, heat flow, and magnetism; and off-shore drilling, by which to sample deep sediments. Thus the rocketry program was paralleled by probes to the deep ocean. Shortly before the first manned rocket flight to the Earth's outer atmosphere—an elevation record—the bathyscaphe *Trieste* plummeted 36,800 feet into the Marianas Trench, the deepest descent below the planet's surface. In the United States, essentially the same generation pioneered each realm: Richard Byrd was a contemporary to Robert Goddard, the founder of American rocketry, and to William Beebe, inventor of the bathysphere. Goddard launched the first liquid-fuel rocket in 1926, the same year that Byrd flew over the North Pole; and in 1930 Beebe, assisted by Otis Barton, executed the first deep-sea descent as the Byrd expedition returned from the first flight over the South Pole.

For a while, it appeared that the U.S. would add another unvisited domain to the agenda, the Earth's mantle. But the grandiose Project Mohole—aspiring to drill to the Mohorovicic lithologic discontinuity that segregated the crust from the mantle—was replaced by a less risky and expensive but enormously productive program of deep-ocean drilling. Within a little over a decade the geography, geology, and geophysics of the Earth's oceans were roughly surveyed. Similar remote sensing techniques, particularly seismic profiling and radar echoing, gradually mapped the subice terrain of Antarctica. Between them the submarine geography of the ocean basins and the subglacial topography of Antarctica quadrupled the amount of the Earth's solid surface subjected to mapping.

By any measure IGY was an enormous success. Reviewing its eighteen months—from July 1, 1957, to December 31, 1958—during his closing presidential address to the last IGY congress, Chapman predicted with British understatement that "the time will come when the International Geophysical Year will be viewed as an important but primitive contribution to the exploration of the cosmos."[37] Others were less reticent. Hugh Odishaw, head of the U.S. National Committee, announced with American hyperbole that IGY was "the single most significant peaceful activity of mankind since the Renaissance and the Copernican Revolution."[38] Like other times during which exploration had suddenly opened up large areas to inquiry, this one produced an information explosion. The U.S. Antarctic program alone brought back seventeen tons of data. To house that information, three World Data Centers (WDC) were established—one in the U.S., one in the Soviet Union, and one divided among several European nations. A massive publication effort was launched, *The Annals of the IGY*, but dozens of additional specialized journals and new scientific societies in the earth sciences, from glaciology to tectonics, were needed. Most would persist beyond the formally designated duration of IGY. The U.S. bibliographic effort on IGY and Antarctica would

evolve into the massive *Antarctic Bibliography*. Similarly, the
international committees and the pattern of multinational expeditions celebrated by IGY would continue.

So, after a fashion, would IGY. It is not always simple to scale
down a large scientific program, and in some instances it is not
desirable, either scientifically or politically. Many nations—the
U.S. and the U.S.S.R. chief among them—wanted to maintain a
permanent presence in Antarctica without engaging in territorial claims or recognizing those of other nations. The scientific
program of IGY had granted entree to Antarctica, and if that
program could be institutionalized, it would help justify a continued political presence. Moreover, once the Soviet Union declared its intention to remain in Antarctica, the U.S. was com-
mitted to an equally substantial presence. Almost immediately,
a reduced IGY program was extended for another year until the
aegis of the International Geophysical Cooperation (IGC). To
replace the CSAGI Antarctic committee as a governing body of
international coordination, a Scientific Committee on Antarctic Research (SCAR) was established within the International
Council of Scientific Unions. Other similar institutions were
created for ocean (SCOR) and space (COSPAR) research. Antarctic exploration proceeded through a combination of coordinated national programs and multinational projects, both large
and small. The IGY exemplar was likewise succeeded by a host
of global programs from the International Year of the Quiet Sun
to the International Biological Year. Meanwhile, loudly proclaimed as a "high ground," endowed with military implications, and inflated by concern over national prestige, space exploration, not Antarctic research, collected and channeled the
international rivalry between the U.S. and the Soviet Union.

More was involved than a reformation of institutional style.
IGY signaled a generational change in the character of Antarctic research, best symbolized by the death of Byrd in 1957.
"The Moses of America's Antarctic frontier," as Paul Carter put
it, "had not made it all the way to his Promised Land."[39] Though
Larry Gould, the science officer for Byrd's first expedition, remained influential for several decades with the U.S. program
and SCAR, the American IGY program was the last hurrah for
"Byrd's boys." A continuity with previous Antarctic exploration
remained, but IGY trained a new generation for which there
was a loss of individual identity. Remarkably invisible, a corporate body shaped by Big Science and Big Education and usually

known by the programs under which it worked, this new group shaped future research. Likewise, IGY symbolized a change in the character of information collection. Instead of the hand-held barometer or thermometer, remote sensing devices and their platforms became increasingly fundamental. Ideally, in the ocean basins and across interplanetary space, remote probes could substitute for human observers. These were areas not only unoccupied by native peoples but never before visited by humans and in which humans could exist only within wholly synthetic environments. Antarctica would be assimilated into civilization, but not into the civilization known to the eighteenth century of Cook or the nineteenth century of Wilkes or the early twentieth century of Byrd.

Not only exploration but the whole syndrome of Western thought had altered the way in which exploration as an enterprise and knowledge as its product were conceived. Modernism was firmly established as an "official culture" in art, science, and philosophy. The acceptance of a chance universe; the relativity of time, space, and perspective; the blurring of the observer with the observed; the delight in abstract, minimalist art—the intellectual apparatus at last existed with which to comprehend the alien ice terranes of Antarctica. Modernism and The Ice were perfect complements. Critics who observed that the IGY era of discovery did not have the same attributes as previous epochs of exploration were right. Yet those earlier eras had often been ill equipped—intellectually no less than technologically—to discover and assimilate the new realms of geographic exploration. IGY accompanied a delayed revolution in metaphysics and scientific theory about the Earth. The same year, 1969, that volcanic rocks were brought back from the Moon, *Lystrosaurus* fossils were discovered in the Transantarctic Mountains, confirming the theory of continental drift; and it was calculated that the information-handling capacity of the world's computers exceeded, for the first time, the information capacity of the world's population of humans.

The situation was well illustrated by the curious conjunction of the IGY assault on Antarctica and the simultaneous, but independently conceived, British Commonwealth Trans-Antarctic Expedition. Self-styled as the "last great land expedition on earth," the latter was a much-publicized trek that sought to realize Shackleton's ambition for an overland traverse of Antarctica. The main party, led by Vivian Fuchs, set out with

tracked vehicles and dog sledges from the Weddell Sea region,
while an advance party under Edmund Hillary established re-
supply depots on the Ross Ice Shelf. The journey succeeded, although it was difficult to say just what it succeeded in; its principal contributions to science were the gravity and seismic
readings it conducted on behalf of IGY. An enterprise separate
from IGY—distinct not merely in its origins but in its emphasis
on the personalities of its leaders—the Trans-Antarctic Expedition was an anachronism. Its meaning to exploration was defined less by its realization of the transantarctic traverse than
by the new matrix for discovery established through IGY. Its
real counterpart was not the coordinated interrogation of the
Earth represented by IGY, which also sent out several overland
traverses to the interior of Antarctica, but the concurrent voyages of the USS *Nautilus* and *Skate* beneath the North Pole.

This metamorphosis was more than a case—common in the
history of science—of an overload of information deforming
existing theories. Exploration accompanied a profound re-
definition of nature. Traditions of landscape painting like those
of Humboldt devotee Frederick Church were meaningless on
the great whiteness. The geologic and biologic sciences were
baffled in dealing with a geography of nihilism that banished
life and buried data beneath an ice sheet two miles thick. Lock-
ean empiricism, epitomized by the fanatic collection of specimens—a metaphysics that had thrilled to abundance and
thrived on placing a multiplicity of objects into proper categories—vanished in an epistemological whiteout on The Ice.
What began as an unknown white spot on the map of the known
world would, paradoxically, end up as a known white spot. The
whiteness would be reified and named—"a proof of something,"
pondered Katha Pollitt, "though only in the end white chalk in-
visibly scribbled on a white tabula rasa."[40]

Writing of the new perspectives IGY offered on the Earth,
Berkner suggested that "it is like coming from outer space and
finding a new planet."[41] There was more to the image than perhaps he realized. As the space program matured it would be possible, literally, to see the Earth from the outside in. In photos of
the planet taken from interplanetary space, the obsession of
modernism with self-reflexivity would find geographic expression. But the turning of the mind of the Earth back upon itself
would actually begin earlier with the ice mirror of Antarctica.

The Shelf

It presented an extraordinary appearance, gradually increasing in height, as we got nearer to it, and proving at length to be a perpendicular cliff of ice . . . an obstruction of such a character . . . [that] we might with equal chance of success try to sail through the Cliffs of Dover, as to penetrate such a mass.

> —Sir James Ross, *A Voyage of Discovery and Research* (1847)

But, after all, it is not what we see that inspires awe, but the knowledge of what lies beyond our view. We see only a few miles of ruffled snow bounded by a vague wavy horizon but we know that beyond that horizon are hundreds and even thousands of miles which can offer no change to the weary eye, while on the vast expanse that one's mind conceives one knows there is . . . nothing but this terrible limitless expanse of snow. . . . Could anything be more terrible than this silent, wind-swept immensity when one thinks such thoughts?

> —Robert Scott, *The Voyage of the Discovery* (1905)

Everywhere it forms a rampart of white—sometimes small and finely drawn, elsewhere massive and enormous—that envelops the continent like the icy crust of the Jovian moon Europa.

Not its land but its land ice establishes the true coast of Antarctica. This is an ice continent, a *terra glacies*, bounded by an ice littoral. Only about 3 percent of both continent and coast are not submerged beneath ice, but along the coast there is everywhere an ice shore. Some of the ice is the product of local processes, the action of sea on ice and land or the outcome of local stresses along the terminus of larger ice masses. There are ice grottos, ice caves, ice stalactites, ice beaches, and ice foots. The latter may be extensive, fringing rock or ice with a terrace of ice, snow, debris, and sea-spray icicles 1.8–3.0 meters high and 6–60 meters wide. Ice foots can grow into ice fringes, and ice fringes into ice piedmonts. Elsewhere the interior ice sheet extends directly to the coast. Some of this coastal ice results from sea and land ice accumulations: seasonal fast ice, drift ice, anchor ice; quasi-permanent pockets of fast ice, extensions of local glaciers, beached remnants of former ice shelves and sheets, ice cliffs shaped where the interior ice dome meets the shore. But the bulk of coastal ice emanates from the interior ice sheets, some of which filter through a matrix of land, while others spread directly from source to sea. Perhaps 30–40 percent of the Antarctic littoral consists of ice bound to rock; the rest consists of floating ice shores, ice tongues and ice shelves, often of immense proportions. Collectively, this ensemble of floating ice—call it the shelf—equals 10 percent of the entire area of Antarctica under glacial ice. It is the shelf that effectively etches the outer boundary of land ice, that defines the inner crystalline sphere of The Ice.

As an ice terrane, the shelf has some functions of the pack and some of the ice sheet. Like the pack, it segregates hydrosphere from atmosphere. There is some surface accumulation from snowfall and ablation from wind scour, as well as some bottom buildup by sea ice and removal by melting. But the shelf does not exhibit a seasonal life cycle, and it is not itself the product of air and sea interaction. Instead it represents a seaward extension of continental ice, a massive sheeting that eliminates even partial exchange between atmosphere and ocean. Like the ice sheet, the shelf couples ice to land, and it 119

The

Shelf

extends the range of the ice sheet to offshore islands and submarine rises. Land and sea share a common surface of ice. The
effect is to simplify in a colossal way the complexity of the Antarctic coast. The reductionism of the pack is intensified to include more directly the attributes of the ice sheet: internal
creep substitutes for the motion of floes; a frozen memory of ice
deformation supersedes seasonal cycles of ice growth and decay; a vast emptiness replaces information, as the simplicity of
an ice cover supplants the complexity of air, land, and sea.

Yet the shelf has its own identity and functions. Paradoxically, it is the principal source of both continental ice stability
and instability. As the point of ice wastage, where glacial ice is
melted, broken, and liberated into the pack, the shelf is a zone
of instability and disintegration. But, equally, the shelves and
tongues are the crystalline ligatures and ice buffers of Antarctica. More than any other ice terrane, the shelf joins ice to
ice: glacier to glacier, glacier to ice stream, ice stream to ice
stream, sea ice to land ice, ice sheet to ice sheet, ice source to
iceberg. The shelves, moreover, form reservoirs of continental
ice, massing various ices into great retaining basins that regulate the ablation side of the Antarctic ice budget. Even more
significantly, they underpin and restrain the ice sheets; they
physically grapple the West Antarctic ice sheet to the lithosphere, help weld an island archipelago into an ice craton, and
connect West Antarctica with East. The shelf forms a kind of
crystalline exoskeleton that shapes, binds, and protects the ice
continent. Between the constant sloughing off of ice and its
constant replenishment there exists an unstable, dynamic equilibrium of change and permanence. The hybrid functions and
attributes of the shelf account for much of its glaciological and
esthetic interest.

Consequently, the shelf is both special and generic. It possesses some of the attributes of the other ice masses of Antarctica yet organizes those physical and esthetic traits into a
unique whole. Some of its features are inherited from the
glaciers, ice streams, and ice sheets that contribute to the shelf;
and some are acquired from new processes of accumulation and
ablation, from new stresses associated with floating, calving,
and the tension and compression of colliding ice streams and
creeping ice sheets. In brief, the shelf retains an inherited com-

position, structure, and motion to which it adds and subtracts and which it reshapes. The shelf mixes, incompletely, the ices that congregate around it into new forms with unique structures, dynamics, and esthetics. It contains the complex memory of the precalved berg, but without the berg's additional experiences or its free-water dynamism. It exhibits the severity of the ice sheet, but without the ice sheet's originating quiescence. Where it forms a triple junction with land and sea, the shelf is among the most exciting of Antarctic ice terranes. But where it is isolated from the other terranes—an icy steppe remote from exposed land or open sea—the shelf becomes perhaps the least engrossing of Antarctic icescapes. Under these circumstances, the shelf is most valuable as an introduction to the esthetics of the pure icescape, to the domain of the interior ice sheets—the source regions—to which it is coupled directly without mediating earth, air, water, or life.

It comes as no surprise that the most immense and accessible of the shelves, the Ross Ice Shelf, was first named the Great Ice Barrier and retained that label for decades. The Barrier was the ne plus ultra of maritime exploration. Once the pack was breached, the open Ross Sea brought a party as close to the pole as possible anywhere around the circumference of Antarctica. The Weddell Sea pack prevented access to the complementary Ronne Ice Shelf; interminable small shelves, glacial tongues, fast ice, ferocious winds, and an ice dome that extended completely to the shore discouraged landings in most of East Antarctica; and the offshore islands of the west coast of the peninsula, though often accessible, led nowhere. The Ross Sea was the most prominent embayment by which to enter Antarctica, and it ended abruptly at the Barrier. Once humans reached the continent, it was on the ice shelves that, for the most part, they encountered The Ice.

In return, humans became the only organisms to live on the shelf. This did not occur, however, without accommodations: new forms of adaptation were needed, and individual adjustment was psychological and cultural as well as physiological. The shelves were a barrier to the mind no less than to the body, to the noosphere no less than to the biosphere. The process of adaptation demanded new, often elaborate forms and institutions for acquiring and assimilating information. The shelf was both entree and barrier.

And a voice came back from a soul that seemed sick,
Came back from the Barrier;—Go!
For the secrets hidden are all forbidden
Till God means man to know.

—Edward Wilson, "The Barrier Silence" (1911)[1]

Glaciology of the Shelf

An ice shelf proper is a floating slab of land ice. On some sides it is confined by rigid borders, but other sides form dynamic boundaries at which ice enters and leaves the system. An ice shelf is both stable and unstable. Its rigid margins confine and pin the ice, promoting stability. Ice flows past or over these sites by shear, but the volume of ice is conserved. The dynamic margins, however, introduce instability to the shelf by controlling the amount and rate of ice movement. The critical boundaries are two: the grounding line or hinge marks the plane at which the glacier or ice sheet begins to float, while the ice front identifies the plane at which the floating shelf disintegrates into bergs. In addition, the shelf has a history and its ice a memory. The shelf becomes a complex ensemble of ice masses and ice movement. Not only are ice and new snow acquired and shed, but the various ice streams and dynamic boundaries must interact among themselves and respond to long-term climatic change. The actual geography and movement of a shelf thus depend on those factors that govern the discharge of ice into and out of the system and on whether the shelf's dynamic boundaries are advancing or receding. Rarely are all these components balanced: at any instant, the shelf displays a crude dynamic equilibrium, while over time it is metastable.

Ice shelves vary widely in their shapes and movements. The morphology of a shelf or tongue depends on the amount of ice and snow brought into it, the topography of the land around it, and its history. Small glaciers emptying into an unconfined sea create small ice tongues; larger networks of glaciers or ice sheets that discharge into confining embayments develop into vast shelves; and both grounding line and ice front may be retreating or advancing as a result of a history of heavier glaciation or deglaciation. Consequently, the larger shelves congregate around the furrowed coastline of West Antarctica, where ice shelves smooth out the irregular littoral of the continent and compensate for the gross asymmetry between West and East Antarctica.

In general, East Antarctica lacks the right combination of ice sources and receiving basins. Its contribution to the huge Ronne-Filchner and Ross ice shelves is secondary. Instead, ice sheet flow is shaped by subglacial topography and mountains into broad ice streams and large outlet glaciers. Where protected, the glaciers form ice tongues like the Koettlitz, Mertz, and Dibble. In a few areas, ice streams empty into unconfined but sheltered areas to form ice piedmonts or small ice shelves, such as the Shackleton, West, Fimbull, and Riiser-Larsen shelves. The best-developed shelf in East Antarctica, the Amery, appears where the gigantic Lambert Glacier empties from the polar plateau directly into an enormous fjord. The ice shelf that results is not large in area so much as in volume.

By contrast, West Antarctic is almost wholly rimmed by continuous ice shelves and ice tongues. A crenulated coastline, innumerable offshore islands, and adequate sources of snow and ice make floating ice the coastal norm. Large shelves include the Abbot, Getz, and Larsen; but the dominating shelves are the two that flood the deep embayments between West and East Antarctica, the Ronne-Filchner and the Ross. The Ross Ice Shelf—roughly the size of France—alone accounts for 30 percent of all Antarctic shelf ice. The great embayments offer numerous sites for subglacial grounding and lateral pinning, which are essential for ice shelf thickening and stability; tides and currents are weak, diminishing stress fractures on the shelves; cold, closed seas inhibit excessive melting; and storms tend to pass across the shelves frequently, depositing snow. The geometry of the shelves means that their grounding lines are substantially longer than their ice fronts, that ice tends to coalesce rather than dissipate.

The relationship of grounding line to ice front is vital to the dynamics of the shelf. A shelf depends on the balance between the ice added to it and the ice it loses and on the extent to which the shelf is pinned to rocky shores, islands, or submarine rises. Here ice shelf and ice tongue differ. Under stable conditions ice tongues show a cyclic history of growth, rupture and removal, and regrowth. The periodic calving of ice tongues across their grounding lines probably accounts for the super ice-

bergs of Antarctica. Operating under stable conditions, shelves
show a dynamic equilibrium in which the amount of ice discharged across the ice front roughly equals the amount of ice
brought across the grounding line and the snow subsequently
acquired. The outcome is a relatively constant production of
tabular bergs.

But few shelves are truly stable. Neither grounding line nor
ice front is fixed. Both are dynamic boundaries, not only because ice passes across them but because they themselves move.
Moreover, they respond not only to different conditions but to
the same conditions in different ways. Changes in snowfall, in
the amount of ice brought into the system, in the amount of
ablation, in iceberg discharge; fluctuations in sea level; variations in ice shelf temperature; the thinning or thickening of the
shelf due to realignments of anchor points—all will influence
the location of grounding lines and ice fronts and their relative
rates of discharge, recession, and advance. The movement of
grounding line and ice front is of great importance to the whole
system. If the ice front lengthens (advances), then calving will
accelerate. The shelf will shrink until a new equilibrium of accumulation and ablation is reached or until new grounding
lines are developed. Conversely, a retreating (shortening) ice
front may allow individual ice streams or glaciers to punch
through the shelf, fracturing an interdependent system into separate ice masses. The shelf loses the stability that normally results from the interaction of its constituent ices. It is also possible that both ice front and grounding line will advance or
retreat. The outcome will vary accordingly. A grounded ice
sheet may replace a floating ice shelf, a new equilibrium of ice
movements may develop, or the shelf may simply disintegrate as
a coherent ice terrane. Shelves are thus rarely balanced: on a
macroscale, they are metastable, and on a microscale, they are
vibrant with transient motions that are temporarily uncompen-
sated, retained within the frozen memory of the ice.

The basis for the shelf is the glacial ice brought to it from ice
sheets and local icesheds. Mountain glaciers spill into the shelf;
outlet glaciers and ice streams transport huge volumes of land
ice from the polar ice sheets. In fact, a relatively few ice streams
and outlet glaciers account for most of the glacial ice. The Lambert Glacier, whose iceshed taps the source regions of the polar
plateau, supplies most of the shelf ice to the Amery; the Slessor
and Recovery glaciers largely sustain the Filchner; the Founda-

tion ice stream and Evans (and associated) ice streams support the Ronne; and five subparallel ice streams from the West Antarctic ice sheet contribute disproportionately to the Ross Ice Shelf, with secondary sources from outlet glaciers threading through the Transantarctics. This ice not only comprises most of the mass of the shelf but provides the rigid matrix that is essential for trapping additional snows, saline ice, and other additives to the composite.

These secondary sources are varied. Snow is contributed by the frequent storms that circle around the coast and, locally, by wind drift from mountain snowsheds. Paradoxically, snowfall is heaviest along the ice front where ablation is most rapid. This heavy snowfall accounts for the high buoyancy of shelf-formed bergs as compared with those calved directly from glaciers. Seasonally open water also encourages rime, glaze, and hoarfrost to form, in places amounting to 5–10 percent of the total ice mass. Bottom processes proceed in the reverse direction. Bottom freezing of saline ice is most pronounced toward the grounding line, while bottom melting dominates in regions closer to the ice front. The effectiveness of bottom freezing varies considerably among shelves. On the Amery the process is vigorous (perhaps 0.5 meters per year) and extends well toward the ice front; on the Ross, it may amount to 2 centimeters per year and is restricted to the thicker, more inland portions of the shelf. Of 416 meters retrieved from a borehole through the Ross Ice Shelf, some 6 meters consisted of basal saline ice. It is estimated that in places on the Amery Ice Shelf saline bottom ice may be 150 meters thick. Still other sources of accumulation—volcanic debris, sea spray, algae, and dirt—are locally important as stratigraphic horizons and confer color and shape to their receptor ices. Anchor ice is a sometimes important mechanism for adding basal ice and for conveying material from the bottom of the seafloor upward to the floating ice shelf. But the contribution of these miscellaneous sources to the overall thickness or dynamics of the shelf is negligible.

Near the coast, the sea transforms shelf ice by melting and fracturing it and by impregnating it with brine. In complexes of fast ice, brine saturates firn and snow when floes are temporarily submerged. The brine slush freezes to make lenses of amalgamated sea, snow, and infiltration ice. In shelves, however, the brine enters through other mechanisms—by percolation upward within bottom crevasses to the firn strata, by an upward diffusion along ice-crystal boundaries within the ice fabric, and by lateral infiltration from the ice front at the firn-ice boundary. Penetration along the ice front seems to contribute the most seawater by volume, and it produces a peculiar geometry of brine and firn. At a new ice front—the result of recent calving—brine penetrates the firn as a wave. Each new ice breakout induces a new brine wave, and each new wave is superimposed over previous ones so that the inland boundary can be characterized by a sequence of descending steps. The brine, moreover, is quickly concentrated by a process of fractionation. Interstitial freezing and transport remove water and certain mobile elements, leaving lenses of concentrated brine.

Not accumulation alone but the net balance between growth and decay determines the thickness of an ice shelf. Almost immediately there is some wastage, and ablation of all kinds increases toward the ice front. To the processes that lead to surface, basal, and cross-sectional accumulation, there are counter processes that determine the magnitude of ice loss. Barrier winds and katabatics blow snow out to sea. Basal melting, which may account for as much as 25 percent of total ice wastage, thins the shelf near the ice front and assists the process of fracture and calving. On the Ross Ice Shelf, basal melting is important within 100 kilometers of the ice front, with as much as 1 meter per year wasted away. The underside of the shelf takes on a graded appearance: water forced down around protuberances encourages melting, while rising water promotes freezing. In this way land ice, which melts, is exchanged for sea ice, which congeals. But the great bulk of shelf ice is, of course, lost as icebergs. Since the shelves drain more than half of the entire Antarctic ice sheet, icebergs are the most important of all the means by which Antarctica sheds its ice. The grounding line marks a place at which ice streams converge, and the ice front marks the point at which ice streams diverge.

Calving, large or small, relies on common mechanisms of ice fracture. But the processes that guide it, the products that result, and the periodicity of berg liberation depend on the nature of the shelf or tongue. Small glaciers emptying directly into deep water will calve rapidly into irregular, prismatic bergs. Ice tongues, forming in more protected bays, will fail periodically according to the attributes of the glacier that feeds them and the sea that disintegrates them. And because ice shelves are laterally supported by rigid sides, they fracture in more complicated, but still characteristic, patterns.

Essentially, ice tongues fail in two ways. As an elongated slab of glacial ice thrust out from the coast, the ice tongue inherits a heavily crevassed texture. Some calving results from fracture failure as these crevasses widen and deepen around the perimeter. The more spectacular bergs, however, result from rupture near the grounding line or at some intermediate point between the hinge and the tip of the tongue. Here is a source for the enormous superbergs—the true ice islands—of Antarctica.

Rupture depends not only on the properties of the ice but on the peculiar circumstances of the tongue. As it extends outward, the tongue thins, partially because of internal creep and partially because of basal melting. The ice is already latticed with crevasses from its history as a glacier. Several stresses act on these fracture sites—the natural warping of the ice beam as its weight grows, the flexing of the ice at its grounding line because of tidal oscillation, the impact from collisions with large icebergs, and the vibrations induced by ocean waves, oscillations that can approach the natural frequency of the slab. These different stresses, in turn, promote different fracture patterns. Calving at the grounding line most often results from tidal action and the geometry of the bedrock. Marginal calving follows from the ceaseless downwarping of the ice front caused by the imbalance of hydrostatic stress in the ice mass and the pressure of the seawater. Intermediate calving occurs from vibrational stresses. Where the failure occurs near the grounding line, the conditions that lead to fracture can obey a certain periodicity. At the same time, there are elements that retard rupture. Its perimeter of foreign ice—fast ice, drift ice, and grounded icebergs—may protect the ice tongue by acting as a breakwater and by coupling the sides of the slab to land, thereby reducing flexing. Moreover, fracture and liberation do not always coincide. The ice tongue can be imagined as a cantilever beam, supported partly by the buoyancy of the sea and partly by the rigidity of the glacial ice. When the beam breaks, the typically shallow sea along the coast is not always able to support the entire draft of the ice slab. The iceberg grounds, sometimes for decades.

These same stresses apply to the ice shelf, but the sheer areal dimensions of the shelf and its lateral confinement dampen their effects. Theoretically, a free-floating sheet of ice responds only to internal creep, with a degree of deformation that depends on the thickness of the ice. But Antarctic ice shelves hardly approximate such an ideal. The ice sheet is homogeneous in neither composition nor structure. Instead, it amalgamates land ice with basal sea ice and surface snow, and it retains for some distance the characteristics of the separate ice streams that contribute to it. Nor is the shelf an unconfined sheet of floating ice. It is pinned to shorelines and submarine protuberances in such a way that, both locally and across the entire ice field, the shelf imposes powerful new stresses. Fracture and structural deformation are the inevitable results.

There are many mechanisms for failure. The cracks caused by shear stress along rocky coasts or over submerged rises can reseal. This takes time, however, and if the ice front approaches before the fissures are closed, the cracks may propagate through the entire ice sheet—an excellent mechanism for calving. In some cases, ice streams can simply pierce the entire shelf. At the same time, the ice sheet as a whole thins as it departs from the grounding line, partially because of creep and partially because of basal melting. The ice fatigues, longitudinal stresses arise, tensile cracks develop on both surface and bottom. Local stresses that cause a sheet to warp and crack include erosion by wave and current along the ice front. The unequal hydrostatic pressures of ice and ocean cause the ice front to warp down and the shelf, somewhat inland, to arch. Tides induce flexing; ocean waves, oscillations; and collisions with icebergs, vibrations. Brine infiltration near the ice front weakens the slab and bottom melting hardens it, increasing its brittleness.

Thus a variety of fractures contribute to calving. Some fractures are fresh, the outcome of new stresses. Some are residual, the product of stresses that have since been removed but for which the ice has not yet fully readjusted and resealed, such as crevasses formed around an ice rise or from shear between ice streams of differential velocity. Shelves can preserve rifts several hundred kilometers long and several kilometers wide, the outlines of feeder ice streams. While some fractures reflect only local stresses, some reflect general strains in the ice field—creep fatigue in the thinning ice, sheer rupture between different ice streams or between floating ice and rigid boundaries, upstream buckling from the backpressures set up by grounded anchor points. Some fractures develop from the surface down and some, the larger, from the bottom up. Both types—surface and bottom—tend to form at regular places related either to stable sites of ice pinning or to dynamic boundaries, such as the ice front and grounding line. The cracks may fill with seawater or meltwater, both of which are denser than ice and can exert hydrostatic pressure outward and widen the fissure. And in both surface and bottom fracturing the tendency is for the crack to propagate to sea level. This means, however, that surface crevasses in high-density ice will penetrate only about 7 percent of the ice thickness, while bottom crevasses may represent failure through nearly 78 percent of the shelf.

Because they can be up to 250 meters long and 100 meters wide, bottom crevasses are especially critical. Once initiated, the crack propagates according to two competitive processes: ice creep tends to open the crack and the freezing of sea ice tends to close it. Only in the thickest shelves (greater than 400 meters) does creep dominate. But if freezing does not proceed quickly enough, the crack becomes subjected to other stresses near the ice front that also encourage it to open. As the ice front approaches, bottom melting increases, eliminating the potential for the crack to seal by the freezing of the seawater that infiltrates it. If a bottom crevasse joins a surface crack, the outcome is a fracture that may penetrate the entire ice mass. Though less deeply developed, surface cracks are also abundant. They originate from internal deformations in the ice sheet and from local stresses, such as those from tides and waves, that are superimposed over the general stress field. Once established, sites of weakness are exploited by the array of stresses along the ice front; and as a consequence, great plateaus of ice—the celebrated Antarctic tabular bergs—break off. The multiple fracturing, ice faulting, and outright calving cause icequakes, singular and swarming, that eerily shatter the silence of the Barrier.

The behavior of the ice itself contributes mightily to its dimensions and dynamics. Once it is no longer attached to ground, the ice sheet thins, spreading laterally under the impress of internal plastic flow or creep. This kind of behavior has mixed results. Thinning encourages the shelves to melt more rapidly and fracture more easily. Yet it allows a given volume of glacial ice, as measured across the grounding line, to occupy a much larger area by floating than it could when it was frozen to land. Thus the shelf traps more snowfall and affects storm patterns by shutting off air-sea exchanges. More important, the enlarged area increases the likelihood that the shelf will strike, and be anchored to, land. It is not simply the huge quantity of ice introduced into the system that determines the shelf's ultimate geography and allows the shelf to perpetuate itself, but the arrangement of coastal, offshore, and submarine lands that pin the floating ice sheet. Against these rigid bodies, the ice is caught or jammed; this sets up backpressures that cause the ice behind the point of contact to thicken. The thickness of the ice shelf will be proportional to its width, and its width (or extent) will depend on the lands that confine the ice shelf. The Ross Ice Shelf—by far the most intensively studied—varies in thickness from 700 meters at its grounding line to 200 meters at the ice front.

The shelf is a dynamic, interdependent system. A change in grounding line or ice front can lead to a thickening or thinning of the shelf, both of which will cause a relocation of grounding and calving lines. If the ice thickens, or the submarine topography elevates, or the sea level rises, the grounding line will advance. Such changes occur constantly. But since the ice behaves plastically, it does not respond instantaneously. The instabilities are temporarily preserved, and the shelf as a whole tends to be metastable. Eventually the properties of the various ice streams approach a common value, but few shelves offer undisturbed conditions for the length of time necessary to achieve an ideal accommodation. Field stresses are too forceful, the ice front too close, and the processes of mixing too slow. Moreover, the shelf is a historical entity. The present ice shelves of Antarctica did not achieve their current dimensions simply because of outward growth from source glaciers and ice streams. More likely, they would have disintegrated before they reached their current anchor points. Instead, their present geography represents a line of retreat from a time of more intense glaciation, when grounding lines advanced to points beyond the contemporary locations of the ice fronts. As these grounding lines retreated, the floating ice locked onto its present anchor points which, for the moment, are apparently adequate to preserve the shelves.

There is another paradox in the relationship of a shelf to its anchor points. The ice shelf does not cease to move when it strikes ice or land; it shears along the blocking ice stream or rocky shore, and it overrides small islands or submarine protuberances. The movement of the shelf slows, sets up backpressures that cause the ice flow behind the shelf to thicken, and fractures. The fracture zones, which assume patterns, may be on a vast scale. The Grand Chasm identifies one such region on the Filchner Ice Shelf, the Crary ice rise another on the Ross Ice Shelf. Their fracture zones make the anchor points places of weakness within the shelf as a whole, a paradox that the phenomenon of the ice rise illustrates well. The ice sheet locally flows up and over a submarine obstruction, a deformation transmitted to the surface. The resulting structure behaves like a small ice cap embedded within the shelf, but it is a zone of intense deformation—of ice folds, ice faults, and ruptures. Though the bottom ice is frozen to the submarine bed, the upper ices display a radial flow that is ferociously crevassed and full of ice anticlines and ice synclines.

A consequence of these stresses is that the shelf displays a surprising number of mesoscale structures, which are complemented by other features that are the product of differential accumulation and ablation; rarely are the two processes balanced at any one site. Snow does not fall evenly across an entire shelf, basal erosion and sea-ice deposition are most effective in different portions of a shelf, and land ice enters a shelf in distinctive ice streams or glaciers. The ice does not mix readily; each stream retains its own internal properties; and the contours of the ice streams are marked by flow lines of debris, by crevasse patterns resulting from shear along the flanks, and by a broad topography of narrow, elongated ridges and troughs—some longer than 450 kilometers. The fast-moving ice stream thins, while ice trapped between streams thickens. In some places on the Ross Ice Shelf, abrupt, almost steplike changes in ice thickness are apparent. The shelf ice has a memory; its constitution preserves its inherited ice momentum no less than its inherited ice composition and ice structure.

The ice shelf is most interesting along its perimeter. Here its deformation features are best developed and are constantly renewed. The ice front, the junction between shelf and ice sheet and between shelf and glacier, the frozen weld between sea ice and land ice, the interaction of glacial ice against land and land ice against sea—it is around the shelf border that structural variety and contrast are possible. Compression leads to ice rumples, ice haycocks, and ice hummocks; tension leads to crevasses and jumbles of ice blocks. Especially where land and sea meet, shore ices show a variety and delicacy out of character with the purified interior of the shelf. Crevasses, ice erosion,

and the refreezing of meltwater can lead to ice caves and ice
grottos brimming with ice stalactites. Sea moisture entering
large fissures encourages prodigious displays of crystal growth.
Frozen sea spray adds other, lacy forms to the seaward front; an
ice foot terraces land and shelf with mixed ice shapes; grounded
icebergs and remnant shelf ice, mixed with dirt, algae, and
glacial drift, compound the scene with bizarre colors and weird
erosional sculpturings; meltwater ponds of turquoise mix with
grey leads and yellow sea ice, with snow-bright bergs and blue
glacial ice.

Yet this ice shore is not the essence of the shelf. What over-
whelms every observer is the vast sameness, the enormity, singularity, and simplicity of the shelf surface. That surface is not
invariant but reforms constantly as new snow falls, snow crust
forms, hoarfrost grows on exposed points, rime collects during
coastal fogs, diffusion growth reshapes snowflakes into mirror-
like plates, and wind redistributes snow masses. In some places,
the wind causes snow to accumulate into drifts; elsewhere, it
scours depressions and gouges the surface into a fine ridge and
ravine topography known as sastrugi. Sastrugi forms most often
where the surface is thick and crusty, the snow hard and granular, and the winds strong and constant in direction. Wind,
sun, and snowfall alternately abrade and build up the surface
into a texture like that of a collage.

But these are mere decorations. What dominates the appearance of the shelf is its surface. Everywhere it replaces complexity and depth with simplicity and flatness. Over most of the
shelf, snowfall buries surface irregularities into a deceptively
planar horizon; a hard crust of snow preserves the effect. The
monumentally flat appearance of the surface camouflages completely the internal redistribution of stresses caused by ice flow,
accumulation, and deformation. The ice fabric of the surface
constantly recrystallizes; the size, shape, and orientation of the
ice crystals and the distribution and configuration of entrapped
air bubbles are reworked incessantly. Yet the snow covers all:
shelf bottom, shelf surface, shelf interior. The shelf exists
largely as a geometric plane of white, as regular as the geoid.
Only along the perimeter, where the homogeneity of the shelf is
terminated by contact with other ice terranes, is there relief
from the domineering character of the surface. The Great Ice
Barrier was first named for its ice front, but it became identified
with its ice surface. That surface controlled not only the his-

tory, exploration, and settlement of the shelf but its esthetics. It became the grand, unsettling introduction to a geography of nihilism and to the esthetics of The Ice.

Projective Geometries

The Great Ice Barrier ends, once and for all, a direct connection between sea and air. Unlike the pack, the shelf is not itself the product of air-sea exchanges. That connection is severed and its complicated dynamics simplified. Instead the ice responds separately to sea and air. The interaction between shelf and sea is limited. Bergs calve along the ice front; relatively subdued ice erosion and deposition occur along the shelf bottom; subshelf water is chilled, ocean currents and tides diminished. Similarly, the shelf reduces the complex interactions of ice and air that characterize the pack. An intense inversion layer is superimposed over the ice surface, and this sheath of air largely reshapes the mechanics and appearance of the Antarctic atmosphere over the shelf. The meteorology of the shelf is by and large the meteorology of its surface inversion.

The shelf ice is hardly impenetrable to storms or wind. Cyclonic systems can pass over even the largest shelves, the Ross and the Ronne-Filchner. Offshore systems can influence wind flow and precipitation over the shelves. West Antarctica—not only the Antarcandes that form the peninsula but the west ice sheet—occupies major storm paths which make the region famous for its bad weather. In addition, the deep embayments that favor ice shelves also encourage stationary cyclones. The Weddell, Ross, and Bellingshausen seas are important residences for cyclonic storms, sometimes leading to storm decay and sometimes to rejuvenation. The Ross, in particular, has a reputation as a cyclone graveyard. The storms are significant sources for the snowfall essential to the growth of the ice shelf and to its surface appearance, and they influence the direction and velocity of the surface winds that sweep the shelves. Not a source for winds, the shelves collect, modify, and channel the inversion and katabatic winds that are funneled into them from the bordering ice sheets and glaciers. Ice and wind become inextricably intertwined.

The shelf not only simplifies atmospheric processes but distills even the appearance of the ice shelf to new minima. Only

clouds or ice crystals in the air intervene between sunlight and
snow plain. Frequently—more often closer to the ice front than
distant from it—low clouds obscure the sky for days or, when
storms approach, strong surface winds whip loose snow into
blizzards. The icescape becomes uniformly opaque. The sun is
visible as a dull glow, an iridescent cloud, or a radiant disk of
light diffracted through the cloud deck into, at most, the au-
reole of a corona. But when the clouds part, thin, or rise, the
interaction of light and ice can produce a marvellous array of
optical effects. These phenomena are not unique to Antarctica,
but on The Ice they are characteristic. There are few competing
effects, as there are outside the polar regions, to overpower
them. Even the diurnal effects of sunrise and sunset, and the
multiple positions of the sun as it arches across the sky, are
slowed and reduced to a single annular cycle. For much of the
polar year there is only daylight; for much, only night; and for
the rest, varying degrees of twilight. The Sun remains low in the
sky, enhancing the importance of the surface layer of air. With
common atmospheric processes stripped to their bare essentials,
the optical effects of light on sky and surface increasingly dominate the scene. Alone, these atmospheric displays populate and
inscribe a geometric order on an otherwise boundless, barren
sky. Their esthetic appeal is immense.

Some of the displays are the direct result of sunlight or moonlight on ice crystals in the sky as well as on the surface. The
intensity and angle of incident light interact with the shape,
orientation, and abundance of these crystals to inspire a host of
dazzling optical phenomena. The effects are simplest for snow
cover, which merely reflects the incident sunlight. The high albedo of Antarctic snow and ice explains the development of a
temperature inversion near the surface and the lack of surficial
melting, but it is also responsible for the blinding brightness of
the Antarctic surface. So overpowering is the brightness that
moonlight and starlight are often preferable to sunlight and
give the polar night an enchantment altogether lacking in the
polar day. Occasionally, because of partial sublimation or because of recrystallization, the surface crystals grow into elongated plates and filigree patterns of hoarfrost. The surface is
dusted with millions of infinitesimal mirrors and prisms. But
the most dramatic of optical effects involve ice crystals in the
air, crystals that may or may not be organized as clouds. Especially in the interior, they simply saturate the air, even under

cloudless skies. These fine crystals—diamond dust—simultaneously reflect, refract, and diffract light into both single and compound forms.

The colors and patterns that result depend in part on the characteristics of the crystals and in part on the orientation of the crystal to the source of light and to the observer. On all counts there is considerable variety. Ice crystals can assume many habits, they can fall through the air in various ways, and they can be viewed from several perspectives. The diffraction of light through this sheen of ice prisms creates coronas, aureoles, and cloud iridescence. Refraction inspires other, more geometric effects: halos—22-degree, 46-degree, and circumscribed; arcs—Parry, Lowitz, upper-tangent, circumzenithal, circumhorizontal, supralateral, infralateral, and contact; and parhelia—colloquially known as sun dogs or false suns (or paraselenae, if the light source is the Moon). All show regular patterns of light and color as the incident light is bent by ice prisms of different sizes, shapes, and motions. The 22-degree halo, for example, requires randomly oriented crystals; the parhelia, platy crystals falling with their base level to the horizon; upper-tangent arcs, pencil crystals. But these same ice crystals also reflect light. After first being refracted or reflected within the crystals, incident light bounces off their outer sides and ends, their interior sides and ends, and their interior sides. A spectacular, abstract art results: vertical streaks of light, sun pillars; concentrations of light into subsuns; partial arcs and circles, parhelic circles, subsun dogs (22-degree subparhelia), subparhelic circles, 120-degree parhelia and paraselenae; and, in a direction opposite the light source, anthelic arcs, anthelic pillars, and anthelions. Thus a single atmospheric display may combine several patterns of reflection and refraction into a compendium of light geometry.

During IGY a display was observed in which most of the sky was simultaneously inscribed with circles, arcs, streaks, and concentrations of light that represented the concatenation of a dozen separate optical phenomena. Among refractions there were 22- and 46-degree halos, Parry arcs, parhelia, a parhelic circle, and a circumzenithal arc; and among reflections, the sun pillar, anthelic pillar, subanthelic arcs, and heliac arcs. At the South Pole, ensembles of optical effects have been photographed that include the 22- and 46-degree halos, 22-degree parhelia, a parhelic circle, an upper-tangent arc, an upper-suncave Parry arc, and a circumzenithal arc. During a sledging journey

over the Barrier, Edward Wilson observed a display that involved "no less than nine mock suns . . . and arcs of fourteen or
more different circles, some of brilliant white light against a
deep blue sky, others of brilliant rainbow."[2] Apsley Cherry-
Garrard includes a passage from Bowers's diary that describes "a
splendid parhelia exhibition . . . [with] a 22° halo, with four
mock suns in rainbow colours, and outside this another halo in
complete rainbow colours. Above the sun were the arcs of two
other circles touching these halos, and the arcs of the great all-
round circle could be seen faintly on either side. Below was a
dome-shaped glare of white which contained an exaggerated
mock sun, which was as dazzling as the sun itself. Altogether a
fine example of a pretty common phenomenon down here."[3]
Byrd recorded an ensemble of atmospherics that occurred on the
Barrier when "the air suddenly became charged with ice crystals, which fell like rain."[4] Haloes, arcs, mock suns, sun pillars,
an anthelion—all proliferated until the air thickened into an
obscuring grey. In fact, sunlight and crystals are indiscriminate: every refraction and reflection that can occur does occur.
What is actually seen depends on the location of the observer
relative to the display.

The Ice affects light indirectly, too, through the powerful surface inversion it creates. The atmosphere stratifies into layers of
air, each of which has a different density. Light passes through
each of these layers at a different velocity. One effect—most
pronounced at sunset—is to stratify and segregate the incident
light as it passes at low angles through the atmosphere. Normally, sunlight is bent and slowed as the sun sets, distorting the
outline of the sun and shifting its color to the red end of the
spectrum. In Antarctica these effects are accentuated: the reddening sun appears to consist of rectangles stacked one upon
the other. Where the inversion is strong, sunlight may be ducted
in a series of waves along the upper boundary of the inversion,
and the distortion of the sun may be dramatic—the Novaya
Zemlya mirage. The refraction affects colors, too. A distinct
twilight wedge, a flexed prism of light arching over the submerged sun; earth shadows, an inverse crepuscular ray that
likewise bends across the sky; layers of pastel blues and reds that
wash in bands across the horizon; the famous green flash of the
sunset—all typify the low-angle solar phenomena that are enhanced by the awesome surface inversion.

On the Antarctic desert, conditions are ideal for mirages. The classic desert apparition, the inferior mirage, occurs when the surface layer is warmer than the air above it. The image of a distant scene is cast on the near horizon. But the polar desert has much colder air near the surface and features the inverse phenomenon—the superior mirage, in which the distant image is projected above the horizon. It is visible amid all the ice terranes of Antarctica. To sailors navigating in the pack, the effect was referred to as "looming." If the image was compressed, the mirage "stooped"; if it was elongated, it "towered." Where the horizon itself seemed to stretch into long ice walls and spires, or "icewalls," the mirage was the famous fata morgana. Even on clear days, then, the horizon of ice and sky was difficult to determine exactly. The Great Ice Barrier itself was first manifest by the massive ice blink above it. Everywhere the horizon could be warped, projected, overlaid, and multiplied into two or more false horizons. Not only is a foreground denied because of an obscuring patina of snow, but the background deceptively blurs sky and ice. The vanishing point so fundamental to Western representational art itself vanishes.

Nowhere is this better exemplified than in that most dreaded and complete of Antarctic atmospherics, the whiteout—in metaphoric Russian, the white darkness. Loosely, a whiteout is any condition in which visibility vanishes. But more precisely, a whiteout occurs whenever light becomes so diffused, scattered, and reflected that all shadows disappear and the horizon as an identifiable feature is lost. Clouds at all levels can produce the effect, though high cirrus clouds are perhaps the most notorious because they appear so innocuous. The whiteout is the ultimate intensification of the reductionism that is the essence of The Ice. Light becomes an obscuring rather than an illuminating medium. Everything is brightened and nothing can be seen. All contrasts dissolve in a fog of light—a "milky, trembling nothingness."[5]

So hazardous is a whiteout that travel becomes impossible, but other properties make it the quintessence of Antarctic atmospherics. Unlike the blizzard, which is more common along the coast, whiteouts occur in the interior and are ominously passive, not active. Unlike snow blindness, which can be prevented by wearing glasses, the obscuring effects of a whiteout do not result from a failure of will. The whiteout is more insidious and more mentally disturbing than snow blindness because it makes consciousness difficult and convolutes rational thought.

Space, time, and the presence of an other against which one can define self all dissolve. The observer is left with literally nothing to observe. Art and science, mind and sight, require contrast; without some darkness there is no meaning to daylight. Instead the whiteout produces a sweet light, an unpleasant mysticism that illuminates everything and enlightens nothing.

The Icemen Cometh:
Human Adaptations to the Antarctic

The Great Ice Barrier is also the great biotic barrier. A few birds fly over it en route to somewhere else, and some fish and marine invertebrates swim beneath it, but no species, with the exception of *Homo sapiens*, attempts to live on it. Instead the shelf divides the ecosystems of air, sea, and land into separate spheres. The one organism that has inhabited the ice does so not by virtue of evolved biological adaptations but by means of cultural and technological inventions. Humans occupy the ice in a cultural not a biological sense, and they live on the ice, not off it. They have arrived only recently, with survival skills learned elsewhere; they occupy Antarctica only as transients; and they live, in the interior, only through synthetic environments for which everything must be imported.

In contrast to other environments, there is no mutual adjustment between organism and environment. There is no ecosystem. There is no real society or indigenous culture. Life is sustained in artificial environments not unlike space capsules. The occupation of interior Antarctica by life is not a product of on-site adaptation but an extension, with modifications, of a human society developed elsewhere. Antarcticans are the remote sensors and probes of a scientific civilization: inhabitants are selected not for their preadaptation to the physical environment of Antarctica but for those skills that will contribute most to the civilization that sends them. The fact is that The Ice *qua* ice cannot sustain life. It lacks water, food, energy, information. Instead The Ice receives, reflects, reduces, and preserves. This is not merely the simplest environment on Earth but one that aggressively simplifies. The quintessential Antarctic experience is of something taken away, not something added.

That experience, of course, will vary according to where Antarctica is encountered, to what ends it is observed, and on the temperament of the observer. Life on the western side of the Antarctic Peninsula may not differ much in its physical circumstances from what one might experience in Alaska or Norway. Nearly everywhere, except in the most blizzard-ridden terrains, the coastline offers conditions superior to those of the interior. But the physical environment is not only among the harshest in the world, it is the simplest; the social environment is not only small, it is isolated. And an individual's adaptation to the Antarctic icescape includes both a physiological and a psychological dimension. Acclimatization seems to proceed in stages. A period of initial adaptation and disruption lasts two to four weeks. A general feeling of being unwell, lethargy, disorientation, sleep arhythmias, and, if at high elevations, signs of altitude sickness are all elements of an Antarctic syndrome. The major phase of acclimatization occurs over a four-to-six-month period, after which a relative degree of adjustment persists. Thus most summer transients are never acclimatized, but neither are they subjected to the rigors of the polar night. Some people do return for additional tours of duty, though each tour usually lasts a single year, and never more than two. It is doubtful that a full adaptation to Antarctica—its interior, not its coast—has ever been achieved or that it would even be desirable.

Antarctic life does offer some advantages. The environment is relatively free of pollutants and diseases. There is ample time for work and leisure. Many of the anxieties and complications of industrial society are absent. Life at a remote station involves a kind of voluntary incarceration, but like a religious retreat it is freely chosen; and many of the amenities of modern life, though filtered by remoteness, are available. For those who need to study some phenomenon of The Ice—who are extracting information from it—there are psychological rewards. But even here it is the relationship of the researcher to the larger civilization, with all its complexity, and the significance of the data to the larger intellectual culture that is modern science which are critical, not the relationship to The Ice. "The Antarctic offers little enough solace, stimulation, and satisfaction to the scientist and explorer with work to do," Byrd wrote candidly. "When that work is done, it seems the loneliest, most God-forsaken spot on this globe. Doubtless it is."[6] Intellectually no less than physically, Antarcticans are sustained by civilization. Gould observed that "it was the men of mental resources, men with backgrounds of culture and education who best kept their poise."[7] In return, Antarcticans have contributed to the sum of experiences by which Western civilization defines itself. An International Biomedical Expedition to the Antarctic has even been organized to study the physiological and psychological reaction of humans to Antarctica.

The record of acclimatization is overwhelmingly one of dysfunction and deprivation. The reports begin early, with Frederick Cook's lugubrious dirge to boredom and the psychosomatic disorders of sensory deprivation, *Through the First Antarctic Night*. A physician with considerable experience in the Arctic, Cook documented ruthlessly a "part of the life of polar explorers [that] is usually suppressed in the narratives." The *Belgica* party did not want or plan to spend a winter in Antarctica, but they became trapped in the pack; the depression that followed was physical, mental, and "perhaps moral." Humans accommodate themselves "sluggishly and poorly to the strange conditions of the polar seasons . . . to the awful despondency of the long winter night," observed Cook. "It is possible to close your eyes and befog your brain after a time, when all the world is enveloped in prolonged darkness, but this is not physiological adaptation; it is abnormal education."[8] The *Belgica* expedition was itself abnormal in the degree of its malady. Subsequent expeditions—with the *Belgica* nightmare as an unblinking warning—went to great lengths to provide work, entertainment, and social comradery by which to overcome the malaise. Above all, the early expeditions had the prospect of an approaching summer of adventures to sustain them.

To the cold, the wind, the altitude of the plateau, the humidity of the coast, the disruption of diurnal patterns of darkness and light, the deprivation of sensory stimuli, there are physiological and psychological responses. Weight gain, dehydration, hypothermia, decreased blood circulation in the extremities, sleep arhythmias, minor frostbite, and imbalanced blood pH affect nearly everyone who remains in the Antarctic. On the polar plateau, one can suffer altitude sickness, a dry morning-cough, a continually running nose, skin cracking and chapping, and shortness of breath. Snow blindness and hypothermia are occupational hazards of outdoor existence. But more typical are the hazards of boredom arising from a progressive and pervasive lack of sensory stimuli. Sights, sounds, smells, and feels erode away. What did he miss most, one Antarctic explorer was asked? "Temptation."[9] For many of these effects the pattern of light and darkness characteristic of the polar year is an adequate explanation. Peary observed that "to nine out of ten the word polar is synonymous with cold. To one who has spent a year within the Arctic or Antarctic, it is likely to be synonymous with darkness . . . [which] renders a polar night so trying."[10] The special circumstances of Antarctica compound these effects and strengthen the need for cultural enrichment. "Like the camel's lump," noted a Russian commentator, "the memory proves to be a storehouse of spiritual nourishment" by which to survive the deprivation of Antarctic existence.[11] More important is the knowledge that the polar night will end, that the Antarctic vigil will pass and the Antarctican return to civilization. The two most joyful events in a polar voyage, one Norwegian wryly observed, are the first and last sight of the ice.[12]

Initially, Antarctica adds new impressions that can excite mind and body. Shackleton gave this sentiment its classic expression when he wrote that "the stark polar lands grip the hearts of the men who have lived on them in a manner that can hardly be understood by the people who have never got outside the pale of civilization."[13] Shackleton, however, had the ultimate explorer's thrill to support him, the knowledge that his eyes were the first to view a scene. Less majestically, Paul Siple observed that Antarctica "generally wields a profound effect on personality and character and few men are the same after a stay there." Yet the effect, though powerful, is short-lived: the impress of Antarctica results from a limited number of effects reduced to stark simplicity and given enormous dimensions. Nothing so awesome can be seen in temperate and tropical zones, where each effect must interact with others in more complex but muted forms. The Antarctic scene lacks these intermediate processes, and its impression is immediate and overpowering. Ultimately, however, the huge becomes commonplace and the unusual an invariant. Disorientation and boredom result. Siple qualified his assessment by observing that Antarctica was "both a hateful and a fascinating place."[14]

There are no external biological or social systems by which to regulate, structure, or compare Antarctic life. Biological rhythms exist only in the individual, sleep disorders become endemic, and a sense of time disappears. The vast emptiness of the polar plateau eliminates spatial complexity. There is no alternative geography to that of the tiny quarters; a sense of space

is erased. There is no society, no cultural tradition. Information
requires order, and order contrast. But the only structure is that brought from the outside and, in defiance of reductionism, preserved. Among the "insidious" qualities that "lurk in the winter night," Byrd reflected, was that "Antarctica is the last stronghold of inertness." Inertness was a kind of sink; and on Antarctica, "inertia governs a vast empire . . . [drawing] by centripetal action, into a dull, stupid, dispirited monotony." Of course, he hastened to add, this was "largely a condition of the mind"; it was not Antarctica that was dangerous but "man . . . who makes it dangerous."[15]

Psychosomatic and psychosocial disorders of the winter-over syndrome include depression, outbursts of hostility, sleep disturbance, social withdrawal, and impaired cognition. The reappearing sun is universally greeted with jubilation. During both the austral summer and the austral winter, sleep disorders—especially insomnia, the Big Eye—are rampant. They bring on a kind of unrelenting jet lag. Many summer Antarcticans never get over the problem; they leave before they can acclimate or before the twilight returns. Antarcticans who winter-over, however, do experience altered states of sleep. The number of hours spent sleeping averages out to eight per day, but sleep habits evolve into different patterns, and some stages of sleep are apparently lost. The complementary effect during the waking state, the Long Eye—vividly described as a "12 foot stare in a 10 foot room"—encompasses both transient and more persistent altered states of consciousness, including staring and drifting. In brief, Antarcticans in remote interior stations experience a general slowing down of physiological and mental processes, a kind of proto-hibernation. The better motivated the persons and the more structured their activities, the less severe, in general, are the reactions.

But the maladjustments do demonstrate a fundamental fact of Antarctic colonization. It is not the brief outbursts of furious activity during the austral summer—the stuff of Antarctic sagas—that limit the settlement of Antarctica but the relentless passivity, silence, emptiness, and deprivation inherent in The Ice. The greatest of adaptations to Antarctica may be the knowledge that a stay there is transitory, that there are other worlds in which to live and against which to understand The Ice, that a ship or airplane will take one beyond The Ice after a defined period of time. In brief, colonization can be sustained only by active civilizations, cultural dynamos that can transmit themselves with enough intensity to survive the cold reductionism of Antarctica. No one demonstrated this fact better, perhaps, than Richard Byrd when he elected to spend much of a polar night in isolation.

Byrd had wintered once before on the Barrier, at Little America. For a variety of reasons that are difficult to ascertain or justify, including a longing for a kind of rational mysticism, Byrd occupied Bolling Advance Base some 160 kilometers south of Little America II during the deepening polar twilight. There were Thoreauvian overtones to the gesture (literary critics had rediscovered Thoreau during the 1920s). But the Barrier, though "world enough," was no Walden Pond. "Austere as platinum," in "cold and darkness as complete as that of the Pleistocene," the Barrier would simplify being to its essentials. "I should be able to live exactly as I choose," Byrd imagined in reverie, "obedient to no necessities but those imposed by wind and night and cold, and to no man's laws but my own." He would sink his roots in a "replenishing philosophy." "My whole life here," he elaborated in an early burst of euphoria, "in a sense is an experiment in harmony, and I let the bodily processes achieve a natural equilibrium." He did experience moments of exhilaration while watching the twilight wedge or a meteor shower, but the "natural equilibrium" of the Barrier was entropy, the heat death of mind and body. The experiment fell apart when Byrd suffered chronic carbon-monoxide poisoning; yet that was part of the lesson, too. In "approaching the final enlightenment," Byrd concluded, "how little one really has to know or feel sure about."[16]

There is much to commend about simplifying a life made needlessly complex or about reducing the hype of an overstimulated environment. The desire to discover essences through deprivation is an ancient one, as old as the fast in the desert. But the Antarctic desert is a ruthless reducer, not an originator: it suffers from understimulation not overstimulation, from information underload not overload. On The Ice the Thoreauvian gesture must be reversed: stimulation, complexity, information must be constantly added to such an environment or else one will succumb to solipsism or a whiteout of personality. As Byrd analyzed the centripetal inertness of Antarctica at Little America, his instincts were correct; at Advance Base, they went almost fatally awry. The challenge of Antarctica was to bring civilization, not to withdraw from it. In a self-referential world where everything is isolated, there is no meaning in withdrawal. Neither Byrd nor anyone else has ever repeated the act.

In the end it may not be so critical how individuals or small groups adapt to Antarctica. A voyage to Antarctica has always been a collective enterprise, and the output of an expedition has always been intended for broad, even international consumption. Here the Antarctic experience diverges from the eremitic tradition: it has never had as its principal objective self-discovery or the achievement of a particular individual state of consciousness. These things may come about, but they are incidental to the Antarctic expedition. There is no need to adapt people over the long term to Antarctica; Antarcticans are not autonomous actors but remote sensors, human probes. The critical relationship is not Antarcticans to Antarctica but Antarcticans to the civilization that sends and sustains them. There is not enough information in Antarctica to support an indigenous culture, any more than there is enough water or food. Antarcticans exist only through a pervasive system of prosthetics. The crucial question is not how Antarcticans adapt to their physical surroundings but how the information they collect is assimilated into the art, science, literature, and institutions of the informing civilization. After all, the purpose of outposts on Antarctica is not to eliminate the complexity of modern civilization but to add to its depositories of information.

Humans get from Antarctica what they bring to it. Those who value the Antarctic experience—and they are many— have usually occupied areas of Antarctica that were less ruthlessly simplified than others, or had specific projects that could be accomplished only there, or found something in themselves that they valued. Antarctica provided a means, not an end. There does not seem to be a unique Antarctic experience, only intensifications of other experiences. And it takes a sophisticated culture—not only technologically but intellectually—to sustain itself on The Ice. Only part of the strange harshness of Antarctica is attributable to the maladaptability of the human organism to polar ice sheets. The more important difficulty concerns the ability of the larger civilization to convert The Ice into a cultural source rather than a natural sink. Much of the alienness of The Ice lies in the Big Eye, and much of its emptiness in the Long Eye, of the beholder.

To James Ross, the first man to see it, the Great Ice Barrier presented an "extraordinary appearance . . . a mighty and wonderful object, far beyond any thing we could have thought or conceived."[17] To Ernest Shackleton the Barrier epitomized the "Great Loneliness," a "whole place and conditions so strange and so unlike anything else in the world in our experience . . . as though we were truly at the world's end."[18] To the pragmatic Amundsen, the Barrier—"so still, so still"—appeared as a "mighty desert," an "endless plain, that was lost in the horizon on the extreme south" and over which there were "disagreeable" grey fogs, whiteouts, or "a bright, white, shining light, so intense that it dazzles the eyes." When on his return journey he sighted two skuas, the contrast was overpowering. "They brought us a message from the living world into this realm of death—a message of all that was dear to us."[19] To Robert Scott, who ultimately perished on it, the Barrier was a terrain of wretched cold, strong wind, bad light, and poor surfaces, a "terrible limitless expanse of snow." There is "no doubt," he wrote, that "the middle of the Barrier is a pretty awful locality." And it "was the surprise which awaited us on the Barrier," Scott informed the public, that did his party in.[20] To Laurence Gould, who conducted the longest geologic sledging trip across it, the Ross Ice Shelf was "the most distinctive" of all Antarctic features, "unique in all the world," whose "charm lies not so much in its actual scenic beauty as in the feeling that it gives one . . . an intangible something that is intriguing."[21] To Richard Byrd, who built a town on it, the Barrier was a "forsaken tableland of ice . . . as quiet as in a tomb," with a "spaciousness . . . of the raw materials of creation."[22] Yet it was also a refuge, and the reductionist tendencies of The Ice could purify a society, or a man, to the essences.

The shelf defines an esthetic no less than a geographic Barrier. Its actual appearance, of course, depends on where it is viewed. Along its margins, an ice shelf can present a dramatic study in contrasts—ice sheet to sea, ice sheet to mountain, ice sheet to glacier, berg, and pack. The shelf abruptly segregates land from sea, the biotic from the abiotic, color and shape from white homogeneity. The ice front rises sharply from a blue-black sea—a glistening white cliff, scalloped into rough alcoves and dappled with blue shadows. Around the shelf there are

abundant picturesque niches: the meltponds and bizarre erosional forms of the dirty-ice regions, the gingerbread decorations of the shore-ice foot, the wonderful colors, shapes, and
perspectives offered by ice caves and crevasses.

But the real esthetic challenge of the shelf is its interior. Here
gradation and contrast are lost, and the shelf becomes unbounded. A few colors—white, black, grey, and blue—define
sky and surface. A snow crust covers subsurface textures.
Where clouds do not obscure the horizon, a persistent surface
inversion distorts it: blue sky and white ice blur into each
other. The shelf becomes a vast ice steppe, extending endlessly
in all directions—a cold desert of sun and snow, a surface hued
in whites and grey, a sky radiant with iceblink blue and pale
yellow; a monotonous white plain where color, shape, composition, perspective, horizon, and moral lessons are erased into
a minimalistic surface. Any variety, color, and patterns that
exist in the scene derive almost wholly from its one real variable: the atmosphere.

When the sky is clear it arches across the shelf with an
emptiness that echoes the voids of interplanetary space. Even
the long-awaited sun can become oppressive by its constancy.
Gould complained that the "bright light of the all day summer
became more monotonous than was the darkness of the long
night." Under transparent skies there is only "light, light,
light—brilliant, blinding, dazzling light for weeks and months
on end."[23] Everything is drenched in light, bleached of color
and form, until all that remains is a cold yellow sun and a radiant white land—a kind of esthetic and mental snow blindness.
Compared to such a scene, the polar night has its charms,
an eerie, otherworldly grandeur of platinum snow and grey
shadow. It is no accident that as many night scenes of the Barrier as day scenes have been painted and described. In the
muted glow of moonlight, starlight, airglow, and aurora, light
and dark exist in some manageable proportion.

During the polar day, however, the only regulators of sunlight
are clouds. A low cloud deck transforms everything into a duotone of leaden grey or into coolly illuminated swirls of white
and grey. The sun becomes a pale disk, a corona of lunar-like
luminescence. By contrast, high clouds or fog can immerse the
scene in a whiteout. But mixed clouds can fashion an ensemble
of light and shadows, and cascades of diamond dust can produce prisms of color and light that inscribe a welcome if ab-

stract geometry across an otherwise unbounded scene. Atmospheric optics thus have an important role in the esthetics of the shelf: they take the place of perspective, of a chosen vantage point.

On the shelf the elements of the scene are few, but they are vast, stark, overpowering. Phenomena that would be minor components of a scene elsewhere are here accented by a process of subtraction, made prominent because competing and moderating phenomena have been eliminated. While the resulting effects tend to be singular and bold, they are also abstract and invariant. Colors are impressive in a recondite and mechanical way, like the spectral lines of a distant star. Byrd's feeling that the twilight wedge over the Barrier was "inexpressibly strange" conveys the sense by which the familiar is ruthlessly reduced and magnified into the exotic. Nor can individual effects be organized into varied perspectives. There is generally only one perspective—that which is set by the incident light of Sun or Moon. The field of vision—like colors and shapes—is powerful but limited. Only on the polar plateau, of which the shelf is a prelude, are the elements of the Antarctic scene so purely exhibited.

For information and real esthetic appeal, the uniformity of the shelf must be broken apart. Optical displays provide a welcome, quasi-mathematical perspective where none could otherwise be found. Broken clouds can mix light with shadow, giving to sky and ice the surface fabric of abstract expressionism. Mountain and ice dome divide an indistinct horizon by bold strokes of color and form, like the lines of a minimalist painting. The austral twilight—with low sunlight fractured into broad bands of pastel blues and reds, minor surface relief contorted by monstrous shadows, and the prismatic twilight wedge—far exceeds in interest the vast bleakness typical of the shelf during the austral winter or summer. Not surprisingly, early explorers consistently favored the picturesque graphics of the Barrier margin over the sublime vacuum of the shelf interior. Ice caves, crevasses, ice stalactites—anything that framed the field of vision or gave it a distinct foreground and background was photographed, painted, and visited endlessly. Similarly, the juncture of shelf with sea and of shelf with land introduced contrasts of form, color, and perspective that made art, as it was then understood, possible.

More massive than the pack, less varied than the glacier, less sublime than the ice sheet of the polar plateau, the shelf is an ice terrane as unique esthetically as it is geographically. Some of the features of the icescape are introduced in the pack, but the shelf both simplifies and magnifies them. The canons of representational art are adequate to report on the margins of the shelf—and on the shelf as the margin of The Ice—but they break down in the interior. This is more than a problem of mathematical perspective or an impoverishment of color, objects, and shape: it involves the shrinking of the observer to an infinitesimal size relative to the enormity of the observed ice. There are no intervening systems by which to arrange a human observer within the icescape: The Ice is confronted one-to-one. The effect can be overpowering. Not an intimation of the sublime, which can awe and terrify but ultimately inspire, the shelf offers only the vision of a huge emptiness that absorbs rather than emanates. Not only does the horizon vanish before the observer, but the observer shrinks within The Ice from a place of privileged omniscience to nothingness. "One's dear self," pondered Lieutenant Prestrud of Amundsen's party as he stared over the Barrier, "becomes so miserably small in these mighty surroundings." [24]

To some that seemed an opportunity. Byrd initially relished the reductionism of the shelf, first at Little America, then at Advance Base; it offered an occasion to strip away the nonessential trappings of civilization. Yet a journey to Antarctica ended, for Byrd, with a "drift off into a dream of horrors." [25] The Ice is not a wilderness in which nature can replace or inform civilization but a cold cosmic sink, an alternately white and black hole that drains away motion, life, and meaning. The prostheses and platforms provided by civilization are not impediments but essentials; they alone make the experience of the shelf meaningful, and the richer they are the greater the significance of The Ice. To stare unaided at the endless white results only in snow blindness. So it is with the mind. Without the concepts of science, art, and literature, without the institutions of society which constrict the enormity of the scene and color it, The Ice would be unviewable, unthinkable, unassimilable. No one journeys to such a world alone or acquires its essence as he would pick up a specimen or gaze at an idol. Only with Virgil as a guide through the deepening despair of the Inferno did Dante dare enter "the circle—'twas the third— . . . eternal, cold, accursed: / Its measure and its nature never change."

The surface of the shelf rumples, rises, and falls; crevasse fields and ice falls lace the terrain; ice ridges and ice streams shear and mix against a backdrop of peak and plateau.

After rising imperceptibly because of internal thickening, the floating shelf approaches its grounding line. Its arbitration between sea and land, Southern Ocean and Southern Continent, finally ends. Through the medium of the glacier, the shelf joins ice to Earth, and through the medium of the ice stream it connects ice to Ice. From shelf to ice sheet there is an intensification of those attributes special to the icescape. The reductionism continues until the simplest of all environments on the globe, the source domes of the polar plateau, are reached. But from shelf to glacier there is an interruption. Earth and ice interact in rigid mosaics not unlike those more mobile ensembles of sea and ice that characterized the pack. The uniformity of ice shelf and ice sheet locally disintegrates; great fractured streams of ice rise from the shelf and climb, glistening with blue and white, through transcendental passes to the polar plateau.

4

Heart of Whiteness
The Literature and Art of Antarctica

"Be granted to me to utter what I heard
And with your heavenly sanction to disclose
Things deep in earth and in its darkness
drowned."
Dim forms in lonely night they went along
Amid the gloom . . . and the realms of
nothingness—

—Aeneas, in Virgil, *Aeneid*, Book VI

There was great beauty here, in the way that
things which are also terrible can be
beautiful.

—Richard Byrd, *Little America* (1930)

It is the most intellectual landscape on Earth, yet Antarctica has never really known the full attention of high culture. Although art—literary and visual—has always been an important mechanism for conveying the discoveries of exploration, The Ice was too remote geographically to participate in the outburst of Romantic interest in nature and too distant culturally to develop a liaison with modernism. There has been no Antarctic school of literature or painting. Antarctica was never made into a Xanadu, a Hudson River, a Montparnasse; no art colony flourished there, no cultural icon emerged from its discovery, no archetypal images emanated from its scenery; no artist or period made Antarctica its own. In art, as in other matters, The Ice would drive conventions to their extremes. It was an esthetic sink, not an inspiration. Its landscape erased those elements which provided the artistic conventions that made other newly discovered worlds accessible, and its fantastic isolation seemingly defied any but self-referential attempts to assimilate it.

Yet for those who traveled there and for the civilization that sustained them, it would always be important to convey the image and meaning of Antarctica. "Every one who has been through such an extraordinary experience," Apsley Cherry-Garrard wrote, "has much to say, and ought to say it if he has any faculty that way." Exploration was a full-fledged cultural activity: the "physical expression of the Intellectual Passion."[1] Writing a few decades later, Richard Byrd was more modest in his assessment. Explorers *qua* explorers were "men of action who serve science only [as] a reflection in a mirror," little more than "glamorous middlemen between theory and fact, materialists jobbing in the substance of universal truths." It was the "scholars sitting in bookish surroundings" who really "tell us where to go, what to look for, and even what we are apt to find," and "who pass judgment on whatever we bring back."[2] Antarctica gave exploration a special quality: it simplified severely the relationship between an exploring expedition and its sponsoring civilization. Even so, that relationship went beyond mere jobbing, as Byrd himself demonstrated. There was more to an expedition than geographic exploration, and there was more to learn than could be contained within science. On the whole, Antarctic exploration was designed to see that as much information was collected and as many experiences given expression as possible.

Illustrators and writers accompanied expeditions, and the explorers and scientists who conducted the actual process of discovery themselves produced books, paintings, and photographs. Others appropriated the images bequeathed by this group to other artistic purposes. Thus the phases of Antarctic literature and visual art follow closely, in both volume and style, the phases of Antarctic exploration. The arts and sciences responded to the same stimulants of exploration, the same abundant novelties and information explosions. Both art and science helped assimilate the new information within approved conceptual systems and artistic conventions. Each shared a common cultural environment, the same pervasive philosophies of nature, science, art, and ethics. It was a milieu that valued exploration and that, in turn, exploration helped to shape.

Yet the assimilation of Antarctica by art was no less problematic than its assimilation by science and politics. The special attributes of its physical geography, the timing of its exploration, and the overwhelmingly scientific character of the information that emanated from it all kept Antarctica on the periphery of intellectual history. It did not contain information that was vital to Western civilization, it did not challenge the fundamental assumptions of intellectual culture, and the whole intellectual culture of the West would never be applied to it. The Ice would receive, not instigate. Its intellectual attraction, like its esthetic appeal, derived not from huge reserves of information, natural or cultural, but from its sheer geographic dimensions and the absence of any human presence other than the exploring party. From the beginning, science was a motivation and a vehicle for other forms of inquiry. The intellectual assimilation of Antarctica became, paradoxically, radically simplified and enormously difficult.

The very simplicity of Antarctica made it alien. Many scenes around the peninsula were "highly exciting," thought James Eights. Yet the "effect produced on the mind by their general aspect is cold and cheerless to an unusual degree, for on their lonely shores the voice of man is seldom heard. . . ." Icebergs, Eights admitted, could be "sternly sublime" amid the "turbulence of cloud and storm," but the shore was barren to such an extent that it could not uplift, only depress.[3] To those who wished to find analogues of a European or American landscape, the Antarctic presented formidable difficulties. The pastoral landscapes of Europe—the classical Arcadias of Claude and

Poussin—had no analogue here. The wilder Alpine scenery of
Romanticism had a few equivalents in the isolated, deglaciated
oases and in the coastal fjords and glaciated peaks of the continental perimeter, populated by throngs of peasant penguins and
the nobly savage seal and killer whale. But there was no preexisting esthetic for the interior ice terranes. The shelf and the
polar plateau had nothing of the beautiful, the pastoral, the picturesque, or the sublime. Illustrators with Cook could draw the
great bergs as ice islands, white equivalents of the volcanic
atolls common to the Pacific. Artists with Ross could make the
front of the Great Ice Barrier resemble the white cliffs of Dover.
But the interior icescape could not be made to look like any familiar landscape. In fact, the whole convention of representational art, with which the landscape had been identified since
the Renaissance, breaks down as one moves into the interior.
Mathematical perspective becomes impossible, the customary
icons of landscape art cannot be found, color and shape are
bleached from the scene, and inherited artistic conventions become meaningless. Instead the landscape is abstract, minimal,
conceptual. Interior Antarctica is nature as modernist.

The artists of Western civilization had accommodated, even
celebrated, the revelation of other strange lands. The absence of
natural scenes that could mimic existing esthetic ideals or that
contained ready-made icons of pictorial conventions did not by
itself determine whether a geography could be made into a
landscape. After all, Romantic painters had commonly distorted topographic reality and selected particular pictorial elements and rearranged them according to their effect on the
observer. Thomas Moran had successfully transferred the conventions of the Alpine landscape to the Grand Canyon. T. W. M.
Turner had painted sunrises and mists that resembled floating
smears of color. Gustave Doré had brought a transcendental horror to the Gothic world of the Ancient Mariner. Even Arctic icescapes had offered a proper subject to the right imagination.
The search for the Northwest and Northeast passages to Asia
had invested Arctic discovery with an almost mythological
aura. The melancholy saga of the Franklin expedition had combined wild nature with tragic aspirations—an ideal tableau for
Romantic art. Caspar David Friedrich had discovered the sublime in a ridge of pack ice. Frederick Church had transformed
the Greenland ice coast into a chromatic Andes and found a
macrocosm in an iceberg. In fact, the conventions of Romantic

landscapes had themselves evolved in good part because of the novel scenery unveiled by explorers and travelers.

Nothing equivalent occurred in Antarctica. In part, the attributes of The Ice are an explanation. This is not merely a landscape that has been simplified to a minimal state, but one that relentlessly simplifies whatever ideas are brought to it. In part, too, the problem is that Antarctic art—like the rest of Antarctic history—is dominated by Antarctic science. Scientific terms provide a descriptive language; scientific reports substitute for an indigenous folk art or folktales; scientists, as communicators and illustrators, replace a population of professional artists. The enduring literature of Antarctica consists of exploration memoirs; its principal art, of scientific illustration. Under these circumstances all forms of inquiry tend to become documentary in purpose. It is possible to construct moral universes out of such material, as Poe and Cooper did, but the act requires a belief in the moral order of nature—a belief that tended to be lost in the twentieth century, when Antarctic exploration got seriously underway.

Instead the Antarctic has been largely a wasteland for imaginative literature. Thomas Kenneally, in explaining how he wrote his Antarctic novel *The Survivor* (1969), described the "standard works on Antarctica" as "disconcerting." They say "nothing of the gulf between man and man," give "only the most paltry indications of character-clash and neurosis, which are the novelist's meat," and fail to record "human conflict, which is the only ultimately interesting conflict."[4] Traditional fiction could not compete for sheer adventure with the real-life memoirs of explorers, and it could not find enough material in the Antarctic experience or the Antarctic environment to construct typical novels. There was no real society on The Ice, no native ·people with whom European intruders could conflict and who could serve as a moral template, no tension between colonials and mother country. The range of potential experiences was much smaller than elsewhere, the opportunity for surprise much less. A small population of explorers could quickly sample those experiences and, without competition, could dominate the subsequent literature. The Antarctic experience was powerful but invariant, intense but limited. Antarctic travel literature tended instead toward the interior monologue. Like others, Kenneally returned to the Scott tragedy, while imaginative literature persisted in its early association of

Antarctica with scientific fiction, which could exploit the raw data of scientific discovery and found in the blankness of The Ice a screen on which to project alternate worlds.

Another explanation is needed, for the special isolation of Antarctica lies less with properties intrinsic to The Ice than with developments internal to Western civilization; and this is a matter of timing. Antarctic exploration typically came at the conclusion of major epochs of discovery and intellectual ferment. Antarctica was a scene to which conventions were applied, not out of which new contentions were generated. Consider the case of landscape painting. Throughout the nineteenth century, the painting of natural landscapes and the study of natural history had proceeded in tandem, with painters and litterateurs often enthusiastic consumers of natural science. Natural history paintings had supplanted historical paintings of the Grand Manner as the highest genre of visual art, and it had been common for landscape painters to journey to distant lands or even join scientific exploring parties. That did not occur with Antarctica—partly because of the rigors and limitations of expeditions and partly because of changes in the character of art and science. Even as the heroic age of Antarctic discovery met The Ice, modernism was sweeping the intellectual culture of the West.

Art experienced an internal revolution that would not only validate new techniques and repudiate many old ones but would redefine the role of art as an intellectual pursuit. Landscapes had first thrived in the Renaissance because they were part of the Book of Nature, and hence a companion to the Book of Scripture, in the reading of Providence. By the nineteenth century they became glorious panoramas of Design, testimonials to the plenitude and complexity of Creation. Natural theology seemingly became a branch of natural history, and landscape artists were important practitioners of both. In painting nature, they ultimately painted a moral order. But by the early twentieth century, revolutions in science broke the alliance once and for all. Modernist art renounced as illegitimate the insistence that art could provide moral instruction through its rendition of the natural world. The whole belief in Design— in the reading of nature to learn about God—was in shambles. Art would investigate art; the morality of art would be determined by the character of the artist's internal search, not by his or her ability to render the external world. Just at the time when Antarctica challenged landscape art with new, alien scenes, landscape painting and the moral energy that sustained it were languishing. Representational landscape painting would endure as scientific illustration, not as art. The prospects for discovering a moral universe in Antarctica were reduced to Scott's vision of Antarctic exploration as an exemplar of the noble life and, later, to Byrd's eccentric vision of a utopian society in the Antarctic.

Yet there is a paradox to this scenario. The modernist triumph equipped Western art with techniques that were ideally suited for The Ice. Modernism provided the words and images and perspectives necessary to venture into the interior of Antarctica, and Antarctica offered a "ready-made" modernist landscape as disturbing as any of the signed shovels that Dadaists like Duchamp declared to be a ready-made art. While the exploration of Antarctica and the maturation of modernism occurred simultaneously, no important exchanges occurred between them. The development of techniques was not matched by the commensurate creation of an intellectual or moral purpose. Instead modernism, like The Ice, looked to itself.

In the nineteenth century the great American landscapist Frederick Church could eagerly follow Humboldt's steps through South America in order to paint his glorious *Heart of the Andes*. It was a sentiment that Shackleton could echo, perhaps unconsciously, when he titled his memoir of the *Nimrod* expedition *The Heart of the Antarctic*. A journey into the far reaches of the external world had meaning for the interior world of mind and morals. That belief broke down with the advent of modernism, which was more inclined to study the observer than the observed, more likely to project the internal world outward than the outer world inward; representational art only distracted the visual artist and deceived its observer, and representational science, based on everyday imagery, led only to intolerable paradoxes when applied to the atom or the universe. Modernist literature was more inclined to follow Joseph Conrad into a heart of darkness than to pursue Robert Scott into the Antarctic's heart of whiteness.

Drawn from Nature

When James Cook witnessed the ice islands and pack ice of the Southern Ocean, he was with a company of savants as well as sailors. Several centuries of exploration by Western civilization had established expectations that certain kinds of information would be discovered and that certain intellectual disciplines would process those data. The map, the ship's log, the captain's (or chief naturalist's) travelogue, the collection of specimens, and illustrations of peoples and places—all comprised the intellectual stuff of exploration. All shared forms that had been established during the Renaissance and were reinforced, and in some cases redirected, by the scientific revolution. For a few of these pursuits, such as cartography and travel literature, exploration had been fundamental; for subjects like art, it was largely a beneficiary. But the alliances that all these disciplines had known with exploration were, by the time of Cook's voyages, approaching a culmination. No longer were the products and results of exploration to be simply brought back to scholars: it was one of the reforms of the Cook era, and one of the measures of scientific power, that intellectuals became members of the exploring company.

The Renaissance had developed a pervasive curiosity about nature which evolved into the belief that reading the Book of Nature was complementary to reading the Book of Scripture, that both were forms of knowing and worshipping. This sentiment climaxed with the scientific revolution. But it inspired, equally, traditions of representational art and naturalist landscape painting, and it sustained new literary genres modeled on the concept of experimentation. In the essay, for example, one tested ideas by experience, and in the travelogue one recorded impressions and facts for purposes other than their spiritual symbolism. When the new subjects and new data were combined with the accelerated recovery of texts from antiquity—and especially with the revival of Platonism and mathematics—the ramifications were widely felt.

The same elements that transformed Western painting also permeated Western science. The combination of empiricism and mathematical perspective that characterized late Renaissance paintings was exactly analogous to the amalgamation of empiricism and mathematics that culminated in modern mechanics, astronomy, cartography, and anatomy. Portolan charts were reorganized and abstracted by mathematical projections such as Mercator's; Ptolemaic geographies of heaven and earth were recalculated on the basis of new sightings and redesigned in accordance with better geometries; symbolic landscapes of

medieval art—little more than typological backdrops—were
redrawn into richly empirical naturalist landscapes organized by mathematical perspective. Natural philosophy, epitomized by mathematical principles of natural laws, replaced theology as the model of rational inquiry. The dialectic had been adequate for organizing and interpreting the inherited texts of Scripture and the ancients, but it was inadequate to cope with the inundation of data about the natural world that now coursed through Western civilization. Inherited systems of knowledge, concepts, and perspectives were all profoundly reworked.

In its development, modern science shadowed representational art. Both subscribed to similar philosophies about knowledge, and each frequently served the other. The sciences and geographical discovery brought new images and information into intellectual discourse, while the arts lavished some of their new skills in support of natural philosophy. Thus the year 1543 witnessed the recovery of important mathematical texts of Archimedes and the publication of Copernicus's *De revolutionibus* and Vesalius's majestic anatomy, *De fabrica*, in which drawing became a tool of empirical inquiry. A persistent tradition of drawing—not merely representational drawing but documentary—was established that would eventually become a staple of exploration. In the twentieth century that tradition would be denigrated—dismissed as illustration, not art. Modernism pursued art not only as a means of inquiry but as its end. Yet for centuries exploration had been both a stimulant and a recipient of the visual arts. Artists had been an integral part of exploring companies.

The Enlightenment was an age of reasoned synthesis and methodical codification, epitomized by Johnson's dictionary, Linnaeus's systematics, Pope's exposition on the chain of being, Arrowsmith's maps—and Cook's voyages of discovery. Those voyages produced a prodigious quantity of new information and, in the case of the mythical Southern Continent, removed some misinformation. Collectively, the output of Cook's voyages brought the inherited traditions for processing information to something of a climax, a neoclassical canon. After all, the voyages had been prescribed by the needs of Enlightenment learning: to measure the transit of Venus, to investigate (or disprove) the existence of a Southern Continent and a Northwest Passage, to fill in the missing parameters of a generally known world ocean. The voyages' collections, Cook's journals, the reports by the expeditions' naturalists, the *mappa mundi*, the illustrations drawn by the expeditions' artists, the design of the expedition and the reasoned skepticism of its captain—all represented an apex in a style of exploration and an important episode in the intellectual history of the Enlightenment.

The synthesis did not come easily. Intellectuals were often a querulous, troublesome lot. "Curse the scientists, and all science into the bargain!" Cook reportedly blurted out as he prepared for his third voyage.[5] But there was no avoiding modern science and representational art. Cook's problems with the second voyage began after a brooding Joseph Banks, the naturalist on his first voyage, huffily backed out of the second. As replacements, John Reinhold Forster and his son Georg were accepted. The tempestuous elder Forster proved to be a tribulation to everyone, but his son quickly revealed himself as an enthusiastic collector, a talented draftsman, and a frequently inspired writer. A quiet student of Linnaeus, Anders Sparrman, came at his own expense. And in what had become typical, the voyages included artists and artist-draftsmen to render in line such important coastal features as harbors and headlands, illustrate the artifacts, flora, and fauna discovered by the expedition, and record important occasions of exotic scenes. The resulting "graphic record" of the voyage included works by William Hodge, a professional artist; by cartographers and draftsmen such as Joseph Gilbert; and by virtually all the ships' officers, who possessed varying degrees of skill.

Cook's voyages had a major impact on the literature and science as well as the political economy of the day. For Antarctica the outcome was fundamental: most of the basic formulas for Antarctic art and science were all contained within the published output of Cook's second voyage or in the reactions to it; less obviously indicated in these published works was the tradition that Antarctic exploration was as often an exercise in discovering what was not present as in revealing what was. Most of the major participants wrote books about the voyage, of which Cook's *A Voyage towards the South Pole and Round the World* (1777) and Georg Forster's *A Voyage around the World* (1777) were the most important. Both included visual records, the most fundamental parts of which were perhaps the landscapes of harbors and the maps, especially the "general chart" of the voyages done by Henry Roberts. South of New Zealand and a few subpolar islands, the map was blank. The routes of the

Resolution and the *Adventure* were inscribed across a perfectly gridded polar projection, but the south polar regions were a blank, reflecting what the literal-minded Cook knew of the area. He thought that a continent existed—there had to be some source for the gigantic tabular bergs—yet the region remained a tabula rasa for empirical geography.

More important for shaping popular images of Antarctica were the engravings in Cook's book, based on watercolors executed by William Hodge. In particular, *The Ice Islands* became one of the first enduring images of Antarctica. The picture is full of information. A gigantic berg, weirdly eroded, dominates the panorama, while one of the ships rides to the side and small boats of sailors chip away at growlers—a source of fresh water—with huge axes. In another small boat a man—probably Forster—blasts away at seabirds, doubtless to collect specimens. There is some exaggeration with respect to the berg, but the outcome is, all in all, pure representational art. The picture continues the whole tradition of natural landscapes and scientific illustration that emerged out of the Renaissance; it could have come from the voyages of Henry Hudson. That its human figures are shown eagerly collecting and quite literally tearing into the ice is a perfect expression of what the expedition and the picture were all about. The picture is an art of record, a landscape of objective information. Hodge gave the picture a suitable imprimatur when he wrote that it was "drawn from Nature." Its style would be recapitulated by the nineteenth-century expeditions to the Antarctic. The illustrations accompanying the narratives of the Bellingshausen, Ross, d'Urville, and Wilkes expeditions were all the product of a common tradition. These maps and drawings successfully applied cartographic and artistic conventions to the scenery, bringing the Antarctic coast into the visual imagination of Western civilization without seriously challenging those techniques and without suggesting that Antarctica was, for the visual arts, anything unique.

Yet like all culminations, the voyages of Cook helped initiate the transition to a successor. Interestingly, that process began during the second voyage, which had Antarctica as a fundamental objective, and it found its principal expression in literature. Cook became the first of many visitors to accuse The Ice of sublime ugliness. Not only must the navigator confront "thick fogs, Snow storms, Intense Cold, and every other thing that can render

Navigation dangerous," but the difficulties are "heightned by the enexpressable horrid aspect of the Country, a Country doomed by Nature. . . ." Speaking of the South Sandwich Islands, Cook could not credit the scene with even much information. To explore the coast "would have answerd no end whatever, or been of the least use either to Navigation or Geography or indeed any other Science. . . ."[6] But the other great chronicler of the voyage, Georg Forster, made more of the experience. The metaphysical sensibilities of Romanticism were feeling their way into articulation; Jean-Jacques Rousseau died a year after Forster and Cook published; new artistic genres were being recreated out of old forms. While neoclassical styles and sensibilities had been adequate for the Grand Tour that had become a staple of intellectual education, they could not cope with the scale, the exotica, and the sheer volume of information that the new voyages of circumnavigation or, on their example, the exploration of the continental interiors were bringing back to Europe any more than the old scientific theories like the Great Chain of Being or artistic conventions like the Arcadian landscapes of Claude or the Grand Manner of Joshua Reynolds could assimilate the new data and images. A novel style of exploration would be accompanied by a major intellectual reformation.

The Romantic revolution did for the intellectual culture of Europe what democratic revolutions did to its politics and industrialization to its economics. The new voyages and overland travels tremendously expanded European notions of space. The discovery of lost civilizations, the exhumation of the relics and ruins of natural history buried within geologic strata, the debate over the age of the Earth, and the preoccupation with embryology all greatly enlarged the known domain of time. The proliferation of natural history specimens, of encounters with other cultures, and of experiences forced an amplification of consciousness. As these domains enlarged, the old connections that had linked previous data bases together so stretched and deformed that the nature of causality had also to be rethought. Etiology became temporal as well as spatial. Historicism entered philosophy through Hegel's reconstruction of the dialectic; science, through geology, biology, and the concepts of evolution and entropy; literature, through historical prose, from the writing of Romantic history to the narrative structure of the novel.

Nature, it was decided, contained important information for human understanding and morality. Natural history became all the rage among the sciences, and Romanticism emerged as its artistic counterpart. On the basis of the abundance and organization of the natural world, natural theology advanced its argument from Design, that the order of nature proved the existence of a rational God and a providential purpose. Landscape art took on new meaning, now endowed with the power not only to convey this information but to dramatize its emotional and moral effect on the viewer. With these developments exploration would be intimately connected, and a single episode of discovery could be reflected across a range of disciplines. Without creating the slightest dissonance, the accounts of an expedition could take a dramatic personal travelogue stuffed with exotic scenes and sentiments and combine it with the ship's log, filled with navigational data, winds, and temperatures; atlases could incorporate paintings amidst mathematical maps and charts.

Accounts of Cook's voyages—and travel literature of all sorts—were widely read by intellectuals and excited a generation much intrigued by nature and the sublime. Andrew Kippis wrote perceptively in 1788 that Cook's discoveries "have opened new scenes for a poetical fancy to range in, and presented new images to the selection of genius and taste."[7] Out of their experiences and new data, much of it scientific, Forster and his American counterpart, William Bartram, recast the travelogue genre and influenced a generation of Romantic litterateurs. For a time the restless Forster, who traveled through central Asia and Persia as well as the Pacific, became a father figure to Alexander von Humboldt, shaping his determination to become a scientific explorer and providing a model for his widely influential *Personal Narrative*. Humboldt's more scholarly output—the multivolume, encyclopedic *A Voyage to the Equinoctial Regions*—would establish modern geography and furnish a pattern that most explorers of the nineteenth century would emulate in packaging their own data. But the impact of Cook's and Forster's accounts went well beyond science. They became models and source books for a host of popular volumes—some legitimate, some counterfeit—about voyages to the south polar regions and around the world. They expanded travel literature from the Grand Tour of Europe to a wider world that demanded—and got—broader forms, a fresh energy, and revised purposes. The quest replaced mundane travel; a Promethean desire to know the unknowable and to encompass everything as well as a sense of passionate participation replaced the picaresque structure of *Candide*, the precious sentimentality of *A Sentimental Journey*, the moral didacticism of *Rasselas*, and the pervasive satirical voice of the essayists.

The travelogue—in part, contributor to the literary imagination of the day and, in part, recipient of the new forms—was joined by a cognate literary form, the novel. The structure of the modern novel developed along strikingly similar lines to that of new historical sciences. Both provided a form by which an abundance of data could be organically related. Stories showed a beginning, middle, and end. Subplots would be integrated in much the same way that new strata of rocks or genera of extinct plants could be accommodated within evolutionary epicycles. At first, the travelogue and the novel did not differ significantly in their moral purpose. The description of primitive peoples always conveyed a lesson, stated or implied, about comparative morality; and the feeling of awe that suffused the traveler as he stood before a sublime, God-inspired nature was a religious sentiment and a moral act, a secular transfusion of grace. Between them the travelogue and the Romantic novel outlined the realm of Antarctic literature.

Still, even Forster's account was not itself imaginative literature. That transformation came at the hands of Samuel Coleridge. His allegorical narrative poem, "The Rime of the Ancient Mariner" (1798), was the travelogue of a spiritual journey. Coleridge relied on Cook's accounts (and those of Arctic explorers) for much of his information about the southern voyage of the Mariner into the realms of ice. But Coleridge found new meaning in prosaic events. Hodge had been content to paint Forster among the ice islands, routinely collecting specimens, and the younger Forster obligingly drew an albatross for the voyage's scientific record. Coleridge remade the episode into a wanton act that condemned the Mariner to a spiritual hell, and he made the albatross into a symbol of mischosen destiny. Antarctica's literary potential, as the Ancient Mariner realized, lay in its alienness and inaccessibility. The limit of geographic exploration was equally the limit to rational knowledge; the pack was an entree into an unearthly world. The act of collecting specimens—the pursuit of useful knowledge and the contemplation of Design—had consequences on The Ice that were less benign than similar pursuits in Tahiti or Virginia. In demonstrating how Antarctic nature could be reshaped into a fictional, moral universe, Coleridge introduced many of the enduring images associated with Antarctic literature—the polar spirit, the whirlpool, the spectral mists of snow, the haunted traveler who escapes to tell the tale. When Gustave Doré illustrated an edition of the poem in 1875, the Mariner's vessel became a ghost ship in a land of shades, illuminated by the Moon, with throngs of penguins like the massed souls of the damned that he had imagined for his earlier illustration of Dante's *Inferno*.

Sealers, whalers, and later explorers soon supplemented Cook's travels with fresher accounts of the peninsula and its ancillary islands. Benjamin Morrell's *A Narrative of Four Voyages* (1832) and Edmund Fanning's *Voyages Round the World* (1833) and *Voyages to the South Seas . . .* (1838) enjoyed wide circulation. Poe extracted material from Morrell's embellished narrative for his own Antarctic stories. Fanning was in large measure responsible for publicizing the voyages of his protégé, Nathaniel Palmer. Although others probably saw land at the same time—the place was swarming with sealers—they lacked a commensurate desire or talent for publicity. Once the barrier of pack ice was breached, however, the published descriptions of the south polar domain combined with speculations that the polar regions contained an open, semitropical sea. While Cook effectively capped real scientific speculation about a populated *terra australis* near the pole, the notion persisted in folklore. In the United States, through the baroque wit of John Cleaves Symmes, the belief metamorphosed into the concept that there was a "hole at the pole" which opened up to the center of the Earth and its central fires. Fanning campaigned tirelessly for the U.S. to sponsor an expedition on the Cook model to the Antarctic and the South Seas. Symmes's theory and Fanning's advocacy were soon taken up by Josiah Reynolds, the most aggressive of the proponents for what became the U.S. Exploring Expedition, under the command of Charles Wilkes. In an effort to keep popular enthusiasm high, Reynolds wrote incessantly about the south polar and South Pacific regions. One article, published in 1839, retold the sailors' tale about a white whale known as Mocha Dick. Interestingly, the narrator is accompanied by "Captain Palmer" (probably the ubiquitous Nathaniel

Palmer). Herman Melville reworked this material, as Coleridge had Cook's, to make his famous allegorical novel *Moby-Dick* (1851).

But it remained to Edgar Allan Poe to really develop fiction dealing with Antarctica. An avid consumer of natural history, Poe had dedicated "with very profound respect" his metaphysical prose poem about the cosmos, "Eureka," to Alexander von Humboldt. At the same time, Poe was skeptical of the power of scientific inquiry to explain the natural universe. The influence of Coleridge is unmistakable, as twice Poe discovered in Antarctica a suitable imaginative geography and in the explorer a suitable vehicle for Gothic romance on just these themes. In his "MS. Found in a Bottle" (1833, 1845) Poe envisioned a dark side to Tennyson's "Ulysses," with which the story is an exact contemporary. A rational skeptic, a self-proclaimed Pyrrhonist with no room for any knowledge but that of natural philosophy, the narrator undertakes a voyage of curiosity. It becomes, of course, a journey of horrors, as the ship is swept by a typhoon to the Antarctic, where the narrator encounters the "blackness of eternal night" and great "ramparts of ice . . . like the walls of the universe." Here is the ne plus ultra of science and reason. Not even Cook had believed that the dreadful scene was worth the risk to explore further.

The prudent Enlightenment hero, however, has been replaced by the Faustian Romantic. The desire to discover "some exciting knowledge," a "curiosity to penetrate the mysteries," propels the narrator onward, "perhaps . . . to the south pole itself." Instead, "horror upon horror," the ice opens up to a gigantic whirlpool. "Amid a roaring, and bellowing, and thundering of ocean and of tempest," the narrator cries out that "the ship is quivering, oh God! and—going down."[8] The Antarctic becomes a symbol not merely of the unexplored but of the unexplorable— a realm beyond the purview of reason. There was no justification for the journey, any more than for the Ancient Mariner to slay the albatross. At the last instant, the narrator commits to a bottle the "message" of his travels—almost a parody of the scientific note common in the journals of the day.

The *Narrative of A. Gordon Pym* (1838), written as the Wilkes expedition got under sail, was even more insistent. Pym also foolishly decides to indulge his personal curiosity with sea travels. He is secreted on a ship captained by the father of a friend and co-conspirator, Augustus. But instead of a voyage of scientific discovery, the journey becomes a hideous descent to an underworld. Pym's experience as a stowaway becomes an allegorical death; horror follows unthinkable horror, and even Pym's guide, the Virgil-like Augustus, dies, leaving the survivor to continue his nightmares without the aid of reason. Eventually the ship passes through the ice barrier, then enters a moderate polar sea, populated by islands and natives. Marvels and wonders continue, but so do the nightmares; natural disasters and natives apparently kill off all but two of the crew, one of whom is Pym; although the sea warms, polar darkness descends. Farther south, a "chasm" and "cataract" open up before the ship, a shrouded figure whose skin is "the perfect whiteness of the snow" looms before them, and the narration abruptly ends. Somehow Pym returns to the United States and writes down his story. Again, Poe transforms the genre of travelogue and uses it for the unexpected purpose of revealing what reason cannot explain and geography cannot assimilate. The inconclusive ending, together with the random succession of episodes, threatens to turn the novella into a shaggy-dog story. But it does contribute to the effect that the Antarctic, as symbol of a Gothic geography beyond human exploration, is unassimilable. No representational art or literature could hope to express it.

Poe's bizarre tale became more than a model for Antarctic fiction: it offered the kind of a challenge to writers that Fermat's Last Theorem presented to mathematicians. To explain Pym's fate would not only satisfy the sense of literary business left unfinished by Poe, it would demonstrate the superiority of the writer who accomplished it or the progress of a later age that could, unlike Poe's, actually penetrate Antarctica. In particular, science fiction writers accepted the challenge. Writing on the eve of the heroic age, as Poe had written at the onset of the Wilkes-Ross-d'Urville era, Jules Verne picked up where Pym's narration had left off for his *Sphinx of Ice; or Antarctic Mystery* (1897). Verne had used aspects of Antarctic geography for other novels; the harbor Captain Nemo uses in *Twenty Thousand Leagues under the Sea*, for example, was modeled on the submerged caldera of Deception Island. But the conceit for *Sphinx* was, according to the narrator, "that veracious narrative of Arthur Gordon Pym, which I read and re-read with intense attention, fascinated as I was by the ideas that I might be permitted to behold with my own eyes those strange phenomena of nature in the Antarctic world. . . ." The objective of the voyage is a search for lost members of the Pym party, including Pym himself, as well as "for the awful white giant of the South Pole!" The party reaches the pole, finds the remnants of the Pym party, even the ossified Pym himself, and concludes that "discoveries of great value still remain to be made in those waters!"[9] Improbably, the narrator congratulates Arthur Pym for "showing the way" for "others to follow" in the solving of the Antarctic mystery. The novella is really nothing more than an obiter dictum on Poe, chiefly valuable for demonstrating the continuing effect that Poe had on imaginative literature about Antarctica.

Poe was not alone in exploiting knowledge (or ignorance) about the region for literary purposes, and Romantic literature did evolve beyond the Gothic tale. James Fenimore Cooper set the last of his nautical novels near the Bransfield Strait. Though best known for his forest romances, the Leatherstocking Tales, Cooper also adapted the romance form to sea stories, almost singlehandedly inventing both the western and the sea novel. Just as the values which the eighteenth century attributed to historical paintings came over the course of the nineteenth century to reside in paintings of natural history, so Cooper transformed the historical romance of Walter Scott into a romance of natural history. Nature became an expression of the fundamental order and morality of Creation. Cooper understood that reason was not faith, but along with most of his contemporary intellectuals he believed that knowledge of nature could easily lead to knowledge of the Creator. Cooper thus became an avid consumer of exploration literature. And much as he converted the geographic data of the Long expedition into a moral geography for the Old Trapper in his novel *The Prairie*, so he relied on the published accounts of sealers, whalers, and scientific expeditions to sustain the geography of Antarctica in which he set *The Sea Lions* (1849). In particular, he paraphrased Wilkes for many of his descriptive passages of the Antarctic sea, icebergs, and pack.

The story revolves around a set of doubles: two captains, two ships (both named the Sea Lion), and two locales with two sorts of wealth—buried pirate treasure in the West Indies (an illicit wealth) and sea lions and seals in Antarctica (a natural wealth). During his voyage to undiscovered sealing islands in the Antarctic, the hero, Roswell Gardiner, must purge himself of his greedy, materialistic, faithless double, Daggett. He does, during a bitter austral winter, when both ships are trapped on an island by pack ice. Daggett dies, his ship is dismantled, and the true treasures of nature, not those of piratical humans, become the basis for Gardiner's prosperity and his revivified faith in a Christian God.

Even by Cooper's standards, *The Sea Lions* is ponderous and didactic. But the Antarctic islands are sketched in authentic detail, and the purpose of the Antarctic setting—nature at its purest and most sublime—would become a staple of Antarctic literature. Herman Melville thought that "few descriptions of the lonely and terrible . . . can surpass the grandeur of many of the scenes here depicted."[10] Like Poe, Cooper used the Antarctic as a geography beyond the simple compass of human reason. "The icy barriers," he wrote, "become the analogues of the mysteries which ultimately confront all rational inquiry and mark its farthest limits."[11] But where Poe abandoned his narrators to the self-destructive horrors of an inscrutable nature, Cooper granted nature the power to inspire and his protagonists the power of faith. The extremity of Antarctica became a means to supplement reason with faith, not to abandon reason for solipsism. In this way, Cooper could use—in fact, required—scientific accounts; through fiction, he could transcend them and create a moral universe. It is significant, too, that Cooper narrates the story from the privileged vantage point of the omniscient author and that other voices (notably a character who functions as a Christian conscience) enter into dialogue with the protagonist, Gardiner. By contrast, Poe's narrators tell their stories in the first person, without aid from objective guides, seemingly lost in a subjective nightmare. While Cooper buried the corrupt Daggett but brought his hero back to civilization, Poe abandoned his narrators to the polar vortex.

Unlike Poe's stories, Cooper's novel had no real successors. For this kind of novel to work, more was required than the persistence of the romance genre. There had to exist also the belief in rational and benevolent Design which made complements of the scientific and artistic imaginations of the era. Those who lived during the heroic age generally accepted these beliefs and bolstered them by a vastly improved science. But high culture, as literature, did not. Instead, the successor to *The Sea Lions* is Jack London's *The Sea Wolf* (1907). Set on the sealing islands of the North Pacific, the novel matches Wolf Larsen against his double, Death Larsen. It depicts a structured universe, but its design is not infused with a benevolent spiritual-ity. Rather, the novel features a Dark Design, a wholly materialistic world that operates according to immutable natural laws. Within this world, humans must struggle without a greater purpose than simple survival. London successfully brought naturalism to the frozen northland, and Antarctic explorers, in turn, took London and his Alaska contemporary, Robert Service, to The Ice as popular additions to their libraries. No equivalent work emerged from the heroic age. The tradition of imaginative literature about Antarctica remained, lamely, where Coleridge and Poe had left it. The great literature of Antarctica continued to be that of the explorers who told their stories in journal form, published quickly, and attached scientific reports as appendices. The sagas were as gripping as the plots of any naturalist fiction. The science of the heroic age brought a powerful sense of purpose, a peculiar morality, to Antarctic endeavors. It was difficult to romanticize the death of the Enlightenment explorer Cook, who had been trying to reason with Hawaiian natives; it was all too easy to romanticize the death of Scott, struggling with The Ice.

Heroic Age

Besides a particular mode of exploration, the heroic age brought to Antarctica a style of literature and art. A monumental amount of information emanated from the score of major expeditions to the Antarctic, and that experience was processed not only by the earth and life sciences—often in massive encyclopedic tomes—but by conventions of literature and the visual arts. This was the great era of Antarctic journals, paintings, and photographs. Yet all of it—scientific reports, memoirs, watercolors and chalks, photographs—shared a common metaphysical universe. There were different genres, of course, each of which best described particular aspects of the experienced world, but they all broadly agreed on what the natural world was like and on how one could describe it.

They also agreed that the experience was unique and important, quite apart from its scientific data. "My story," Frederick Cook wrote, "is, I hope, a contribution of new human experience in a new, inhuman world of ice."[12] As always, there would be some special qualities. One could not simply wander into Antarctica as one could tramp across Italy or the Alps or the

American West. The isolation of Antarctica strongly filtered out
the kind of art that had accompanied the exploration and settlement of other lands by Europeans. But, equally, high culture was venturing into the interior landscapes of modernism just as the heroic age broke through the Great Ice Barrier. Unlike the information brought back from the exploration of other continents, the empirical data gathered by the heroic age of Antarctic discovery would not be worked over by intellectuals other than scientists who had not themselves traveled to the Antarctic. There would be no Coleridge, Poe, or Cooper. Apart from the geographic remoteness of Antarctica, the idea of Antarctica—the belief that Antarctica held information vital for civilization—was distant from the minds of the age's formative intellectuals. There would be popularizers and historians of the heroic age, and T. S. Eliot would incorporate an image from Shackleton's *Heart of the Antarctic* into *The Waste Land*. But by and large the original art would be what the participants themselves made of their experiences. There would be no imaginative literature.

Explorers conveyed their experience through the traditional form of the journal or travelogue, written in diary form as the expedition progressed, then hurried into print to help pay for incurred debts. Writers followed a chronological narrative, painted word pictures, substituted stories of encounters with penguins, skuas, and killer whales for anecdotes about picturesque natives, and gave the story drama and human interest by describing the struggle of a band of men against the alien Antarctic landscape. These were sagas of a sort, paeans to the strenuous life, real-life versions of the kinds of storied naturalism Jack London was imagining for the Klondike. Yet these accounts lack real society: The Ice strips experiences to a minimum and turns them inward to monologues.

British accounts, in particular, never lose a certain literary flavor; they are not just Romantic in spirit but are full of references to classical learning. "We felt like Argonauts," wrote Frank Hurley, "whose quest had led to the World's brim."[13] A member of the *Nimrod*'s Western Party that fought its way to the south magnetic pole, surgeon Alistair Mackay reported open water around the coast with the chant, "Thalassa, thalassa!"— the famous cry uttered by the advance guard of Xenophon's Ten Thousand when they spied the Black Sea.[14] But what spared Antarctic literature from quaintness and endowed it with a power beyond the naturalism of Jack London or Émile Zola was undoubtedly the tragedy of Robert Scott's polar party.

In his "Message to the Public," written as death closed upon him in his tent on the Barrier, Scott observed that the journey, which he did "not regret," had "shown that Englishmen can endure hardships, help one another, and meet death with as great a fortitude as ever in the past." When Titus Oates, unable to continue and unwilling to burden his failing comrades, deliberately walked out of their tent to his death in a blizzard, Scott "knew that it was the act of a brave man and an English gentleman. We all hope to meet the end with a similar spirit. . . ."[15] Their journey had been an exercise in frustration and hardship; their one prize, the pole, had been preempted by the daring Amundsen; but even as Scott's own death approached, his faith in Providence never faltered. There was a purpose to these events, an unquestionable value to the science that had sent them to The Ice.

Scott's diary, his "Message to the Public," and his letters to friends and relatives of those who perished with him all claim the status of moral epistles. They are meditations on character, on how one faces death, for which there are no real equivalents in Antarctic literature, with the possible exception of Byrd's soliloquy, *Alone*. Almost by themselves, Scott's writings made a moral universe out of The Ice which no literary artist who has selected Antarctica as a setting has ever approached in intensity. It matters little that the diary was edited for publication and some unflattering passages excised: the moral drama remains. The exploits of Shackleton, Mawson, Amundsen, Wilson, Priestley, Nordenskjöld, and others were wonderful tales of adventure—rattlin' good yarns of survival. But only Scott—and in a different way, Byrd—moved beyond that stripped-down naturalism. The story became one not simply of man against nature but of man against himself. The odyssey of the Polar Party is the great moral drama of Antarctica, and except for science fiction, which has followed Poe's example, imaginative literature has never moved beyond the episode. Scott's meditations seemingly paralyzed serious literary treatment of Antarctica, from Kenneally's novel *The Survivor* to Ted Tally's drama *Terra Nova* to Ralph Vaughan Williams's musical word painting *Sinfonía Antarctica*.

Scott the man, like the assembled company of the *Terra Nova* expedition, was of a piece: the beliefs that sustained him as

death inexorably approached were the same that motivated his
scientific curiosity. Yet they date the tragedy of the Polar Party—make it a period piece—as much as a Cooper novel of the New York wilderness or a Bierstadt painting of the Rocky Mountains. Scott's writings and the cinematographs produced by the *Terra Nova* photographer, Herbert Ponting, would be delivered to British troops in the trenches of the western front for their inspirational message. "The unselfishness, the sacrifice, the fight against hopeless odds immortalized by Scott in that last message and in those letters which he wrote as he died," observed Cherry-Garrard approvingly, "had their effect upon the Great War. . . ."[16] By the end of the war, however, they would appear quaint, as criminally anachronistic as Sir Douglas Haig's bayonet assaults on German trenches. Scott became a British Custer, and the tragedy of the Polar Party became a British equivalent to the massacre of the Little Big Horn. Whether Scott was a hero or fool, attitudes toward him would reflect the state of British self-esteem and change with generations. The dying Scott, like Orwell's dying elephant, became a parable for the dying British Empire.

The tragedy of the Polar Party touched a deeper chord than the propaganda of strenuous endeavor, and it celebrated a nobler dimension of the age. The same year that the *Terra Nova* expedition sailed to Antarctica, Joseph Conrad published his brooding damnation of European imperialism and intellectual self-complacency, *Heart of Darkness*. Here geography is transmuted into a landscape of the self and soul. The explorer-entrepreneur Kurtz and his double, Marlowe, plummet into the core of darkest Africa, there to discover their true motives and the black depths of the human soul. "His was an impenetrable darkness," Marlowe observes of Kurtz. During their return voyage down the Congo, as Kurtz lies dying in the black hold, there occurs a "supreme moment of complete knowledge" and Kurtz "cried in a whisper at some image, at some vision—he cried twice, a cry that was no more than a breath: 'The horror! The horror!'" Returning to England, also "one of the dark places of the earth," Marlowe confronts Kurtz's betrothed and lies about Kurtz's final words. "I couldn't tell her," he confesses. "It would have been too dark, too dark altogether. . . ."[17]

Scott's was an alternative journey to self-revelation: he could tell—and he did. "Great God!" he cried at the pole, "this is an awful place." In Conrad's Africa there had been a riot of sensation and temptation, no less than of vegetation and peoples. While the passivity of The Ice was potentially more damaging, it simplified and reflected. There was, in truth, little at the pole, but much to the character of Scott and his comrades. Not Amundsen and Scott in a race to the South Pole but Kurtz and Scott in a journey to self-revelation are the appropriate historical doubles. Both were emissaries of their age. Kurtz has been cherished by literary modernism for his critique of Western morality and rationalist faith and for his exposure of the dark, irrational side of humanity. But Scott, who was real, not fictional, and who transformed his experiences into moral purposes that transcended his surroundings and his times, apparently only distanced Antarctica from the literary domain of modernism.

Scott's major literary rival was Apsley Cherry-Garrard, writer of the "Official Narrative" of the *Terra Nova* expedition, which he baldly titled *The Worst Journey in the World* (1922). The story has all the elements of high drama—a noble purpose, a distant land, a brave band enduring the most terrible hardships. Unlike most official accounts, which were rushed into print to pay the expedition's debts, *The Worst Journey* is the product of considerable research, careful writing, and weighed judgment. Despite its "official" standing, the history is a highly personalized account of what happened—a collective autobiography more than a chronicle. At its center, of course, is the Scott tragedy. Yet there is about the book an aura of the contrived, of the preciousness of the literary product. *The Worst Journey* is a period piece that finally says more about England prior to the Great War than about Antarctica. And far from granting Cherry-Garrard immediate admission to the company of literary savants, *The Worst Journey* instantly dated its author. The expedition's members were, as Cherry-Garrard revealingly recalled, "artistic Christians" who "travelled for Science" and shared a life of hard work and purpose.[18]

The Worst Journey is a massive book, dense with information and Anglo-Saxon monosyllables. The vocabulary, and the temperament it conveys, has more in common with the lyric poetry of A. E. Housman than with the literature of naturalism, with which the story might have been instinctively allied. The incredible concatenation of detail, the lengthy verbatim passages lifted from diaries, and the steady attention to chronological narrative all belong with the realist fiction of Arnold Bennett. A principal purpose of the book, after all, is documentary. "It was like this," Cherry-Garrard says again and again, then proceeds to list temperatures, food supplies, the character of snow surfaces—a litany of detail which, by its sheer bulk, evokes a mood. The author's assessment of the expedition is similarly stated in direct language, filled with tangibles like the quantity of oil, the character and quantity of rations, storm patterns, and the perils of sledge dogs.

But Cherry-Garrard was not by training or temperament a scientist. It was he who urged the Tennyson inscription from "Ulysses" for Scott's memorial cross. His book has its share of lyric poems, and while it never loses its dedication to Science, Nature, and Art, its purpose is a moral interrogation. Ultimately, the book becomes a disquisition on character, less a report on what Antarctica is than how one responds to it. By that standard Scott, the expedition, and Cherry-Garrard measure up. Antarctica reduces people, no less than scenery, to their essences, and Cherry-Garrard conveys this sense with a vastly simplified vocabulary and syntax. In the tenor and point of view of the book, there is little of the modernist syndrome. The author of *The Worst Journey* refuses to disguise the horror of the multiple tragedies of the expedition: he just wants to see these tragedies turned to good effects. There is nothing heroic, in the Romantic sense, about the winter journey that Cherry-Garrard made with Wilson and Bowers to collect a penguin egg from Cape Crozier. But there is nothing false or ridiculous about it either. There is no irony to the voice, nothing of the mockery of Lytton Strachey's *Eminent Victorians*. The expedition wanted to live up to the memories of its ancestors, not lampoon them.

Cherry-Garrard assumed the roles of both poet and critic. Wisely, he chose not to compete with the journals but to integrate and comment upon them. His sober conclusion was, "Never again. . . . I never want to see the place again. The pleasant memories are all swallowed up in the bad ones." Never again should an expedition go to The Ice under the conditions that the *Terra Nova* party did. Never again should it be necessary to publicly "bait" the value of knowledge with "suffering and death."[19] There were other ways to do science and other, less brutal ways to test one's self.

And there were other ways to write books. One need only compare *The Worst Journey* with E. M. Forster's *A Passage to India*, published two years later, to see the philosophical chasm that divided the *Terra Nova* party from modernism. Forster's work is hardly in the highly experimental vogue of William Faulkner, D. H. Lawrence, or Virginia Woolf, but it does abandon a naive realism and exploit the modernist delight in irony. In this case the contrast between two civilizations, European and Indian, is nearly complete. Forster's authorial voice could be refracted through an alternate culture—in fact, through multiple personas. Writing a historical memoir, not a novel, Cherry-Garrard was less free to experiment with different voices, quoting instead from a dozen diaries. But there is no evidence that he wished to do otherwise. He addresses directly the facts of the expedition's history and his reaction to them, and he narrates with the same straightforward quality with which he sledged across the snowfields.

Sledging is not a bad metaphor for the prose of *The Worst Journey in the World*. For Cherry-Garrard, the sledging expedition was the supreme expression of the Antarctic experience, just as the Polar Party was the supreme response. Sledging reduced life to essences. There was no faking character under its strain. And there was no faking of language. The descriptions of sledging trips are among the finest passages in the book. The story proceeds with simple words, uncomplicated syntax, a direct voice, and elementary emotions along a narrative line as straight and strenuous as the motion of a man-hauled sledge. The going might be difficult, and it might be necessary for the author to call his midwinter sledging trip to Cape Crozier the worst of all journeys, but he would face it squarely and narrate accordingly.

It is ironic, then, that Forster rather than Cherry-Garrard perhaps best conveyed the sense of reductionism and passivity that is the essence of The Ice when he took his fictional party of Englishmen to the caves of the Marabar Hills. Every sound introduced into the famous caves echoes back with the same nondescript *oumn*. One could say much the same about the Great Ice Barrier and the polar plateau. The experience was profoundly unsettling to the English. Years later a critic asked Forster what the caves meant. Why, nothing, he replied with mischievous evasion. For all his prissiness, Forster could evoke that emptiness by ironically playing one culture against the other, while the more vigorous Cherry-Garrard, operating within one tradition as it confronted The Ice unaided, could not. No participant could distance himself sufficiently from The Ice or the tragic drama. Cherry-Garrard had no sense that The Ice demanded a new style of literature: The Ice only simplified the old ones and made them more strenuous. Yet *The Worst Journey in the World* did bring a literary sensibility to the epic events of Antarctic exploration, and it assured those stories—and to a lesser extent itself—a permanent place in Western literature.

A journey to The Ice is a journey to the Earth's underworld. When epic heroes traveled to the underworld, they had guides to take them through the horrors—Odysseus had Tiresias, Aeneas had the Sibyl, Dante had Virgil. But the first explorers to the interior of Antarctica had no such guides—neither native guides to assist with the techniques of survival nor moral advisors to interpret the significance of the scene. They confronted The Ice face-to-face, with all its terrible passivity unmitigated by precedent. Unlike Kurtz, Scott told his own story; but Cherry-Garrard retold it, gave it a broader context, and reinterpreted it. Journeys to the underworld had often become part of creation myths, educating heroes to the dark side of existence, to the call of duty, and to the hard fate that might await them. For those who came to Antarctica after the heroic age, the Polar Party became that needed guide and *The Worst Journey* that valued myth.

In some respects, the situation was even more distressing for those who sought to render the Antarctic into visual images. It had long been customary to include artists (and later photographers) on exploring expeditions to describe the scenery, draw natural history specimens, and illustrate the narrative report of the expedition. A good portfolio of landscapes was not only a logical complement to an atlas of maps: it was an invaluable means of publicizing the work of the expedition and, when the expedition relied on public subscription for funds, of paying off its debts. Virtually every expedition of the heroic age had at least one artist and an official photographer among its number, although the men usually served in some other capacity as well. Their function was illustration, not art per se; but it was a part of the intellectual syndrome under which the visual artist operated that the distinction between art and illustration was not finely drawn. Each had its own conventions and techniques, yet both accepted the philosophical assumptions that sustained representational art as a form of intellectual inquiry.

As always, the Antarctic posed special problems, some of them technical. It was impossible to sketch with fingers exposed to the open air for long; oils and watercolors would freeze outdoors; rarely was an artist allowed simply to paint or draw without also sustaining the larger work of the expedition; photographic equipment, which in those days could total 100 kilograms, required separate sledges and extra manpower. George Marston, for example, found it necessary to use chalks, which wouldn't freeze, to convey the colors of the Antarctic sky. Edward Wilson filled sketches with word labels to inform a later conversion of pencil drawing to watercolor. The generally poor weather, sudden blizzards, cold, and awkwardly laborious means of transporting gear brought even the much-traveled Herbert Ponting to admit that he "found the Antarctic a very disappointing region for photography."[20] But, as Ponting also confessed, some of the problems associated with Antarctic art were conceptual.

No landscape school or convention was suitable, unmodified, for The Ice. The pastoral landscape tradition had emphasized the artifice of humanity in nature; the Romantic landscape, the untrammeled artifice of wild nature; the Impressionist landscape, the evanescent play of light as a symbol of the transience of experience and the characterization of mood. All of these schools manipulated light and shadow to evoke mood. In Antarctica, however, light was either too brilliant or missing altogether. Foreground and background were difficult to establish, and there was often no horizon on which to organize perspective. The objects, scenes, and symbols that normally populated a painting were absent. None of the stuff of the pastoral was evident. The conventional icons of Romantic scenery—the wild crag, the deep gorge, the blasted tree, the melancholy ruin, the violent eruption of natural energies by earthquake, storm, or volcano—none were available. Storms did not enhance the depth of sky, they obliterated it. To move deeper into the interior of the Antarctic yielded a purer nature but not a more sublime scene. Mood and light were not reflected through multiple objects to establish a coherent mood: there was one mood dominated by a single light and a monolithic object, ice. On shelf and plateau the vision was of an immutable nothingness. Representational art became exceedingly difficult. Consequently, the artist remained on the coast, where analogues to traditional Romantic Alpine scenes could be found and where life brought a degree of color, contrast, and form. In the interior, artists focused on human figures.

Among photographers, two in particular stand out: the Australian Frank Hurley, veteran of the Mawson and Shackleton expeditions, and the English-American Herbert Ponting, who recorded the *Terra Nova* expedition. Each, in his own way, went beyond a simple illustration of scenes and people to convey a sense of the Antarctic experience. And though the two shared the general intellectual syndrome of that restless age, each accented a different dimension of it. Ponting was the more self-conscious and contemplative. A self-proclaimed "camera artist," he was at his best in portraiture, and many of his best landscapes are more portraits of natural features or creatures than they are conventional landscapes. The tableaus emphasize the interior strenuousness of the heroic age: they are studies of character rather than of deeds. By contrast, Hurley excelled in photographs of action and valued the arduousness of the exploring life as much as its products. When he did photograph landscapes, the vastness of the Antarctic scene tended to dwarf his human figures, who are indistinguishable from (and often less interesting than) other inhabitants of the coast, such as seals and penguins.

Hurley's most famous photographs are those he made on Mawson's Australasian (*Aurora*) expedition and Shackleton's *Endurance* expedition. He took plenty of informative landscape photos—after all, illustration was a primary purpose for bringing a photographer—but generally speaking the landscapes are not successful as art. Many of their perspectives are too obviously contrived, their subjects too artificially picturesque, and their human figures too small in proportion to the backdrop. All of this says something about Hurley's sense of the enormity of the Antarctic. In later years, Hurley experimented with combination printings to enhance the sense of perspective and to introduce further contrast (and drama) into his prints. Romantic painters had done no less with the landscapes they selected, but by the time Hurley applied the techniques the photos appeared artificial. They lacked the vigor of their creation and the metaphysical justification for manipulating landscape for its effect on the viewer.

Hurley's great achievements were his action photos: the famous picture of two members of the Mawson expedition in the midst of a blizzard, crouched low to the ground, desperately grappling the ice with axes, fighting through the wind to read the weather instruments; the dramatic scene in which Shackleton and his crew of five put to sea in the *James Caird* for South

Georgia Island; the day and night (flash) photos of the *Endurance* locked in a fatal struggle with a pressure ridge of ice. The photos convey instantly the sense of strenuous excitement and the contest of man against nature that so typified the heroic age. They are complements not only to the best of the Antarctic sagas but to the watercolors of Winslow Homer and the oils of Frederic Remington, with which they are contemporary in philosophy as well as history. "To a man," noted Hurley, the Shackleton *Endurance* party upon its return to England immediately volunteered for the western front. "Emerged from a war with Nature we were destined to take our places in a war of nations," he noted prosaically. "Life is one long call to conflict, anyway." [21]

For Hurley, who personified his own assessment of man as "a discontented creature," photography was an act, not an image. [22] And his memory is best served, perhaps, by one of his own acts. When, during the *Endurance* expedition, it became necessary to lighten the burden of the small ships, Hurley had to choose between taking food and taking photographic plates. He and Shackleton selected those plates that they wished to preserve; then Shackleton—to forestall second thoughts by Hurley— smashed all the rest. Hurley brought the plates through. It was a deed perfectly in keeping with the temper of the age, every bit as instructive as the images it protected and perhaps more revealing of the man.

That was not the kind of choice that Herbert Ponting faced. Ponting came to the *Terra Nova* expedition with solid experience as a traveler and photographer of exotic lands and peoples. Portfolios on India and Japan, in particular, assured him of an international reputation as a "pictorial reporter." His Antarctic collection—both stills and motion pictures—not only rounded out this legacy but perfectly complemented the tenor of the expedition. Most of the expedition, including Scott and Edward Wilson, were enthusiastic about Ponting's prints; he was allocated a generous portion of the Hut for his photographic lab; and he was included, in some capacity, on most of the activities of the expedition so that he could record the events, the people who conducted them, and the scenery within which the work was done. Scott wrote admiringly that Ponting was "an artist in love with his work." Not merely his technical skills impressed Scott, but Ponting's "eye for a picture," his sense of composition, his "instinct" for the value of foreground, background, and the "introduction of 'life.'" At the right time, with the proper elements for a picture, Ponting could be "the most delighted of men."[23]

Yet Scott recognized that Ponting was "not very fit . . . his nervous temperament is of the quality to take this wintering experience badly."[24] In fact, Ponting was often frustrated. The winter deprived him of light, so essential to photography; the weather prevented many occasions for otherwise desired sessions; the cumbersome photographic sledge was so large, at 100 kilograms, that it required additional men to transport, with another 100 kilograms of baggage to support them; and the Antarctic scene was peculiar. All of this perplexed a photographer of Ponting's temperament and eye. At times, Ponting engaged in word-paintings, as though to compensate for his black-and-white film and poor field conditions. Elsewhere he resorted to toned carbon prints as a means to introduce color. At times, too, he discovered at Cape Royds a fine array of pictorial possibilities. He could speak movingly of the "pageantry of the skies," "the serenely beautiful" mountains of Victoria Land visible across McMurdo Sound, and above all the most "simply magnificent" spectacle he saw anywhere in all the lands he had visited—the Antarctic iceberg. But mostly he sought ways to overcome the deficiencies of the Antarctic scene.

He was at his best as a portraitist, and no one has approached the clarity and honesty of his individual and group portraits from the expedition. Applying similar techniques to the landscape was problematic. It is instructive in this regard to consider the two episodes that most excited Ponting. One concerned an iceberg, Arch Berg, that had eroded into the shape of a great bridge. The collapse of the arch "dejected" Ponting, who considered the sight a "magnificent subject for the camera," yet the "ruins" that resulted so "resembled a castle" that the berg "was now a more perfect medieval fortress than ever."[25] The other episode involved an ice cave near the Hut that "ravished" Ponting with its pictorial possibilities. From within the cave one could look out, past dripping icicles, to the *Terra Nova* at bay and the Royal Society Range in the distance. Ponting eagerly "worked up" the composition with the help of two members of the expedition who agreed to let him position them at the cave mouth. (Debenham recalled how the verb "to pont" was coined to describe "our worthy photographer's frequent demand for someone to stand into his pictures to act as a human scale."[26])

The result had everything the typical Antarctic scene, even along the coast, lacked: there was a natural frame to an otherwise boundless landscape, a foreground of distinct objects in recognizable proportion, a middle ground occupied by an identifiable figure (the ship), and a mountain backdrop. The iceberg offered a pictorial subject, especially if it were eroded into something like a ruin that resembled the normal icons of the Romantic landscape because it could fill up a scene by itself. The ice-cave perspective on the *Terra Nova* was almost obsessive in its amassing of pictorial dimensions, as if to make up for their absence elsewhere. Not surprisingly, the picture became an expedition favorite and remains one of the most often reproduced photographs of the era. In *Death of an Iceberg*, perhaps his other best-known landscape, Ponting shot essentially the same view except that he was able to exploit the rotting, castellated debris of a berg as a foreground. Elsewhere he resorted to telephoto lenses, which gave him the horizon and backdrop he needed. There was no problem with the elimination of perspective which results from telephotography, he insisted, because Antarctica had already distorted or annihilated perspective to begin with. The remark recalls Mawson's frustration in trying to describe the earth shadows that arched from Mt. Erebus. "To illustrate this remarkable 'shadow,'" Mawson lamented, "it is necessary to make a diagram in which perspective is everywhere violated." [27]

When informed that he would not make the journey with the Polar Party, Ponting reluctantly acquiesced. "After the party reached the Great Ice Barrier," he admitted, "there would be nothing to photograph but the level plain of boundless, featureless ice, or the long caravan stringing out towards the horizon." [28] It did not appear to Ponting that the icescape itself was suitable for landscape photography either as an object or a background. Instead he searched out images of the picturesque, suitably sublime panoramas, or penguins, whales, and seals. Nothing special in The Ice merited a new photographic style. This was an issue of philosophy as much as technique. Even as he struggled to carry his photographic kit up mountainsides for a better telephoto position, Ponting thought of the result as both a "remarkable feat of photography" and an item of "lasting value to geography." However much he "worked up" (or "ponted") foregrounds, explored for picturesque scenes, or struggled to introduce (or overcome) perspective—however much he insisted that he was a "camera artist," not simply a photographer—

Ponting remained firmly a practitioner of representational art.
He was there to record, to illustrate, to document.

One of his most celebrated landscapes, a view from Mt. Fuji, is taken from behind two Japanese who stand at the brink and survey the panorama, a scene partially flooded with clouds. The perspective echoes Caspar David Friedrich's famous painting *Wanderer above a Sea of Mist*, in which a Humboldtean traveler is viewed from behind, thunderstruck, while he stares across a spectacle of mountains and mists. The artist, Ponting, was there to record the effect not simply on himself but on the persona in front of him. The vantage point this omniscient photographer enjoyed was thus correlative to that enjoyed by an author like Cooper as he recorded the actions and thoughts of his sealers or, in another way, by the corporate diarist Cherry-Garrard, as he stitched together a chronicle from the literary and artistic documents of the expedition. That the artist was a participant rendered his voice and eye more authentic, not intrinsically unreliable. The experience and the scenery might beggar language and strip photography of its stock of conventions, but there is no sense that a larger, privileged perspective was impossible or unnecessary.

The most remarkable artist of the heroic age, however, was undoubtedly Edward Wilson. Already a veteran Antarctic explorer, Wilson was the Renaissance man of the *Terra Nova* group and a perfect example of the kind of explorer-intellectual that this era of discovery featured as its highest expression. Physician, naturalist, sledger, diarist, artist—"Uncle Bill" Wilson was the expedition doctor, its second-in-command and chief scientist, leader of the winter party sledge journey to Cape Crozier, participant in the depot journey, member of the ill-fated Polar Party, and illustrator par excellence. Wilson felt no discord among his multiple talents: his art served his science, as his science served his faith. Wilson embodied a single, if complex, philosophy that united all these endeavors into a style of exploration, writing, art, and science which was itself a manifestation of an intellectual syndrome. The *Terra Nova* expedition expressed that syndrome more completely than any other exploring party, and Wilson expressed it better than any other individual.

He had joined the *Discovery* expedition to "kill or cure" a serious case of pulmonary tuberculosis. Like so many intellectuals of his generation, he discovered in vigorous activity a prescription for mental and somatic health, and he readily returned with Scott for a second tour of duty. His curiosity and enthusiasm involved Wilson with everything, and he drew everything. He painted landscapes, sketched scenes of expedition sledging parties, designed sledge flags, drew the anatomy of penguins, illustrated the Hut's literary paper, *The South Polar Times*. On the *Discovery* voyage south, Scott wrote Clements Markham that Wilson "has quite the keenest intellect on board, and a marvelous capacity for work." Wilson did everything: "He is called to see and sketch the sunrise. He is on the spot when a new bird is seen. The next moment he is at a microscope sketching."[29] When he traveled with Scott and Shackleton over the Barrier during the southernmost effort of the *Discovery*, Wilson constantly sketched the mountainous horizon, even while he suffered from snow blindness. He estimated that the resulting portfolio, if pasted together, would stretch for 80 meters.[30] Even during the descent down the Beardmore Glacier, while he was dying, he continued to draw mountains and label their geologic features. The amassing of realist detail that Cherry-Garrard achieved with words, Wilson matched with line and color.

By comparison, the photographs of Ponting seem staged and stuffy. Wilson's watercolors, for which he is best known, don't show the final polish of the studio; there is nothing painterly about them. He had to work outdoors with rapidly numbing fingers, sketching in pencil and indicating with words what colors should go where. Later, securely within the Hut, he would clear off a table and under acetylene light complete the painting—often several at once. But apart from his choice of a medium and his cramped "studio," where others watched over his shoulder, the simplicity of his paintings derives from a naive realism that seems unchanged from the days of Thomas Reid and the Scottish Enlightenment. One need only contrast Wilson's watercolor of the *Discovery*, resplendent with parhelia and ice floes, to Doré's brooding rendition of the Ancient Mariner's vessel enveloped with a paraselene to see the strengh of Wilson's vision. What in Doré was Moon and gloom and nightmarish, toothed ices becomes for Wilson the Sun and a self-evident naturalism. Where Doré's darkness reveals a ship bound to the unknown and a landscape bound to Antarctica only by allegory, actual exploration reveals a less threatening world lighted by reason. The Sun seems to guide the ship, and the ship seems to bring the

Sun. This world may be unknown, but it is not unknowable. To compare Wilson's Antarctica to Doré's is to witness the triumph of reason over rhyme.

When Wilson lectured on art to the expedition members one evening, Scott recorded the principal themes: that "Nature's harmonies cannot be guessed at," that "accuracy" was of "extreme importance," that the doctrines of Ruskin were as applicable to Antarctica as to everywhere else.[31] As a youth, Wilson admitted, he had been "smitten to distraction" by the landscapes of Turner. He quoted Ruskin tirelessly. He praised Ponting for the clean lines, composition, and solidity of his best landscapes, and he chided the amateur painters of the party for their habit of introducing excessive lines or for painting snow as pure white when it was more often a tint of grey or yellow. He shared with the other members of the expedition a delight in those picturesque scenes made possible by eroded icebergs or playful penguins. Yet he never tried to incorporate everything within a single panorama, as many nineteenth-century landscapists did, or to manipulate the elements of a scene to produce the proper effect on the viewer. The purpose of his art was to record—in all their detail and abundance—the actual scenes, creatures, and wonders of Antarctica. Wilson's sketches and paintings are less an artistic portfolio than a pictorial counterpoint to his voluminous diary.

Other expedition members marveled at Wilson's precision. Scott wrote that "his sketches are most astonishingly accurate; I have tested his proportions by actual angular measurement and found them correct."[32] Cherry-Garrard, who served as Wilson's assistant, confirmed that the purpose of the drawings was "scientific and geographical." Although he dutifully quoted Wilson as dismissing his skills as low in "artistic capacity," Cherry-Garrard also testified that no one ever captured the strange, delicate "atmospheric effects" and colors of Antarctica as Wilson had.[33] That attention to accuracy was not accidental. Wilson painted the scenery and creatures of the Barrier for the same reasons he sought a midwinter penguin egg from Cape Crozier: for information and out of a mutually reinforcing faith in science and God. Accuracy was essential to science and to the measure of Design, but it was also a moral act, a sign of character.

Here was no dilettante, no member of an avant-garde who wished only to explore the nature of art. Life did not exist for art: art existed to serve life, to explore and record the natural world. Both art and science worked in their own ways toward the same purpose. "Free will in the eyes of God," wrote the indomitable Wilson, "means the willingness to do one's best at whatever comes our way and however difficult it may seem."[34] Before setting off on the winter journey, recognizing that nearly a year would pass before he would see her letters, he wrote his wife that "it all seems cruel and cold but it is God's will to make good stuff of us both."[35] The books he carried to the pole were a pocket Testament and Prayer Book given by his wife and Tennyson's "In Memoriam," lent by Cherry-Garrard—a "perfect piece of faith and hope!" They would be found "in my hand or in my breast pocket when the end comes," he wrote his wife from their final camp on the Barrier. "All is well. . . ."[36]

As an artist-illustrator Wilson was not alone in his style, although he was the most dedicated of the common-sense realists who illustrated for the heroic age. The crayons of Van Waterschool van der Gracht, who traveled on the *Aurora* with Mawson; the chalks of George Marston, the artist on Shackleton's *Nimrod* expedition; the oils of F. W. Stokes, who accompanied Nordenskjöld and was a veteran of Peary's Greenland expedition— all tend to be somewhat more in the expressive tradition of northern European landscape. Yet there is no mistaking the era, or the continuity of these artists' work with that of Alexander von Humboldt and William Hodge, George Catlin and John Audubon, Karl Bodmer and William Henry Holmes, and the legions of others who freely combined scientific and artistic purposes and who transformed the newly unveiled continental landscapes into visual images. Within the art of the heroic age there is a remarkable homogeneity of purpose and style. Ponting and Wilson planned to exhibit together when they returned to London. Ponting's photos, Wilson's watercolors, and Scott's diary all come together in Cherry-Garrard's account with a degree of harmony that goes beyond the fact that these men were friends and colleagues. The works of the three men express a broadly shared philosophy and faith.

Time and again fresh landscapes, novel and abundant information, and unexpected visions had inspired new genres of landscape art, but this would not be the case with Antarctica. The scene *qua* scene was never sufficient. The Alps, the Hudson River gorge, the Rocky Mountains had all had to be viewed at the right time, by someone with the proper sensibility and the appropriate techniques. That kind of timing did not occur with

Antarctica, and Antarctica, with a few adjustments, was incorporated within the existing conventions. Apparently no one conceived of The Ice as anything more than a special or extreme case of traditional pursuits. Wilson, for example, got around the perspective issue by drawing specific scenes or objects, by treating them as specimens. With regard to color he wrote matter-of-factly that "there are no similes in everyday life that describe the pale brilliance of the lights produced by the sun down here. . . ."[37] Instead he alluded to the radiance of incandescent metals, such as potassium and strontium, which he recalled from his days as a chemistry student. The appeal to scientific experimentation as a solution to an artistic problem was symptomatic. When confronted with baffling perspectives or difficult weather, Ponting likewise appealed to the "geographical" value of the product, and Cherry-Garrard justified the expedition's hardships because the expedition did "Science." There might be doubts that a penguin egg was worth the horrors of the winter journey, that the data brought back were equal to the compounded tragedies of the expedition, but few doubted that better-financed expeditions could overcome those limitations.

There was no sense that Antarctic exploration ought to be abandoned, any more than that the intensely personal experiences that tested his "character" led Cherry-Garrard to scrap realist prose for stream-of-consciousness narrative, or that Ponting's problems suggested to him that he forsake representational art for an abstract and subjective art, or that Scott's suffocating agonies on the Barrier led him to renounce his belief in Providence for an ethical relativism. The breakup of the heroic age involved more than a change in the techniques and purposes of exploration. It paralleled a revolution in intellectual syndromes that rendered the old common-sense realism inappropriate and questioned the value of geographic exploration. For the succeeding era there would be no single figure, no Edward Wilson, who could embody the many strands of the new intellectual syndrome of the age and apply them to Antarctica. Yet it was this remarkable unity of purpose and perception, not merely sledging parties, that qualified the age as "heroic."

Lost Horizon

When Antarctic exploration reestablished itself during the 1920s, the precepts of modernism were sweeping physics, biol-

ogy, philosophy, mathematics, painting, sculpture, music, literature, and ethics. It was an intellectual revolution that reconstructed the epistemological foundations by which Western
civilization had come to know itself and the world around it.
There were profound dislocations in the understanding of space,
time, causality, and meaning that went even to the core of natural philosophy. The principle of relativity challenged not only
assumptions about absolute space and time, and thereby the
universality of physical laws constructed out of them, but the
belief in the existence of a privileged position for observing
the world. Yet that was only a start. Heisenberg's principle of indeterminacy questioned the nature of observation; Bohr's principle of complementarity, the ability to represent the atomic
world in terms of common-sense images; Gödel's proof, the capacity of mathematical logic to describe systems that are both
consistent and complete. Chance became an accepted presence
in the natural world—not simply a failure of understanding but
an irreducible component that finally destroyed the concept of
Design.

There were parallel developments in the arts. Just as mathematics became obsessed with the nature of proof, so painting
brooded over the identity of the painted canvas and the role of
the visual artist, and literature pondered the nature of the authorial voice, narrative structure, and the relationship of the
reader to what was read. Historicism lost its metaphysical vitality; storytelling seemed to demand something beyond chronologies and life cycles, and literature required something more
than stories. Eventually literature was seen to consist of self-
contained texts encoded with signs and information. Painting
was broken into its constituent parts—lines, colors, canvas surface. No longer could physics, mathematics, art, or literature be
considered simply as representations of an external world.
Painting made statements about painting, and literature about
writing. Reality became a peculiar alchemy between observed
and observer. As disciplines turned to explore that phenomenon—as they tried to define themselves by reference to something other than an external universe—they confronted the
paradoxes of self-reference. A period of extravagant experimentation ensued as the modernist syndrome struggled to establish
a new synthesis or, more often, to complete the destruction of
the old.

The inherited genres were never abolished, of course. Newtonian mechanics was still used to build bridges, Gothic novels were still published, and cowboys and mountains were still painted. But the forms became formulas; they lost their vitality as modes of intellectual inquiry. These older, now traditional canons of art and philosophy, however, constituted the intellectual baggage that the successors to the heroic age brought to Antarctica. In particular, the reportorial urge persisted: the great bulk of Antarctic images and descriptions consisted of memoirs, reports, journalism, histories, photographs, and maps. The dominant images, however, were shaped by popular magazines like *National Geographic* and *Audubon* and by documentary films for television. No one carried modernism to the newly accessible polar plateau as James Cook had brought the Enlightenment to the pack or the *Terra Nova* expedition had transported a Romantic realism to the Barrier. The moral imperative to geographic discovery had, it appeared, receded; high culture was mesmerized by things other than the high latitudes of the south; and apparently only the inherited momentum of science, a sense of unfinished geography, and the new momentum of technology—symbolized by the airplane—propelled the new era.

It is a curious lapse—this absence of modernism—and it says as much about modernism as about Antarctica. Many of the technical difficulties that had plagued the artists of the heroic age were solved by the modernist revolution. Representational art had broken down beyond the Barrier, where there were few ways to escape the lost horizon, powerful surface effects, leached colors, and nihilistic scenery of the pure icescape. But modernist art could freely handle abstractions, minimalism, and abolished perspective. Writing early in the nineteenth century, John Constable could say of painting that it "is a science and should be pursued as an inquiry into the laws of nature. Why, then, may not landscape painting be considered as a branch of natural philosophy, of which pictures are but the experiments?" This esthetic position was not much different from that of the artist-illustrators of the heroic age.[38] The Ice might make the experiment difficult, but that only enhanced the value of the effort.

A dramatically different esthetics had emerged by the mid-twentieth century. Frank Stella remarked that he always got into arguments "with people who want to retain the old values in painting—the humanistic values that they always find on the canvas." They "always end up asserting that there is something there besides the paint on the canvas," that the colors and lines represent something else. Instead, argued Stella, "only what can be seen there *is* there."[39] Robert Motherwell, explaining the relationship of art to instruction, stated that "in the greatest painting, the painter communes with himself."[40] Here, it seems, were a pictorial language and an introspective philosophy ideally suited for the interior of Antarctica.

It was not quite that simple. Modernist artists no longer joined expeditions of geographic discovery, so modernist art never made it to The Ice. Equally, it was not obvious that modernism could have really coped with the geographic reality of the Antarctic. For all its rebelliousness, for all its clamor about purity, about returning painting and literature to their elementary forms, about dissolving the distance between observer and observed, about the existential nature of the moral life, modernism had demanded a rich texture of civilization, a dense tradition of art and information as an agar in which to thrive. Without that culture there was no purpose in the modernist rebellion, in its urge to reconstruct and purify. Without the old tradition of naturalism, perspective, and realist detail there could not be a modernist reconstruction, any more than an avant-garde could exist without a bourgeois society. One had to understand naturalist painting in order to understand the abstractions of modernism; a minimalist canvas resembled nothing significant until it was mentally contrasted with the art that had preceded it. Thus, while the techniques and some of the esthetic presumptions of modernism seemed applicable to The Ice, and while Antarctica seemed to present a ready-made geography of modernism, the larger social context apparently did not exist to sustain the effort to unite them.

Modernism did not look to nature for its foundations but to culture. Exploration, as a means of searching the external world, was foreign to it; modernism preferred to look inward, ultimately absorbed in questions of self-reference. Almost exclusively it occupied a synthetic landscape—a universe populated at first by other works of art, then by competing images from the synthetic landscape of an industrial society. Modernism excelled at purifying, at reducing and distilling. But Antarctica had already done that. It was one thing to take a world rich, or overripe, with information and a multiplicity of viewpoints and simplify it; it was another, more difficult task to take a visually and experientially impoverished environment and enrich it. Perhaps modernism could not modernize itself. Thus, while many of its techniques and concepts were well suited to Antarctica (no surrealist imagined a stranger nightmare than the aurora over the snows of the polar night; no minimalist drew a more severe surface than the polar plateau; no op artist matched the mirage-filled horizon of the icescape), modernism failed to see in The Ice a mirror image of its programs. Even apart from intellectual problems, the social context was impossible: modern art was done in lofts, not on sledging expeditions. Antarctica would be left to science or to science fiction, which could populate The Ice with lost worlds and alien creatures or inject some moral principle by threatening the Earth with an oblivion of cold, an ice invasion brought on by humanity's environmental sins.

In this matter, as in others, the Byrd expeditions are revealingly transitional. Modernism really announced its presence as an official culture in America about the time Byrd first established Little America. In the same year that Byrd voyaged to the Barrier, the Museum of Modern Art opened in New York; it was the first institutional expression of modernist art. The same year that Byrd flew to the pole, Joseph Wood Krutch published his manifesto of the modernist movement in American letters, *The Modern Temper*; William Faulkner published *The Sound and the Fury*, one of the formative experimental novels of modernism; and American architects joined the International School at the Barcelona Exhibition. But there were always American eccentricities to modernism. Americans never abandoned for long their acceptance of an external world, the hard reality of objects, or the impulse to record them. And then there was a native philosophy, pragmatism, whose emphasis on chance, on life as experimentation, on pluralism, and on truth as something done and reality as something internally felt made it the first modernist philosophy and a rebuttal to the despair of European existentialism. Even as they toyed with new techniques and concepts, American artists remained reporters, and American scientists remained experimentalists rather than theoreticians. America's purists of modernism would be, by and large, European emigrés to America.

The Byrd expeditions brought a modernizing of technique rather than a modernist philosophy. Only science, Byrd wrote, could justify an expedition to Antarctica, and it was science, shorn of its old liaisons with the arts, that Byrd's expeditions brought back. Byrd took Cherry-Garrard's recommendations to heart—not simply the call to use newer transportation but Cherry-Garrard's insistence that Antarctic exploration had to have a broader base than a sledging trip and that scientific information, not simply the testing of character, had to be the foundation of organization. Yet there was no alliance between the exploring party and exponents of American modernism, no equivalent to the unified intellectual syndrome that had animated the heroic age, only an aggressive pragmatism intended to finish an incomplete task. Antarctica remained as remote from high culture as the dark side of the Moon.

The expatriation impulse rampant among American artists; the search for those modernist species of refuge from middle-class philistinism, bohemia and the artists' colony; the fascination with self and psychological analysis—all of this was alien to a group that unabashedly sought to establish a small town on the Great Ice Barrier and to publicize portions of the yet-unseen external world through those most direct of all mediums, geographic discovery and aerial photography. At a time when the American intelligentsia was busily expatriating itself to Europe, in loud flight from a debased commercial culture, Byrd was successfully soliciting funds from Fords, Rockefellers, and Walgreens and laying the foundation for future land claims by which American civilization might be permanently established on Antarctica. Russell Owen, a journalist from the *New York Times*, joined the party and won a Pulitzer prize for his stories; but this was news, not art. By the time Byrd's second expedition established itself on the Barrier, the dissonance was somewhat less pronounced. Modernism in America experienced a retrenchment. Social realism marched with experimental literature, and American Scene and Magic Realism restored something of genre painting. But Little America was hardly the Stone City, Iowa, of Grant Wood, and the Barrier was impossibly distant from the muscular Midwest landscapes of Thomas Hart Benton.

No modernist litterateur or painter believed that a journey to the Barrier could be a means to artistic education, a vehicle to fame, or a useful arena in which to demonstrate the power of modernism. It was more important to study literature itself as a phenomenon and to dwell on the subjective reality that animated literature than to apply literary techniques to the de-

scription of an external universe. Modernism celebrated as one
of its founding myths the story of Sigmund Freud's experiment in self-psychoanalysis, a symbolic journey into the subconscious conducted within the comfortable confines of a Vienna office, not Richard Byrd's exercise in autoexperimentation at Advance Base, where amid the frozen polar night Byrd sought to reconcile his rational consciousness with the great cosmic harmonies.

Byrd's account of that experience, *Alone* (1938), is by far the most interesting and philosophical of the Antarctic memoirs from this period. In many ways it echoes *The Worst Journey in the World*, even at times as though the new Antarctic explorer had to measure himself against the old. "Yes, I learned much," Byrd wrote frankly of the episode, "but I never want to go through that experience again."[41] The nightmare brought into question for Byrd the value and truth of many beliefs, yet in the end he affirmed the eternal verities of family, love, self-knowledge, and a much-muted providence. Similarly, his soliloquy did not require the invention of new literary forms or even suggest the adaptation of the techniques of experimental literature, though the experience seemed to be intrinsically made for them. Instead, *Alone* was written in part as an apologia and in part as a quasi-scientific report. Though it strives for accuracy of detail, act, and feeling, it is more openly philosophical than *The Worst Journey*, while devoid of Cherry-Garrard's overly rigorous prose. Equally, it is free of irony, of archetypal overtones, of rhetorical experimentation. The book is empty of the narrative devices that would make exemplars of thematically similar, but unabashedly modernistic, stories like e. e. cummings's *The Enormous Room* or William Faulkner's *As I Lay Dying*. Modernism, it has been said, is an art of exiles, real or imagined. But Byrd's gesture was traditional, his "exile" that of a novitiate on a spiritual retreat, not that of political excommunication or rabid expatriotism. The mood of his book recalls more the rational meditations of Pascal's *Pensées* than surrealism or psychoanalysis; his voice echoes the Defoe of *Robinson Crusoe* more than the Faulkner of *Absalom, Absalom!* Modernist literature avoided Antarctica, and imaginative literature on Antarctica remained where Poe had left it.

In fact, Byrd's second Antarctic expedition was a direct inspiraspiration for two of the classics of twentieth-century science fiction: Don L. Stuart's (John Wood Campbell) short story "Who

Goes There?" (1938) and H. P. Lovecraft's novella *At the Mountains of Madness* (1939). Both writers borrowed from episodes and accounts published by Antarctic explorers, much as Cooper had from Wilkes, but their spiritual identity descends from Poe and Coleridge. Both discovered in the Antarctic a nebulous landscape, capable of housing (or hiding) an imagined civilization, and both chastised a reckless rationalism that let scientific curiosity replace prudent common sense.

Campbell assumed the editorship of *Astounding Stories* in 1937, devised a new literary prescription for writing about scientific and futuristic topics, and inaugurated a generally recognized golden age of science fiction. "Who Goes There?" was one of the first demonstrations of this philosophy and formula, an immediate classic. An Antarctic expedition discovers in the ice an alien spacecraft and frozen alien beings. A debate ensues over whether to recover the specimens "for science," destroy them, or leave them in blue ice. The scientific argument prevails, and a sole specimen—horribly imagined with red tentacles for hair, a tortured face full of hate at its frozen destiny—is thawed; then the horrors begin. The creature can invade and consume other organisms, taking on exactly their features and memories, and it can propagate. By the time the process is discovered, the party is trapped for the winter, and no one knows who is real and who is an embodiment of the creature. The dramatic qualities of the plot are obvious, and twice the story has been clumsily filmed by Hollywood as *The Thing*.

Yet the story is not pure fantasy. A careless rationalism had unleashed the creature, but only a more disciplined reason destroys it. So, while there are plenty of horrors and abominations, the problem is a cerebral puzzle and the plot has affinities with the English mystery story; the isolated Antarctic camp takes the place of the locked room or the stalled train. There are also philosophical conundrums, perhaps unintended, aroused by the closed environment and by the problems of distinguishing appearance from reality. At times they echo the illogic of self-referential systems. At one point a physiological test is devised to distinguish human from nonhuman, but there is no way in this relativistic world to tell who is really human, only who is different. A crewman paraphrases Russell's famous paradox. "I know I'm human. I can't prove it either. One of us two is a liar, for that test cannot lie, and it says one of us is. I gave proof that the test was wrong, which seems to prove I'm human,

and now Garry has given that argument which proves me human—which he, as the monster, should not do. Round and
round and round and round and—"[42] Eventually, the paradox is
circumvented and the monster destroyed. But here, at least, was
an example of how the isolation and alienness of Antarctica
could be put to literary purposes. Nor were the possibilities restricted to catastrophes on or about ice. Until the advent of real
space travel, published descriptions of Antarctica were commonly extrapolated to the other worlds projected by science fiction writers of the next several decades.

At the Mountains of Madness more specifically resurrects Poe's
Antarctic tales, modernizing their equipment with airplanes
and drilling apparatus while retaining the fantastic geography
of A. Gordon Pym. Lovecraft had read widely in Antarctic non-
fiction, but the story belongs with mythical journeys to the underworld, to lost worlds, or to other planets. The novella is also
an effort to tidy up some unfinished business in American
literature. "Here was I on the other side of that curtain, the side
Poe did not care, with all his imagination, to pierce," thought
Russell Owen.[43] But while the journalist Owen and the Byrd expedition had pierced the veil of sea smoke with scientific fact,
they had left unresolved the literary mystery of A. Gordon Pym.
Lovecraft proceeded to complete the tale. Deep in the polar
plateau, the Miskatonic University Expedition discovers the
loftiest mountain range on Earth, and within that massif is a
buried civilization originally descended from another planet.
Not a single creature but a whole alternate cosmogony is revealed. The exhumation of this civilization, another example
of untamable scientific curiosity gone amuck, only resuscitates
a form of death. The Antarctic presents an implacably alien
and malignant landscape of lethal desolation, disordered time,
and unearthly natural law, filled with unspeakable terrors. The
descent to the bowels of the City of the Old Ones ends with the
narrator pursued by a shapeless black horror emitting a hideous
stench. The story is filled with references to the unresolved
mysteries of Pym, and Lovecraft puts his Antarctic material
into an updated version of the Gothic horror story. Ultimately,
only two geologists escape—like Poe's Pym and Melville's Ishmael—to tell the tale.

One survivor is driven mad by his literally unspeakable vision. But the other, the narrator, writes his account to protest
"this contemplated invasion of the antarctic," which will "bring

up that which we know may end the world."[44] There are limits to science and to rational understanding, and like his mentor Poe, Lovecraft found the Antarctic to be a suitable geographic expression for both. Like Poe's tales, the story is not so much a plot as it is a means to effect a mood. To the extent that the story answers questions, they are those left over by Poe's enigmatic *Pym* narrative—literary questions, not larger questions in philosophy. In a curious way, Lovecraft's motivations in tidying up a mystery left by an old genre parallel those of the explorers who sought to complete the geographic exploration of Antarctica begun by Poe's contemporaries. In both cases the endeavors led, in a sense, to dead ends. Once Antarctica and the ocean basins had been generally explored, there were no unvisited geographies within which to set a lost civilization; fantasy writing had to resurrect old problems, tour other planets, or plunge into the depths of the human soul. For Lovecraft, Antarctica was a place to locate old, if luxuriantly imagined, themes. Although in *At the Mountains of Madness* Lovecraft temporarily updated an old genre and revived old curiosities, he did not invent a new style or inaugurate a school of Antarctic literature.

When IGY dramatically announced a change in the scale, style, and purposes of exploration, one result was a great outpouring of Antarctic literature of the traditional sort—scientific articles, journalistic essays, memoirs—a variety of new perspectives, principally through aerial photography and satellites, that brought the visual imagery of Antarctica into resonance with contemporary painting; and at least one art book, Emil Schulthess' *Antarctica* (1960). The Swiss Schulthess had, as "an old dream," wanted to do a "photographic documentation of Antarctica." In particular, he longed to "take photographs of the sun and its course in this extreme Southern part of the world."[45] As the scientific agenda for IGY took shape, he recognized the opportunity, attached himself to various American expeditions around Antarctica, and brought to The Ice the German tradition of photojournalism, with its ambition that photos could by themselves record the scene and narrate the story. It was a style that Schulthess had worked out in other grandly scaled books on Africa, America, Europe, and Asia, and it was a vogue that *Life* magazine had popularized at the time.

"He was everywhere," marveled Adm. George Dufek, who supervised the American logistical program for Antarctica during IGY, "shooting pictures from all angles and from every position."[46] For the first time since Edward Wilson, Herbert Ponting, and Frank Hurley, a visual artist traveled to Antarctica to record the place and its people. In many respects, Schulthess was the successor to the heroic age. His camera seemed indiscriminate. Everything needed to be recorded: people, icebergs, floes, penguins, skuas, snow crystals, huts, haloes, rocks, Sno-Cats, airplanes, crevasses, icebreakers, and of course the Sun. For the first time an artist journeyed to the polar plateau and lived to tell about it. There was no tradition of plateau art to rebel against, no need to fuss over the moral baggage of modernism. Instead Schulthess combined the modernist freedom of perspective with the ambition of the journalist-explorer to document; he was more a modernizer of techniques than a philosopher of modernist art. No need for contorted strivings after novelty: here everything was new. Schulthess liked the "surprising and interesting effects" of the Antarctic clouds, "fascinating endless snowscape," the "symphony of splendor" that was the crevasse, the "incredible wealth of forms produced by the changes of the weather." None of his previous journeys had been so revealing, he exulted, and he was accordingly "spurred into making the utmost of every piece of photographic equipment." No artist since has ranged so widely over the Antarctic.

Schulthess used polarizing lenses to filter the overpowering summer light, telephoto lenses to shorten the empty distances that broke down perspective, wide-angle lenses to create an illusion of depth, and fish-eye lenses to capture the circular trajectory of the polar Sun and the disorienting sense that, at the pole, one looks north to all horizons. Closeups were thrust next to sweeping vistas. Where foregrounds did not exist, they were created. While Ponting had framed Erebus through the aperture of an ice cave, Schulthess framed it through the housing of a helicopter tail-rotor. His use of linear composition was very much in the vogue of the representational artists who had illustrated Western exploration. A cover photo of ice floes and bergs—staggered strips of blue-black sea, white ice, and grey sky—could pass for colored engravings from Ross' *Voyage*. The book was an especially happy thesaurus of Antarctic images—evocations of traditional scenes mixed with new perspectives and new subjects.

Schulthess' photographs of the polar plateau are perhaps his most important. Schulthess dealt with the "monotony" of the "Antarctic desert" by establishing perspectives that could bring the scene into the tradition of representational art. At the pole he photographed a dramatic solar halo. The Sun gave the scene a vanishing point, while a vehicle track across the snow brought depth to the foreground. On an overland traverse, he used the crevasse detectors in front of the vehicle—like an array of antennas—to organize the foreground, while a lone figure provided an object to focus on in the mid-distance. Elsewhere, caravans of Sno-Cats and sledges mark a distinct, figurative horizon, a narrative of the journey. In an aerial view of the South Pole station, vehicle tracks inscribe a weird pattern of shadowed lines on white. Forming a kind of abstract expressionist figure, the lines converge on the minuscule black specks that are the buildings of the pole station. And in what may be the only pure icescape ever published for the plateau, Schulthess relied on natural features to sketch an almost perfect geometry of mathematical perspective: sastrugi in the foreground and streams of cirrus clouds in the background converge to a common vanishing point along a starkly linear horizon. Like thick brush strokes, the sastrugi bring a degree of depth and shade to the scene, while the rays of whitish clouds add some color by brightening the sky to a royal blue near the center and darkening it to a navy blue around the fringe.

Perhaps the most curious photographs are those taken with the fish-eye lens, then a novelty, at the pole and from aircraft. The distortions, the abstract geometry of the Antarctic landscape and seascape, and the surface-dominated flatness of the icescape are all vividly apparent. But this was not novelty for its own sake; Schulthess intended the photos to inform, and his success at capturing the whole sky answered some of the old laments by artists of the heroic age that they needed a circular perspective to convey atmospheric effects. Schulthess plotted the Sun's path at the pole with an exposed plate, but he framed the photo with a protractor so that the arc could be plotted mathematically. Similarly, he had no esthetic compunction against drawing lines of longitude across an aerial photo of the pole. The result not only instructs and orients the viewer but gives perspective to the otherwise flat plane of the polar plateau. This is no self-referential image: the artist, not the photograph, eagerly places the image within the intellectual context of Western science; and where appropriate pictorial references are absent from the scene, he manufactures them.

More recently, nature photography has rediscovered Antarctica. During the course of "more than a dozen expeditions to the antarctic and the Subantarctic in as many years," Roger Tory Peterson assembled a magnificent portfolio of penguin photographs, drawings, and paintings. Not Antarctica but the penguin was the subject, however, and not art but documentation was the principal purpose. In a sense, Peterson's work is a lineal descendant of Edward Wilson's; Wilson had also begun his career as a scientific illustrator with studies on birds. As art, Peterson's pictures are genre pieces in many ways indistinguishable from Wilson's. What does distinguish Peterson's portfolio is its comprehensiveness and its introduction of a new moral curiosity to the study of wildlife. A belief in a providential design has evidently been replaced by a belief in an ecological design. Accordingly, nature lectures humans about proper behavior, but its moral didacticism says less about the behavior of human to human than about the relationship of humanity to all of life. Thus the penguin—a creature that seems to be a comic eccentric in nature's economy—becomes a "litmus paper of the sea, an indicator of the health of our watery planet. If they fail to survive, by what arrogance do we think we can survive?"[47] A report on penguins is no exercise in indulgent hobbyism but a selective study in the conduct of humans and an appraisal of the legitimacy of human claims to a future. Appropriately, Peterson recounts that his introduction to the penguin occurred in the hideous aftermath of an oil spill.

Although animated by similar sentiments, Eliot Porter made Antarctica itself central to his portfolio. Like so many other artists to the region, Porter began as a scientist, with degrees in chemical engineering and medicine from Harvard. For a while he taught biochemistry. Progressively, however, he was drawn to photography, to friendships with Ansel Adams and Alfred Stieglitz, to the artistic canons of the Group f/64, and to the transcendental nature philosophy of Thoreau. In 1938 his first show opened at Stieglitz's gallery. He never lost his early naturalism, advancing first to a photographic study of birds in the wild, then to color photography, and then to a full-blown series of landscape studies, most published through the Sierra Club, beginning in 1962 with *"In Wildness Is the Preservation of the World," from Henry David Thoreau.* The books were a perfect blend of Porter's artistic and naturalistic philosophies. As part of its contribution to the American bicentennial, the U.S. Antarctic Research Program invited him to visit Antarctica.

Most of Porter's travels took him along the coast, where life was abundant, and to the Dry Valleys. A flight to the South Pole resulted in some photos of the polar plateau margins. But the contrast of Porter's work to Schulthess' is almost perfect. In *Antarctica* nature is portrayed as an old master, The Ice as a precious object, and Antarctica as a last great wilderness. There is no paraphernalia of science (or congeries of scientists) in the photos, no omnium-gatherum of miscellaneous images. These are not simply pictures of Antarctica but works of art, and this is not so much a book as a gallery. Although Schulthess conveys a truer representation of the Antarctic scene, Porter is perhaps truer to the esthetic power of Antarctica: its role as reducer, abstractor, and mirror. Unlike Schulthess, who not only wrote explanations for his scenes but cheerfully inscribed lines on the prints to better inform the viewer, Porter supplies only a general narrative of his travel, completely separate from the gallery of prints. Images and words are joined in the same way that the photos of Walker Evans complement the text of James Agee's *Let Us Now Praise Famous Men*. The book's captions, Porter explained apologetically, "have been written by my publisher to offer additional information on the human and natural history of Antarctica."[48]

Its vast distances, reliance on air transport, and notorious weather made Antarctica "a frustrating place for a photographer."[49] Early on, the elderly Porter, then seventy-three, broke an arm and had to return a second time to complete his travels. But Porter's tendencies toward a flattening of perspective, abstraction, and self-consciously esthetic purposes resonated well with the pictorial possibilities of the Antarctic. In fact, some of his best-composed photos are still lifes of anchors, tie posts, and hut interiors, cherished not for their information about Antarctica as for their inherent appeal to Porter's esthetic sense. Yet there is a peculiar mixture of interests and techniques. At times, Porter evokes nineteenth-century Romanticism. He presents the Dry Valleys as a lost world, a Machu Picchu of bare rock and ice. The Erebus ice caves—silent, isolated, immutable—"where the process of crystallization, atom by atom, is the only change, recall forbidden sanctuaries on other continents, where mysteries of long-forgotten cults were celebrated."[50] At the same time,

Porter could turn an iceberg into a stunning minimalist portrait, approvingly compare cavernous boulders in the Taylor Valley to the "works of Henry Moore," celebrate the painterly qualities of crevasse fields and green ice, and transform a group of crabeater seals into a scene out of Dali.[51] In one of his more dramatic life studies, Porter has his subject, a seal, stare back at him in a way that seems to dissolve the modernist conundrum of observer and observed. No other observers are photographed in the book—only Porter, who remains a powerful presence known indirectly by his effect on the observed object. The result is a portfolio of some of the most haunting of all Antarctic photos.

Even so, Porter never abandons the solid world of real objects for pure abstraction, and his desire to simplify seems to reflect more a Platonizing philosophy than a modernist one. He imagined pictures much as the Transcendentalists conceived of words, as "an abstraction from the natural world."[52] And like Thoreau, he relished synecdoche, the selection of a part to stand for the whole. Instead of panoramas, there are detailed studies of particular features, an obsession with abstract forms. His photos, that is, work best by reducing abundance to essences. Revealingly, there are no photos of the polar plateau other than along its mountain-shredded borders, and while one object will dominate a picture, only rarely is that object missing altogether.

Similarly, Porter's motivations reflect a curious mixture of old and new. He disavowed any "ulterior purposes," including conservation. "I photograph for the thing *itself*—for the photograph—without consideration of how it may be used." Documentation in the service of science is no longer adequate, nor will Porter allow his work to become simple propaganda. The modernist impulse justifies only "personal aesthetic satisfaction."[53] Yet the esthetic urge to photograph nature has clearly found a new moral imperative: an ideology of wilderness. Porter's esthetic interest in landscape merges with his conviction that Antarctica must be spared the travesty played out in Alaska. "Already," Porter mutters in his introduction, Antarctica is "threatened by the pursuit of natural riches that human beings have carried on almost since the beginning of their history—not merely to meet their needs but because of an appetite for wealth, the source of power over one's fellow man." Unless somehow checked, Antarctica will be "corrupted by trash and pollution."[54]

Here is a new moral perception of Antarctica, perhaps the only serious challenger to the Scott legacy. The wilderness movement in the United States, with which Porter had been associated, gave a moral urgency to Antarctica as another place to be "saved." It validated an artistic interest in landscape and natural objects. It is hard to conceive of an endangered Antarctica in the same sense as an endangered grove of redwoods or a not-yet-overrun-by-tourists Baja California. This most wild landscape on Earth is, for humans, also the most predictable and artificial. The Platonizing Porter—almost Emersonian in seeing Antarctica as a saving wilderness—misses completely the dark reductionism of The Ice. But the wilderness ideology justified his interest in Antarctica, and his attention to natural objects spares the book from being too painterly and his vision of Antarctica from becoming too precious. The contrast between the photographer Porter, aboard the research vessel *Hero*, and the sealer Nathaniel Palmer, first captain of the original *Hero* after whom the ship was named, quietly informs the whole book.

In terms of sheer volume, however, no imagery of Antarctica can match aerial photographs. Without any artistic intention aerial photogrammetry introduced a new perspective on the Antarctic landscape. Some of the trimetrogon images taken during Operation Highjump, for example, are almost Escheresque in their effects. But appropriately, it was IGY that made possible perhaps the most important visuals of Antarctica: satellite imaging. For the first time it was possible to see Antarctica whole, to have its outlines bounded, to overcome the distortions of the surface. In what was almost a parody of pop art—Warhol's "I am a machine"—the satellite *was* a machine, a platform for cameras. It could frame the icescape in its entirety and see wavelengths of light that the human eye could not. False color imagery further enhanced the abstract figurations of Antarctica, and although false coloring had been designed to improve the information content of images, its visual effects were as dramatic as those of a Fauvist painting. If art was information, as the pop propagandists held, then no human artist could cope with the torrents of encoded data that came back from remote sensing platforms. Here was no precious image, no overextended sculpture designed to frustrate museums, no piddling monument of earth art: this was the Earth as modernist landscape. No modernist or postmodernist could match The Ice for coolness.

Whiteout: The Esthetics of The Ice

An alliance with modernism didn't happen, although it might have and might still. The exploration of Antarctica and the creation of the modernist syndrome proceeded in tandem, and by the time the interior was being seriously surveyed, modernism had become an official culture. The esthetics of modern art could accept the abolished perspectives, abstract geography, and simplified iconography of Antarctica. The Antarctic ice-scape realizes perfectly Joseph Stella's dictum "What you see is what you see." The total reductionism of the ice sheet mimics Barnett Newman's insistence that "it is only pure Idea that has meaning. Everything else has everything else."[55] The source regions are self-referring to a degree unrivaled by any other landscape on Earth. The pictorial and literary possibilities are there, and some esthetic is necessary if the full potential of The Ice as a cultural and intellectual problem is to be realized. Here is an opportunity for modernist adventure. What is lacking, apparently, is a compelling reason to go. While science has worked avidly to assimilate Antarctica, modernist art has, by and large, ignored it, preferring the synthetic landscape and the landscape of introspection. Only a handful of works have attempted abstract or conceptual treatment of Antarctica.[56]

One reason, of course, is the relative geographic inaccessibility of Antarctica. Travel inland from the coast almost always means dependence on some national science program, few of which support artists, preferring instead to hire photographers to document activities. The U.S. program, for example, insists that an artist must be "well established," must have plans to "show the resulting works to an audience of significant size," and must avoid work that is "excessively abstract, or not recognizable as having come from the Antarctic." Clearly, this is hardly an invitation for modernist art, but the National Science Foundation is not the National Endowment for the Arts, and its criteria for the application of public monies for public purposes are hardly out of line. Even so, "few artists ask to go."[57] There are other sources of funding (the artists of the heroic age usually performed other roles to justify their participation in an expedition), and a visit is hardly essential to make Antarctica a subject of artistic inquiry. The problem is less the physical inaccessibility of Antarctica than, ironically, its conceptual distance. Instead of making a direct contribution to the images of Antarctica, the liberation of art from its former conventions has found indirect expression through a more experimental journalism.

From the time it examined the new worlds unveiled by the Renaissance voyages of discovery, Western art had thrived on information. Exploration and science both set in motion an information explosion that challenged the mind and the senses; and it had been the role of the illustrator and the artist, as it was of the scientist, to process that information. Again and again, the challenge was not simply that the information was novel but that it was abundant. The information base of Western civilization grew, and art coped with—indeed thrived on—that explosive growth. The process did not abruptly end with modernism. Rather, new devices were promoted by which to cope with abundance. With abstraction, modernist art discovered a means by which to distill and express ever more information; with multiple principles of organization, it had a pluralism of artistic styles that could expand experiences; and with the belief that the morality of art resided in the process of being an artist, not in the material objects an artist produced, it found a way to avoid choking on the sheer quantity of information available to its civilization. In the nineteenth century it was still possible to fill up a landscape with replicas of all the objects in the scene, with discrete packets of information. By the twentieth century, this endeavor inevitably distorted, then destroyed, that system or any system which sought to absorb every datum. No canvas—no museum of canvases—done in representational style could hope to contain the information available. Modernism sought different means of processing that information flow—not simpy the quanta of actual data, but the whole process by which data were produced. Even pop art and its offshoots did not attempt to dispose of information, which they celebrated to the point of idolatry, but only to redirect art toward the largely unexplored information content of the synthetic landscape.

But Antarctica presents special problems. It is already abstracted, minimalist, conceptual. Here is not another case of

information overload but of underload. The Ice has already filtered and reduced the landscape to the simplest environment on *Literature*
Earth. So minimal is the information content of the ice sheet *and Art*
that the very notion of information as structure, as negative
entropy, becomes difficult. The iceberg is a densely textured
message; the polar Plateau, a study in inert uniformity, the absolute disinformation of absolute zero. The only color is the aurora of the polar night and the bleached blue sky of the austral
day; everything else involves tints of black and white. Apart
from stratiform clouds, furrows of sastrugi, and an indistinct
horizon, there are no forms or figures. Viewed from the ice or
the air, the ice sheet is only a flat surface, an almost isotropic
plane. Everything is abstract and invariant. Optical displays are
rigidly prescribed by mechanical laws of optics. The range of potential scenes and experiences is restricted, the degrees of freedom in the scene limited. The classic images and sages of Antarctica are so overpowering because there is nothing else to compete
with them.

Yet information is not solely inherent in the material world: it
is created by the mind. The complexity of an object resides not
wholly within itself but in the complexity of the ideas the object stimulates in the mind of the observer. There is a hierarchy
of information content to the ices. Some terranes are denser and
more accessible than others. Those terranes that display the
sharpest and most abundant contrasts, that produce more information for less energy, are the most attractive. This abundance
disappears toward the polar plateau. In a sense, the information
content of even the interior ice sheets is infinite or at least unbounded. Yet there is more information in a single penguin than
in all the polar plateau. In the same way that transfinite numbers allow a hierarchy of mathematical infinites, so natural systems may offer a hierarchy of infinite information bases. The
Ice is the simplest of these systems. Increasingly, the contrasts
that make the plateau meaningful do not reside in the structure
of the scene: the observer brings them to the scene. Information
is not to be picked up, like specimens of birds or rocks, or recorded by representational images; it becomes a dialectic between idea and ice.

At its source, The Ice is the sum of its negations. It is meaningful only in terms of its contrast to other landscapes. A civilization rich in information, full of esthetic traditions and landscape arts, will see much in the polar plateau because it can

bring much to it. Such a civilization can contrast what is in the scene with what the mind says ought to be there or can be there. In the case of the plateau, so lean is the obvious information content that the surface becomes an almost perfect reflector: its information albedo is high. Its information content is the result not of extraction so much as reflection. The more that is brought to the surface, the more it radiates back. The Ice compares by reduction, and its comparisons end in negation. Much has to be brought to this information sink so that something may be taken away.

Some episodes in modern art resonate with the character of Antarctica and suggest how an esthetic for The Ice could develop. Consider some of the early work of Robert Rauschenberg. There is nothing to·suggest that Antarctica was a subject or even an inspiration for them; they originated in the internal evolution of the modernist esthetic, the reaction of painting to painting. But Rauschenberg's all-black and all-white paintings (1952) and his erased de Kooning (1953)—created while IGY was being planned—curiously anticipated the esthetic questions of Antarctica that IGY would indirectly pose. All-white paintings had been a staple of modernist art since Malevich executed his. Rauschenberg's works, however, went beyond experiments in coloration. The white paintings were intended to be a receptacle, a sink for shadows or other events to act upon— not a bad expression of The Ice. The companion black paintings, with their intention to create complexity without revelation ("that there was much to see but not much showing"), parallel the esthetic problem of the polar plateau.[58] The de Kooning episode is even more instructive. The incident occurred at a time when de Kooning was a reigning guru of abstract expressionism, a movement that imagined itself as the apex of Western art. Rauschenberg decided to erase a de Kooning drawing. This was not vandalism but a creative and symbolic act. Accordingly, it required the participation of de Kooning, who eventually agreed. Rauschenberg laboriously erased the entire picture and framed the result.

The picture itself is nothing but a white paper with a frame and a title. Without the story behind its creation, it is meaningless, at most a joke or an exercise in guerrilla theater. The success of the picture depends on what the viewer brings to it. The "painting" is a negation, and its significance varies with the magnitude of the negation. The more associations one brings to the surface, the more intense its negation and the richer its meaning. It is much the same with Antarctica. Inexorably, The Ice erases all the normal expectations of a landscape. What remains is so sparse, so stripped of sensory impressions, that it can hardly be witnessed as a landscape at all. Only someone, or some civilization, that approaches it with a complex tradition of landscapes and art can invest enough in the scene to generate information out of it. There must be a confirmation before there can be a negation. The polar plateau becomes a great negation of landscape—actively erasing the normal lines of information and passively reflecting back the shadows of its observer.

*Gustave Doré, scene from Coleridge's "Rime of the Ancient Mariner" (1878).
There are elements of hope—here, as the poem opens—with the solar arc and
the white bird, but the ship is clearly entering an ice Hades. Compare the
gloom and allegorical mood with Edward Wilson's "Discovery" with Parhelia.*

William Hodge, The Ice Islands *(1773). The scene was, Hodge notes
approvingly, "drawn from Nature." Reproduced from James Cook,* A Voyage
towards the South Pole, and round the World.

Frank Hurley, Pushing against a Gale. *Two members of the Mawson (Aurora) expedition fight the ceaseless blizzards of Cape Denison to get ice for use as domestic water—a nice photographic expression of Hurley's philosophy of naturalism. Courtesy Mawson Institute for Antarctic Research.*

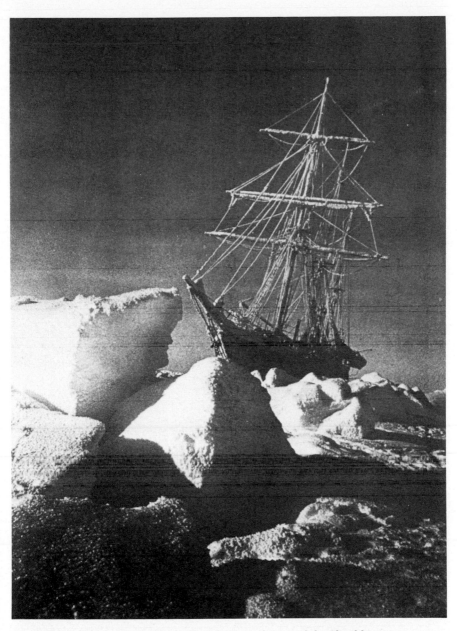

Frank Hurley, Endurance. *The extraordinary odyssey of the Shackleton expedition began when its ship,* Endurance, *became trapped in the pack of the Weddell gyre. Here the ship fights a pressure ridge—another vivid testimony to the world as struggle. Unlike its crew, the ship was eventually crushed and sank. Courtesy National Gallery of Victoria.*

Herbert Ponting, the Terra Nova *seen through an ice cave. One of Ponting's most popular photographs, it has everything the typical Antarctic scene lacks—perspective, a frame, picturesque objects of human interest. Courtesy Scott Polar Research Institute.*

Herbert Ponting, portrait of Captain Titus Oates and C. H. Meares. Most of Ponting's portraits show their subject with a prop suitable to his assignment. In this case, the two men are in the stables. The subdued light from a blubber stove overcomes the difficulty of photographing outdoors in the Antarctic summer, when there is too much light. The effect is a powerful evocation of interior moods, of character. Courtesy Scott Polar Research Institute.

Edward Wilson, "Discovery" with Parhelia. From the first Scott (Discovery) expedition. The scene has organization, perspective, a varied foreground, and a sense of confident rationality that contrasts perfectly with Doré's rendition from the "Ancient Mariner." Courtesy Scott Polar Research Institute.

Edward Wilson, field sketch of parhelia over Ross Ice Shelf, November 14, 1911. Drawn while Wilson was en route to the pole on the Terra Nova expedition, a journey from which he never returned. Note the use of a pony and sledge. Courtesy Scott Polar Research Institute.

Emil Schulthess, the Byrd Traverse Party, an overland caravan on the polar plateau. The tractors give a linear organization to the scene, and the solar halo provides a dramatic perspective. Courtesy Emil Schulthess.

Emil Schulthess, The Axis of the Earth at the South Pole. *This photograph was taken with a fish-eye lens suspended from a tall tripod, with the lens pointing downward. The camera is visible in shadow, and in the lower right corner is the shutter release. The picture has an abstract, self-referential quality that is heightened by the geographic inscriptions along lines of longitude. Courtesy Emil Schulthess.*

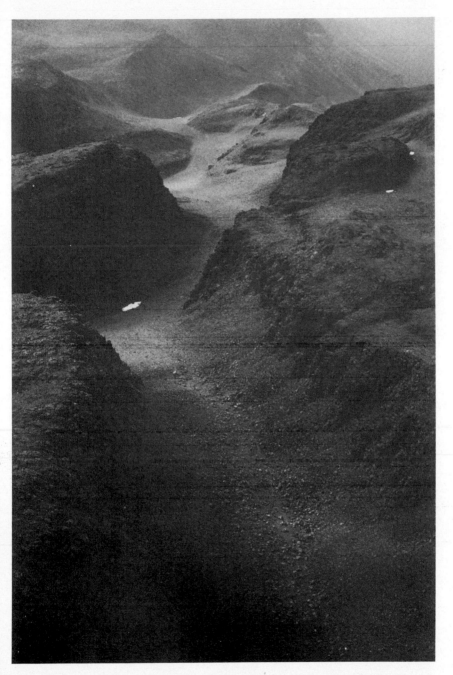

Eliot Porter, Labyrinth, Wright Valley. Old channels—long since abandoned by ice and water—make an abstract but romanticized pattern in the Dry Valleys. Courtesy Eliot Porter.

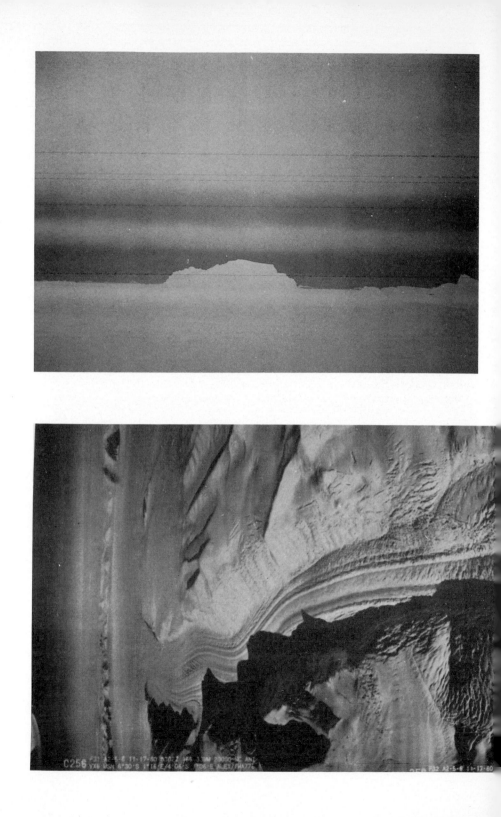

Eliot Porter, Iceberg, Ross Sea. The vigorous linearity of the picture quickly identifies it with much nineteenth-century American painting, but the stunning emptiness of the scene conveys a twentieth-century message. Courtesy Eliot Porter.

Glacier, Transantarctic Mountains. A composite of three photos (trimetrogon) taken as part of the photogrammetric mission of Operation Highjump. The effect of even simple representation, however, is profoundly disorienting, almost Escheresque. Courtesy U.S. Geological Survey.

The Dry Valleys from space. Even in this—the largest of the deglaciated oases—LANDSAT conveys a sense of the valleys as little more than a precious enclave in a vast ice field. Courtesy U.S. Geological Survey.

The Glacier

We have now traversed nearly one hundred miles of crevassed ice, and risen 6000 ft. on the largest glacier in the world . . . and we have an extended view of glacier and mountains. . . . These mountains are not beautiful in the ordinary acceptance of the term, but they are magnificent in their stern and rugged grandeur.

> —Ernest Shackleton, *The Heart of the Antarctic* (1909)

The mighty glacier opened out before us, stretching, as we could now see, right up from the Barrier between the lofty mountains running east and west. It was by this glacier that we should have to gain the plateau. . . .

> —Roald Amundsen, *The South Pole* (1912)

The ice field rises and shreds into a mosaic of mountain and glacier, like a mixture of planets, all rock and ice, among stars.

It is the smallest, the most fragmented, and most Earthly domain of the Antarctic ice field. As an ice terrane, the glacier is transitional. Geographically, it exists not as a coherent ice terrane but as a multiplicity of scattered ice masses. Some ice masses join ice sheet to shelf and tongue; others exist as systems without a direct link to the larger ice terranes. Historically, the glacier occupies an unstable equilibrium between mountain and ice sheet. During episodes of major glaciation, the ice sheet thickens and overrides its mountain impediments; the glacier disappears as a distinct system. During interglacials, the ice sheet thins, local glaciers become more prominent, and some locales may become relatively ice-free. Esthetically, the glacier contributes to, but does not define, the character of The Ice. Because of its association with mountains, it introduces a new level of complexity and contrast to the ice field. Ice is proportioned rather than absolute.

Ice interacts with rock. In some places mountain ranges effectively dam the continental ice sheets, forcing ice to drain through selected passes as outlet glaciers. In other places, mountains act as collectors of snow, sustaining alpine glaciers. Such mountains are outcrops, as valuable as Moon rocks, from the geology of a subglacial continental landscape nearly as distant as another planet. And in a few places, the mountains are sufficiently elevated and massive to black out locally the fringe of the ice sheets. The result is a startling inversion, a rock oasis. Anywhere else on the planet such enclaves would be celebrated for their glacial displays. Local glaciers lattice the mountain flanks and form ice deltas in the valleys. Periglacial phenomena abound. Features like these caused a North Atlantic island to be named Iceland, but in Antarctica the oases are considered ice-free sanctuaries. The processes of The Ice are locally and temporarily reversed; the terrane does not acquire a cohesive unity but fractures into an archipelago of ice masses; the scene is shaped by periglacial as much as glacial processes.

The outcome is a stunning inversion: a reduction in the size and singularity of ices means a diminution in the power of Ice reductionism. There are more colors, forms, patterns, and information in one such system than anywhere else on the continent. The ice of the glacier experiences a variety of motions second only to that of the iceberg, and it acquires a host of internal and surface structures only approximated in number and variety by the shelves that receive and eliminate them. The geologic information content and the ice information content of the terrane are high, and the two exist in immediate contrast.

Here—poised in equilibrium between sheet and shelf—the proportions are humanly absorbable. As a glacier, ice can be mentally assimilated in ways that The Ice as a whole cannot. Instinctively, it is to these oases that humans are drawn. Systems of understanding developed elsewhere on Earth work best here, where there are a geology, a terrestrial biology, a landscape. Here, where The Ice is temporarily in remission, its utter alienness is reinforced. The other ice terranes contrast ice with ice or ice with sea. The glacier starkly pits ice with land. At their best, the ice terranes of the glacier and the pack show similar mosaics—the pack, between sea and ice; the glacier, between land and ice. As the pack introduces the shelf, so the glacier introduces the sheet.

The mountains are beacons of familiarity amid the icescape, points of reference for the earth sciences and welcome icons for estheticians. They were also natural corridors, geographic points of entry and egress to the polar plateau. A few of the early explorers, such as Mawson, reached the polar plateau directly by climbing the slope of the ice dome, but most entered it only through the great outlet glaciers that poured through the Transantarctics; and even Mawson first reached the East Antarctic plateau through the outlet glaciers of Victoria Land. It is perhaps the best way. The mountains are the icy Pillars of Hercules that announce entrance to The Ice, and the outlet glaciers are the Sibyllic gateways to the underworld of the Earth.

Glaciology of the Glacier

The glacier collects, transports, and dissipates ice. As a physical system, it miniatures the processes of the entire ice field. Everywhere in the system there is some wastage and some aggregation, but the general budget includes a zone of net accumulation, where snow and ice are gathered, and a zone of net ablation, where that mass is lost. The classic sources of glacial ice are snow, freezing rain, refreezing meltwater, ice condensed directly from the vapor state, drift snow, and avalanches. The processes that govern ablation include melting, sublimation, calving, wind erosion, and the removal of snow by avalanches. The geographic dividing line between these two sets of processes marks an equilibrium line altitude (ELA), the ideal plane where accumulation and ablation are momentarily balanced. Below this line the glacier is composed of glacial ice; above, it is composed of snow, firn, and ice lenses of various origins superimposed on glacial ice. Glacial dynamics describe the movement of ice from accumulation to ablation zones.

The ice moves like a frozen river. No other ice mass is subjected to such vigorous stress fields or exhibits so many deformations. In small glaciers such as cirques, a solitary basin can contain both accumulation and ablation zones. In valley glaciers, the ice flows outside its originating basin, not unlike the outflow of a river that drains a lake. The outlet glacier, however, is more characteristic of the Antarctic. It represents the reduction of a complete dynamic system to a means of transport between ice terranes: the accumulation zone is an ice sheet, the ablation zone an ice shelf or ice tongue. This is less a glacier, in the classic sense, than a temporary change of state in an ice sheet. Its size, not its intrinsic complexity, makes the outlet glacier impressive.

The stuff of the glacier is ice and sky—fine ice crystals and trapped air. To these constituents may be added minor salts, microparticles of dust, and more substantial debris picked up during transport. The glacier shows a varied composition because of the way in which these materials are deposited and the complex metamorphoses they experience during transport. The transformation of snow into glacial ice is analogous to the transformation of sediments into rock. There are geochemical peculiarities that depend on the special properties of ice and thermodynamic simplifications that result from the fact that unlike rocks, which consist of ensembles of minerals, glaciers contain only ice and air. Lithification involves primarily densification. Molecular diffusion, particle rearrangements, mechanical deformation under changing stress fields, settling and sintering, and mass transport of water by sublimation and condensation all operate at slightly different times and rates to encourage the metamorphosis of snow crystals and trapped air into a tough ice fabric called firn, and firn into glacial ice. As lateral motion, not simply vertical settling, proceeds, new stress fields act on and reconstitute this ice fabric.

In general, firnification rates increase with warm englacial temperatures and with the presence of meltwater. Where ambient temperatures are near freezing, snowflakes are large, snow is heavy, and snow falls in great quantities, the process by which ice crystals are converted into glacial ice speeds up. In those environments in which surface snow can melt, percolate through lower layers, and refreeze, metamorphosis is rapid. With increased stress, ice grains and air bubbles tend to segregate. Simple glacial ice evolves into ice slates, ice schists, and ice gneisses—contorted bands of blue ice alternating with stripes of white ice.

These internal structures only reflect a complex external structure. The ice mass as a whole is shaped into a confined flow; it is stretched, compressed, and sheared. Sheet flow becomes stream flow. Part of the flow occurs as internal deformation—from processes of plastic flow, creep, and regelation. The polycrystalline structure of the ice fabric initially resists stress until, over time, the fabric recrystallizes with new glide-plane orientations, better suited for the prevailing stress field. Englacial temperature is an important variable. Part of ice flow, too, takes the form of mass movement—by kinematic waves, a mass transfer analogous to the passage of a flood wave, and by basal sliding, the displacement of the glacier as a whole while it is lubricated by films and streams of basal meltwater. Accordingly, glaciers creep, flow, and surge.

Since velocity is proportional to the net loss and gain of mass, high rates of accumulation and ablation are required for high rates of flow. The greatest velocity occurs at the ELA, and flow lines there will be parallel to the glacier surface. Above the ELA, in the accumulation zone, flow lines tend to move downward—both down into the ice and downhill. Stress is tensile, flow is characterized as extending, and the rate is known as the submergence velocity. Conversely, in the ablation zone, flow lines tend to move upward toward the glacier surface as well as downhill, and it is appropriate to speak of compressive stress, compressing flow, and an emergence velocity. In the case of cirque glaciers, the flow lines show a rotational movement centered about the ELA. To these movements, however, there are resistances—the opposing surfaces of bedrock sides and bottom.

Along the flanks shear stress builds up, crevasses form, and the rate of flow is slowed. Basal motion may be more complicated because of the presence of meltwater. Thus the center of the glacier moves more rapidly than the edges, the top more rapidly than the bottom, and the rate of flow at the ELA is greater than the rate at either the accumulation or ablation zones.

Because ice does not respond to a change of stress instantaneously but deforms as a plastic solid, the process is spasmodic, and there are lags to any change within stress fields. Movement is never smoothly continuous but is a series of unsynchronized jerks. Glaciers respond differently to the same event, and a given glacier may respond to innumerable events with a different response time for each. The scale of ice mass becomes significant. A small glacier may respond within 3–30 years; the Antarctic ice sheet, on a scale of 5,000–10,000 years. In addition, local glaciers have no other ice terranes to buffer them, while outlet glaciers are modulated by ice shelf and ice sheet. Under such conditions equilibrium is a transient phenomenon. The various processes work at different speeds, with different lag times; different tributaries contribute different amounts of ice to a glacier, so that the glacial stream consists of ice ribbons of different velocities; different events, which are responded to in different ways and with different lag times, move the glacier beyond the status of a physical system to that of a historical document. This variety of motions, actual and preserved, also promotes a great abundance of glacial structures and shapes.

To this flow of ice the confining rocks offer resistance, and between them force and resistance sponsor a host of deformation structures. Under intense compressive stresses, the ice folds and buckles; glide planes within the ice fabric take on a preferred orientation; ogives sculpture the glacier into wave terraces; transposition occurs as folds tighten, foliated layers thin, and stratigraphic layers are rearranged. Under tensile or shear stresses, the ice simply fails, resulting in an ice fault. The faulting may be normal, as around ice falls; strike-slip, as along crevasses; or organized as thrust planes, as around such impediments as termini and moraines.

When the failure results from tensile stress, however, the ruptures form crevasses, the dimensions of which depend on ice velocity, density, and temperature. Crevasses vary in width from hairline fractures to rifts several meters wide and in depth from a surface break to chasms 30 meters deep. The cold, dense ice of

Antarctica supports the deepest crevasses on Earth. Since the
informing stresses compose a field, crevasses tend to occur in patterns. Chevron crevasse fields collect along the margins, transverse crevasses form across the glacier, splaying crevasses develop from longitudinal fractures that are rotated by down-glacier flow, and radial splaying characterizes the glacial snout. Combinations are legion, and fast-moving glaciers, glaciers traversing rugged topography, and glaciers composed of multiple ice streams of differing velocities will be choked with shear stresses and a nearly universal grid of crevasses. In places, the ice and the stress field interact to form large surface features—crevasse chasms, ice pinnacles (seracs), ice falls, ice-stream flow lines, and buckle folds. Among ice masses only the glacier rivals the iceberg for variety.

The Antarctic glacier, however, is a simple glacier, and the compexity of the glacier terrane is in some ways an aberration. Compared to the petrology of rocks, the petrology of the glacier is naive. Compared to the glaciology of glaciers in subpolar and temperate regions, that of the Antarctic glacier is unsophisticated. Accumulation and ablation proceed slowly. Virtually all ice derives from snow or atmospheric ice crystals, and wastage is dominated by iceberg calving and sublimation. As a consequence of the absence of melting or ablation other than calving, the ELA resides near the glacier terminus. In this polar desert the quantity of snow decreases sharply inland, the size of snow crystals diminishes, and the density of snow decreases. There is little melting. Firnification is retarded, flow sluggish, and in the general absence of basal meltwater there is little opportunity for true glacial surging. Antarctic glaciers tend to be dense, cold, thermally invariant—perpetually frozen from bedrock to surface. Only in special cases do they exhibit either surface or basal melting. The Wilkes Glacier, which experiences a little summer melting, makes the transition to ice nearly ten times as rapidly as the ice sheet at Vostok, deep in the polar plateau, where melting never occurs. Yet such melting is atypical—restricted to areas of the coast, to portions of the peninsula, to rock oases, to the lower reaches of coastal outlet glaciers such as the Lambert and Rennick, and to those locales where exposed rock warms enough to induce local melting.

What makes the terrane fascinating is the relative variety inherent in the glacier as compared with the ice shelf and ice sheet. Considering the geologic processes that could go on in these mountains if they were located anywhere else than at the poles, the glacier is a simple system. The mountains, too, would be more complicated landscapes were they not in competition with, and intermittently buried by, the ice sheets. Compared with other glaciers the Antarctic glacier is almost ingenuous. The apparent surging behavior (or velocity) of large outlet glaciers is most likely a result of the peculiar function of these glaciers as conduits from the ice sheet.

Rather, what excites the mind is not the Antarctic glacier but its larger context. The vast uniformity of the ice sheets and ice shelves is fragmented; ice and earth can interact much as sea and ice can in the terranes of the pack and the berg. The presence of dynamic ice masses makes the mountains far more interesting than mountains in a polar desert without ice, and the mountains give the ice stream a character it would never possess if it remained embedded within a continental ice sheet. Unlike bergs or floes, however, the glacier is constantly confined by rigid borders, so that any motion involves both internal deformation and the displacement of the ice mass as a whole. The character of The Ice is internalized. As with the pack and berg, too, the reductionism of The Ice is only abated, never completely absent: some glaciers are fed by ice sheet and empty into ice shelf, and all are influenced by katabatic winds; yet the juxtaposition of glacier and mountain makes the regional glaciology and geology, simple in themselves, more interesting. The segregation of the glacier from homogenous ice sheets, its external shapes (from wind-driven snow fields to transsectional systems of valley glaciers), its surface carvings (the result of deformation and erosion), and its internal structures all result from the fact that Ice does not overpower Earth, and they all account for the special identity and appeal of the glacier as an ice terrane. As elsewhere, the mountain makes the glacier. In most regions, however, it does so by providing a source of snow; in Antarctica, the mountain makes the glacier by interrupting the ubiquity of The Ice.

Nunatak: Antarctic Geology

In Antarctica the glacier is a geological no less than a glaciological system. It exists as a distinct ice terrane by virtue of the geological structure of the continent—the geography of its

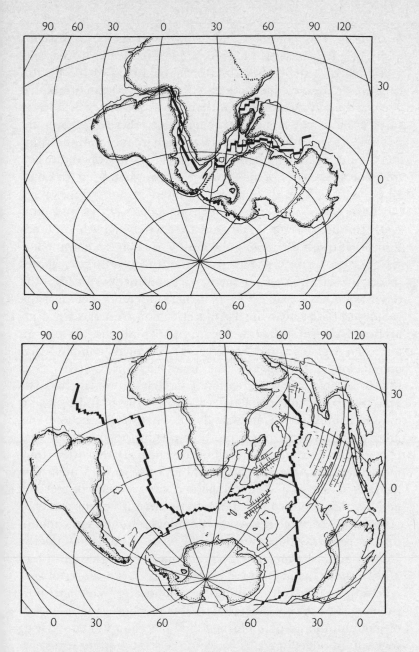

Antarctica and Gondwanaland. Top map shows the position of the Gondwana supercontinent circa 115 million years ago (early Cretaceous). Since then Antarctica has drifted toward the South Pole, where it has remained stable, while the other continents appear to raft away from it (bottom map). The critical event for the formation of an ice sheet, however, was the opening of the Drake Passage, which established the Antarctic circumpolar current. Redrawn, original courtesy University of Wisconsin Press.

mountains. The mountains, in turn, reflect the curious asymmetry of East and West Antarctica and the history of the Antarctic plate, which is apparently the cold core of the Earth's lithosphere. Knowledge about the rocky substratum of The Ice depends largely upon the less than 3 percent of the Antarctic surface that is not submerged beneath ice. These exposures are not large geographically, but they are rich in information. Ironically, more is known about the geologic history of Antarctica from cores taken out of the Southern Ocean than from rock outcrops. Moreover, in this terrane ice interacts not only with ice but with earth—directly through glacial activities and indirectly through periglacial processes and wind regimes. The landforms that result are among the most varied on the continent.

Geology is history. The crustal structure of Antarctica shares its origins with the rest of the Earth's continents. Yet from the onset there has existed a fundamental difference between the geology of East (or Greater) Antarctica and West (Lesser) Antarctica. East Antarctica evolved from a continental shield, an ancient (Archaean and Proterozoic) basement complex that once belonged to Pangaea, the amalgamation of sialic rocks that broke up to form the cores of the Earth's continents. The first great rift fractured Pangaea into northern and southern masses, Laurasia and Gondwanaland. What would become Antarctica occupied a central position within the ancestral complex of Gondwanaland: it alone touched all the other fragments—South America, Africa, India, Australia, and New Zealand. Their shared Pacific border was an arena of tectonic activity that accreted new lands to the margins of the shields.

From this heritage the Antarctic shield retained some mountainous regions—the mountains of Queen Maud Land, Enderby Land, MacRobertson Land, and the American Highland and, in all likelihood, some of the elevated areas in the center of East Antarctica, such as the Gamburtsev Mountains, which are now submerged by the ice sheet. Each subsequent orogen, or episode of mountain-building, deformed and metamorphosed existing rock suites, added igneous rocks to the stratigraphic sequence, and enlarged the continental craton from an East Antarctic shield to a larger East Antarctica and a newly created West Antarctica. Each tended to cut across the boundaries of contemporary continental perimeters. The Ross orogen of the Cambrian-Ordovician age, which established the Transantarctic Mountains, coincides with the Adelaide orogen in Australia

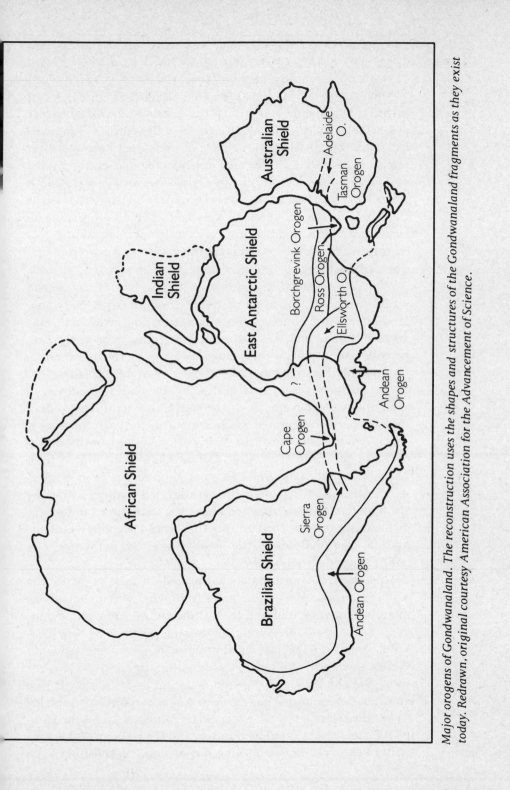

Major orogens of Gondwanaland. The reconstruction uses the shapes and structures of the Gondwanaland fragments as they exist today. Redrawn, original courtesy American Association for the Advancement of Science.

and perhaps with the nebulous Pan-African event. A second orogen, probably peaking during the Devonian era, affected Australia, Tasmania, New Zealand, and Antarctica. In Antarctica, where it is known as the Borchgrevink orogen, it is best manifest by a fragment of mountains added to the distal corner of Northern Victoria Land. In Australia the episode is referred to as the Tasman orogen. A third major orogen, known collectively as the Gondwanide orogen, affected the entire Pacific margin of Gondwanaland during Permo-Triassic times. In South America it is known as the Sierra orogen, in South Africa as the Cape orogen, and in Antarctica as the Ellsworth orogen. These events, which involved a prolonged series of thermal and geotectonic activities, began the creation of West Antarctica and signaled the breakup of Gondwanaland.

That disintegration proceeded in stages. It probably began with the slow rifting apart of a west from an east Gondwanaland, with South America and Africa spreading away from Antarctica, India, and Australia. In late Jurassic or early Cretaceous times, Africa then rifted away from South America, India pulled away from Antarctica, and some spreading occurred in northwestern Australia. By the late Cretaceous, a spreading ridge developed in the southern Pacific and Indian oceans, and as it migrated westward during the early Tertiary it controlled the breakup of the New Zealand microcontinent, India, and Australia. The New Zealand plateau separated from Antarctica in the late Cretaceous and from Australia soon afterward; Australia rifted away from Antarctica completely during the mid-Tertiary, India exited about the same time, and severe dislocations occurred in the area that would become West Antarctica. The final act in the breakup was the detachment of South America from Antarctica.

This involved more than what a modern map suggests, the simple translocation of a segment from what was a continuous mountain chain extending from Chile to the Antarctic Peninsula. The Andes, the Antarctandes, and portions of New Zealand constitute the last of the major orogens, the Andean, which assembled the land mass of Antarctica into its present form. But the Drake Passage did not form by a simple rift in a continuous mountain chain joining Andes and Antarcandes. Instead, the tectonics of the Scotia plate more resembles the complex history of the Caribbean plate, and the geology of the Antarctic Peninsula shows it to be not a simple extension of the

Andes but a similar, yet distinct magmatic arc of Mesozoic and
Cenozoic age that differs in tectonic style. The history of the West Antarctic microplates is further complicated by the apparent staggered subduction of a spreading center during Eocene and Miocene times. The segregation of Antarctica from South America, complicated by the tectonics of the Scotia Arc, was completed during the Oligocene or early Miocene, 16–17 million years ago. The event inaugurated the Antarctic circumpolar current.

But if the relationship between the peninsular mountains and the Andes is complicated, the relationship between West Antarctica and East is even more baffling. The differences between East and West are profound and the link between them uncertain. In nearly every geophysical trait they differ. The crustal thickness of East Antarctica, for example, is significantly greater than that of West (35–40 versus 25–30 kilometers). The Ross orogen, epitomized by the Transantarctics, divides the two Antarctics geographically and structurally. The boundary between the Transantarctics and West Antarctica shows major discontinuities of crustal thickness, gravity, and magnetism and is probably traced by a large fault. East Antarctica shows a continental composition, building upon a Precambrian shield. West Antarctica reveals a more active history and a more recent stratigraphic column. Its basement complex is not Precambrian but consists of Paleozoic, Mesozoic, and Cenozoic rocks accreted to the Antarctic segment of Gondwanaland as a magmatic fore-arc terrain. Virtually all of East Antarctica was in place before the start of the Gondwanaland breakup, with the exception of some igneous intrusives that were probably generated by the fragmentation. Most of West Antarctica dates from events subsequent to the major suntering of Gondwanaland. The volcanics so characteristic of West Antarctic rock suites continue to the present day with such active volcanoes as Mt. Erebus and Mt. Melbourne.

Though it has experienced perimeter growth, East Antarctica is essentially a single continental craton, easily inserted among the contemporary fragments that once made up Gondwanaland. By contrast, West Antarctica is the great anomaly in the reconstruction of Gondwanaland. The Antarctic Peninsula does not fit readily anywhere. In place of a single, more or less homogeneous craton, West Antarctica may be composed of as many as three (or more) microcontinents, a mobile mosaic of plates that have accreted, rotated, and translated their positions over time. A large fault rift apparently segregates the plate which encompasses the Antarctic Peninsula and Ellsworth Land from the Greater Ellsworth plate, which contains the land between the Ellsworth and Whitmore mountains. In addition, a large subglacial basin probably parallels the boundary between those two plates and the Marie Byrd Land plate. The most reasonable history is one that places the Ellsworth to Whitmore chain of mountains within the Transantarctics and posits a much reduced peninsula as a Gondwanaland appendage to it. During the Ellsworth orogen, either this region fractured into separate plates (or microcontinents) or a single Greater Ellsworth plate split into at least three large blocks under the impress of vast crustal extension. Either way the entire region was stretched, translated from East Antarctica to West, and rotated perhaps 90 degrees. The fragments that comprise the West Antarctic mosaic have thus moved strenuously relative to one another and to East Antarctica.

Except where mountains protrude through the ice sheets, the contemporary surface of Antarctica is a vast, gently sloping ice plain. The subglacial topography is something else. Even East Antarctica is far from a peneplainal shield. Completely buried beneath the ice sheet, for example, are the Gamburtsev Mountains, two large block-faulted massifs, intracratonic basins (Wilkes and Aurora), and pronounced trenches, perhaps a failed rift valley. Between these features, so far as remote sensing can tell, there are plateaus and plains, many carved by fluvial or glacial erosion prior to the advent of a permanent ice sheet. West Antarctic is yet more rugged, almost an island arc system. Were its ice sheet removed, most of East Antarctica would lie above sea level. Portions of the Wilkes Basin would likely be flooded, but the craton would retain its unequivocally continental features. Much of West Antarctica, however, would be submerged. In combination, a deglaciated West and East Antarctica would not appear to be unlike Australia and the large islands of New Guinea and Indonesia. What welds West Antarctica together—and to East Antarctica—is the ice sheet. The presence of ice shelves reduces further the asymmetry and irregularities of the two Antarcticas. The Ice makes the continent.

Ice, of course, dominates the more recent geologic history of Antarctica. In the McMurdo Sound area, the onset of glaciation, crustal bending from the weight of glacial ice, and massive glacial scour and alternative offshore deposition are the prominent geological events. Where volcanism continues, it does so within a glacial environment; hyaloclastites typify volcanic rock. The geomorphology of the area—where any rocks are even exposed—is controlled by glacial and periglacial processes, the advance and retreat of the ice. But the effects go far beyond local circumstances. The weight of the ice sheet has continental, even global consequences, and a symbolic no less than a physical meaning. The complex geology of Antarctica is replaced by the simpler glaciology of its ice terranes. Rock exposures seem little more than interludes among the ice or misplaced glacial erratics; except at nunataks and oases, geomorphology becomes meaningless. The Ice simplifies, abstracts, and removes from the realm of common-sense understanding.

Its ice cover is more than a veneer for Antarctica: it is a powerful geologic and geophysical agent. Soviet geologists have suggested a mechanism whereby the ice sheet promotes crustal rifting by a combination of crustal deformation, which increases temperature, and ice insulation, which preserves high temperatures in the upper mantle. As part of an attempt to explain the unusually high number of continental rift features, the mechanism suggests that, should the ice sheet collapse suddenly, the continent itself could disintegrate into blocks. More certain is the isostatic adjustment of the Earth to the weight of the ice. The Earth itself is deformed, flattened by its ice burden. The magnitude of this effect, noticed by tracking satellites in polar orbit, gave rise to the description of the planet as slightly pear-shaped. Were the ice cover removed, two competing processes would restore the land to a more normal continental elevation: isostatic rebound would raise the continental land, while the melting of the ice would raise sea level. Paradoxically, its ice makes Antarctica the lowest of the continental land masses and the highest of continents.

Antarctica is the most seismically quiescent of all the continents. In its geology no less than its oceanography and meteorology, Antarctica is apparently a cold core of the Earth. Within the context of the Antarctic plate, the Antarctic continent is positioned at some distance from the rifts and spreading centers that define the plate boundary. That boundary surrounds the continent like its seas and air masses; it is a kind of lithospheric convergence. Plate motion is relative, but it makes more sense to consider the Antarctic plate stable and to have the African, South American, and Pacific plates move away from it than vice versa. Consequently, the Antarctic, as Walter Sullivan observes, is the "pariah among plates—the one from which all others are fleeing."[1] No large earthquakes have been reported within the Antarctic plate, and minor quakes are about ten times more abundant in West than in East Antarctica. Most seismic activity relates to icequakes—to ice motion rather than earth motion. Though its fossils testify to an ancestrally subtropical locale, Antarctica has been a polar continent since the early Tertiary. But not until its complete isolation, with its rupture from South America, did it begin to acquire the ice that now defines it. It became a cold sink, converting liquids and vapors into solids, exchanging heat and motion for cold and immobility, and transforming Earth into Ice.

The actual expression of this transformation depends on the relative proportions of ice and mountain. The most extensive mountain ranges, the Antarcandes and the Transantarctics, have the most glaciers. In some places, notably portions of the Antarctic Peninsula where the mountains are isolated from the main ice sheets, the ice terrane is dominated wholly by local glaciers. The higher temperatures and greater moisture of the west side of the peninsula make it more active than the east side, and some ice masses here show the properties of temperate glaciers. On the east side, lower temperatures encourage the development of ice piedmonts and ice shelves, ice fringes and ice cliffs. In other regions, such as the Prince Charles Mountains, which are surrounded by the East Antarctic ice sheet, the mountains do little more than channel major ice streams, and the tallest peaks toward the interior barely rise through the ice sheets into nunataks, like rock pyramids lost amid a snowy Sahara; local glaciers are dwarfed by the ice sheet. Intermediate in scale are the outlet glaciers—ice streams that drain interior ice sheets through deep mountain valleys.

The Transantarctic Mountains, in particular, display the entire kaleidoscope of ice masses that comprises the ice terrane of the glacier. Where the ice sheets of East and West Antarctica meet, the range is virtually submerged beneath ice, a tiny atoll of nunataks that merely channels ice streams. An ice divide connecting east and west ice sheets even passes transversely across the summit of the range. As the ice sheets thin slightly toward the Ronne and Ross ice shelves, isolated mountains such as the Dufek Massif, the Pensacola Mountains, and the Ohio

and Wisconsin ranges develop ice caps on their plateaus, local
cirque glaciers on exposed rocky enclaves, and small valley glaciers to drain the cap; these mix with the major ice streams that surround them. Further north, flanked on one side by the East Antarctic ice sheet and on the other by the Ross Ice Shelf, the mountains display a mixture of local and outlet glaciers. The Reedy, Scott, Amundsen, Shackleton, Beardmore, Nimrod, Byrd, and Mulock glaciers are prominent, fast-flowing outlet glaciers by which the East Antarctic ice sheet breaches the mountains. Of these the Byrd is the largest, discharging more ice annually to the Ross Ice Shelf than all the other outlet glaciers combined. The entire terrane, however, is mantled with snow and ice that form local glaciers or that simply slough off into larger accumulation basins. Beyond the Ross Ice Shelf, local glaciers begin to dominate the scene. The mountains thicken toward Cape Adare, the ice sheet thins, and the continent bends away from the range. There are outlet glaciers: the Ferrar, Wright Upper, Taylor, Mackay, and Mawson. But the local glaciers, their névés well supplied with snow, are abundant and varied. Some of them are tributary to outlet glaciers or ice shelves; some end in independent ice tongues; some form piedmonts; and some, in the famous Dry Valleys, exist as complete, self-contained systems.

Thus ice and rock interact in the Antarctic mountains with a variety of effects. The glacier scrapes, plucks, erodes, and reshapes the rocks that contain it. Striations, grooves, polished surfaces, friction cracks and gouges, roches moutonnées, potholes, and plucked surfaces are all the rock-preserved products of glacial movement. Erosion is concentrated within ice falls, where plucking can be most intense, and within the shear zone of the glacier, where ice and rock mix to produce a rough abrasive and where shear planes can act differentially on rock debris and protuberances of varying sizes. Along with other materials that the glacier simply transports, the eroded debris must be deposited. Most is organized along the perimeters of the glacier, as lateral and terminal moraines. Where there is basal meltwater, fluvial processes can combine with glacial processes to produce such landforms as eskers, kames, kettles, outwash plains full of moulin and coarse debris, ice-dammed lakes, and intermittent streams. As ice moves down a river valley, it widens the gorge into a broad, U-shaped landform.

There is evidence of all these features within the glacier ice terrane of Antarctica. Most of it remains buried by ice. What is visible represents past, larger glaciations that crossed over the mountains, then subsided to their contemporary levels. Just as a flood leaves a high-water mark and debris to mark its passage, so the ancient glaciations have left behind striations, grooves, sites of plucking, boulder erratics, and pockets of drift. Where substantial areas have been momentarily deglaciated, the whole spectrum of glacial and fluvio-glacial landforms may be present. But the cold glaciers of Antarctica are typically frozen to their beds, and rock oases are rare. The glacial geomorphology of Antarctica is powerful not because of its diversity and accessibility but because of its purity and continental dimensions.

So, too, with periglacial landforms—an aura of ice-related features that envelop rock exposures of all dimensions. Where soils exist, the landforms are poorly developed, slowed by the dryness of the Antarctic atmosphere, the unremitting cold, and the absence of vegetation. Ground is perennially frozen. Where water penetrates, it becomes permafrost—lacing the soil crust with needle ice, ice lenses (segregated ice), vein ice, intrusive ice; organizing the loose detrital mantle into geometric patterns and the internal mix of soil and ice into involutions; and when melted, generating a variety of collapse features. Frost wedging (or shattering) applies the expansive power of ice to break rocks apart along jointing and other sites of weakness. In some cases, the result is weirdly eroded bedrock piles, known as tors; in others, the debris is carried away by glaciers; and in still others, it is piled up beneath cliffs in ramparts of talus, or in stratified slope deposits, or in stone-banked lobes and terraces that testify to mass movement; or where ice, topography, and talus permit, it forms rock glaciers. The degree of slope, size of debris, and vigor of the freeze-thaw cycle determine whether gelifluction, frost, slope wash, or block creep dominate as geomorphic processes, and whether polygons, stripes, sorted steps, or ice-debris flows become the characteristic microrelief. Frost heaving leads to patterned ground features in which the seasonal expansion and contraction of ice veins, which are themselves organized into geometric shapes, gradually segregate ground debris so that large debris collects in the depressed vein. Among the features that result are large and small sorted circles, sorted polygons, sorted stripes, debris islands, and stone pavements. Frost creep moves talus and soils downslope. Moraines, whether active or dormant, typically feature ice cores. Even disorganized snow patches have geological consequences, and so-called nivation processes include stone pavements and ava-lanches. Debris exposed by deglaciation or lowered sea level will soon be reworked by periglacial processes.

The scene is impressive. The sharp, angular rocks, dark with color, contrast with the more plastic white and blue ice. The glacier is the most contorted of ice masses, its shape the product of active deformation, not (as with the berg) the outcome of erosion. There is even a component of life to the scene. Lichens occupy many rock exposures, especially those not far inland, so that some maritime influences can be seasonally felt. Endo-lithic cyanobacteria burrow into porous rocks. And on ice that does undergo some surface melting, cryoalgae—red, yellow, green—can blossom briefly. Since most of the mountains border coastlines, they have interesting ensembles of meteorological processes—some influenced by the ice sheets, some by maritime air, and some by local circumstances of heating. Under the un-blinking sun of the austral summer, the exposed rock warms; local melting can occur along the snow-rock fringe; and in cer-tain locales, perennially frozen lakes have been reported at the junction of mountain and glacier. Powerful katabatic winds sweep off the polar plateau through the mountains, scouring, shaping, and sublimating snowfields. The interaction of wind and peak creates a turbulent regime—made more so as seasonal maritime flow inland interacts with local topography and off-shore katabatics. Out of these processes come special ice masses, including ice cornices, wind scoops, and ice scoop avalanches.

Yet the scene, so startlingly complex for Antarctica, is rela-tively ingenuous compared to other regions of the Earth. The cold Antarctic glaciers are simpler glaciologically and geologi-cally than their subpolar and temperate counterparts: they have less mass input, less mass loss, and less activity. They exist under a cold environment more uniform and extensive than any other; the surrounding environment, with which the ice terrane must interact, consists of other ices. Within this polar desert the freeze-thaw process is poorly developed; fluvial ac-tivity is restricted as nowhere else on Earth. Except in special places and certain times, sublimation replaces melting, and the abundance of glacial and periglacial land features—rich by the standards of an icescape—is poor in comparison with processes in Norway, Alaska, or Tibet. The microbiosphere of Antarctica has more in common with Mars than with Earth. Only in the oases, which are strange enough by Earthly standards, is there a geology that can match the complexity of Antarctica's glaciology.

Oasis: The Dry Valleys

Rock oases constitute a minuscule fraction of Antarctica's geography. But they are opulent with information, they harbor a terrestrial and lacustrine biota, and it is at the oases that humans naturally congregate. The oases differ from simple rock outcrops, nunataks, and clusters of mountain peaks: their scale allows them to reverse the radiation balance typical of the surrounding ice and to establish self-reinforcing processes that permit the environs to remain at least partially free of ice. Yet the connection with the informing ice sheets is never severed completely. At times, the ice sheets advance across the oases; at other times, ice expansion and retreat influence the patterns of moisture that dictate the magnitude of local glaciation; and katabatic winds, which pour off the ice sheets, are among the most prominent mechanisms for removing snow before it can develop into ice. Paradoxically, the ice sheets are a source not of accumulation but of ablation.

The inversion that Ice works on Earth is here itself inverted, though the outcome is not to return the landscape to a preglacial condition so much as to transform it into a netherworld that is vaguely but not quite an icescape and almost but not quite a landscape. This most Earthly of Antarctic scenery is, in reality, among the most alien of Earth landscapes, of a piece with such Arctic islands as Svalbard, Novaya Zemlya, Pearyland (Greenland), and Iceland, which fringe Earth geography. But the isolation of the Antarctic oasis is more complete; the geology of the Antarctic oasis could be transported to the polar regions of Mars without dissonance, and its microorganisms could pass for an exobiology. That the Dry Valleys appear familiar testifies to the metamorphosing power of The Ice, to which the exposed rocks stand in harsh contrast.

Among the score of recognized Antarctic oases, only half a dozen are significant. The Bunger, Vestfold, Amery, Ablation, and Grearson oases all occupy sites along the coast. The Dry Valleys are etched out of the mountains of South Victoria Land. Collectively, the oases account for 1/2,000 of the total surface of

Antarctica. In every case, ice sheets that once covered the areas
have retreated to the perimeter of the contemporary oasis. Mountains have risen, the ice sheet has lowered, outlet glaciers have diverted the main ice streams away from the site. Once delivered from glacial ice, the triumph of ablation becomes self-reinforcing: the exposed surface warms sufficiently during the summer to melt off winter snows, and katabatic winds blow away and sublimate snowfall. An order of magnitude larger than any other oasis, the Dry Valleys epitomize the Antarctic oasis, exhibiting a gallery of geologic features and processes without parallel elsewhere on the continent. When these features are combined with the volcanics of the offshore Ross Island (Mt. Erebus), it is as though Iceland had been set down amid the Transantarctics.

Ice abounds, and the scene is rife with glacial and periglacial phenomena. Ice sheets and ice shelves border the region. Local glaciers—alpine, cirque, valley, and piedmont—drape down mountainsides, block off valley entrances, and abut sea ice. Permafrost and ice lenses underlie the soil, and ice wedges core the various moraines. Lake ice frosts the permanent ponds that join, like an icy chain, the otherwise disjunctive outlet glaciers. Precipitation takes the form of snow. There is no process that does not connect to ice, no landscape feature that does not depend on the ancient and present distribution of ice. Ice is the universal presence, dictating its principles of reductionism and preservation. The Dry Valleys are a geochemical tomb.

Yet the oases exist within another context, that of The Ice. Consequently, an equilibrium between glaciology and geology, ice and rock, appears to put ice into remission. In any other Antarctic ice terrane, there is only ice. In the Dry Valleys there are competing landscapes and competing geomorphic processes that act on rock as well as on ice. The valleys have been glaciated and deglaciated several times; flooded with seawater and locally with meltponds, swept by ferocious winds, frozen to bedrock and subjected to meltwater streams or groundwater percolation. The upshot is a spectacular anomaly. The oases are as foreign to Antarctica as Antarctica is to the Earth.

The Dry Valleys contain a good sampling of glaciers and glacial landforms. The glaciers form self-contained systems; they accumulate on the mountain ridges and ablate in the valleys, spilling into the valley floors like icy deltas fringed with spectacular ice cliffs. Most of the ice wastes away through sublimation, some by dry calving. Most landforms, however, are relics of bygone eras when the valleys were flooded with ice and when, on occasion, there was some meltwater to shape glacio-fluvial features. The valleys themselves are classically U-shaped and asymmetrical troughs, scoured by ancient glaciations. With their decorative pattern of striations, erratics, and roches moutonnées, the valleys show evidence of glacial erosion; with moraines of all sorts, they show signs of glacial deposition.

The moraines are almost all ice-cored, some with fresh ice from active local glaciers and the rest with relic ice. The ice coring is extensive enough to significantly inhibit soil development. In some cases, the moraines and hummocks grade into rock and even into sandy glaciers, of which the valleys have over thirty examples. In others, the moraines temporarily dammed the meltwaters and sediments of retreating glaciers, generating deltas and mantles of loose debris. From meltwaters, far more prevalent in the past than at present, there are kames, eskers, river terraces, meander scars, ice-wedge furrows and levees, and even relic-pitted valley trains—all evidence of Antarctic sandars, the outwash plains of glaciers. They form down-valley from glacial snouts or below hanging glaciers. The continent's largest streams—intermittent and braided—flow through the valleys, reworking older deposits. The Onyx River in the Wright Valley flows over 30 kilometers through moraines, terraces, lakes, and a sequence of valley-train features.

Even more active than proglacial processes are the peri-glacial. Permafrost is ubiquitous, and wherever talus and out-wash debris collect, there is patterned ground. In the Dry Valleys a hierarchy of polygons can be found, with larger polygons (containing the largest stones) enclosing smaller polygons with progressively smaller stones. Frost heaving helps transport stones to the surface, and the formation of ice veins and ice lenses helps sort them into shapes. The ice inclusions have a history, as interstitial ice fragments evolve into ice wedges and an ice core. The process resembles the conversion of snow to glacial ice, except that rocky debris takes the place of air bubbles, and expansion-contraction cracks replace crevasses. Polygons and stripes mechanically inscribe designs onto barren till and al-luvium. Because the valleys are too arid, the active layer, un-like Arctic permafrost, does not freeze; water *qua* water does not survive long. Winds strip the surface clean of all but larger stones—desert pavement.

If not rapidly moved, debris is quickly broken down. Frost
wedging disintegrates exposed rocks. Frost cracking—caused by the differential heating of boulders produced by the intense solar radiation of the austral summer—mechanically fragments large detritus into small. The absence of water slows frost action; but an abundance of salts, and the process of salt crystallization, more than compensates. The valleys are enclosed basins, without a drainage outlet. Precipitation and glacial runoff collect, evaporate, and leave a residue of mineral salts. Some salts derive indirectly from the ocean, through the medium of precipitation; others, through various geochemical separation mechanisms that segregate selected cations from limited surface and groundwaters. Salt production is high, and winds constantly redistribute the salt. Perhaps the most spectacular example of salt-assisted weathering is the cavernous erosion of granite erratics—lumpish shapes like rock bones in a desert or an outdoor sculpture garden of modern art.

In place of fluvial or glacial transport there are eolian processes and mass movement. Gelifluction and frost creep move debris downslope, assisted by the permafrost surface, which functions as a permeability barrier and allows debris (and even, in some locales, groundwater) to seasonally move across it. Gelifluction lobes and sheets form near sources of moisture, such as glaciers, though these sources are necessarily ephemeral. Fresh talus and rock blocks, as well as reworked outwash debris, move downslope. If organized by a contiguous core of ice, they may form a rock glacier.

Across everything in the Dry Valleys sweeps the wind. Eolian processes abrade and deposit, and everywhere the wind influences geomorphology by desiccating whatever landscape it passes over. Katabatic winds, rushing down the polar plateau, warm as they descend through the trough valleys, sublimate snow and ice, abrade exposed rocks, deflate outwash plains of fine debris, and establish pebble dunes, transverse sand dunes, and whalebacks. Where the sand intercalates with ice, ice-cored dunes are formed. Especially in winter, the winds scour the rigid rock surfaces of the valleys and rework their mobile sedimentary sites. The power of the winds to sublimate is total; their power to abrade, awesome. The winds blow fine debris away, leaving a desert pavement of large stones. Blown sand abrades the stones themselves into ventifacts, the polished facet invariably facing toward the plateau from which the winds come. Small boulders that protrude above the surfaces of their stone embedments will be gradually sheared off. Even on the lee side, there are eolian effects. The arid winds promote the desiccation of the upper surfaces of the rock; as the moisture leaves, geochemical processes encourage a veneer of iron oxides—desert varnish—to coat the surface. Boulders are thus selectively varnished, abraded, striated, pitted, spalled, and fractured.

Among the most surprising features are those made from water. There are a number of sources, though none are more than intermittent: snow, glacial meltwater, permafrost, buried ice. Most of the solids sublimate rather than melt, but in exceptional years some melting can occur; most glacial melting is restricted to protected areas of the sides or top of an ice mass. Water, of course, is extremely sensitive to temperature. During the summer the unending insolation, exposed dark rocks, and warming winds combine to induce at least some selective melting. A few intermittent streams can flow, the longest being the Onyx River in Wright Valley, before they enter playas and saline lakes. Most of the discharge is from groundwater, where the flow is shielded from the winds. But even the simple melting of ice-cored debris can produce a pseudokarst (thermokarst) environment of collapse features and deranged drainage—of melt dolines, tunnels and caves, sinking streams and dry gullies, subsurface flow, springs and natural bridges, knob and kettle topography. The regolith is already broken; once the ice cement is melted, the debris can wash, creep, or waste away. Where circumstances are favorable, the permafrost is not monolithic but fractured into frozen and temporarily unfrozen parts—ice aquicludes and sandy aquifers—that maintain a weak groundwater system. Collectively, these flows sustain an array of lakes and ponds.

The lakes are among the great puzzles of the Dry Valleys. Some depend on glacial melt for sustenance; others, on underground flows or a mixture of sources. The lakes are highly saline, rigorously stratified according to density, and perennially frozen. An exception, tiny Don Juan Pond, is unfrozen most of the year; but it occupies the only known Antarctic occurrence of groundwater discharge from a confined aquifer, and it sports a unique mineral, antarcticite (a hydrated calcium chloride). The source of the lake salts is equally baffling. Some of the salts are relics of an earlier era in which seawater invaded the valleys. A few lakes, those characterized by sodium chloride, apparently derive their salts from concentrated glacial meltwater and precipitation. But the calcium chloride lakes have dense brines unrelated chemically to adjacent lakes or to meltwater streams that enter them. Moreover, the lakes may be chemically layered, with each stratum possessing a different chemical constituency. The best explanation is that their waters derive from ground flow, and that the peculiar dynamics of groundwater recharge and discharge in an unendingly arid and frozen landscape leads to a geochemical separation process that delivers the salts to the lakes.

The frozen surface layer of the lakes, 4–6 meters thick, is translucent. Light penetrates, and against all expectations simple forms of life thrive. Blue-green algae congeal into organic mats attached to the lake bottoms. Eventually, the mats fill with waste gases, segments rise and break off, melt through the surface ice, dry and blow away. There—on the valley floor— they join other microorganisms that, illogically, persist in the detritus of the Dry Valleys. Lichens are the characteristic terrestrial life form of Antarctica, and they are most abundant in the maritime coastal regions. In rock oases they disappear in their normal form. The Dry Valleys become a biological no less than a geochemical mausoleum. Their sterile soils contain a host of exotic microorganisms blown in from elsewhere that survive, torpid and comatose, without growing. Indigenous microorganisms include rare chasmoendoliths that live within the fracture zones of rocks, as well as cryptoendoliths—bacteria and lichens—that enter the porous subsurfaces of sandstones. The endolithic lichens are the most common specimens, survivors not because they have evolved unique biological adaptations but because they have discovered special niches, protected from the wind, in which they can live. Their total biomass is perhaps surprisingly high. But this remains a hugely simplified ecosystem, without higher consumers and predators. The lichens, too, are survivors of the last glaciation, which flooded the valleys with a succession of ices and waters. That life could survive such catastrophic changes encourages exobiologists to speculate that a landscape like that of Mars, once more favorably endowed, might have preserved life in ways similar to those apparent in the windswept deserts of the Dry Valleys.

For their relative complexity the Dry Valleys can thank the present state of ice-sheet recession. More earth is revealed here than in all the other rock exposures of Antarctica combined. A rock, which consists of a suite of minerals, is always more interesting than an ice mass, which consists of a single mineral, no matter how complexly deformed. But there is also the matter of history: the geomorphology of the valleys derives not from a single episode or process but from several. Many of the features are vestiges, only partially reworked, of past glaciations. There appears, initially, to have been a phase of local, alpine glaciation. Eventually this succumbed to (and perhaps helped establish) a general ice sheet which overrode the mountains at least twice, gouged the valleys into glacial forms, and flowed cross-grained at least once to the trend of the valleys and ridges, abrading the north valley walls and plucking the south valley cliffs. Yet this connection was pinched off. The old outlet glaciers, Taylor and Wright, were largely sustained by a local accumulation dome, and the entire Dry Valleys region became susceptible to the dynamics and history of the West Antarctic ice sheet and its floating appendage, the Ross Ice Shelf. The East Antarctic ice sheet came to contribute to the valleys indirectly—through its general influence on Antarctic climate and its katabatic winds, not through its ice. As the outlet glaciers receded, there were extensive glaciofluvial processes and lacustrine formations; stagnant ice and ice-cored moraines dammed glacial melt into lakes.

With the recession of the ice sheet, there occurred a rise in sea level; more expansive open seas encouraged greater precipitation, which enhanced local glaciation; marine water invaded the Dry Valleys, forming ice-covered fjords. As the West Antarctic ice sheet waxed and waned, the Ross Ice Shelf saw its grounding line advance and retreat. At maxima the grounded ice entered the valleys. It reshaped debris at the mouths so that the valleys became enclosed basins, higher at their heads and mouths than at their centers. At the same time the expansion of the grounding line to the margins of the continental shelves shut off an important source of regional moisture. Local glaciation predominated, and the network of alpine and piedmont glaciers that now frames the Dry Valleys became established in quasi-equilibrium. The Ross Sea synchronized local and regional glaciation. When the sea was open, local precipitation increased; when the sea was iced closed as a result of major glaciations, local precipitation decreased.

There is no escape from The Ice. The Dry Valleys exist in un-

certain equilibrium between the two great ice sheets of Ant- 233
arctica, and they are alternately shaped by the preeminence of *The*
one or the other. At present, neither is powerful enough to in- *Glacier*
vade the region: the East Antarctic ice sheet cannot swell over
the Transantarctics, and the West Antarctic ice sheet is safely
grounded across the Ross embayment. Instead, a milder ice regime, the glacier rather than the sheet, and a smaller scale of
ice, local rather than continental, shape the valleys. The significance is apparent when one compares a local glacier like the
Meserve in Wright Valley to one of the East Antarctic outlet
glaciers such as the Byrd, which breaches the Transantarctics to
the south.

The Meserve Glacier is one of a series of alpine glaciers that
decorates the flanks of Wright Valley. Sustained by snowfall ultimately derived from the moisture reservoir of the open Ross
Sea and organized as a cirque, with a tongue that extends partially downslope, it exists in rough equilibrium, displaying an
ice budget that is perhaps slightly positive. At its maximum, the
ice is about 80 meters thick, more commonly 30–50 meters. The
glacier is cold, frozen to its bed. It moves slowly, at a pace of
15 millimeters per day. Its basal structure consists of two zones:
clear ice, with a velocity near zero, and a layer of amber (dirty)
ice that is sandwiched between a bedrock of ice-cemented rock
debris and the clear ice. The dirty layer consists of moulin and
salts, and it moves with a basal velocity an order of magnitude
greater than that of the clear ice. There are cavities around the
large boulders caught within the basal debris; some of the cavities are filled with soil-like materials and others with sublimation ice crystals. Among ablation processes, sublimation dominates (55 percent). The ablation zone is surrounded by exposed
rock that heats well during the summer. There is some melting,
though only 2–3 percent of ice (water) that is lost escapes in a
liquid state; 40 percent is evaporated.

Abrupt ice cliffs define the glacier sides. The margins consist
of hard, semirigid ice that acts as a retaining wall, buckling the
surface back up the glacier and undergoing occasional dry calving. Sedimentary layers of snow, firn, sand, and dust—creating
a nonhomogeneous strain field—fold into ogives; and trains of
ogive waves, like mountain terraces, shape the glacier's longitudinal profile. A part of the local hydrological cycle, the Meserve Glacier does little if any geologic work. It exists because
water can survive long in the Dry Valleys only as ice. Among

the ice masses of Antarctica, it is a potted plant, a species of decorative art.

Not so the mighty Byrd Glacier. The difference is one not simply of scale but of importance in the overall dynamics of The Ice. The Byrd Glacier is a synopsis of the entire ice terrane. In ice dynamics, it embodies a series of rapid transitions: from ice sheet to grounded ice stream (glacier) to floating ice stream (tongue) to ice shelf. Flow converges as the ice is drawn from the névé into the glacier. As the flow passes through its confining rocks, it is stretched, sheared, warmed by friction, and softened by strain. It is uncoupled from its sides, then ungrounded from its base. As it enters the ice shelf, flow decelerates and diverges, an icy delta spreading into an ice lake. The larger flow of the Ross Ice Shelf then shears off the stream, directing it southward as a more or less definite flux embedded within the shelf. Tensile stress dominates the transition from sheet to stream, compressive stress characterizes the transition from stream to shelf, and everywhere lateral shear stresses transform the ice surface into a collage of crevasses and pinnacles, ice blocks and rifts that extend to sea level. Brash ice collects in some of the fracture zones and sea ice congeals on the base; the entire panorama of ice terraces is gathered into one wildly deformed, miniaturized package.

The Byrd Glacier moves about 25 percent of all the East Antarctic outflow that enters the Ross Ice Shelf. The characteristics of that flow, however, are determined not merely by the enormity of the ice sheet that feeds it but by the entire complex of ice terranes that the glacier connects. There is ample evidence that the East Antarctic ice sheet here, as further north at the Dry Valleys, has overridden the Transantarctics and that the direction of this flow was determined by a significantly higher ice dome, so that the ice passed cross-grained to the preestablished ridge and valley system of the mountains. The Byrd Valley was occupied by an ice sheet, not an ice stream. More recently, the last glaciation saw little growth in the East Antarctic ice sheet but considerable enlargement of the West Antarctic ice sheet and the grounding of the Ross Ice Shelf. As the floating ice shelf converted to a grounded ice sheet, it thickened; it pushed into the Dry Valleys and caused outlet glaciers, such as the Byrd, to slow and swell in their lower reaches. The dynamics of the ice sheet crept upward into the Byrd ice stream. When the grounding line retreated and the Ross Ice Shelf assumed its present con-

figurations, so did the Byrd Glacier. It became a grand ice cor-
ridor to the polar plateau. Unlike the Meserve Glacier—almost
quaint in a rocky sanctuary, its connections to the informing
ice sheets indirect—the Byrd Glacier dramatically proclaims
the universality of ice sheet and ice shelf, reducing nunataks
and arêtes to rocky litter and the Transantarctics to the status
of a moraine. The glacier, as straight as a sluice; the rock
nunataks, like navigational beacons; and the ice falls, the point
of transformation from ice sheet to ice stream, all point inward
to the Source.

A Gallery of Earth Art: The Esthetics of Glaciers

The glacier abruptly compresses and reshapes the esthetics of
The Ice. For this ice terrane there is no single esthetic characteristic. A single glacier may include a spectrum of esthetic qualities, and multiple glaciers can steadily transform landscape into
icescape. For this ice terrane as a whole there is no single esthetic characteristic; appearances vary according to the relative
proportions of ice and earth. In the Dry Valleys, impressions are
generally dictated by the local geology. Ice masses shape and
frame the scene only indirectly: this is landscape, analogous to
the rift valleys of Iceland or the frosted desert mountains of the
Great Basin. In the high névés of Victoria Land, mountain and
glacier exist in a kind of scenic equilibrium, the esthetics of
icescape and landscape in counterpoint. At the Portal, where
the polar plateau and the Transantarctics meet, ice dominates
the scene. Every vestige of Earth progressively vanishes beneath
the ice sheet.

Overall, the effects are often startling without being unique,
unique without being overwhelmingly impressive. No esthetic
characterizes the scene wholly. Where one looks for landscape,
the ice interrupts with white voids. Where one looks for icescape, the rock fractures the surface into a broken ice-mirror.

Nussbaum Riegel, Wright Valley, might at first sight be any
range of arid mountains. The rocks and landforms are utterly
exposed, providing structure, texture, color, perspective. The
Nussbaum Riegel—a small plateau elevated above the more pre-
cipitous valley—even provides that rarest of Antarctic phenomena, a vantage point. A single panorama can encompass all the

elements of Antarctic geology and glaciology. There are mountains to all sides, the Kukri and Asgard ranges within the Dry Valleys and distant Mt. Erebus across McMurdo Sound; glacial and periglacial landforms, in a rich tapestry of history and shapes; the ice masses that comprise the glacier ice terrane; and hints of the ice terranes that here come together—the glacier, the pack, the shelf, and the sheet. Glacial action has shaped or scratched rock surfaces into Earthly pictographs. Detrital surfaces are organized into patterned ground, regolith counterparts to the atmospheric optics that geometrize the sky. When the sea ice that fronts the mouth of Taylor Valley breaks up, it does so in polygonal blocks. Ice and soil pattern the ground; ice and water pattern the sea; ice and light pattern the sky. Cirque glaciers drip down the valley sides like white and blue stucco, and valley glaciers spill into the valley floor like daubs of ice on a rock palette. Lakes splotch blues, whites, and greens across a brown and yellow drabness. High translucent clouds screen the sky; fluffy cumuli, pumped with moisture from the open Ross Sea, pile up above peak and glacier. Angular mountains mingle with soft clouds, tangible rock with abstract snow.

It is an impressive display of near-alpine esthetics. Its colors, warmth, intricate perspectives, and endless shapes make this environment instinctively attractive. Yet the scene palls and ultimately disappoints. The expression *dry valleys* was first applied by Shackleton to the great oases of Victoria Land, then revived by the Rymill expedition to describe smaller features in the Antarctic Peninsula. The scene reminded the Britons of Welsh valleys with their streams removed. Here, as always, reductionism is at work; the site is less interesting for what it contains than for what it lacks. In particular, the Dry Valleys lack many of those features that make alpine landscapes so interesting: water and life. They are utterly soundless and motionless. In Alaska, Norway, or the Alps, glaciers and mountains would roar with the seasonal sound of meltwater. The Dry Valleys scenery wants some features that are necessary to qualify it as truly alpine, and it lacks the essential element, ice, that it needs to become an icescape.

The reductionism of The Ice is incomplete and indirect: it does not lead to a new kind of scene so much as to an impoverishment of more familiar landscapes. The ice is fragmented into disjunctive masses. The rock facades are a stripped-down version of desert mountains. There is too much ice for the scene to

be typical of Earth scenery and too little for it to belong to the
Icescape. Compared to the polar plateau, the valleys appear to be an Earthly refuge, yet compared to Earth scenery they seem otherworldly. If the Dry Valleys are a respite from The Ice, they serve nevertheless as an introduction to exoesthetics. The channeled valleys, thermokarst landforms, rugged mountain and valley terrane, and windswept rock desert are an analogue of that most Earthlike of other planets, Mars.

Anvers Island, Antarctic Peninsula, is a classic scene: towering mountains and coastal glaciers, rocky coastline and rough sea, heavy cloud and broken sunlight. Ice drapes everything. It mantles mountainsides, spills into glaciers, spalls into ice shelves, bergs, and névés. Grounded bergs, blue as pale sapphires, mix with rocky shoals. Penguins, seals, whales, and seabirds crowd the scene with life and sound. Here the glacier is at its lowest profile and the mountains at their highest. Ice and snow are wholly local, contained within the island. Land, sea, and ice mix in dramatic proportions.

But there is little that is unique. The scene could pass for the northern fjords of Norway, Iceland, Greenland, or coastal Alaska. It is a remote land but not an esthetically alien landscape, a hostile environment but not an abstract one. The ice is a cover, not an informing principle. The scene is well suited for tourists who want enough spectacle to make it exotic but not the reductionism that would remove it from understanding. And to scenes like this the tourists go, but it is an aspect of the glacial ice terrane that, like the Dry Valleys, leads nowhere. Neither geographically nor conceptually do the glaciers of Anvers Island connect to the ice sheets or lead one, either glaciologically or esthetically, to the Source.

Evans Névé, in Northern Victoria Land, is a broad, irregularly shaped basin. It feeds a number of local glaciers and contributes, along with the East Antarctic ice sheet, to the giant Rennick Glacier. Around its perimeter is some of the most interesting scenery in Antarctica. Antarctica is most unique when it is most bleak and bleached, when ice and the Sun's savage light drain away all color, perspective, and shape. But Antarctica is most magnificent when, as around the Evans Névé, the purity and emptiness of those effects are modulated by the interaction of Sun, snow, rock, and wind. It is a mixture of the tough and the delicate, epitomized by mountain and cloud, rock and snow. Under the right circumstances, hoarfrost feathers new snow on mineral ice or on crusted firn into soft micaceous crystals that glisten iridescently.

Common snow is hard and granular, blown like desert sand into dunes and abrading the firn into cross-bedded textures. Glacial ice is the most contorted of ice masses, and everywhere away from the névé proper it is largely scoured of surface snow to expose powder-blue ice streaked with swaths of white bubbles, an ice marble. Snow collects within crevasses or adheres in splotches; the ice becomes a mirror of blue sky and white cloud or, where the crevasses form an organized field, a patterned ice. As a complex ice mass, the organized field is second only to the berg; but at the Evans Névé it is only a contributor to the scene, not a definer of it. There are other, less organized ices and other esthetics. As exposures warm, larger layers of fresh snow slough off as avalanches. Where the névé feeds glaciers, ice falls counterpoint nunatak with ice block. The smooth surface of snow—its undulations and contortions masked by the absence of perspective—is interrupted by crevasse fields, as though painted in heavy brush strokes. Katabatic winds from the plateau sweep around nunataks and exposed strings of mountain summits. Snow patches on rock sublimate into weird erosional sculptures, wind-scooped depressions of blue ice surround the peaks, and snow grains shape dunes.

The sky stratifies into shades of blue, forming a kind of continental iceblink. Near the horizon the sky rises in a light powder-blue, deepens to a royal blue, and ends overhead in a grim navy-blue as rich and empty as that of the Southern Ocean. The austral Sun circles the névé, throwing shadows from the peaks; refracts, when sufficiently low on the horizon, to bathe the scene in pinks, lavenders, and greys; dances a strange minuet with a ghostly Moon. But the great influence on the scene is the clouds. Northern Victoria Land experiences the same high stratiform clouds that are ubiquitous over the rest of Antarctica. But its proximity to the open Ross Sea seasonally encourages thick fogs of low cloud to rise up glaciers, and as mountains warm, moist air is raised and isolated piles of cumulus clouds collect over peaks. To the atmospheric optics and whiteouts that characterize icescapes, then, the Evans Névé adds an abundance of cloud forms, and with clouds, shadow. The shadows of peak and cloud give the surface a striped and

mottled appearance, modulating the intensity of sun and ice. At
one extreme, the névé has a lunar quality, a clarity and hardness of form and color like white steel, a topography of snow marias and rocky uplands. At the other extreme, clouds, shadows, textured snow, and dark peak break up the singularity of the scene and evoke a soft, enchanting mood, glassy rather than adamantine. The scene is minimal but not wholly abstract.

Similarly, the Evans Névé bridges the two ice terranes that define the region. Toward the coast, the névé becomes the glacier. With icefalls and ice streams it passes dramatically around nunataks and drops precipitously through the mountain ranges of two orogens, the Ross and the Borchgrevink. The scenery is wild and white, not unlike that which envelops Anvers Island. There is enough ice in the névé to move beyond a simple alpine or nordic scene, however, though not so much that all variety is lost to the relentless reductionism of The Ice. Meanwhile, toward the interior the névé threads slightly upward, through a tangle of increasingly separated peaks, to an indistinct frontier with the polar plateau. Clouds dapple the scene with grey shadows, confusing their color and shape with those of scattered peaks. A solitary nunatak marks the boundary with the plateau. Then nothing.

The Portal, in Southern Victoria Land, is perhaps one of the two most dramatic scenes of the glacial ice terrane. Both occur at the glacial termini. Where the glacier ends, where it looks out through ever more looming mountains across ice shelf or ocean, the scene resonates with the esthetics of mountains, glacier, shelf, and sometimes pack. Ice provides a platform from which to see features that are not wholly ice; one surveys complexity from a site of simplicity. The spell of The Ice is momentarily interrupted. But the spectacle faces away from, not into, the ice source.

Not so the conjugate panorama, at the site where the glacier forms. Reductionism unbalances the scene. The definition of the rock-confined glacier is exchanged for the diffuse presence of the sheet. At the Portal, which is situated along the border between the Transantarctics and the polar plateau, ice from the plateau is funneled through ice-fall amphitheaters into colossal outlet glaciers. Where mountains rise to significant heights, they form earthly ramparts that dam the ice sheet. On the interior side, the ice rises to the summits of the range. On the other side, as with all dams, the ice is far lower, spreading out in vast, quiescent lakes of windswept blue ice. The Portal proper occupies a broad breach in the mountains. To its south stretches the Skelton Névé, which partially nourishes the huge Mulock Glacier; to the north lies a mosaic of local glaciers and névés only slightly fed by the ice sheet.

There is little color, nothing but white snow and blue ice, buff rocks and blue sky. There are, at best, muted forms, and they dissolve across the threshold of the polar plateau. There is perspective and, if one views the scene from within the Transantarctics, there are vantage points. Toward the coast, the scene is a tangle of mountains and glaciers. Toward the interior, however, there is a vast simplification before the erasing power of The Ice. Yet the scene has a hidden complexity, here where ice sheet and glacier meet and metamorphose. Through its contributed ice and katabatic winds, the ice sheet extends its influence deep into the ice terrane of the glacier; in return, the mountains disrupt the flow lines and fabric of the ice sheet for some distance inland. But here is an undeniable border of ice terranes: the border between the final two distinct terranes in Antarctica, the innermost of the crystalline spheres that comprise The Ice. Across this frontier, there is no other.

Earth and Ice
The Earth Sciences in Antarctica

The geological features that these islands [Shetlands] present in those highly favored situations, where the continuous power of the winds has swept bare the rocks, correspond in a great measure with their desolate and dreary aspect.

  —James Eights, "Description of a New
    Crustaceous Animal" (1833)

The role of the Antarctic is a vital one . . . the shield of East Antarctica constitutes the "key piece" . . . around which, with wonderful correspondences in outline, the remaining "puzzle-pieces" of Gondwanaland can with remarkable precision be fitted.

  —Alexander Du Toit, *Our Wandering
    Continents* (1937)

Antarctica is not only a land for science but a land of science. Without the scientific revolution Antarctica would have remained unexplored. Science alone justified expeditions of discovery; the information brought back was cast into the sciences or was generated specifically by the sciences; and science directed the course of geopolitical no less than intellectual assimilation. In a sense, scientific exploration has not simply revealed Antarctica but created it. Eliminate those expeditions sent for scientific purposes and Antarctica would be no better known than Pluto. Strip away scientific concepts and the scientific lexicon and one is left literally speechless before the continent. The scientific establishment might well be sustained for reasons of national interest, a geopolitical compromise with motivations quite beyond the intrinsic pursuit of knowledge; but modern science remains the vehicle for the assimilation of The Ice, the means by which high culture of all sorts arrives.

Yet Antarctica was as much a challenge to the sciences as to other institutions of Western civilization. Some phenomena of scientific interest were unique to the polar regions or Antarctica. Expeditions would be mounted to study the aurora, geomagnetism, glaciology, Antarctic geography, the special dynamics of the Antarctic atmosphere and the Southern Ocean, and the nature of biological adaptations to the Antarctic environment. But the exploration of Antarctica began at a special time in the history of the sciences, and timing would condition the understanding of Antarctica. The voyages of Cook coincided with a transition in intellectual syndromes, an exchange of exemplars. Natural philosophy, which had informed the most dramatic products of the scientific revolution, would be challenged by natural history, which acquired an intellectual and social urgency. Between the voyages of Cook and the heroic age, the earth and life sciences—modern geology and biology— would achieve a theoretical and institutional synthesis equivalent to the one mechanics and astronomy had enjoyed earlier. The first scientist to see the region, James Eights, was a naturalist who reported on the organisms, rocks, and ice of the South Shetland Islands.

To this larger intellectual transformation, however, Antarctica remained peripheral. That the land was visited at all is a tribute to the escalating importance of natural history within Western civilization. But The Ice did not feature the kinds of data upon which natural history thrived. Terrestrial life was al-

most nonexistent; ice obscured rocks, mountains, landforms,
and fossils; there were no native cultures, and the only ruins of ancient civilizations were those a fanciful imagination pro- jected onto icebergs or writers of Gothic horror stories insinu- ated beneath The Ice. Antarctica offered, at best, an archi- pelago of rock outcrops, and such elementary questions as whether East and West Antarctica were physically coupled re- mained unanswered (or unanswerable). Scarcity, not intrinsic significance, made those limited exposures of rock enormously valuable. Yet as fragments of Earth structure and history, those mountain outcrops made possible an intellectual entry into the continent as fully as the outlet glaciers made feasible access to the interior plateau.

Nor was the south polar region fundamental to theories of the Earth: the relevant information and the important questions were apparently to be found elsewhere on the globe. Not until the earth sciences underwent another revolution, in metaphys- ics as much as in conceptual structure, did Antarctica become a central feature for geoscience. By then Antarctica was as valu- able an analogue for exogeology as it was for terrestrial geology and geophysics. Antarctica became a point of departure for the study of planets. What the Mediterranean and Baltic seas had been for maritime discovery and the interior of Europe for con- tinental exploration, Antarctica and the ocean floor became for the epoch of interplanetary science. Its cold lithic plate, sim- plified geomorphology, and hostile atmosphere made it a natu- ral terrestrial analogue for planets and moons composed of rock and ice.

Yet even as the evidence mounted for the multiple geophysi- cal connections that bound Antarctica to the rest of the Earth, the most important ligatures were those of thought. Science did not merely discover those processes that Antarctica and the Southern Ocean shared with the atmosphere, hydrosphere, and lithosphere; the act of doing science brought Antartica into the noosphere. The earth sciences, in particular, not only demon- strated the physical basis for the presence of The Ice on Earth but created many of the intellectual terms under which hu- mans could understand it. In this matter, as in others, The Ice was an information sink: the assimilation of Antarctica would require an enormous intellectual effort and the presence of a powerful information gradient, made possible by a highly devel- oped science. Too much in a class by itself to provide a general model of intellectual inquiry suitable for other topics, and too little endowed with information to become a scientific source, The Ice was nevertheless necessary to complete systems of thought in the same way that a heat sink complements a heat source to make a true thermodynamic system. The Ice would be a place to which scientific ideas would go, not a place from which they would come.

Theories of the Earth

The voyages of James Cook coincided with a revival of interest in Earth cosmology and cosmogony and with the resuscitation of a genre of scientific literature, the theory of the Earth. In France, the Comte de Buffon abstracted from his encyclopedic *Histoire naturelle*, especially its initial volume, *The Theory of the Earth* (1749), and revised it into the *Epoques de la nature* (1778). In Germany, Abraham Gottlob Werner published the manual of mineralogy, *Von den ausserlichen Kennzeichen der Fossilien* (1774), which became the basis for his general *Theory of the Origin of the Earth* or, as he preferred to call it, Geognosy. Immanuel Kant speculated on the origin of the Earth from an incandescent cloud of gas (1755), a theory given more precise mathematical and mechanical formulation as the nebular hypothesis of Baron Laplace in his *Exposition du système du monde* (1796) and *Celestial Mechanics* (1799). And in Britain, James Hutton wrote *Theory of the Earth* (1788, 1795), founding his theory on such processes as erosion and thermal metamorphism. Collectively, these were Enlightenment modernizations of a much-ridiculed genre of cosmology and cosmogony.

Yet these new versions were different, too. They operated not only against a rising tide of information but within a revised metaphysics of nature. They included new data from travel, discarded much misinformation (or, more properly, misplaced information), and recast the structure into a format more to the liking of an age of reason that delighted in codification and in the deductive analysis of great mechanical processes such as gravitation. What has been said of the *philosophes*—that they did not abandon utopian theorizing but simply built the old City of God out of more modern materials—was equally true for the new theorists of the Earth. Moreover, just as the political and social context of Enlightenment theories about the

state and society made the theories into programmatic mani-
festos for an age of democratic revolution, so the cultural context of these new theories of the Earth became fundamental to
a new perception of nature. Questions about the Earth acquired
a new intensity and significance for both popular and intellectual culture. There were new subjects, especially the domain of
geologic time; new principles of organization, all versions of
historicism; and new sciences, particularly geology.

Cook's voyages epitomize this transition. They began with
the international program to measure the transit of Venus,
the eighteenth-century counterpart to the IGY. They occurred
within a predominantly geographic and geophysical tradition,
a tradition of natural philosophy rather than of natural history,
though their inclusion of such naturalists as Joseph Banks and
Georg Forster would help change that. Their purpose was a mixture of novelty and skepticism, to chart new lands and seas
and to disprove, if necessary, the existence of such legendary
geographic phenomena as a Northwest Passage and a *terra australis*. Their use of cartography as a method for organizing
information was a quintessential expression from an age of
systematizers. Cook's maps parallel those other codifications
that typified eighteenth-century natural history: the biological
systematics of Linnaeus and the mineralogical systematics of
Werner. As Cook inspired other explorers to emulation, so Linnaeus and Werner animated a host of travelers to interrogate the
Earth in their name and to collect specimens.

But as much as anything, the purpose and character of the
voyages are encapsulated in Cook's use of John Harrison's chronometers to measure longitude. Those clocks are part of a tradition of geophysical measurement that has been fundamental to
Antarctic exploration, the antecedent to the magnetic studies
that motivated Ross and his cohorts and an anticipation of the
geophysical inventories and remote-sensing program of IGY and
its successors. Equally, the paired-pendulum clocks may be
taken as symbols of the Newtonian order that underwrote the
Enlightenment understanding of nature—a world of immutable
parts organized into complete hierarchies and of varied yet balanced forces. In natural philosophy, this perception was well
expressed by the Newtonian model of the solar system, in
which nature was dynamic but stable, a vast mechanism of
countervailing forces. In natural history, the ancient concept of
a Great Chain of Being attained its grandest expression. Accord-

ing to its informing principles of plentitude, degree, and sufficient reason, every object in the world formed part of a vast,
unbroken chain which joined that object precisely to all of its
subordinates, added some distinctive trait that differentiated the
object from those below it, and bestowed upon every object a
purpose. Nothing was lost and nothing was gained; nothing was
missing and nothing was superfluous. Moral philosophy, too,
was suffused with a belief in the permanence and benevolence
of nature. Just as planets revolved endlessly in their orbits, so
societies experienced cycles of change from degeneration to virtue and back to degeneration. Upon these perceptions were
constructed the principles of natural theology, the argument
from Design: that the presence of an intricate artifice was evidence of an Artificer; that nature shared in the morality of God;
that the Deity, although the ultimate creator, was removed from
the ordinary processes of nature and acted through secondary
causes such as the laws of mechanics.

This was the celebrated clockwork universe, a powerful analogy that underwrote nearly two centuries of intellectual endeavor, from the mechanics of Isaac Newton and Christian
Huygens to the theology of William Paley. The symbolic value
of the Harrison chronometers that Cook carried on his second
voyage, however, goes beyond this cosmic metaphor: they characterize a perception of time. Newtonian time was cyclic, like
the swing of the pendulum; immutable, between the act of
Creation and the final Conflagration; and reversible, lacking a
compelling direction. The instruments for measuring time—the
pendulum clock and the secular revolutions of the Earth in orbit—perfectly expressed this perception. In practical matters
these chronometers and concepts were adequate. There were no
questions in natural philosophy that they could not answer, and
with them the last conundrum of applied geophysics (the measurement of longitude) was answered. The Earth itself was reasonably young. In the seventeenth century, Newton and the
more famous scholar Bishop James Ussher calculated the age of
the Earth from the genealogies listed in the Bible. In 1650
Bishop Ussher arrived at the date 4004 B.C. as the time of Creation, with the Noachian Deluge coming in 2349 B.C. The Newtonian revolution in mechanics and astronomy had replaced
the vision of a closed universe with one of infinite space. The
complementary discovery of infinite time became a ruling in-

tellectual concern only with the revival of the theory-of-the-Earth genre in the late eighteenth century.

A new cosmology had been a consequence of the scientific revolution, and such philosophers as Leibniz, Descartes, and Newton had offered at least portions of one. But many others—among them Athanasius Kircher (1664), Thomas Burnet (1681), William Whiston (1696), John Woodward (1695)—wrote separate cosmogonies on the Earth that brought together the known data about the planet within the context of the new natural philosophy. In retrospect, these treatises seem an exercise in scientific mythmaking. At their worst, they are indiscriminate miscellanies of information from scriptural, classical, and scientific sources organized into a mythopoeic vision, cosmogonic equivalents to Cotton Mather's *Magnalia Christi Americana*. They retain the themes of classical authors, problems dominated by the geology of the Mediterranean—volcanism, earthquakes, fossils, the rise and fall of sea and land, and the geography and origin of precious metals and stones. An important legacy of the classical authors was the belief in a central fire within the Earth.

To this intellectual inheritance, circumscribed by the books of the ancients, new data were added in during the Renaissance. For a time a kind of information inflation raged, the intellectual counterpart to the flood of precious metals from the Americas that upset the European economy. Medieval lapidaries, bestiaries, and herbals were inadequate to contain it. The medieval synthesis had been the product of typological thought and scholastic logic acting on a limited number of texts, but the swelling of data demanded organizing principles beyond the logic of Aristotle's organon or Abelard's dialectic. "Correspondences," the doctrine of signatures, the use of typology and allegory, and the concept of the microcosm all gave spiritual, symbolic, and providential order to a data base that threatened to overwhelm the rules of formal logic. The scientific revolution replaced this Renaissance exuberance with a new set of metaphors (mechanical), new principles of organization (mathematical), and new sources of data (experimental).

But the synthesis was achieved in mechanics and astronomy, not in natural history. The seventeenth-century theories of the Earth—heroically conceived—were soon denounced as wild speculations; natural history settled down to a period of consolidation, patient codification of specimens, and calculated travel by gentlemen-scholars on the Grand Tour and a handful of scientific savants on expeditions of national and international consequence. The need for organization and standardization was great: between 1664 and 1775 some twenty-seven different taxonomies of natural history were proposed. By the time Cook eased his ships through the edge of the Antarctic pack, a new round of discovery and theorizing was under way. At its center was Abraham Werner, inspirational lecturer at the University of Freiburg, systematizer of minerals, and promulgator of the subject of *geognosy*, which intended to "treat of the solid body of the earth as a whole and of the different occurrences of minerals and rocks of which it is composed and of the origin of these and their relations to one another."[1] Soon afterward, in 1783, Jean Deluc coined the rival term *geology*.

To none of these developments was Antarctica fundamental. It existed on maps as a relic of ancient learning, a geophysical contrivance of indeterminate dimensions to render symmetrical the land masses north and south of the equator. It was irrelevant to the debates that raged among European savants about new cosmogonies; a growing number of natural philosophers doubted its existence, and Cook had been dispatched to disprove the wilder speculations about its geography. Similarly, Antarctica would be peripheral to the era of exploration and earth science that unfolded during the 150 years after Cook's exemplary voyages. When intellectuals turned to the polar regions with important questions, they looked north to the scene of the vestigial ice sheets that had invaded Eurasia and North America; to the ore bodies of Siberia, Canada, and Alaska; and to the presumed westward displacement of Greenland.

Ages of the Earth

The theories of the Earth that appeared in the late eighteenth century brought together a number of disciplines, from the study of minerals to the study of mountains. What integrated these disciplines was the shared geography of the planet, a persistent cosmogonic tradition, and a reformation in mineralogy that made the study and classification of minerals into an empirical base and a methodological model for geognostic inquiry and synthesis. Werner defined in mineralogical terms the concept of a formation, which served the new earth sciences in the same capacity that the concept of a species served the life sciences; he developed an empirical and comparative method for the theory of the Earth, founded on his mineral systematics; and he urged that correlations between geognostic events and phenomena be made according to mineralogical properties.

A brave beginning, but one that would be swept aside by a more profound discovery, a medium capable of integrating all the phenomena of the Earth: geologic time. Between the mid-eighteenth century and the mid-twentieth, the known age of the Earth increased a millionfold, from roughly 6,000 years to 4.6 billion. The discovery of this *terra nova* had an intellectual impact as powerful as that of the geographic discoveries of the Renaissance. It was a New World, as vast as astronomical space, that demanded exploration, new methods of measurement and reasoning, and new principles of correlation and integration. Geologic time became the medium on which Earth history performed; it was to earth science what the subtle ether was to classical physics. The measurement and organization of geologic time became the special province of geology, its raison d'être and its claim to cultural significance. Nor was the issue solely academic: on the calculated age of the Earth depended the rates and character of geologic processes, and on geologic agency depended the rate and character of organic evolution. For more than 150 years, the debate over the age of the Earth was the informing question of geology.

The realization that the Earth was wonderfully ancient came slowly. In the eighteenth century a few theorists had dared to suggest that the Earth was much older than commonly held. Buffon plotted his *epoches* over a span of 75,000 years, Kant gave the age of the universe as 100,000 years, and Mikhail Lomonosov speculated that perhaps hundreds of thousands of years had passed since the Creation. James Hutton based his theory of the Earth on the proposition that the Earth was unimaginably old, with "no vestige of a beginning,—no prospect of an end." But this begged the question: it was not enough that the Earth be old; its history had to be organized as well. The resolution to this dilemma developed simultaneously from two disciplines, each of which established characteristic new chronometers. From natural philosophy came the entropy clock, and from natural philosophy emerged the evolutionary clock. The two approaches were not only contemporaneous but complementary.

The laws of evolution, based on the life cycle, were natural-
history equivalents to the laws of thermodynamics, which were
based on the heat cycle and governed the natural philosophy of
the Earth. The nebular hypothesis, which described the progressive development of the Earth from a primordial swirl of
gases, gave natural philosophy a conceptual focus and presented
a suitable methodology. Geology acquired an equivalent method
and theory during the second decade of the nineteenth century,
as William Smith in England and Georges Cuvier in France
established the principles of stratigraphic correlation and
produced the first geologic maps—a cartography that summarized Earth time, not merely Earth space.

In neither system was there room for chance. Historical
causality was as rigorously deterministic as Newtonian mechanics. The entropy clock assumed that Earth systems were
thermodynamically closed, so that each event inexorably increased the entropy of the system. Secular refrigeration of a
once molten globe, tidal friction on a rotating planet, the decay
of solar radiation—all were means by which to measure the
longevity of Earth processes and ultimately of the Earth itself.
Not least, the contraction of the globe from cooling or gravita-
tional collapse offered a comprehensive process by which to relate important geophysical topics, and for this task the infinitesimal calculus offered an ideal mathematical instrument.
Like geologic time, it could be unspeakably tiny at any instant
of differentiation but suitably vast when integrated over long
terms.

Similarly, evolution was not assumed to be a random process—that specter was raised only with Darwin's *Origin of Species*. Instead, it was modeled on embryology, and the two scales
of the life cycle, individual and species, were finally reconciled
with Haeckel's biogenetic law that ontogeny recapitulates phylogeny. The Chain of Being was temporalized, its links were
filled with historical species, and the metaphor of the clockwork universe was transfigured into the tree of evolution, the
metaphor of an organic universe. Fossils became chronometers
of organic evolution; paleontology became an alternative mathematics for geology; and stratigraphy, the first specifically geologic subject that paleontology organized, became the mechanics of the new science. Just as physics had advanced from the
seventeenth century by steadily "mechanizing" new phenomena, so geology progressed by "stratigraphizing" the phenomena

of the Earth. Exploration unveiled new strata, fragments of
Earth history, which geologists organized into a grand chronology. The first era of the geologic timescale was the Jura (proposed by Humboldt in 1799); the last was the Ordovician (1879). But the power of this technique was too great and the domain of Earth time too vast to limit this method to strata. Relentlessly, brilliantly, geologists discovered fossil-equivalents that could be ordered according to the same principles and correlated with the same universal timescale. The shape of landforms, for example, was a kind of Earth-fossil that could reveal the planet's state of development and age; mountains and rivers experienced life cycles; particularized mineral species evolved out of undifferentiated magma according to regular principles of selection; even planetary motions could be considered "dynamic vestiges," fossil-equivalents of the Earth's origin.

Though differences in methodologies and results meant that natural philosophers and natural historians quarreled over the exact age of the Earth, they both agreed that the question of time was fundamental. The Earth had a beginning, a progressively complex middle, and an inevitable end. Each agreed on the validity of new chronometers and on the necessity for new principles of correlation among otherwise disparate phenomena. Both agreed that Earth time was directed, progressive: their "cycles" were really spirals, in which something was progressively added (evolution) or removed (entropy). Together they synthesized an otherwise incoherent array of Earth-based objects and events. Through a shared metahistory, the physical and the biological poles of geology could be reconciled: the contraction of the Earth made for increasingly complex geologic environments; these, in turn, provided more ecological niches, a prerequisite for more complicated biological evolution; and the progress of biological evolution made possible the vista of cultural, spiritual, and moral evolution by humans and their institutions. It became possible to project from an evolutionary past to an evolutionary future.

These ideas were not isolated, either in origin or in effect. They contributed mightily to questions of significance to Western civilization, especially the problem of biological evolution and the Darwinian acceptance of chance as an integral component of nature. As concepts of history, they were part and parcel of the historicism that infected virtually every form of intellectual inquiry throughout the nineteenth century. In moral philosophy they were manifest as the idea of progress; in literature, as the emergence of historical writings, from Romantic histories to the novel; in philology, as the tracing of linguistic families; in natural theology, as the substitution of growth for mechanism as evidence of Design. The resulting metahistory proposed, in effect, a new order of creation myths for the natural and social worlds.

The landscapes of time that geology revealed, moreover, were consonant with the Romantic syndrome of the day. Peter Pallas exhuming mammoths and woolly rhinoceroses in the Urals; Gideon Mantell and Mary Anning digging up their "terrible lizards," the dinosaurs; hard-rock geologists discovering the fossil roots of ancient mountains, now worn to oblivion; Louis Agassiz mesmerizing audiences with the specter of a catastrophic Ice Age; geomorphologists labeling the shards of ancient landforms that make up a modern scene, like archaeologists projecting the contours of ancient Rome—all resonated well with an era that exulted in and puzzled over lost civilizations in desert and jungle, an enlargement of esthetic consciousness, and a cascade of information that demanded another axis, history, to organize it. Thus, in the United States the same year (1836) that saw Thomas Cole paint the first of his great landscapes, The Oxbow, and Ralph Waldo Emerson publish his transcendentalist manifesto, "Nature," also witnessed the establishment of the Army Corps of Topographic Engineers, which would pioneer the exploration and intellectual assimilation of the new territories of the American West, and the first congressional authorization for the Wilkes expedition.

It was important that an Earth chronology be universal and that geology be applicable to all terrestrial landscapes. The original models, such as Werner's, had characterized particular scenes. They needed to be expanded to encompass Europe as a whole and to accommodate the other newly revealed continents. Indefatigable Werner students soon became celebrated travelers. Leopold von Buch, in particular, claimed Europe; Alexander von Humboldt carried geognosy to South America and Asia; and others studied regions in North America, Asia, and eventually Africa. The comparative method so critical to the study of natural history was applied to geology, not merely on the scale of formations but on the order of continents. Coarse geologic maps were published, cross-sections of continental geology sketched the gross outlines of Earth history, and pro-

gressive explorations filled in the blank spots of Earth time with
stratigraphic precision. New sciences like evolutionary biology
and thermodynamics reinforced the methods and purposes of
geology. The old theories of the Earth became little more than
hollow shells—emptied of previous speculations and "facts"
drawn principally out of books—to be refilled with new data
and structured with a new conceptual order. Inherited theories
were deformed and elevated as thoroughly as the compression
of the Earth's crust, by the collision of continents, had raised
the Alps.

An excellent illustration of how geology came to be indis-
solubly bound with exploration and larger cultural trends is the
intellectual history of the Grand Canyon. The canyon had been
discovered with little consequence in 1540 by conquistadores
with Coronado; rediscovered in the 1770s by Spanish padres on
Indian missions; and duly noted by Humboldt, without comment, as the "Puerto de Bucareli" on his map of New Spain. Fur
traders traversed the area and swapped stories about a "Big Canyon." Not until the mid-nineteenth century, after the character
of exploration had changed and the receptivity of intellectual
culture to natural spectacles had improved, was the canyon
properly "discovered." Thanks principally to the creation of
geology and the concomitant development of landscape art, the
Big Canyon could be considered a Grand Canyon. It became an
emblem of American nationalism and an exemplar of what the
earth sciences were all about.

The first monograph published by the U.S. Geological Survey,
Clarence Dutton's *Tertiary History of the Grand Canyon District*
(1882), brought everything together. Dutton narrated the geologic history of the canyon country through a series of "imagi-
nary journeys," each illuminating a scientific and scenic high-
light. Chapters on canyon geology alternate with chapters on
canyon esthetics, just as in the accompanying *Atlas* geologic
maps interleave with brilliant panoramas by Thomas Moran
and William Henry Holmes. The journeys are stages of evolution, each climax leading to a larger perspective. The entire series culminates in the perspective from Point Sublime, where
Dutton synthesizes the varied geologic themes into a grand narrative of Earth history and consolidates the esthetic lessons into
the evolution of a scenic day, while Holmes illustrates the text
with three beautifully wrought panoramas executed with lithologic detail and careful perspective, marvels of representational

art in the service of science. In one of the panoramas, two figures are visible in the foreground: an artist, sketching, and a geologist, looking over his shoulder and instructing on matters of realistic detail. They are, of course, Holmes and Dutton, represented within the omniscient perspective that also characterizes Dutton's narrative.

It is appropriate that the *Tertiary History* was published in 1882, the same year that the English philosopher Herbert Spencer made his triumphal tour of the U.S. Dutton had recapitulated—with geologic topics and a suitable landscape—the Spencerian epigram that evolution involved an inexorable and progressive change from a state of incoherent homogeneity to a state of increasingly coherent heterogeneity. Dutton's narrative, an epitome of nineteenth-century geology, began with broad brush outlines that were refined stage by stage and evolved into a grand synthesis. Here were Earth history and heroic Earth biography, and with the *Tertiary History* Dutton joined the ranks of the great historians, biographers, and novelists who accepted a similar narrative structure, authorial perspective, and realistic detail. Appropriate, too, was the fact that the *Tertiary History* appeared almost simultaneously with the Reverend Osmond Fisher's *Physics of the Earth's Crust* (1881), a compendium of geophysical thought, which Dutton reviewed enthusiastically for American audiences. Critical of the contractional theory of Earth cosmogony, as was Dutton, Fisher agreed fully that geologic history was a powerful synthetic medium and that the question of the Earth's age was an informing topic. There were landforms other than the canyon that posed important questions for earth science, but no other so completely summarized geologic time and, particularly for Americans, no other scene so fully intersected intellectual culture.

None of this would be true for Antarctica during the heroic age. Eventually, The Ice would in some ways become as powerful an Earth emblem for the twentieth century as the Grand Canyon had been for the nineteenth century, but only after major reformations in the mode of exploration and in intellectual syndromes. Certainly no one would do for Antarctica what Dutton had achieved for the canyon. The landforms themselves (strangely enough, Grand Canyon excavation and ice-sheet formation had occurred about the same time) were different: the canyon revealed and The Ice obscured; the canyon had obvious links to themes of Earth history and organic evolution,

The Ice did not. The canyon was revelatory, The Ice reductionistic. Equally, modernism did not encourage the kind of Spencerian evolutionism that Dutton could assume. Unlike a journey to Point Sublime in the Grand Canyon, a journey to the source regions of The Ice was a study in lost time, space, perspective, and empirical detail, not a progressively more complex synthesis of increasing detail within firm parameters of an objective geography and history.

By the time the heroic age dispatched scientists—and a significant number were earth scientists—to Antarctica, the larger theory of the Earth had been accomplished. In 1904, Eduard Suess completed the fourth and final volume of his summa of nineteenth-century earth science, *The Face of the Earth*, and a year later Thomas Chamberlin and Rollin Salisbury brought out the first volume of their three-volume synthesis, *Geology*. Chamberlin found it necessary to reconstitute the nebular hypothesis into an alternative cosmogony, the planetesimal hypothesis, and others worried about how to incorporate the new heat source discovered in radioactive decay within geophysical theory. But both developments were internal reforms: the planetesimal hypothesis retained planetary contraction as a fundamental process, and radioactivity became less a threat than a long-sought "natural chronometer," as Arthur Holmes put it, an ultimate entropy clock that kept a "more magisterial register of time, after the manner of an hour glass."[2] In fact, the iron rule of time created a growing philosophical conundrum. In the seventeenth century, the realization had grown that, unless the Earth was rejuvenated from time to time, erosion would destroy a habitat created expressly for humans—a theological no less than scientific quandary known as the denudation dilemma. By the early twentieth century, a modern version had been posed with the concept of the Earth's inexorable heat death, the paradox that even as the Earth progressed biologically and socially it was irreversibly deteriorating into a cold, inert rock incapable of supporting life. This was, in fact, a geologic analogue of the Dark Design common to the literary naturalism of the day. Both shared a philosophy that the Earth obeyed rigid material laws, principally the laws of time.

In 1910 F. B. Taylor and in 1912 Alfred Wegener proposed global tectonic theories that would eventually become the theory of continental drift. But none of this was accomplished with material from Antarctica. In his two thousand pages of dense geologic observations, culled from world literature, Suess offered only a passing reference to the mountains of the Antarctic Peninsula. The planetesimal hypothesis did not look to Antarctica for important data. When Rutherford proposed in 1905 that radioactive decay could measure geologic time in an absolute rather than a relative scale, and when John Joly saw in radioactive heat a source for periodic orogenies, neither had Antarctica in mind. Wegener predicted that the crucial experiment for his theory of continental drift would be found in the displacement of Greenland, and he eventually died sledging across the Greenland ice sheet.

Yet the Antarctic was a piece of unfinished business for earth science. To the casual observer, it seemed as peripheral to earth science as to the Earth, but it was there and it needed to be investigated. Naturalists like James Eights had occasionally accompanied sealers, and others had examined the scene from afar on the Ross, d'Urville, and Wilkes expeditions. Dredgings from the *Challenger* expedition, taken some 2,000 miles from the Antarctic coastline, brought up a mixture of continental rocks that indicated the composition of the continental crust. John Murray used these continental shards to summarize the geologic evidence for the existence of an Antarctic continent in the famous paper he delivered to the Royal Society, in 1893, the speech that served to renew scientific purpose in Antarctic exploration. Murray's treatment of the *Challenger* data, moreover, demonstrated the intellectual triumph that the alliance between geology and continental discovery had made over the older association of maritime discovery and geography. Through their bottom sediments the oceans became a source of geologic data, and they were interpreted within the context of geologic history, not simply geography.

Other samples of Antarctic rock were hurriedly gathered by a shore party (which included Borchgrevink) from the Bull expedition. Borchgrevink returned on the *Southern Cross* expedition (1899–1900) to inaugurate the first serious geologic work. In time-honored fashion, he brought back specimens that petrologists at scientific institutions, such as museums and universities, then analyzed. Many of the most significant reports would, in fact, be written not by members of exploring parties but by academics to whom specimens and observations were brought. Borchgrevink's role as a field geologist was quickly amplified by others associated with expeditions of the heroic age: Henryk

Arctowski on the *Belgica* expedition, Otto Nordenskjöld and Gunnar Andersson on the Swedish National Expedition, E. Gourdon with the Charcot expedition, W. S. Bruce with the Scottish National Expedition, H. T. Ferrar with the *Discovery* expedition, T. W. Edgeworth David and Raymond Priestley with the *Nimrod* expedition, F. L. Stillwell, A. D. Watson, and C. A. Hoadley with the Australasian Antarctic Expedition (*Aurora*), Wilhelm Filchner, Erich von Drygalski, E. Philippi, and R. Reinisch on the German National (*Gauss*) Expedition, and Geoffrey Taylor, Frank Debenham, and Raymond Priestley (again) with the *Terra Nova* expedition. Borchgrevink brought back the first rocks; Andersson sketched the first geologic map (1906); Ferrar effectively outlined Antarctic stratigraphy; and Priestley and Taylor, working from the Dry Valleys, plotted the earliest geomorphic history. Most expeditions summarized the various ices they encountered with a veritable thesaurus of ice types, and glacial geology bridged the domains of geomorphology and glaciology. In 1914 David and Priestley consolidated Antarctic geology into a masterful memoir, *Geology*, published as part of the scientific work of the *Terra Nova* expedition.

When they arrived at the continent, expedition geologists already possessed a well-developed chronology, techniques for geologic exploration, and an understanding of what constituted a geologic explanation—a geologic map and a narrative of Earth events in the region in question. As a new science, geology had already been pioneered, strengthened by comparisons among the six explored continents. Since Antarctica offered far less potential information than other continental bodies, it soon became apparent that perhaps the most remarkable fact about Antarctic rocks and geography was not their novelty but their familiarity. The most prominent Antarctic fossil, *Glossopteris*, was well known from other locales throughout the Southern Hemisphere. Antarctic mountains were quickly aligned with others: the Antarcandes with the South American Andes, and the Transantarctics of Victoria Land with the Great Dividing Range of Australia. The petrology of Antarctic rocks looked like those of any other suite, even to the point—moderately puzzling—of showing not only similar processes but similar paleoclimates. West Antarctica was readily matched with Pacific-American patterns of orogeny, East Antarctica with continental shields like those in Africa, Australia, and India. Speaking of the *Terra Nova* expedition, Debenham remarked that its "geological work" was "particularly comprehensive and was one of the chief items in the scientific syllabus of the Expedition."[3] Such an emphasis was itself traditional: for a century, geology and geography had been inextricably allied with the exploration of the world's continents.

But there was, equally, a constant stream of apologias about the value of this work. In Antarctica, geology in the service of national empire offered little beyond national pride and the intrinsic value of public patronage for the sciences. There were laments that the public really wanted sagas of adventure, not science; that "no *scientist*," as an exasperated Taylor once put it, "ever needs to be converted to a belief in the value of Antarctic exploration."[4] Yet it appeared that few geologic breakthroughs would occur as a result of Antarctic geoscience, no intellectual equivalents to a march on the pole. The Ice received ideas: it did not originate them. At the end of the heroic age, half a dozen sites around Antarctica had been rapidly sampled. Ferrar noted that he had one month in which to explore 600 square miles of the Transantarctics—a difficult reconnaissance, the data from which were effortlessly assimilated into larger conventions of petrology, stratigraphy, glacial geology, and Earth chronology. As far as geologic inquiry was concerned, Antarctica was less a continent than an archipelago of islands in a sea of ice or a scattering of Earth meteorites. It simply did not possess the magnitude of information that the geologic discovery of other continents did, or anything like the ease of acquisition during the eighteenth and nineteenth centuries in Europe, Asia, Africa, Australia, or the Americas.

The troubling status of Antarctic science and exploration is nicely illustrated by the notorious winter journey to Cape Crozier, undertaken to collect the egg of an emperor penguin. The embryology of the penguin would, in theory, enlighten science on the mysterious divergence of primitive birds from the reptiles, a matter of significance in the evolution of life. When Cherry-Garrard dutifully brought the egg—now a memorial to the martyred Wilson—to the British Museum, he was met with a comfortable indifference. The episode dismayed more than disillusioned Cherry-Garrard: he successfully argued that the intellectual ennui displayed by the museum in no way diminished the moral value of the winter journey as a test of character.

But the scientific value of the penguin egg had justified the journey, and ultimately the issue of scientific importance did bear on the character of the expedition. The last of Edward Wilson's sketches, executed on the Beardmore descent, had been of geologic features, and the Polar Party had burdened their man-hauled sledges with some 37 pounds of rock specimens. If the geology did not matter, then the polar journey had been mere sport, and the party's demise the fate of good losers. If science mattered deeply, however, then those rocks and sketches were testimonials that ennobled the Polar Party as much as the final epistles of the dying Robert Scott. Moreover, correctly placing the emperor penguin in the great chain of evolutionary being was an exercise not only in science but in history: science was something more than data-gathering and history went beyond simple chronologies. How the heroic age saw history accounts, in part, for how history has viewed the heroic age.

Dead Ice

Most of all, perhaps, the Antarctic discoveries suffered from bad timing. The old metaphysics of nature was being rapidly reconstituted. But the modernist reformation that swept discipline after discipline seemed to pass by geoscience with hardly a seismic tremor. The prospect of continental drift, with its promise of a new global tectonic system, had little effect on other themes of geoscience and no demonstrable effect on its informing problem—geologic time and the age of the Earth. Radioactivity, at first a radical source of heat, was quickly absorbed into geoscience paradigms and became the ultimate instrument for geochronology, an entropy clock for determining absolute ages. The old alliances of geoscience with physics and biology seemed unaffected by the revolutions that raged through the latter two disciplines in the early twentieth century. More important than penguin eggs for evolutionary inquiries was the cascade of discoveries in modern genetics. Almost quaintly, geology remained a bastion of historicism, a kind of genre piece, long after most of the sciences and the arts had abandoned that philosophy.

By the heroic age of Antarctic exploration, the rate of data production in geoscience was slacking, the library rather than the field had become the source for the resolution of conflict, the discipline of the laboratory was superseding the rigors of exploration as a test of character, type areas were being obsessively resurveyed, and geoscience became preoccupied with a grand synthesis of its inheritance. The geologic puzzles of Antarctica were important to Antarctic geoscience, but apparently not to questions and regions outside The Ice. The earth sciences entered a period of intellectual dormancy, in part the product of exhaustion after the labors that had produced a global inventory and in part the outcome of massive complacency.

By 1928, as the first Byrd expedition brought Laurence Gould, a geologist, to Antarctica, the American school of geology orchestrated a coherent vision of the Earth from its microcosm, the mineral, to its macrocosm, the solar system. Norman L. Bowen published *The Evolution of the Igneous Rocks*, which brought to a culmination the great laboratory tradition of American mineralogy. Bowen argued that the abundance of igneous mineral species could be explained by various selective mechanisms, such as fractional crystallization, that differentiated a primitive magma. The analogy to organic evolution was unmistakable, and the connections to geophysical theories of the Earth that depended on contraction and at least local melting strengthened the thesis. At the same time Thomas Chamberlin published *The Two Solar Families*, the final installment of a cosmogony and cosmology which extended geologic methods beyond the Earth. Considering planetary motions as "dynamic vestiges"—fossils—of planetary history, Chamberlin replaced the "hot" globe of the nebular hypothesis with a "cold" globe of the planetesimal hypothesis, but left contraction more or less intact and organized the history of the solar system in strict evolutionary order. Nor were the intervening landforms of the planet ignored. William Morris Davis published his *Coral Reefs Problem*, further extending a geomorphic synthesis in which every landscape experienced an invariant evolution of form from "young" to "old," from a system full of potential energy to one of maximum entropy (a peneplain). G. K. Gilbert's posthumous *Studies of Basin-Range Structure* completed the record of America's great explorer-geologist by formally developing the theory of a new mountain-building mechanism. And the American Association of Petroleum Geologists (AAPG) printed the proceedings of an important international meeting, *The Theory of Continental Drift: A Symposium*.

The symposium, held in 1926, had assembled many of the leading geologists of the day, including American theorists, for a debate over the proposal by the German Alfred Wegener that large-scale continental displacement had occurred, that the present distribution of the continents was the product of the ancient breakup of a single continental craton, Pangaea. An Arctic explorer, Wegener had apparently conceived the idea by watching the fragmentation and drift of ice floes. His idea, first presented in 1912 and published in 1915 as *The Origin of Continents and Oceans* (but best known from the many translations of the 1924 edition), was almost universally denounced. The symposium moderator was sympathetic, and Wegener found disciples of varying credibility elsewhere; but Americans in particular exhibited a barely suppressed outrage. "If we are to believe Wegener's hypothesis," Rollin T. Chamberlin, son of Thomas, remarked, "we must forget everything which has been learned in the last 70 years and start all over again." The "planetesimal hypothesis," he continued scornfully—angered that Wegener was "oblivious" to the contractional formula of the planetesimal model—"is an integral part of comprehensive geological philosophy, but Wegener's hypothesis is not."[5]

The theory was far less drastic than that: it proposed a new tectonics of sweeping proportions but left untouched the great bulk of geologic topics and did not, like the controversies of old, attack the metaphysics of Earth time. The British geologist Arthur Holmes had in fact just revised his celebrated treatise *The Age of the Earth*, and he found no dissonance between his conclusions about Earth history and his support for Wegener's theory; at the time of the symposium's publication, he proposed a model for convective flow in the Earth's mantle that bore on the question of continental displacement. More symptomatic, perhaps, was the fact that the symposium had been sponsored by the AAPG and that the most visible member of the American earth science community, former mining engineer Herbert Hoover, had been elected president of the United States. It appeared that earth science was a subject whose theoretical synthesis had been accomplished and whose credentials were accepted, and it entered into an era of vast application. Except for Antarctica, much of which was inaccessible to geologic methods anyway, the Earth's continents had been explored. In 1931 the National Research Council officially vindicated the technique of radiometric dating; by the mid-1930s the riddle of the Earth's age was rapidly approaching resolution; in 1956 Claire Patterson of the California Institute of Technology convincingly announced the Earth's age as 4.55 billion years.

The achievement of earth science was enormous, the triumph of the historical method complete. To measure the intellectual distance that had been traveled, one need only compare the personalities, concepts, and instruments from the beginning of the era to those at the end: the paired Harrison chronometers Cook used to establish longitude with the isotopic clocks Arthur Holmes employed in the radiometric dating of rocks; the artificial systematics of minerals Abraham Werner used to the sophisticated physical chemistry and evolutionism of N. L. Bowen; the specter of a timeless, endlessly cycled planet outlined by James Hutton to the Earthly progressivism of Thomas Chamberlin; Alexander von Humboldt, the gentleman-scholar as Romantic explorer, to Richard Byrd, the machine-dependent explorer as business manager. Geology had begun as a derivative branch of cosmology; by the 1920s cosmology had become, in Chamberlin's words, the "foreign department" of geology.

Antarctic studies, too, achieved a kind of climax at the same time. A sudden outpouring of publications concerning Antarctica gave some credence to the otherwise orphic remark by Griffith Taylor, a *Terra Nova* veteran, that "never has so much interest been taken in Antarctic exploration as at present."[6] In 1928 the American Geographical Society published a new map of Antarctica, an English translation of Otto Nordenskjöld and Ludwig Mecking's *The Geography of Polar Regions*, and an anthology of invited papers, *Problems of Polar Research*. J. Gordon Hayes wrote his historical synthesis, *Antarctica*. A year earlier Rudmose Brown had published *The Polar Regions*, the first English textbook on Antarctic geography. Britain had institutionalized its Antarctic science with the establishment of the Falkland Islands Dependencies Survey and the Scott Polar Research Institute under the direction of geologist Frank Debenham. Soon afterward Taylor, now a professor of geography at the University of Chicago, wrote a popular synopsis, *Antarctic Adventure and Research* (1930), while "three major expeditions, those of Byrd, Wilkins and Mawson, are still in the field." He noted that thanks to Ferrar, Debenham, and David, there existed an "almost complete series of geologic formations surveyed in Antarctica."[7] The outstanding geographic riddle, the connection between East and West Antarctica, would soon be solved.

Not everyone agreed. Nordenskjöld recognized the thinness of geologic materials, and Raymond Priestley and C. E. Tilley concluded that "at best, our present knowledge of the continent is not sufficient to provide more than the barest outline of its geological and paleontological history and the barest hint of its geological constitution."[8] They concluded that "the problem of the future" was "the filling in" of the missing data and the testing of contemporary hypotheses, normal rather than revolutionary science. Mawson warned that "geographical knowledge concerning the Antarctic is yet exceedingly fragmentary—far more so than those unfamiliar with the subject are likely to realize."[9] Everyone thought it appropriate to extend existing geologic techniques and theories to additional Antarctic outcrops, to complete at least a first-order reconnaissance. Antarctica was important, but more as a nagging epiphenomenon than a geologic climax. No one at the AAPG symposium on continental drift thought that Antarctica possessed unique information for Wegener's theory; Wegener himself thought that the test would come in Greenland; and Priestley and Tilley argued that on the contrary, the "paleoclimatological evidence" from Antarctica "presents an insuperable obstacle to the acceptance of this most fascinating and all-embracing theory of modern geology."[10] Even the world's oldest rocks belonged to the continental shield of Greenland, not Antarctica. Certainly no such motivation extended to Wilkens or Ellsworth, for whom Antarctica was the scene for Lindbergh-like spectacles, or to Byrd, for whom the blank spot on the globe that was Antarctica was reason enough. "Polar exploration," Byrd wrote with Baconian enthusiasm, "is first of all an instrument geared to penetration, whose primary object is fact-finding and observation."[11]

Yet, as Henry Menard has ably documented, American geology was entering a period of both intellectual and institutional dormancy. Growth in American geological literature had been strong until about 1830–1840, as classical geology defined itself and inaugurated broad intercontinental comparisons. From roughly 1840, when the Army Corps of Topographical Engineers embarked on major surveys in the Trans-Mississippi West, up to 1880, with the consolidation of federal geologic science into the U.S. Geological Survey, the scientific literature grew exponentially, doubling every twenty years. That growth remained exponential but slower in pace until about 1915, approximately the end of the heroic age of Antarctic exploration. Then the rate of growth decreased further. From 1925, on the eve of the AAPG symposium on continental drift, until 1955, during preparations for IGY, the doubling period extended to thirty-eight years; for the USGS the doubling time reached, in Menard's words, "an appalling 70 years, or considerably slower than normal expansion of either the national population or the gross national product."[12] By the mid-1950s, however, the earth sciences were being rejuvenated. The number of published papers in American geology from 1945 to 1980 increased 26-fold. Not coincidentally, the earth sciences were participating in a new era of vigorous exploration and experienced major theoretical revolutions.

During the intervening years, however, American geology showed all the classic signs of scientific dormancy. Increasingly it turned to the books of science rather than the book of nature. Library research and bibliographic citations, often involving elaborate literature searches, replaced the kind of field work that had come readily to the nineteenth century, with its host of untrammeled continents and its revelations about geologic time. In 1890 citations rarely included articles older than thirty-five years, roughly corresponding to the onset of the western surveys; in 1940, a large proportion of citations dated to between eighty and one hundred years, and bibliographies occupied a substantial portion of published scientific pages. Suess had demonstrated the power of library synthesis with his encyclopedic *Face of the Earth*, but this kind of endeavor demanded a vigorous base of new data. Instead, American geologists evidently recycled old data, resurveyed sites that had been important during the nineteenth century, and debated endlessly the inherited controversies. The method of multiple working hypotheses, popularized by Chamberlin, lost its vitality as an instrument for sorting out theories in a universe of rapidly expanding information. It became the tool for a new scholasticism, a noncommittal dialectic for systematically comparing contradictory (and irreconcilable) theories with the evidence contained within the canon of published literature. Jargon replaced the pragmatic language and metaphor of active ideas; debate and ritual controversy replaced problem solving; and an admirable scientific caution ossified into conservatism so that, as Menard observes, "an increasingly large fraction of research did not and could not lead to incisive and exhaustive results."[13]

A concern with style, the perpetuation of a classical literature and inherited themes, and long delays in actual publication all gave American geology more the character of the humanities than of normal science. Perhaps it is no surprise that the most innovative use of Antarctic exploration was its contribution to a new genre of literature, science fiction (the passive hero of Lovecraft's *At the Mountains of Madness* was a geologist). In some respects Antarctic exploration was a throwback to a pregeological era of discovery; the endless search for a subglacial graben connecting the Weddell and Ross seas took on the character of a twentieth-century search for a Northwest Passage or Strait of Anian. Only in science fiction, where alien creatures could be suspended in ice, was there a revelation of geologic time. The state of American geology and geography makes the achievement of Richard Byrd all the more remarkable.

Byrd proclaimed with genuine satisfaction that his second expedition "achieved, by a fair margin, the most complete program of scientific research in the history of polar exploration."[14] Airplanes and tractors supplemented dog sledges, and seismic profiling of the ice (a technique suggested by R. A. Daly) augmented rock hammers, but this remained traditional geologic exploration. Geographic and geologic questions merged indistinguishably. Interestingly, geophysical topics such as earth magnetism and upper atmospherics—topics for which the polar regions offered intrinsic advantages—had both a stronger intellectual foundation and, thanks to radio and navigation needs, ties to practical technologies. One of the men connected with these researches, Lloyd Berkner, would be prominent in suggesting the third polar year, which evolved into IGY. The perennial enigmas of Antarctic geography—the persistence of the Antarcandes beneath the West Antarctic ice sheet and the hypothetical presence of a subglacial graben along the border of Greater and Lesser Antarctica—had nothing like the global implications of such baffling oceanic features as the great trench systems of the Pacific or the mid-Atlantic ridge. Perhaps inevitably, the geologic results of Byrd's first two expeditions were largely of a character with the natural-history reconnaissances typical of nineteenth-century American geology at its best. The discovery of geologic features had the kind of excitement and archaic flavor generated by the exhumation of King Tut's tomb.

But the logistical dimensions of the scientific work were not the sole issue: the data had to be significant to the sciences back home, and their significance was often a matter of timing. For all the popular attention the expeditions received, the scientific output was not on an order or of a type that would revolutionize American earth science, that could shake it out of its doldrums. The most important potential use of Antarctic geology, its relevance to the theory of continental drift, was recognized by Alexander Du Toit, a South African geologist who enthusiastically endorsed Wegener's theory and granted to Antarctica a "vital" status as the "key-piece" in a reconstructed Gondwanaland. With the exception of Reginald Daly, however, Americans dismissed Wegener as a geologic hallucinator, Du Toit as a monomaniacal propagandist, and, by implication, Antarctica as a sideshow of geologic inquiry. When Lovecraft's horrified geologist testified that the theory of "continent drift lately advanced by Taylor, Wegener, and Joly" was vindicated by murals and bas-reliefs in the City of the Old Ones, he inadvertently confirmed what respectable American geologists thought of the concept: that it was a fantasy best left buried with its originator.[15]

Perhaps the most important outcome of scientific inquiry during this era was the simple creation of a small cadre of geologists who were interested in Antarctica. Great Britain succeeded much more than the U.S. in institutionalizing Antarctic science. The Science Office of the Falklands Dependency, Scott Polar Research Institute, and a persistent interest in the geology of the Southern Hemisphere, where important British colonies flourished, continued a tradition of geologic field work and perpetuated a genealogy of Antarctic geologists, though attention shifted from the Transantarctics to British Antarctic Territory and the Antarctic Peninsula (Graham Land). Increasingly, as British, German (Nazi), and American (U.S. Antarctic Service) work demonstrated, Antarctic science emphasized geopolitical rather than geophysical purposes. But when intellectual and institutional circumstances changed—when Antarctica became integral to the IGY agenda—American geology had something to build upon, and the strong American program was capable of recruiting many Britons into its ranks; the geophysical sink of Antarctica became part of a global postwar brain drain.

Geology had evolved hand-in-glove with the exploration of the continents, and when this exploration had exhausted new lands, earth science shared in that exhaustion. In this regard, academic geophysics had shown itself every bit as conservative as academic geology; classical geology and geophysics seemed to become more and more a branch of engineering or a valuable subset of techniques within a wider discipline. Antarctica was thus transitional—both the last of the continents to be so surveyed and the first of extraterrestrial lands to be explored. But the geographic base of the earth sciences was only one of the difficulties they faced: equally moribund was geology's metaphysical foundation and its justification as an intellectual enterprise. Geology had acquired an identity as part of a larger intellectual syndrome, and when that syndrome lost its vitality, earth science suffered a crisis of identity. For its entire existence classical geology had developed amidst growth—growth of data and increase in the known age of the Earth. How old the Earth might be was constantly debated; but the organization of that span of time and the experience of having it continually enlarged were constants to the intellectual purpose of the science. The answers geology gave had broad cultural meaning that went far beyond technical solutions in applied geophysics and prospecting. Accordingly, during the heroic age of Antarctic exploration major syntheses had appeared, geochronological counterparts to Suess' *Face of the Earth*: in 1911 from the American Joseph Barrell and in 1913 from Briton Arthur Holmes. But after the heroic age the rate of information had slowed alarmingly, the question that had informed the science (the Earth's age) was solved or no longer vital in a modernist syndrome, and no other question of equivalent magnitude was on hand to take its place.

The issue went beyond geology as an isolated discipline. The entire intellectual syndrome which evolutionism—much of it founded on the exemplar of geologic history—had made possible was in disrepute. The modern synthesis of genetics and Darwinian evolution broke the stranglehold that Neo-larmarckianism had placed over American geology. Boasian anthropology showed how complex cultures could develop without rigid evolutionary schemas. Pragmatism shredded the formulas that evolutionists like Spencer had elevated into "block universes." Literature created new forms of narrative, distinct from those typical of nineteenth-century novels. Everywhere historicism came under attack; time was relativized, linear models of historical causality were transformed into cones of probability, time's arrow was given a feedback loop, chance became acceptable within a scientific etiology, the idea of progress was questioned, and the inherited models of a progressively evolving Earth seemed increasingly anachronistic, the quaint presumption of a science which had lost its self-proclaimed position of preeminence as a synthesizer of Earth knowledge and an exemplar of historical laws. Thus when reformation and

rejuvenation arrived, they came broadly: a new era of exploration, new instruments of interrogation and concepts of Earth
processes, changed political circumstances, and a new metaphysical context.

Revolution: Drift to Antarctica

By the mid-1950s an epoch of discovery was taking shape that
would have important consequences for Antarctica and the
earth sciences. There were new instruments, especially remote
sensing, that would make accessible to scientific inquiry much
of the Earth's solid surface and unleash another tsunami of information. Remote sensing by aerial photography; infrared,
radar, and microwave scanning; radio echo-sounding and sonar
mapping; seismic profiling; airborne and shipborne gravity,
heat, and magnetic sensors; drilling on continents, shelves,
deep-sea floors, and ice sheets; the establishment of distant, au-
tomated devices and platforms such as Earth-orbiting satellites—all of this led to an explosion of information about the
Earth that gutted previous theories of their claim to global synthesis and compelled a new perspective on the Earth as a planet.
Earlier cosmologists like Suess had asked their readers to imagine the view that visitors from another world would have of the
planet as they approached its surface. By the 1960s that perspective was no longer a fictional trope: it had become a popular vision confirmed by a torrential flow of photographs and data
from space-based geophysical sensors.

When a continent had been the largest unit of geologic exploration, the tectonic syntheses of Dana and Suess appeared as
wondrous achievements in holistic thinking and Chamberlin's
cosmogony of the solar system as a nearly universal vision. But
IGY began with a premise of planetary integration, and it annexed whole planets—each with its own global tectonics and
stratigraphy—as the earlier era had new continents. By comparison, the inherited "global" syntheses seemed hopelessly
parochial. In advance of IGY a steady stream of articles and
books, many intended to educate the public, poured out to celebrate the Earth as a planet. During the IGY epoch, whole new
realms of solid-earth geography became known, especially the
global rift and ridge system of the oceans and the subglacial topography of Antarctica; new geochronologies were developed,

the most important one based on paleomagnetism; and whole
new stratigraphies were constructed—from deep-ocean sediments, from paleomagnetic reversals, from the ice sheets, and
from other planets, notably the Moon. International Geological
Congresses during the late nineteenth and early twentieth centuries had lavished considerable effort on the construction of a
universal stratigraphy—one founded on a sense of absolute geologic time, shaped by rigorous principles of historical correlation, and ultimately evolved out of the geologic map of Europe.
Europe was the type continent to which all others were to be
related. After IGY there emerged several planetary stratigraphies, a vaster and more relative sense of history, and a type
planet, the Earth, to which the others could be contrasted.
Ironically, less of Antarctica was exposed to sight than the surfaces of other Earthlike planets. But the techniques that made
possible the surficial mapping of Mercury, Venus, and Mars also
mapped the solid-earth surface, both submarine and subglacial,
of the Antarctic plate.

New political alliances and geopolitical concerns made possible complex international expeditions to the ocean basins
and Antarctica; superpower rivalry was generally confined to
space. The process began, for Antarctica, with the Norwegian-
British-Swedish Expedition (1949–1952), and it expanded enormously from this prototype into the Antarctic programs of the
International Geophysical Year. But the institutional reforms
were matched by an intellectual reformation. A new metaphysics of nature was emerging, highlighted by concepts of information, cybernetics, and systems theory; a new cosmology of the
Earth was ripening, based on the voluminous output of data
from IGY and its successors, a method that would mature into a
science of comparative planetology; and Antarctica, so long peripheral to human society and models of the Earth, would
claim an honored position at the planet's geophysical and geopolitical pole.

IGY did not, of course, originate all the relevant data for this
reformation, and the premier concept to emerge from the earth
sciences during this era, the theory of plate tectonics, did not
by itself constitute a complete intellectual revolution. But IGY
did focus known data, particularly from the ocean basins, that
were otherwise disjointed. It was during the preparations for
IGY, for example, that Maurice Ewing and Bruce Heezen articu-

lated the evidence for a global midocean ridge system. The sheer act of bringing together geophysical concepts and data and of setting research priorities for IGY expeditions compelled a rethinking of large-scale Earth processes and the theories that accounted for them. In the new reconstructions, the "global viewpoint provided by IGY," as Henry Menard recalled, was fundamental.[16] Inevitably, the most enduring of global tectonic models, continental drift, would enjoy a revival. "No one knows with any certainty how the earth behaves," wrote J. Tuzo Wilson during IGY, "why mountains are uplifted, how continents were formed, or what causes earthquakes. . . . Earth scientists are as ignorant of their patient as doctors were of theirs before Harvey disclosed the circulation of the blood"—this from an accomplished geophysicist who had spent a year traveling to IGY outposts throughout the globe and who cultivated a planetary outlook. Wilson believed in and wanted major reforms. "Earth scientists are knocking on the doors of discovery," he insisted hopefully, "they await the answer."[17]

In many ways Wilson personifies the reformation that resulted. He began the 1950s as a "fixist," convinced of the enduring stability of continents and oceans. But by 1959 he had converted to the "mobilist" position, avidly searching for the mechanics of continental drift, publishing a series of critical papers during the 1960s that confirmed continental displacement, and arguing frankly for the necessity of a theoretical reformation for the earth sciences on the model of Thomas Kuhn's paradigmatic treatise, *The Structure of Scientific Revolutions* (1962). As president of the IUGG during IGY, Wilson was in a unique position to correlate the disparate researches for which IGY invited a global perspective. Afterward, he was influential in the Geodynamics and the International Upper Mantle projects, important geophysical successors to IGY, and personally added to their agenda the goal "to prove whether or not continental drift occurred." By 1970 the much-desired revolution was a fact.

The revival of interest in continental drift began in 1956, accelerated in 1962 with a symposium on drift held at Cambridge under the inspiration of S. K. Runcorn and with the publication of theories by Harry Hess and Robert Dietz of what came to be called sea-floor spreading. It reached a fever pitch in the late 1960s and was complete, in the form of plate tectonics, by the early 1970s. When the AAPG published a memoir of invited pa-

pers on plate tectonics in 1974—nearly half a century after its
famous symposium on drift—there had been a reversal of sentiment about continental displacement as complete as those reversals in the Earth's magnetic field that had done so much to establish the new theory. However much a handful of geologic critics might carp or historians hedge their accounts of intellectual change, there was widespread recognition and euphoria among earth scientists about their "revolution." Wilson perhaps deserves the last word. In 1971 he wrote, "Today, many earth scientists believe that, within the past decade, a scientific revolution has occurred. . . ." The revolution, he cautioned, was not irresponsible; it did "not invalidate past observations," and it demonstrated the "interdependence" of geology and geophysics. Nevertheless, "the acceptance of continental drift has transformed the earth sciences from a group of rather unimaginative studies based upon pedestrian interpretations of natural phenomena into a unified science that is exciting and dynamic and that holds out the promise of great practical advances for the future." [18]

But more was involved than the adoption of a single, if stunningly comprehensive, theory about Earth tectonics. Geology had never been founded solely on tectonics, mineralogy, or stratigraphy; what had brought these separate disciplines together in the late eighteenth century was not a theory of orogeny or cosmology but the discovery of geologic time as a medium of Earth processes and the development of a rapidly expanding data base, a development made possible by the opening of the continental interiors to Western explorers. The magnitude of the new earth sciences as an intellectual achievement depended on how broadly they reconstructed the whole subject—from its data base to its conceptual infrastructure to its philosophical superstructure. To a large extent, the new era affected all these components.

The mode of exploration dramatized by IGY overwhelmed the older data base, not merely in the quantity of information it generated but in its rate of production. Not only the scale but the tempo of the earth sciences increased; not only inherited theories but a single geology was incapable of absorbing the information. In a sense, a pluralism of geologies developed, each with its own stratigraphy and chronometers. Geology, which had concerned itself with the Earth's age and with the peculiar processes and regimens of Earthly rocks, could not be expanded indefinitely to accommodate the new realms of planetary exploration. Ultimately, it had to be superseded by a more comprehensive planetary science. Thus in 1962, as the Cambridge continental drift symposium addressed the history of continents and Hess and Dietz invoked a new history of the oceans, Eugene Shoemaker and Robert Hackmann published the first extraterrestrial stratigraphy: a geology of the Moon based on lithic horizons created by the ejecta of impact cratering on the lunar surface. Eventually, this stratigraphy was converted into a lunar chronology. The next year witnessed the first of the major Antarctic geoscience symposia, the harvest of IGY. The earth sciences had always been intimately interdependent with exploration, and the IGY epoch invigorated both. More important than any particular fact, the earth sciences had discovered a new mode of exploration; and, revealingly, the first scientist to the Moon, Harrison Schmidt, was a geologist.

The conceptual infrastructure of the science was certain to enjoy new vitality and to experience an equally thorough reconstruction. Plate-tectonics theory was only the most dramatic expression of this reformation. Although plate theory described a situation apparently unique to planet Earth, it provided a decisive reference for interplanetary comparison, much as Alpine structure had for the nineteenth century theories of mountain-building. But other theoretical and methodological revolutions in the earth sciences were equally profound—for example, in geomorphology. They, too, contributed to the reconstitution of the inherited geologic synthesis and revealed a fresh philosophical perspective. Most fundamentally, the new planetary sciences lacked the historicism that had informed the old; and the modernist syndrome, at last, overtook the earth sciences.

There continued to be plenty of refinements within the general structure of geochronology. The measurement of geologic time continued, of course; the entropy clock (in the form of K-Ar radiometry) was extended to younger rocks; planetary stratigraphies based on impact cratering were rapidly translated into generalized timescales; and novel techniques were invented to order microhistories of very recent or ephemeral events. But the procedures were techniques, no longer axioms of Earth metahistory. Of critical importance was the development of a new chronometer based on reversals of the Earth's magnetic field, which were recorded in rocks. This chronometer

proved critical for the confirmation of sea-floor spreading and,
through the mobile oceans, for the acceptance of plate tectonics. Unlike the timepieces of classical geology, paleomagnetism was not based on life cycles or entropy clocks; there was no progressivism implied in its chronology. It was joined by a host of other Earth rhythms and geochronologies that became important for the earth sciences, such as the Milankovich cycles apparently responsible for ice ages or the oxygen-isotope ratios so valuable for dating ice cores. None of these concepts betrayed the metaphysics of historicism that no nineteenth-century chronometer ever lacked. Similar developments occurred in geomorphology, as it struggled to present landform dynamics within the context of open rather than closed systems and as self-regulating systems in quasi-steady state instead of lithic life cycles and heat engines. There were parallel developments in the life sciences with such chronometers as circadian rhythms, the feedback-laden biotas characteristic of open systems, and concepts like the punctuated equilibria invoked for macroevolution. But more important for the earth sciences was its divorce from the life sciences. None of the new planetary chronometers could appeal to paleontology: they pertained to abiotic worlds, without fossil residues of organic evolution. A planetary science had to conceive of life as a special case, limited to Earth, not the apex of geologic history. Besides, the modern synthesis of genetics and evolution meant that geoscience no longer had to argue for geologic design as a precondition of life.

The application of cybernetic principles, information theory, and systems theory—with logical rigor or simply metaphorically—demanded other, rhythmic chronometers and contributed to the breakup of the older geologic synthesis as fully as did the new tectonics. Even the methodology of geology advanced beyond the evolutionism of Chamberlin and a belief in strict historical causation for the adoption of modeling and probabilism. Curiously, Kuhn's influential theory of scientific revolutions—which earth scientists eager for intellectual ferment seized upon—attempted to explain the nature of scientific progress without progressivism. In brief, while plate tectonics was the most spectacular conceptual synthesis of the new earth sciences and the one most directly related to IGY and Antarctica, it did not constitute a philosophical revolution.

Missing, too, were the vitality of the old metaphysics and the implicit sense of a moral order in nature. During the fifteenth century Caxton's encyclopedist could appeal to the doctrine of correspondences and the concept of the microcosm and macrocosm to compare the structure of the celestial spheres with the anatomy of an egg. Early in the nineteenth century J. D. Dana, arguing that history unfolded according to a purposeful program, proposed that the evolution of North America could be aptly likened to the embryology of an egg. But in updating the analogy after IGY, J. Tuzo Wilson also gutted it of its metaphysical vitality. "Like an egg that has cracked while being boiled so that gouts of white ooze out upon the shell, so has the earth cracked and exuded its continents." [19]

From the beginning, Antarctica was intimately connected with these developments. The desire to bring modern technology to Antarctica had been fundamental in the launching of IGY. The data gathered by IGY and the national and international programs that succeeded it became public just as the debate over continental drift accelerated: the Soviet Union published its *Atlas of Antarctica* (1965); the American Geographical Society, under contract with the U.S. Antarctic Research Program (USARP), inaugurated its publication of the Antarctic Map Folio Series (1964) and released its post-IGY map of Antarctica (1965); the Library of Congress, also under contract with USARP, began the comprehensive *Antarctic Bibliography* (1962); and USARP expanded its newsletter format into a new periodical, the *Antarctic Journal* (1966). Important symposia on Antarctic earth science proceeded in tandem with the exfoliation of plate tectonics. A small symposium was held in 1959 (Buenos Aires), about the time Wilson and others experienced their conversion to some rendition of continental drift. A major symposium in 1963 (Cape Town) explicitly, if eccentrically, put the legacy of Du Toit before Antarcticans at the same time that the critical ideas of sea-floor spreading and the drift symposium were under way. A 1970 symposium (Oslo) concluded with a special section called "Antarctica and Continental Drift." But, revealingly, the 1977 symposium (Madison, Wisconsin) opened with the relationship of Antarctica to Gondwanaland, as explicated by plate tectonics. At the 1982 symposium (Adelaide)—on the centenary of the birth of Sir Douglas Mawson and nearly the centennial for the publication of Dutton's Grand Canyon monograph—plate tectonics saturated the proceedings to such an extent that its reality was never questioned.

Writing in 1952, when the obvious outcrops had been described, Rhodes Fairbridge concluded a comprehensive synopsis of Antarctic geology with the observation that "Antarctica's geological history is full and identical in general pattern with that of all other southern continents. . . . In Antarctica we see geologically a 'normal' continent whose past history is closely comparable with other continents. . . ."[20] Reviewing Antarctic geology after IGY, Arthur Ford (1964) noted that "no other area of its size, except the ocean basins, is so unknown geologically." Ford went on to argue, however, that Antarctic data supported the old theory of continental accretion and that "the structure of this southern continent appears to be consistent with the global structural pattern."[21] That was the traditional American stance. But a volume on British science in Antarctica, published the same year, warily echoed the words of Du Toit. "Until recently Antarctica was the only unknown fragment of the geologic jig-saw puzzle," wrote Raymond Adie, "but now that the history of this continent has been partially unravelled it is apparent that East Antarctica is the true primitive continental shield of Gondwana affinities. . . ."[22] Adie stopped short of an endorsement of continental drift; yet it was clear that British geologists were prepared to look for lithic affinities among India, South Africa, Australia, and Antarctica to match the affinities of their political commonwealth.

Not Antarctica but the larger context of Antarctic discoveries would inspire a change in the scientific status of Antarctica. New data from Antarctica demonstrated that it was a normal continent, easily absorbed into whatever larger theory about the Earth then prevailed. If Antarctica was to acquire special significance, then a general theory would have to develop that targeted Antarctica as important. The meaning of The Ice, that is, would not emanate from The Ice but would have to be brought to it. The theory of plate tectonics did just that: the global tectonics that integrated Antarctica fully into earth science thus paralleled the geopolitical developments that integrated Antarctica into the Earth's political economy. In both cases Antarctica remained somewhat in a class by itself, though not completely; it was unusual but not anomalous. No longer was Antarctic science addressed only within the context of symposia on Antarctica; a series of international conferences on Gondwanaland, for example, assured Antarctica of a firm place in historical geology. In 1977 Campbell Craddock, dean of American Antarctic geologists, affirmed the relocation of Antarctica from the periphery to the center of earth science by blandly noting that "because of its position in the reassembly, Antarctica clearly must play an important role in determining the reality and history of Gondwanaland."[23]

After IGY Antarctica could not easily be ignored. The pattern of magnetic anomalies around the East Pacific Rise, which segregated the Pacific from the Antarctic plate, was important in vindicating the chronology and methodology of paleomagnetism and, thereby, sea-floor spreading. The bathymetry of the Southern Ocean was fundamental to the establishment of global plate boundaries. The discovery in 1969 of a Gondwanaland-type fossil, the Mesozoic reptile *Lystrosaurus*, near the Beardmore Glacier not only affirmed the centrality of Antarctica within a Gondwana supercontinent but emphatically dismissed that conceptual crutch of biogeographers, land bridges, which paleontologists had improbably imagined as spanning whole oceans. The geologic structures and stratigraphy of Antarctica and the contours of its continental shelf matched up brilliantly with the other constituents of Gondwanaland. Where Wegener had made Africa the stable point of reference for continental displacement, Dietz and Holden in their reconstruction of Pangaea (1970) gave that role to Antarctica, envisioning lithospheric plates swirling infinitesimally around Antarctica like colossal ice floes. Antarctica remained a cold core, central but immobile.

Yet the impact of Antarctic exploration should not be overstated. In many respects, Antarctic geoscience gained more from plate tectonics than it contributed. The contemporaneous exploration of the oceans was vaster and more critical; the 1962 symposium that revived continental drift as an academic subject said nothing about Antarctica but much about the enigmas of California; the discovery of Antarctic fossils and paleomagnetic records only corroborated, though in important ways, what had been developed elsewhere. Continental drift theory could not be accepted unless it explained Antarctica, but the explanation for Antarctic geology was not a primary motivation for or against the acceptance of drift. In his panoramic survey of the arguments for continental drift (1963), Wilson noted that "the compelling evidence for the existence of a Gondwanaland during the Mesozoic Era . . . has been reinforced by the findings made in Antarctica since the intensive study of that continent began in 1955."[24] In designing the U.S. Antarctic program, A. P. Crary recalled that "we realized very early in our studies of the Antarctic . . . that the southern oceans, area for area, were as interesting as the continent and possibly of more practical use, scientifically and otherwise."[25] Antarctica was supportive, not germinal: it did not, for example, enter into Wilson's seminal paper on transform faulting, which provided the last geophysical mechanism needed for plate theory. Antarctica did not confirm the validity of plate tectonics: it was plate tectonics that confirmed the status of Antarctica.

After IGY, however, earth science could no longer ignore Antarctica as being remote from important processes and unknowable by scientific methods. Yet Antarctica's prominence in IGY was attributable to the fact that the program evolved out of the suggestion, advanced by an Antarctic veteran, for another polar year and that the IGY agenda never lost that formative bias. Neither plate tectonics nor the larger revolution in planetary science was a response solely or even critically to the modern exploration of Antarctica. On the contrary, the modernizing of earth science reinvigorated the arguments for Antarctic research. Moreover, a strong commitment to Antarctic science was unquestionably an expression, somewhat sublimated, of international rivalry, a Cold War on The Ice.

There is an agreeable symbolism, then, to the story of the most widely heralded geologic discovery in Antarctica: the *Lystrosaurus* fossil that was taken as evidence of the Gondwanaland breakup and thereby of continental drift. The fossil was not simply a relic of Earth history: it represented a vestigial process of the earth sciences, the most ancient type of geologic evidence from the historical core of the earth sciences. The exhumation of *Lystrosaurus* did not stimulate plate tectonics; it "confirmed" continental drift. Not an anomaly like magnetic stripes on the ocean floor or gigantic transform faults that cried out for explanation, the fossil was a traditional type of evidence applied to an inherited problem. Antarctica was once again a recipient more than an originator. The discovery a year earlier in Antarctica of a jawbone fragment (identified as from a labyrinthodont amphibian) and the growing acceptance of continental drift had provided the rationale for Edwin Colbert to search for *Lystrosaurus*.

While the discovery aided the effort to place Antarctica within Earth history, it also helps place Antarctic geoscience within intellectual history. Moon rocks, also recovered in 1969, describe better than *Lystrosaurus* the alliance between high-tech exploration and the new planetary science. Not as evolutionary history but as a validation of continental displacement was this widely regarded "missing link" significant. Earth history had lost its historicism; the fossil might as well have been a unique mineral or a rift valley and served the same purpose. That purpose, too, had changed. It was through the Beardmore Glacier that Shackleton had penetrated into the heart of the Antarctic, and from Beardmore scenery that Wilson had penned his final sketches and the Polar Party had collected the rocks they carried with them to their snowy grave. Big Science had lost its special claim as a test of character, and nature had lost its role as a source of moral legitimacy. Colbert, an authority on reptiles, tried to inject other moral fables into his discovery: the extinction of the dinosaurs, the anthropogenic disruptions of modern biogeography, the lessons of the past for the future. But too many environmental threats—from synthetic chemicals to nuclear war—had no real precedents in the geologic past. The assimilation of Antarctica was well under way, but the world with which Antarctica was integrated was different from the one that had begun the process.

Iceblink: A History of Glaciology

The uniqueness of Antarctica did not reside in its rocks but in its ice. Initially, those ice terranes were an alien presence—the great impediment to geographic exploration, a white obscurantism that screened off intellectual inquiry, and a landscape astronomically remote from Earth processes, a Pleistocene relic as weirdly fascinating as the frozen carcass of a Siberian mastodon. Yet ice terranes control the information level of Antarctica, and if scientific exploration was to progress in the Antarctic, it had to make The Ice into information. It is no accident that the exploration of Antarctica epitomized by IGY coincided with the emergence of glaciology as a distinct scientific discipline.

The study of geologic ice had never been far removed from the study of rocks. Too much of early geologic travel had been to mountains, especially the Alps, for glaciers to be ignored. The rate of movement of the Grindelwald Gletscher was measured in 1760, and natural philosophers proposed two theories to account for the motion—dilation, a form of frost wedging by meltwater in crevasses, and sliding, by which the entire glacier slid as a

more or less coherent slab. Most of the important figures of
early geology—James Hutton and H. B. de Saussure, for example—developed glacial theories. During the 1820s such phenomena as erratics, moraines, and striations came to be associated with glaciers; Johann von Charpentier (after Goethe) argued that glaciers had formerly advanced on a vaster scale than at the present; and between 1837 and 1840 (with his *Etudes sur les glaciers*) Louis Agassiz reworked and popularized this idea and those of others into an "Ice Age," an almost Noachian Deluge of glacial ice across Europe. Agassiz successfully propagated his theory in Britain, where he converted Buckland and Lyell, then brought it with him to the United States. Large-scale glaciation became an accepted geologic fact, and glacial geology evolved into an important subfield, complete with its own stratigraphy, geomorphology, and principles by which it could be correlated to other climatic events. One of the dissatisfactions geologists felt with the nebular hypothesis was that its model for the evolution of an atmosphere made an ice age anomalous. Conversely, one of the presumed strengths of the "cold" planetesimal hypothesis of Chamberlin—who was himself an outstanding glacial geologist—was that it accommodated the Pleistocene ice age and tolerated, if it did not completely explain, its multiple advances and recessions.

The mechanics of ice flow attracted sporadic speculation. De Saussure thought that a glacier advanced by sliding as a rigid slab; Agassiz and his cohorts studiously measured the velocities of Alpine glaciers; and John Forbes (1843) argued for a model of viscous and plastic ice flow. Later, John Tyndall, a physicist, suggested that ice flowed according to the principles of regelation. In 1885 Albert Heim consolidated all these theories in his *Handbuch der Gletscherkunde*. By the end of the century, the Austrian S. Finsterwald had enunciated a theory of flow lines and the American geophysicist H. F. Reid had applied certain analytical methods to ice behavior. The extent to which ice behaved according to plastic, viscous, or regelation flow mechanisms was unknown and somewhat academic. What mattered most was that glaciers were a geologic phenomenon—agents of erosion and manifestations of ice ages, climatic epicycles in the evolution of the atmosphere and of life. What glacial geologists examined, after all, were relic landscapes and vestigial ice masses, the fossils of a lost age. The search for modern analogues of the Pleistocene ice sheets that had swept across Eurasia and North America merged, in particular, with traditions of Arctic and Alpine exploration to bring naturalists to Svalbard, Scandinavia, and Greenland. But not to Antarctica. When he published his famous treatise on climate cycles in 1886, James Croll hypothesized that the Antarctic ice sheet (if it existed) had to be 12–24 miles thick at its center to provide an adequate outward flow of ice to its margins—a statement that revealed a breakdown in glacial physics as profound as its conceptual breakdown in glacial geography.

By the advent of Antarctic exploration, the principles of glacial geology were well advanced and the concept of an Ice Age well established in Earth cosmogony. Antarctica, it was hoped, would offer a laboratory for the study of what Pleistocene Europe and North America might have been like. But the ice terranes were too formidable for traditional exploration; the ice sheets could tolerate rapid journeys to the poles of rotation or magnetism, but they could not sustain their own study. The great compendium of glacial geology of the era, Albrecht Penck and Eduard Brückner's *The Alps during the Glacial Periods* (1909), like Suess' complementary treatise on global tectonics, assumed that Europe and the Alps were type cases, that glacial epochs worldwide would correlate to those found in Europe just as mountain systems and stratigraphic columns conformed to the European pattern. Even the much smaller ice sheet on Greenland was not truly traversed until the Quervain expedition of 1912 and the important Koch-Wegener expedition of 1913. Earlier travels across the south (by Nansen, 1888) and the north (by Peary, 1890s, and Rasmussen, 1912) involved much smaller distances and lacked scientific purposes.

And the question of scale did matter. Ice sheets behaved differently than ice streams, and they formed not simply through the coalescence of mountain glaciers. With 90 percent of the planet's ice contained within the unexplored Antarctic ice sheet, theories about Earth ice behavior and history were severely limited. Yet scale was important in another, symbolic way too. Glacial geology had developed amidst landscapes from which the ice had long vanished or within which mountain glaciers constituted a dynamic fossil. These ices could be understood within the context of their rocks, glaciology within the parameters of geology. In Antarctica, however, ice was the prevailing medium; Earth had to be interpreted through the context of Ice. Accordingly, the enormity, intrinsic poverty of infor-

mation, and self-referential features of the Antarctic ice field
made it difficult to assimilate.

Yet ice was what Antarctica had in greatest abundance, and early Antarctic expeditions described glaciology, in addition to glacial geology. A few explorers—notably C. S. Wright of the *Terra Nova* expedition—addressed questions of ice physics that went beyond glacial geology to intersect themes in Antarctic meteorology and climatology. By the conclusion of the heroic age, the major ice terranes were identified, the magnitude of the interior ice sheets was recognized, and the chief problem of glacial geology in Antarctica, paleoclimatology, was articulated. Nordenskjöld with *Antarctica* (1905), Drygalski with "The Ice of the Antarctic and the Subantarctic" (1921), and Priestley and Wright with *Glaciology* (1921)—their formal contribution to the British Antarctic Expedition—brought together most of what was known and surmised about the ice field. It was soon recognized that the ice sheets had been greater than they were at present and that Antarctica, as a whole, had paradoxically experienced more temperate climates. The fossils of the Beacon supergroup testified to a dramatically warmer Paleozoic and Mesozoic, complete with coal beds—an anomaly seized upon by proponents of continental drift. Equally, the evidence for a much vaster and more recent glaciation was everywhere preserved on exposed outcrops and oases and, according to Scott's theory, by the presence of floating ice shelves like the Great Ice Barrier. An ironic aftermath, however, was the growing doubt (based on its relentless aridity) that Antarctica could serve as a contemporary surrogate for the great Pleistocene ice sheets.

Yet the Antarctic ice field seemed to be exceptional, huge rather than informative. The major developments in glacial geology and glacial ice behavior came after the heroic age and from the ice regimes located in the Northern Hemisphere—the studies of Alpine glaciers by Somigliano, Lagally, Mercanton, and Finsterwald; Demorest's (discredited) theory of extrusive flow based on multiple expeditions to Greenland under the sponsorship of the University of Michigan; the ice sheet researches of Wegener's tragic Greenland expedition; the celebrated Jungfraujoch studies of M. F. Perutz; Hans Ahlmann's and Harald Sverdrup's researches in Scandinavia, Svalbard, Iceland, and Greenland. Breakthroughs in ice-sheet stratigraphy, the measurement of englacial temperatures, the processes of fir-

nification, and seismic profiling all came about during an almost continuous stream of expeditions to Greenland.

Not the size of the ice field but the strength of the information
field brought to it determined the intellectual importance of an
area; information flowed, as though by electromagnetic induc-
tion, as the one field passed vigorously over the other. Despite
its dimensions, The Ice by itself was an intellectual sink, a geographic solipsism. Understanding demanded the presence of an
equally powerful source that could emanate only from major
centers of learning. As the source field intensified, the information gradient of Antarctica gradually steepened. Yet like a
cirque nestled within a mountain flank, the study of ice remained a comfortable enclave of geology.

When the American Geographical Society commissioned its
1928 memoir *Problems of Polar Research*, Priestley and Wright
nonetheless reaffirmed that Antarctica possessed great value,
that it held puzzling information about paleoclimatology, and
that "it is in Antarctica alone that all the main types of land ice
are met with today." Yet they argued for caution. Knowledge
about the interior "was very scanty indeed"; and only "constant
attention to detail" will "render it possible to make the gener-
alizations which are so fascinating but which the present generation of explorers should avoid." Antarctica could answer no
immediate theoretical problems, and no cross-sections of Antarctic glaciology were analogous to the geologic stratigraphy in
the Dry Valleys. Rather, "the time has come when new technique or better equipment will have to be evolved"; an adequate empirical data base about Antarctic ice would require
painstaking efforts; and an "adequate scientific attack," they
pleaded, should involve "international cooperation on the grandest scale." [26] Byrd echoed their concerns. Glaciation was the
"blankest," "most enthralling" chapter of Earth history, and
glaciology was "a glittering edifice of theories" amid a "painful
want of substantive data" for which Antarctica offered a chance
to observe "the mechanism of an Ice Age." [27] The conclusions of
his own survey supported the generally accepted idea that the
Antarctic ice sheet was a relatively thin veneer over an elevated
continent.

International rivalry was a more effective incentive than cooperation to Antarctic glaciology, and new conceptual models,
not geographic flights over *glacies firma incognita*, revitalized
the intellectual structure of the science. Much as it redirected

attention to Antarctica as a geopolitical arena, World War II indirectly revitalized the study of Antarctic ice. War research established cold-weather labs, interest in the polar regions revived (and thanks to the Cold War intensified), and a bizarre scheme to construct an aircraft carrier out of ice imparted to glaciology a new vigor and a heady intellectual and institutional independence. With the enthusiastic endorsement of Winston Churchill, it was proposed in 1942 to use ice floes as an aircraft carrier. Since a pound of explosives was required to destroy a pound of ice, the carrier would be impervious to German submarines, literally unsinkable. But natural floes were too intractable, so special laboratories were set up to investigate the properties of ice with the idea of constructing an artificial floe. Operational plans to construct a prototype ice carrier in Newfoundland were scrapped when the war turned in the Allies' favor.

But the research results and the experience of mixing glaciology with laboratory disciplines such as metallurgy endured. It was realized that glacial ice behaved more like a crystalline solid than a viscous liquid. Glaciology transferred its conceptual and methodological foundations from geology to rheology. An important conference involving the various groups that had investigated ice during the war was held in England in 1948. A year later E. Orowan consolidated that wartime research, and upon his findings during the 1950s J. W. Glen articulated the modern flow law for ice; J. F. Nye and others promptly extended the laboratory results to the world of real glaciers and ice sheets. Glacial geology increasingly became an arena for applied glaciology, rather than vice versa. Glaciologists could now evaluate ice behavior and effects according to physical models of ice deformation, not solely by extrapolating from geological landforms; and theories of ice-age genesis could be corroborated with the physical properties of ice sheets, independent of particular Earth cosmogonies and their ancillary baggage. The kinds of information that could be extracted from the ice expanded enormously. With wonderful irony, the rheology of ice was likened to the rheology of the mantle (aesthenosphere), linking plate theory and ice sheets in a way eerily reminiscent of Wegener's use of ice floes as a metaphor for continental drift. After the war, too, the institutional arrangements that had fostered a robust glaciology were strengthened: military labs for cold-region research were continued, civilian science was boosted, and the exploration of the Arctic and Antarctic, stimulated by Cold War hostilities, reintroduced vast geographies of ice and snow into academic inquiry.

Thus by the late 1940s there occurred a wonderful confluence of events. Glaciology had been reconstructed in its methods, purposes, and theory. Its status was such that it could support the founding of the International Glaciological Society and a separate periodical, the *Journal of Glaciology*—another happy upshot of the 1948 conference. At the same time, Hans Ahlmann's propagandizing for an international glaciological expedition to Antarctica culminated in the Norwegian-British-Swedish Expedition (1949–1952), the primary purpose of which was to investigate ice. The postwar militarization of the Arctic, including Greenland, assured that there would be permanent bases on the island and even on the ice sheet—this was in addition to a revival of traditional expeditions to Greenland. The Norwegian-British-Swedish Expedition was quickly succeeded by the continental-scale explorations of IGY, and to the new analytical techniques transferred from metallurgy were added technologies of deep-ice coring and analysis. The discovery that the ratio of oxygen isotopes (O^{16}/O^{18}) preserved in snow varied between winter and summer led, principally through Willi Dansgaard, to a new glaciochronometer that was distinct from traditional snow stratigraphy—in many ways a glaciological counterpart to paleomagnetic reversals. Similarly, ice-drilling technology improved in parallel to deep-sea drilling. In particular, new kinds of thermo-drills, well suited for ice coring, became available during the late 1950s. Remote sensing supplemented seismic profiling as a means to map the interiors and bases of ice sheets. In less than a decade a separate discipline, glaciology, had been created, a theoretical foundation for ice rheology established, new experimental and exploratory techniques vindicated, vigorous patterns of international coordination confirmed, and robust sources of new data developed. The rapid metamorphosis of glaciology into Big Science through wartime research and IGY was timed exquisitely to make the Antarctic ice field accessible and valuable.

For those interested in ice *qua* ice Antarctica, which contained 90 percent of all the land ice on Earth and most of its sea ice, was absolutely essential. No theory about ice that failed to explain Antarctic ice terranes could hope to succeed, nor was there good reason to ignore the Antarctic data which had sud-

denly blossomed into abundance. The timing had been phenomenal. The American prospectus for IGY Antarctic programs, for example, had exulted that the glaciologist "will be
on the greatest untouched glaciological frontier on Earth."
Even allowing for crowded and disrupted schedules of scientific
activity, "it is inconceivable that the alert glaciologist cannot
find some program of study in almost every situation and at almost any place in Antarctica which will produce useful results."[28] Antarctica and its ice was a premier attraction of IGY,
and instead of being cursed as an obscuring screen, the ice itself
became an object of interrogation.

The reformation came with remarkable suddenness, and the
Antarctic ice field and glaciology became inextricably intertwined. Admiral George Dufek, when asked what he thought of
the Ross Ice Shelf during Operation Deepfreeze, had replied,
"It's a hell of a lot of ice. But what good is it?"[29] After IGY, when
access was no longer prohibitive, glaciology established the
value of The Ice as scientific data. Similarly, Maurice Ewing,
when a student told him that he "had learned a little glaciology,"
replied, "Well, isn't that about all there is to learn on that subject?"[30] Antarctica—now valuable for any number of scientific
and geopolitical reasons—helped validate glaciology by forcing
it to consider the behavior of ice masses other than glaciers. At
the 1959 IUGG Buenos Aires symposium, the chairman on the
glaciological section declared that "the outstanding feature of
the whole symposium has been the reports on glaciological traverse operations over the Antarctic continent and ice-shelves."[31]
A year later the International Association of Scientific Hydrology sponsored the first symposium dedicated to Antarctic glaciology. Glaciological conferences on Antarctica paralleled the
international geoscience conferences. A decade after IGY, at the
International Symposium on Antarctic Glaciological Exploration (1968), A. P. Crary jocularly urged his audience to "have
patience and not be above leaving some real problems for the
future glaciologists"—a quip that would have been unthinkable prior to IGY.[32] In 1976 Johannes Weertman, an outstanding
theorist, formally announced that the stability of the West Antarctic ice sheet was "glaciology's grand unsolved problem."[33]
Glaciology had defined a distinct identity for itself within the
earth sciences, and Antarctica had assumed a critical role
within glaciology.

Institutionally, the IGY example was perpetuated by SCAR

coordination of national glaciological projects and the International Hydrological Decade. Eventually the International Antarctic Glaciological Project, established in 1969, formalized a better division of labor. Orchestrating research from Australia, France, Great Britain, the Soviet Union, and the United States, the IAGP focused first on the East Antarctic ice sheet, then expanded to include the West Antarctic Ice Sheet Project (WISP), the Ross Ice Shelf Project (RISP), the Ross Ice Shelf Geophysical and Glaciological Study (RIGGS), and the Glaciology of the Antarctic Peninsula (GAP). By the early 1980s the subglacial topography of Antarctica was at least rudely known, ice-flow lines had been delineated, an understanding of the Antarctic ice budget was given some quantitative definition, and Antarctic ice terranes were more or less integrated into global models of the Earth's climate, meteorology, and hydrology. Antarctica figured prominently in two symposia sponsored by the International Glaciological Society, one on icebergs (1977) and the other on Antarctic ice terranes (1982). But virtually every discussion of ice now had an Antarctic component.

Through its intellectual liaisons with atmospheric sciences, glaciology extended its range far beyond its geologic origins. In a sense, theories of climate change and general circulation models (GCM) did for Antarctic ice what plate tectonics did for Antarctic rocks. Antarctic data—especially ice cores and ocean sediment cores—figured prominently in CLIMAP (Climate: Long-range Investigation, Mapping, and Prediction Study), a subprogram of the International Decade of Oceanographic Exploration which has attempted to reconstruct selected past climates and ice terranes; in GARP (Global Atmospheric Research Program) and POLEX (Polar Sub-Experiment on Atmospheres), which have examined the role of ice in climate dynamics; and in alarmist models about the impact of atmospheric warming induced by an anthropogenic buildup of carbon dioxide, a warming that could cause the Antarctic ice sheets to melt, surge, or otherwise disintegrate abruptly with catastrophic consequences. With the acceptance of plate tectonics, the paleoclimatic data from Antarctica were no longer a remote anomaly but a further confirmation of continental displacement.

The history of the ice sheet remained an important question, of course, and glaciology never ceased its inquiry into geologic topics, but the segregation of glaciology from geology and the emancipation of geology from historicism refocused these relationships. The classic question about the ice ages had been how to place them within an unfolding historical drama—in particular, how to incorporate the ice deluges in a way that protected the evolution of life. In the nineteenth century, glaciology had been as bound by evolutionary geology as geology had been tied to evolutionary biology. Increasingly, however, the ice sheets acquired meaning beyond their presence as historical events: they were interesting, dynamic systems, full of feedback mechanisms; and the elusive explanation for global glaciation, it was proposed, could be found in the rheology of the Antarctic ice sheets. Glacial epochs could be triggered by the concatenation of astrophysical rhythms and chance events; they were part of self-regulating systems, not simply evolutionary epicycles in the progression of Earth history.

Perhaps more demonstrative were theories of global glaciation based on glaciology. In 1964 A. T. Wilson proposed a theory in which the West Antarctic ice sheet behaved like a surging glacier; global glaciations followed from the periodicity of the sheet's advances and recoveries. Almost a decade later, Terrence Hughes published an analogous theory that sought to explain the termination of glacial epochs through the disintegration of the West Antarctic sheet. The theories helped give intellectual energy to glaciology, brought Antarctica to the center stage of glaciology, and reoriented the study of global glaciation from geologic and climatic models to glaciological models. Meteorological and geological processes, it was argued, had to act through and be integrated by ice; the qualities of ice, ice sheets, and ice shelves were the fundamental facts and processes of global glaciation.

These theories, moreover, allowed The Ice to intersect a growing environmental ethic and conferred upon Antarctica a new moral interest. In its stricter formulations, the naturalism of the heroic age had imagined a designed block universe, structured by immutable laws of history and materialism. Humans either conformed to the laws or were crushed. Religion assured that the Design had a grander purpose and both comforted and inspired actors to pursue life strenuously. But glaciology matured within the context of a nonreligious, precariously open natural world that was all too vulnerable to human environmental meddling. Anthropogenic changes in the Earth's albedo and the carbon-dioxide content of the atmosphere could, in theory, affect global temperatures enough to indirectly initiate a surge or disintegration. Thus, while the study of Ice would not reveal Design, it might prevent destruction. The preservation of Antarctica's ice sheets joined the protection of its penguins and whales as a test of human character. It also challenged geopolitical ethics: arid nations contemplated glacial ice as a valuable mineral resource, and nations pondered how the ice terranes of Antarctica should be governed.

The rocks and ice, however, are chiefly valued for their information content. Antarctica enjoys a political economy based on the extraction of information, and the geopolitics of science are centripetal and stabilizing. While the geophysical isolation of Antarctica has intensified over geologic time, its integration with the noosphere has rapidly accelerated. Originally, its rocks were considered little more than final outcrops in the geologic mopping-up of the continents, its icy mantle an obscuring medium as opaque as deep ocean waters or the clouds of Venus. But as the exploration of the solar system has matured, that mixture of ice and rock has become a beginning rather than an end, a point of departure for the study of those broadly similar bodies which also orbit the Sun—the inner planets (especially Mars), the moons of the outer planets, the asteroids, the comets. Antarctica gave glaciology a continent of its own to investigate, and glaciology helped integrate The Ice into intellectual history. Ice became a medium, and the medium is a message.

The Sheet

I have reached these lands but newly
From an ultimate dim Thule—
From a wild weird clime that lieth, sublime,
Out of SPACE—out of TIME.

   —Edgar Allan Poe, "Dream-Land" (1845)

Great God! This is an awful place.

   —Robert Scott, on the polar plateau (1911)

It spreads to all sides, an unbounded void of alien whiteness and geometric rigor, as though Charon, the icy moon of Pluto, had splashed softly to Earth.

The Ice is everywhere and everything. Antarctica is the highest, windiest, driest continent; its continental shelves are the narrowest and deepest; its continental cratons are the lowest; its topography and dynamics the simplest on Earth—all this because of the ice sheets. They transform the Antarctic into a colossal exercise in reductionism: the sheets and shelves plate over or push out the sea, they submerge the land, and they displace the lower atmosphere. Here are concentrated the paradoxes and singularities of Antarctica.

The polar plateau is the largest yet simplest of the terrestrial landforms on the planet. Practically speaking, an entire continent is constructed out of a single substance, in a single state, manifest as a single mineral. The ice sheet is impressive by virtue of its size and its ruthless simplicity: microcosm joins directly to macrocosm, ice crystal to ice sheet; intervening processes and interactions, shapes, colors, and perspectives are removed. The Dry Valleys, only indirectly bound to the ice sheets, can be viewed as analogues of features on Mars. But the polar plateau can be likened only to less complex ice bodies such as comets and the moons of the outer planets—Europa, Callisto, Ganymede, Charon. The more deeply one goes into the interior, the more tenuous become its ties to the Earth and to human understanding, the more self-referential its processes.

There is an awesome singularity to the ice sheets. Their composition is pure, with few contaminants to adulterate the descending snow crystals. The structure of the sheet is far simpler than that of other ice terranes except for the sheet's floating cognate, the shelf. Within the sheet there is a gradual downward metamorphosis of snow to firn and firn to glacial ice, but little horizontal motion, little deformation, and little mixing of other ices with the ice sheet. Ice flows from the center of the sheet outward. Ice sheets are thus remarkably self-contained systems; no other ice terrane feeds into them; they are a peneplain of accretion, an unevolved ice mass of terrible simplicity, a glacial atavism. These are the simplest of ice masses; the information content of the terrane derives from its vast scale, not its

intrinsic complexity. Mass is reduced to one substance; structure is reduced to a surface of seemingly unbounded scope.

The ice sheets are a planetary sink—a cold vortex of heat,
water, and solar and cosmic radiation—that becomes a source
for virtually all the physical processes that make Antarctica
what it is. Its connections with the Earth are grossly extenu-
ated, but they are never wholly lost: the Antarctic atmosphere
has important bonds to the upper atmosphere; the Southern
Ocean, to the world sea by means of intermediate and bottom
waters; the continental cratons, to the fragmented plates of
Gondwanaland; the polar biota, to the biosphere through the
migrations of mammals and birds. But most of this mixing occurs around the perimeter of the ice sheets proper. As one advances into the interior, ice reductionism intensifies until, at
the eye of the vortex, motion itself slows to an appearance of
absolute zero. This erasure of Earth processes in turn exposes a
nexus with interplanetary space, most pronounced with the
onset of the polar night. The polar vortex is not only meteorological but geomagnetic: the solar wind supplements the gradient and katabatic winds, noctilucent clouds supplement the
cumulus and stratiform varieties, and the aurora supplements
the scattering of visible light and lunar optics.

Even here there is information. The Ice is not a vacuum. The
ice sheets have a history, often complex, and they exhibit internal variations in composition, structure, and motion, though
the effects are often apparent only because of the vast masses and
large distances involved. The ice is not simply an opaque veil
but substance with its own information content, however meager, and a matrix for embalming air, aerosols, microparticles,
and meteorites. The air inclusions that ripple across white and
blue ice are vials containing ancient atmospheres. The ice sheets
are great archives of past climates. The polycrystalline fabric of
the ice contains a history of stress fields. The meteorites that
gather into blue ice placers, the debris of interplanetary space,
and the cosmic ray interactions with the outer atmosphere that
settle into the snow all testify to the power of Ice as a medium
of information. Yet this is information preserved, not generated.
The hydrologic cycle is slowed, frozen, stored, then released on
a scale of tens or hundreds of millennia. A molecule of water in
the atmosphere will cycle every 0.1 year; in the oceans, 10–100
years; but in the ice sheet, 10,000 years. The residence time for a

molecule in the surface oceans is about 5,000 years; for the ice sheets, nearly 100,000 years. Humans can intervene—intercept some data, translate ice into information—before the ice dissolves back into more complex and far-flung Earth systems.

That information comes hard. The Ice replaces complexity with simplicity, variety with hugeness; it removes points of reference, perspective, and comparison. To extract information from The Ice requires a complicated society, a large expenditure of energy, and the capacity to step far beyond the confines of Antarctica to achieve the kind of contrast and perspective necessary for understanding. Other planets are one means of comparison; geologic time is another. Antarctica is a powerful reminder that the Earth belongs with a host of solar system elements that are composed of rock and ice, and it is a vivid analogue for the ice ages of Earth history. The domain of Earth time grants a perspective in some ways equal to that of interplanetary space. Through it the ice sheets of Antarctica find a context.

It was during that final glacial episode, of which the present may be nothing more than a temporary interstadial, that *Homo sapiens* developed—a species that learned to live in an ice age, that possessed, with fire, an antidote to cold; a species that alone has learned to extract from ice its most important commodity, information, and that has found in the source regions of The Ice a reflection of its own identity.

Glaciology of the Sheet

The dimensions are awesome. The ice sheets and their ice shelf extensions cover 13,800,000 square kilometers and occupy a volume of 25–30,000,000 cubic kilometers. The Antarctic ice sheet is about five times the magnitude of the Martian polar ice sheets. There is more water by three orders of magnitude in the Antarctic ice sheet (0.2×10^{17} tons) than in the entire atmosphere. Were the ice sheet to melt, the world ocean would rise 60–65 meters, and the consequences would be greater if so much of the ice sheet were not grounded on continental shelves where they displace seawater. Because of the weight of the ice, most of East and West Antarctica is depressed below sea level. If the ice were removed, even allowing for a dramatic elevation in sea level, most of the continent would rise above the waters. At the South Pole the Earth itself is measurably deformed from the geoid. Moreover, the ice is not only massive but monolithic, more like an overgrown rock than a unified mechanical system.

Yet the ice sheet is more than simply a continent-sized—and continent-defining—mass of ice thick enough to flow under its own weight. It is a complex composite of ice masses that are physically coupled and dynamically interdependent. Much as its ice shelves consist of lobes, streams, rises, and undulations overlain by thick mantles of snow, so the Antarctic ice sheet consists of many ice caps, ice streams, new and old ice, mobile and stagnant ice, structural and dynamic variabilities, and irregularities of shape caused by its geologic substratum. These complexities are greater at the margins than at the center. They are more evident at the base of the ice sheet than at the surface, more apparent in the peripheral ice streams than in the central ice domes, more pronounced in the smaller marine ice sheet of West Antarctica than in the enormous continental ice sheet of East Antarctica.

The geography of the Antarctic ice sheet divides into three general components: the east sheet, the west sheet, and the diminutive peninsular sheet. The east sheet has about ten times the ice of the west sheet, the west sheet perhaps ten times the ice of the peninsular. The peninsular sheet contributes to the Ronne Ice Shelf and supports an array of lesser shelves, most of them tightly bounded by offshore islands. It sustains a variety of local valley glaciers and ice caps with outlet glaciers. Its most important component is the ice dome in Ellsworth Land. Here the Bentley subglacial trough, which apparently defines two microplates, supports major ice streams into the Ronne Ice Shelf and to the Pine Island Glacier that debouches, unconfined, into the Amundsen Sea. This is a critical, dynamic boundary that the stable peninsular sheet shares with the unstable west sheet.

The east sheet is likewise land-based. Because of the ice, much of the continental craton is currently depressed beneath sea level, though melting would cause the land to rebound isostatically to an elevation well above sea level. The ice dome rises to a maximum thickness of 4776 meters; the central ice divide parallels the crudely elliptical shape of the craton. About a fourth of the ice mass drains through the Lambert Glacier to the Amery Ice Shelf. Much of it empties into the Filchner Ice Shelf; some, through outlet glaciers, contributes to the Ross

Ice Shelf; some crosses the great polar breach through the Transantarctics to join the west sheet; the rest flows in sheets and assorted ice streams to discharge points around the continent. The collective ice dome is roughly symmetrical to the circulation of air and water, so that storms rotate around the region rather than pass over it. Its great height and the thinness of the polar troposphere mean that true storms rarely penetrate into the interior. A sheath of chilled air—the inversion—covers the ice surface. Stable, huge, and lethargic, the east sheet contains 80 percent of the planet's ice.

The west sheet is more anomalous. Geologically, the region consists of an archipelago of mountains. The bottom of the west ice sheet consequently rests .5–1 kilometer below sea level; even with the ice removed and the land restored to its isostatic norm, most of West Antarctica would remain beneath the sea. The west sheet, then, is a marine ice sheet. Its bulk is largely grounded beneath sea level, and its flanks are pinned by the Ellsworth Mountains, the mountains of Marie Byrd Land, and the ice rises of the shelves that are contiguous with it. Most of it rests within the giant Byrd subglacial trough that extends from Ellsworth Land to the Ross Sea, and flow along several ice streams within the trough sustains the Ross Ice Shelf. The perimeter of the west sheet consists only partially of rock; the greatest proportion joins ice shelves, the east ice sheet, and the peninsular sheet—a dynamic, plastic border. The base of the west sheet is not frozen to bedrock but overlies films of meltwater. It can move and erode, and the grounding line that demarks the sheet from the shelf can be floated into retreat by a rise in sea level. Storms frequently cross perpendicularly to the west sheet, with higher rates of precipitation than to the east. Its greater accumulation and ablation rates, its watery base, its subice topography, and its smaller, more responsive mass all make the west sheet into a mobile, inherently unstable ice terrane. The glaciology of the continent thus reflects its geology: a stable continental craton to the east, a more active mosaic of microplates to the west.

The gross structure of the ice sheets is that of an inverted plate, a shallow parabola fattened at the ends. The shape is almost that which follows solely from the flow law for ice. So vast are the ice sheets that the topography of their geologic substratum and the mountain ranges that flank them have a negligible impact on their overall profile. The Ice dampens, reduces, homogenizes. But the appearance of homogeneity—so powerful at the surface—does not extend throughout the ice mass. The ice sheet that comprises the polar plateau subsumes an ice topography of ice domes, ice divides, ice saddles, ice streams, and stagnant ice placers. Bedrock topography channels ice into currents of faster flow and transmits disturbed flowlines upward and outward through the surrounding ice-sheet mass. Mountains locally dam the sheet flow, leaving some sites stagnant while directing others into vigorous outlet glaciers. Outflow patterns vary according to whether the ice empties into calving bays or ice shelves. Rates of accumulation and mass transfer are concentrated along ice-sheet margins. The parabolic curve of the ice sheet is the largest—not the only—ice structure, itself deformed by the geography of the craton. There are internal structures and ice fabrics, a profile of temperatures of significance to ice flow, and motions that are far from uniform. The surface is not inscribed with real geometric rigor. Smaller-scale surface features—undulations caused by bedrock relief and thin ice and reworked by winds—are found on the order of 6–20 kilometers. The snow mantle is etched wonderfully by wind deposition and erosion.

The properties of the ice sheet begin with its snow. The Antarctic is cold and arid. Compared to other ice terranes, there is little accumulation and little motion. Ablation occurs primarily by iceberg calving and secondarily by sublimation; a small proportion of snow is blown to sea by offshore winds. On the average, the water equivalent accumulation is 17 centimeters annually, but most of this precipitation is concentrated along the coast and shelves, where storms spiral inland. There is an order of magnitude difference between the accumulation along the coast and that in the interior. At the South Pole, ice crystal accumulation averages less than 4 centimeters per year; at higher source regions within the ice dome, the rate is even less. The blockage of storm paths and the geography of the polar front partly explain this aridity, and the extremely low temperature is another factor. Absolute humidity varies by a factor of 10 between −20 and −40 degrees C.—common temperatures for the interior ice sheets, and they plummet even further during the winter. Hence, although the relative humidity might be reasonably high, the total water vapor is paltry and precipitation sparse. Most of the ice accumulation occurs as snowfall; some develops as hoar (frost or depth) and some is the result of re-deposition by wind; locally, ice fog may leave a surface residue. Along the coast, snow falls in large flakes, the arms of the flakes interlock and meld, and ambient humidity reworks surface deposits. But within the more arid interior, precipitation falls as tiny ice crystals that do not merge easily and that blow like fine sand. The drifts resemble the great heaving sand dunes of the Arabian deserts; where snow and mountain meet, winds carve snow fields into a resemblance of the sand patches that ripple up the mountain flanks of Death Valley or the Tien Shan.

The surface-wind regime has two components: gradient winds, which accompany synoptic-scale storms, and katabatic winds, which develop within the sharp temperature inversion that overlies the snow. The two winds often interact, with low-pressure systems around the continent first blocking then accelerating the outflow of the katabatics. The katabatics derive their mass from the sheath of cold air that originates over the snow surface and their energy from gravity, which pulls that dense air downslope. The inversion is deeper in winter (500–1000 meters) than in summer (200–600 meters), when the temperature gradient between its top and bottom is greater (25 degrees compared to 3 degrees C.). The winds, and their effect on the surface snow, are thus more ferocious during the austral winter than during the summer. The outcome can be aptly described as a low-level jet, with an average depth of 300 meters and the highest velocities concentrated in the lower profile. In its slow mode, katabatic flow has wind but little snow; in its fast mode, the wind surges and is charged with snow—a light avalanche.

The interplay of winds and snow cover generates a host of eolian deposition and erosional features that substitutes for the geographic variety which soils and vegetation bestow on other continents. By comparison, Antarctica's is an impoverished topography, made even more startling by the dramatic juxtaposition of the tiny and the vast, the microrelief of the snow mantle and the macrorelief of the ice sheet. Across the surface of the polar plateau are etched such depositional features as snow patches and drifts, snow ripples and dunes, snow barchans and barchan trains, snow spits, and an abundance of erosional snowforms known as sastrugi. The sastrugi vary according to the properties of the snow mantle (the presence of an ice crust) and the characteristics of the wind-snow flow that sweeps across and chisels it. Sastrugi may be longitudinal or transverse, they show seasonal cycles as the snow crust softens or hardens and the wind intensity rises or falls, and out of snow strata they sculpture a corrugated surface that resembles Lilliputian canyonlands.

At an intermediate scale, undulations with wavelengths on the order of 6 kilometers can develop as the winds respond to changes in slope; and over a scale of 20 kilometers or longer, the general shape of the ice sheet can be affected by katabatic snow removal. Some of the ice-surface irregularities that initiate wind scour on this order are the product of subice topography, transmitted to the surface. For the most part, flowlines disturbed by bedrock do not affect the surface profile; whether or not they do depends on the ice thickness. The thinner ice and higher mountains around the perimeter may be reflected in surface waves with mean amplitudes of 20–25 meters and mean lengths of 12 kilometers. These can be reworked by winds. Moreover, as the winds pour down the ice dome, especially in dense, high-velocity surges, they do not flow over or erode evenly but shape a profile of alternate scour and deposit, much like the rapids-and-pool profile of mountain streams. A gross topography of "whalebacks" or waves can result.

The structure of the ice sheet continues below the surface. The sheet is broadly stratified into snow, firn, glacial ice, and basal debris, perhaps basal meltwater. There are profiles for englacial temperature and ice flow. Ice fabrics metamorphose into new geometries. In fact, the ice sheet is a huge, unconfined glacier; but its size, the relative lack of rigid borders, and the unremitting cold make the sheet special. Everything that occurs happens slowly and on an enormous scale. There is less snowfall than on other ice terranes, the transformation of snow into firn and firn into glacial ice proceeds ponderously, flow is retarded, and ice metamorphosis is simplified by the absence of lateral confinements. The transformation of firn to glacial ice may take 3,000 years, and the firn layer may extend to 100 meters. What the glacier compresses, the sheet decompresses. The information content is dispersed.

Traditional snow stratigraphy is problematic in the interior. Wind deflation and spotty precipitation may eliminate the meager accumulation at a site (half of Antarctica receives less than 10 centimeters per year). Even at a source region like Dome C in the east sheet, there is a 6–10 percent chance of missing a year's accumulation—the result of wind and light, patchy accumulation. At lower elevations on the ice sheet, the accumulation is greater but so are the winds. At the same time, the relatively mild winds of the interior reduce both drifting and sublimation so that accumulation is not smoothed out across an area. The absence of dust and seasonal melting (and refreezing) deprives the snow column of annual growth rings. Instead, stratigraphic information comes from microparticles of dust, of elemental metals, of nitrate and sulfur compounds, and of oxygen isotopes within the trapped air.

At Dome C there is an annual cycle of atmospheric processes, an irregular surface of deposition and erosion, and muted, little understood mechanisms that transform the light, granular snowfall into firn and glacial ice. Inexplicably, fine crusts form over soft snow blankets in the late summer or early autumn. Compression eliminates pore space, and recrystallization organizes new crystal shapes, sizes, and bonds. Most ice crystals are coarse initially and connect to three or four neighboring grains by means of icy necks. Within this porous zone, vapor and heat are transferred to the surface. The driving force is apparently the product of the energy gradient that exists between the large free energy of the crystal surfaces and the free energy of the internal lattice structure; under these conditions, the densification of firn resembles the unconfined sintering of ceramics. While there is some downward compression, recrystallization and densification occur in the absence of confining stress, a simple diagenesis. The upper 10 meters is relatively isothermal, damping out the annual winter cold wave. But the overall process is tedious, infinitesimal: the transition to glacial ice requires 100 meters or more.

This transition is best exposed in the ice cores taken from the sheets. Only one has penetrated the entirety of the Antarctic sheet, the borehole at Byrd Station in West Antarctica. Its location in a zone of relatively heavy snowfall and rapid flow (away from an ice divide) means that the profile of the hole differs from that typical of an ice dome. Particularly on the east sheet, such domes will be colder, drier, and less subject to shear than other portions of ice sheets. The Byrd core augered through 2164 meters of the west ice sheet. The ice fabrics begin near the surface with random crystal orientation. Gradually, under molecular exchange processes, the firn densifies and recrystallizes. As the ice flows and internal shear develops, the ice fabric acquires a strong vertical orientation (around the c-axis). This metamorphosis promotes flow by enhancing nearly horizontal glide planes. With greater depth, internal shear, and improved flow, the fabric becomes more strongly slaty. An intense zone of shear and an ice fabric with a single maximum orientation are found between 1200 and 1800 meters. At the same time, however, the internal temperature of the sheet increases. Friction from shear is one source, terrestrial heat flow trapped by the poorly conducting ice is another, and ice formed during warmer eras and subducted into the sheet is still another. At Byrd the lowest ice temperature occurred at 800 meters (−28.8 degrees C.); at 1800 meters, the temperature had risen to −13 degrees C.; and at the base, the ice was at its pressure-melting point. Thus the temperature of the ice increases with depth, and the warmer ice improves flow. Equally, at greater depths the impact of bedrock irregularities cannot be ignored. The increased temperature, flow, and deformation encourage recrystallization and a multi-polar ice fabric. Thus there are rheological boundaries within the vertical profile of the ice sheet.

One such boundary is the transition between the shear that is controlled by bedrock surfaces and the shear that is controlled by the mean surface slope, the internal deformation of the ice mass due to its own weight. Depending on the stress field—whether the ice flows in sheets or in streams—another strongly oriented fabric may be created in the lower portions (200−400 meters) of the ice mass. Another rheological transition, sometimes found in massive sheets that inhabit mountainous bedrock substrata, marks the boundary between ices derived from different glacial episodes. Old ice from a previous glaciation may underlie newer ice of the present glaciation. The west sheet apparently disappeared during the last interglacial; the ice recovered from the Byrd borehole is wholly the product of the last (Wisconsin-Würm) glaciation, though at 1100 meters there is a change in ice fabric corresponding to the end of the last glaciation. The east sheet, however, never wasted away completely; new snow and glacial ice built up on old, and the boundary between new ice and relic ice is marked by different ice fabrics with distinctive rheological properties. At Dome C, basal ice may be 500,000 years old and may cover even older ice masses. In some cases, this transitional stratum becomes a zone of shear.

The basal layer is the most active. Here the strain rate is highest, the product of high shear stress and high temperature. At Byrd, some basal sliding is likely, although plastic deformation and movement along horizontal shear planes are the major con-

tributors to motion. Perhaps most spectacularly, the Byrd borehole encountered a layer of stratified debris during the last 4.83
meters and struck basal meltwater at bedrock (1 millimeter).
The combination of morainal silt, sand, and pebbles and the frequent deformation (and recrystallization of lower ice strata)
produces a zone of seismic chatter. The most likely explanation
for the debris stripes in the lower column is that they originate
from the refreezing of basal meltwater. Unlike snow-derived
glacial ice, this basally accreted ice lacks air bubbles; it is refrozen water, not compressed snow. Nor are these layers deformed by shear—a further indication that the captured debris
was not abraded from the local bedrock but simply frozen into
the filmy meltpool. The presence of basal water—in some cases,
of basal meltlakes—suggests that the ice sheet or the ice
streams embedded within it can experience basal sliding. Calculations on the potential distribution of subsheet meltwater
sketch a map that features concentric rings of alternately melted
and frozen bases. In the west sheet, the center is melted, and
some refreezing occurs around portions of the perimeter. In the
east sheet, the center source region is frozen, a zone around it is
melted, the zone around that is freezing, and portions of the perimeter are melting. The prevalence of melting, especially along
the more active margins, may be an important mechanism in
explaining the surgelike velocities of major ice streams and
outlet glaciers, and it is significant for the overall stability of
the ice sheets themselves.

If the Antarctic ice sheets were ideal ice slabs resting on a
rigid, level continental platform, they would spread outward by
radial sheetflow according to the flow law for ice. The exterior
profiles of the Antarctic sheets are a good approximation of this
ideal form, but their flow is far from simple. Only locally, or in
some cases on the east sheet regionally, is there anything like
sheetflow from ice domes to ice margins. Instead, the flow is
concentrated by bedrock troughs and mountain barriers into
high-velocity ice streams and outlet glaciers. The ice streams
are segregated from neighboring ice streams by ridges or domes
of slow-moving ice that rest on bedrock ridges. The ice streams
behave like enormous glaciers, except that they are confined
laterally by ice rather than by rock; these glacial streams can
deform, not merely erode, their boundaries, and the confining
ice may preserve deformations for some distance outward from
their point of origin. Basal ice streams, moreover, can flow

around obstacles as well as over them. Depending on the influence of bedrock topography and adjacent ice streams, the flow beneath a single surface point may change directions with depth. The enormous bulk of the ice sheets dampens out most of these disturbances before they can influence the surface profile. But the flow regime is surprisingly complex, in places more like a braided stream than an unadulterated sheetflow. To complicate the picture further, the weight of the ice sheet depresses the base below sea level; in the case of the west sheet, most of the ice would rest on submarine surfaces even if no isostatic depression occurred. Basal ice may thus be frozen to its bed or rest on a film of water, and ice streams may float as ice shelves or ice tongues at their margins.

There are different flow regimes for ice streams, ice divides, and ice pools. It is the ice streams that discharge most of the ice—90 percent for the west sheet. And they are by far the most active portion of the ice-mass composite that makes up the sheet; the west-sheet ice streams and the major outlet glaciers of the east sheet move at velocities typical of surging glaciers. Accumulation rates, basal water, and velocities all increase toward the margins. Where the ice streams experience rigid confining pressures along their sides or bottoms, they are permeated with crevasses. The center of the east sheet, by contrast, is devoid of fractures; the strain rate would have to increase a thousandfold; so mild is the longitudinal strain rate that the response time for the ice dome is on the order of 25,000 years. Because of the low velocities and great thickness of the ice dome, only low velocities are needed to maintain a steady-state regime. In other places, caught between surging ice streams or dammed by mountains, ice may stagnate for millennia, slowly ablating by surface sublimation.

Ice-stream behavior has important implications for the stability of the ice sheets. The driving stress for ice-stream flow depends on ice thickness and velocity. This stress is greatest at zones of convergence, notably the crescentic heads of outlet glaciers and ice streams, and least at zones of divergence or sites where basal shear stress is reduced because of water. In general, the driving stress increases from the ice divide to the ice margin. This rate of increase with distance is greater for the ice streams of the west sheet than for those of the east sheet, although the size of the east sheet means that the highest driving stresses reside there. The presence of ice shelves also reduces and dampens the effect of ice streams; backpressures are set up that retard and thicken the source ice sheet. But because the ice streams carry most of the ice discharge of the sheets and because they move much faster than sheetflow, the stability of the sheet as a whole depends on their flow regime and their interaction with their buffering ice shelves. The east sheet is considered inherently stable because its outlet glaciers cannot retreat beyond the ice falls that mark their grounding lines along the continental shield; the bulk of ice discharge is into a host of small, independent ice shelves; and as the ice sheet thins, the mountains will effectively dam much of the flow. The west sheet is considered inherently unstable for exactly the opposite reasons. The ice-stream grounding lines can retreat indefinitely across the marine-based ice sheet, and the control over ice-stream retreat that the Ross and Ronne-Filchner ice shelves exert is unreliable. Once unpinned, the entire west sheet may disintegrate rapidly. Thus, the east and west sheets behave in fundamentally different ways.

In brief, the west sheet appears to be intrinsically more mobile and unstable than the east sheet. Two major theories about Antarctic (and global) glaciation begin with this potential. The surge theory emphasizes the capacity of the west sheet to advance rapidly, while the disintegration theory emphasizes the capacity of the west sheet to break up catastrophically. According to the surge theory, the west sheet is, in effect, a gigantic surging glacier. Accumulation allows the ice sheet to thicken, the greater depth bringing the base to the pressure-melting point; the west sheet surges out into the Ross embayment; a tremendous expansion of the ice-shelf dimensions and the domain of tabular bergs increases the Earth's albedo, and global climate cools; a glacial period is inaugurated. In this way, a small change can amplify small secular changes in climate so that they have global consequences. Meanwhile, the much-thinned marine west sheet cannot long survive. Calving reduces its dimensions and the process of building up another ice dome begins. In this way, the theory accounts for the periodicity of glaciations and the abrupt onset of a glacial epoch.

The disintegration theory plays on the perceived instability of the west sheet to explain the sudden termination of glaciations. The critical elements of the theory are the submarine bedrock of the west sheet, the poorly pinned ice shelves (notably the Ross Ice Shelf), the ice streams around the margins, and

the presence of basal meltwater under the ice streams, which
encourages surgelike velocities. Fundamental to the theory is the assumption that any ice sheet that is grounded below sea level—as the west sheet is—can be considered inherently unstable because it adjusts irreversibly to climatic change, it experiences surge dynamics, and isostatic rebound is delayed through ice loading. The key is the uncertain metastability of the Ross Ice Shelf. Warming can thin the ice sheet, surging ice streams can then perhaps punch through it, and rising sea levels can float it off grounding lines and submarine protuberances. Once the grounding line crosses a threshold, the entire west sheet begins to break up, and the fractured pieces—colossal bergs—are rafted out to sea. Rather than having heat carried to the ice sheet, as simple models of global warming attempt to do, the disintegration model carries the ice to the heat. Here is a physical explanation for the relatively sudden collapse of glacial periods that the geologic record reveals. An additional attraction of the model is that it couples Antarctic glaciation with that of the Northern Hemisphere. Northern glaciation controls eustatic changes of sea level; as northern ice sheets abstract or liberate water, the grounding line of the west sheet advances or retreats. Glaciation in the Northern Hemisphere promotes a thickened and stable west sheet, while deglaciation in the north encourages a thinning, floating, and unstable west sheet.

The model suggests two modes of disintegration. According to the slow mode, the Ross Ice Shelf expands inland between the calving front and the grounding line. Local ice domes between ice streams become new ice rises, and the ice shelf continues to be buttressed. According to the fast mode, the ice shelf becomes unpinned. The calving line recedes as well as the grounding line, ice streams surge forward without the damping and stabilizing influence of the shelf, and the ice retreats along the streamlines into the heart of the sheet. The ice sheet literally breaks apart. A global warming trend affects the Antarctic indirectly, through a rising sea level brought about by northern deglaciation, rather than directly by melting. A major retreat by the Ross Ice Shelf would affect the largest volume of west ice, since the Byrd subglacial trough empties into the Ross embayment. But the Ronne-Filchner Ice Shelf would similarly crack apart, and the important ice streams that define the boundary between the peninsular and west sheets would be affected. Both the Pine Island Glacier and the Thwaites ice stream calve directly into the Amundsen Sea without the restraining effect of an ice sheet, the bay being kept open by a polynya. The streams could recede catastrophically across the Bentley subglacial trough (a probable microplate boundary), decoupling the west sheet from the peninsula. Once the elaborate network of buttresses around the west sheet is broken, it is thought the ice will rush down surging ice streams, the ice dome will thin, and the entire mass will fragment and raft away.

The idea is plausible on theoretical grounds, and there is an elegant complementarity between the surge and disintegration models. But it is not known whether the models describe the real world. There is evidence from the floor of the Ross Sea and the mouths of the Dry Valleys that the west sheet has spread across the Ross embayment as grounded ice. Other evidence suggests that the west sheet disappeared during the last interglacial, that northern and Antarctic glaciation is broadly synchronous, and that the onset (and especially the conclusion) of glaciations occurs abruptly. The disintegration theory argues further that the west sheet is currently in one of the two modes of disintegration. On this, however, the evidence is mixed. The Ross Ice Shelf and the west ice dome may have stabilized 8,000–7,000 years ago.

The most solipsistic of Antarctic ice terranes, the ice dome is, paradoxically, the vast informing nucleus of the entire ice field. Upon the character of the ice dome depends the entire congregation of ice terranes that comprise Antarctica; upon the stability of the ice sheets depends the history of The Ice. The influence of the sheets spreads to the Antarctic convergence and the polar fronts. By virtue of their sheer dimensions, the ice sheets have become a vital component of Earth climate, atmosphere, and hydrosphere. The relationship of the ice sheets to eustatic changes, to the Earth's albedo, and to the initiation and termination of glaciations makes the white hole that is Antarctica as critical to the climate of the Earth as black holes are to the cosmology of the universe.

Ice of Ages

The ice sheets are more than dynamic systems: they are historical events. The Antarctic ice field is not a permanent feature of the Earth. Antarctica has straddled the South Pole for only

200 million years. The present ice dome is neither the first nor the last of its kind. Periodically, the Earth's cryosphere expands enormously: these planetary ice ages seem to occur at roughly 150-million-year intervals. But they are only part of a hierarchy of ice oscillations that operate on different scales of time— minor, reversible fluctuations in ice masses (25–100 years); major, partly reversible fluctuations (250–1,000 years); stadial and interstadial episodes in which ice experiences significant advances and retreats (2,500–10,000 years); glacial and inter- glacial stages (25,000–100,000 years); and ice ages themselves (on some million-year cycle). These rhythms are compounded with other, stochastic events and with the broad secular pro- gressions of Earth history—the evolution of an atmosphere, hydrosphere, biosphere, and lithosphere. There was no conti- nental glaciation before there were continents, no water ice sheets before there was water. While roughly periodic in their occurrence, the ice ages of the Earth have been distinct episodes because the Earth has changed significantly during the course of geologic time.

Perhaps the first south polar ice existed as a shield of pack ice. By 2.3 billion years ago (Lower Proterozoic), the Earth's crust had thickened enough to be sufficiently high and rigid to support glacial ice. It is likely that the proto-Antarctic craton was involved in these ice ages (the Huronian) on a planet with- out life, with an improverished atmosphere, and upon which continents were lithic atolls amid a universal ocean. There were other glacial epochs throughout the Precambrian, proba- bly three in all, and an ice age during the Late Ordovician that gouged across what is today the Sahara Desert—none of which involved the accreting Antarctic shield. But it was otherwise with the gigantic Permocarboniferous ice age. Centered in southern Africa, it swept across the constituents of Gondwana- land; it buried nearly all of Antarctica, which was then the most polar of the Gondwana shields.

The Permocarboniferous epoch extended over perhaps 100 mil- lion years and embraced at least five major ice ages. It peaked during a span of 40 million years (310–270 million years ago) and seems to have oscillated in stages, each stage radiating far- ther from a central ice dome along the Gondwana junction be- tween South America and southwestern Africa. Antarctica and Australia were caught in the last and greatest surge. In the meantime, the fragmentation of Gondwanaland was just beginning. Antarctica moved into the polar position it would occupy for nearly 200 million years, and as the plates bearing the other continents moved away from it, its isolation intensified and the circulation patterns that could support ice sheets became established. The apparent periodicity of glacial epochs suggests that a global event should have occurred during the Jurassic. But evidence for ice during the period—an exceptionally warm time on Earth—is minor; and if local glaciation occurred in Antarctica, the evidence is buried beneath the present ice sheets.

For the Cenozoic glacial epoch, however, Antarctica was integral, initiating. The Ice is a lineal descendant from those events. Permanent ice began to collect around the early Oligocene (38–26 million years ago). During the Miocene, the lithospheric isolation of Antarctica was completed: Australia rafted northward, and complex microplate movements established the Drake Passage. The development of the Antarctic circumpolar current blocked the old precipitation sources for West Antarctica. By mid-Miocene times (25–20 million years ago), the Antarctic ice sheet was fully realized; ice from the east sheet overrode the Transantarctics (15–9 million years ago), and grounded glacial ice extended to the edge of the continental shelf. By the end of the Miocene, however, the ice was ebbing. Isostatic sinking, the sheer size of the ice sheet, and vigorous subglacial erosion conspired to give the west sheet the properties that make it inherently unstable. The Ross Ice Shelf formed during the recession, about 10–8.5 million years ago. The Pliocene witnessed the collapse of the west sheet, the preservation of the east sheet, and the gradual reclamation of the entire continent by resurging ice sheets. Thereafter the glacial and glaciological history of the ice sheets becomes more complex; northern and southern hemispheric glaciation proceed in rough synchroneity; more detailed information from sea-floor cores and, for the most recent events, from ice cores allows finer resolution, the detection of more subtle rhythms.

The modern ice sheets date from the late Pliocene resurgence (7–3 million years)—ice sheets that were maintained throughout the Pleistocene and in a few instances (most spectacularly in Antarctica) preserved into the Holocene. The maximum volume of east-sheet ice was probably 60 percent greater than at present, and the Transantarctic Mountains experienced at least six major ice events over the past 3.7 million years. The Quaternary glaciation of the Northern Hemisphere got under way 4–3 million years ago; the Greenland ice sheet became established about 3 million years ago; and Arctic sea ice became apparent, at least seasonally, about 3.5 million years ago. An interlocking matrix of ice sheets developed across the north polar and temperate regions: the Laurentide, Cordilleran, Newfoundland, Innuitian, Greenland, Iceland, British, Scandinavian, Barents, Kara, East Siberian, and Putorana ice sheets, with ice shelves coating the remaining Arctic Ocean and North Atlantic around Greenland and Iceland. The Antarctic ice sheet was limited by the geography of its calving perimeter, which coincided with the continental shelf. But the northern hemispheric sheets could spread widely across continents, and by regulating sea level they coordinated events in Antarctica, especially the development of the west sheet.

In both hemispheres the Pleistocene was dominated by a series of glacials; glaciation was the norm for 90 percent of the era, and each interglacial endured for only about 10,000 years or so. The timing of ice rhythms seems to have conformed approximately to the Milankovitch cycles, which describe the amount of solar radiation that strikes the Earth because of various long-term wobbles in the planetary orbit. These mild oscillations in insolation could have been amplified into larger climatic effects because the ice sheets altered both sea level and the overall albedo of the planet. Larger ice masses meant that more insolation was reflected into space, that more of the hydrosphere could be converted into ice, and that eustatic lowering of sea levels could advance grounding lines and allow floating ice shelves to become grounded ice sheets. The establishment of a permanent Arctic ice pack around 700,000 years ago was a major event. Though sea ice has significantly less albedo than snow, the pack provided a relatively stable platform for snowfall, and its albedo was markedly higher than normal land surfaces. That so many of the major ice sheets were marine-based meant that control over sea levels was fundamental to the evolution and synchroneity of glaciation in both hemispheres. Since the establishment of the Arctic ice pack, glacials and interglacials have appeared on a cycle of roughly 100,000 years.

The peak of the last interglacial occurred about 125,000 years ago. Sea level rose 5–8 meters, indicating that either the West Antarctic ice sheet or the Greenland ice sheet had vanished. The land-based Greenland sheet resembles the East Antarctic sheet, except in size, so the likely candidate is the more precarious West Antarctic sheet. The interglacial was ephemeral. By 120,000 years ago reglaciation had reclaimed about half of the lost ice. The East Antarctic ice sheet contains ice of this age, along with pockets and domes of buried relic ice that survived the interglacial. By 75,000 years ago glaciation had reached a maximum—controlled in the Northern Hemisphere by the continental summer meltline and in the Antarctic by a calving line roughly coexistent with the boundary of the continental shelf. The oldest ice from the Byrd borehole dates from this maximum. East Antarctic ice again overrode nunataks and the Transantarctics. The ice receded somewhat during an interstadial lasting from 60,000 to 25,000 years before the present. Then it quickly built up to the last maximum (Wisconsin-Würm glaciation) approximately 18,000 years ago. The Antarctic ice sheets again grounded and reached out to the continental shelf boundary. At last came the recession that has extended, with minor perturbations and fluctuations, until the present.

The grounding line retreated, leaving the major ice shelves as a plastic wake. From 8,000–5,000 years before the present, global temperatures reached a climatic optimum. The relatively sudden collapse of the Northern Hemisphere ice sheets within the span of a few hundred years liberated great quantities of water that raised sea level and transferred the effects of the warming to the Antarctic. Whether the Ross Ice Shelf stabilized during this period, as some believe, or whether it has continued to retreat, as others hold, is a central issue in determining whether the west sheet is stable or is disintegrating. The evidence that ice sheets—especially marine ice sheets such as the Laurentide and Scandinavian of the Northern Hemisphere—can disappear within a few centuries has alarming implications. If the west sheet similarly disintegrates, and does so irreversibly as glaciological models suggest, this will mean a catastrophic increase in sea level, an abrupt discharge of icebergs into the oceans (with significant ocean cooling), and a change in albedo within an uncomfortably brief span of time by human standards.

Yet the issue is far from decided. While the general outline of Antarctic glaciation is apparent, the details are not known. The instability of the west sheet is theoretically sound but not empirically established. Nor is it even understood just how the Antarctic ice sheets formed in the first place or how east and west sheets have interacted with each other. According to

the most common theory—ultimately based on centuries of
glacier-watching in the Alps—ice formed first on the highlands
of East Antarctica, the Gamburtsev Mountains and the Transantarctics. During favorable times these glaciers expanded to
form the giant ice dome of the east sheet. The east sheet not
only influenced the formation of the west sheet by its effect on
regional weather but contributed substantial streams of ice that
became the foundation for the marine-based west sheet. The
west sheet may alternately surge and disintegrate, but the east
sheet endures, no more likely to break up than the craton upon
which it rests. During major glaciations, the ice sheets thicken,
ice streams increase velocity, and calving discharges more icebergs; but the expansion of grounded ice and shelf ice is restricted by the geography of the continental shelf.

Another scenario, however, may be equally plausible, this
one based on the mobility and prevalence of marine-based ice
sheets such as the Laurentide and Scandinavian, which formed
in shallow seas and then transgressed onto land. According to
this idea, the west sheet coagulated by the transformation of
local highland glaciers and fast ice into an ice shelf and then
into an ice dome. West Antarctica has an important element of
ice-sheet formation that East Antarctica lacks: a source of precipitation. In the early Miocene, before the Antarctic circumpolar current became fully established, precipitation was even
higher in the West Antarctic archipelago than it is today. East
Antarctica, by contrast, was a cold, arid desert that lacked sufficient precipitation to sustain more than a smattering of mountain glaciers. The west sheet grounded and expanded to the
edge of the continental shelf—and through the breach in the
Transantarctics created by the rotation of the Ellsworth Mountains. The shelf boundary limited expansion in any direction
but into East Antarctica; more ice flowed from west to east, and
the center of the ice dome shifted toward the South Pole. Unlike
marine-based ice sheets in the Northern Hemisphere, which
were limited in their transgression over land by melting lines,
the west sheet moved into a cold arid desert. Melting would be
trivial. The ice could expand until it reached a calving basin.
When the Miocene maximum arrived, the coalescence of ice
domes and transgressing ice smothered Antarctica everywhere
to the perimeter of its continental shelf. The west sheet could,
and did, surge and disintegrate, but the east sheet was now in
place and stable. By Pliocene times, with the Antarctic cir-

cumpolar current long established and an important source of moisture to West Antarctica cut off, the east sheet became instrumental in the periodic rebuilding of the west sheet.

Even more elementary, there is little consensus on the causes of the ice ages, their baffling apparent periodicity, or their sudden termination. A host of known and suspected contributing causes is recognized: plate movement, which transports continents to polar regions and favorably distributes land-sea patterns; mountain-building, which creates glacial traps, potential source regions for ice; atmospheric changes, especially changes in the Earth's albedo or carbon-dioxide content that can influence global temperature; oceanographic changes, such as the deflection of the Gulf Stream, the creation of bottom water, or the establishment of the Antarctic circumpolar current; periodic magnetic reversals, which may alter insolation and temperatures; astronomical variations such as the Milankovitch cycles, which influence the amount of solar insolation; and glaciological properties, such as the massive instability of the west sheet and the positive feedback that ice has on the creation of more ice. No single cause appears to be adequate to control glaciation. Instead many factors, each with its own rhythm or secular variation, compound with one another to produce effects on the necessary scale. Even here, feedback mechanisms are necessary to amplify small changes into global ones. Here the properties of ice *qua* ice become significant. Ice is such a wonderful instrument of positive feedback that glaciation encourages further glaciation; but, equally, there are often inherent instabilities in the geography and glaciology of large ice masses, so that the masses may contain the dynamics of their own collapse, a historical dialectic of Ice.

A useful concept is the idea of an instability threshold, a compound of climatic effects which separates glacial from nonglacial environments. Constants and variables depend on whether one is in or out of a glacial epoch. Currently, the Arctic ice pack and the ice sheets on East Antarctica and Greenland may be considered constant ice elements; and ice shelves, seasonal sea ice, and unstable marine ice sheets may be viewed as variables. What does seem evident is that simple changes of global temperature are inadequate, by themselves, to instigate and terminate ice ages; that, once the ice is established, periodic ebbs and flows obey the rhythms of orbital variations; and that, given the long spans of geologic time during which ice has been pervasive, glaciation may be considered a normal and enduring feature of the Earth.

The ice terranes of Antarctica obey different rhythms and their behavior may be out of sync. Local mountain glaciers, for example, may retreat in response to warmer and drier conditions that prevail over the course of a few decades, but the ice domes may simultaneously continue to build up as a response to heavier snowfalls that occurred during a previous century. Overall, the ice exists in metastable equilibrium. It absorbs short-term variations and deforms under long-term variations. The stability of the ice depends on the scales involved, and these depend on the size and the response time of the ice mass. Short-term fluctuations are reversible; their periodicity is shorter than the response time of the ice mass. But long-term fluctuations initiate irreversible changes that lead to gross alterations in the size and behavior of the ice mass.

Of particular interest for nearly a century has been the response to known oscillations in the Earth's orbit that affect the amount and distribution of solar radiation. Known since the 1920s as Milankovitch cycles, after the Yugoslav physicist who gave them their modern expression, the theory involves three astronomical cycles: the eccentricity of the orbit (with a period of 93,000 years), the precession of the equinoxes (21,000 years), and the obliquity of the ecliptic of the Earth's orbit (41,000 years). The obliquity variation is especially important because it effects great changes in high latitudes. These cycles seem to correlate satisfactorily with the fluctuations experienced within a glacial and perhaps with the oscillation of glacials and interglacials, but for ice age genesis these insolation rhythms may be inadequate. Even within a glacial, the variation in solar radiation is slight (3–7 percent), no more than the variability experienced in most regions of the world from year to year. At best, the Milankovitch cycles could bring a region across a glacial instability threshold; they could function as relay switches, triggering—perhaps through feedback mechanisms inherent in ice—a quantitatively vaster response.

What accounts for the 150-million-year cycle that seems to govern glacial epochs is unknown. It has been suggested that the movement of the solar system through the galaxy—a spiraling journey on the order of 150–200 million years—may cause the Earth to periodically pass through cosmic dust veils that screen out some solar radiation or to enter zones of comets or meteorites that strike it, explode into palls of debris, and block out enough sunlight for a period of 5–10 years to trigger a self-sustaining glacial epoch.

Precious Stones and Metals: Antarctic Meteorites

Its cosmic connection is perhaps most tangibly realized in the meteorite placers that form in special circumstances on the ice sheet. Mawson discovered the first Antarctic meteorite in 1912, and early post-IGY expeditions located three others. Then in 1969 Japanese scientists chanced upon hundreds of specimens from dozens of meteorite falls scattered across blue ice at the Yamato Mountains. Americans located a similar concentration at the Allan Hills on the ice-sheet side of the Dry Valleys. By 1982 more than 5,000 specimens representing several hundred meteorites had been collected, an increase of more than 25 percent in the world total. As the oldest solar system materials on Earth—rock fossils from primordial times, cosmogenic outcrops—meteorites have become the true precious metals and stones in the information economy of Antarctica.

They probably originated from the asteroid belt. Comets, the source of meteors, show a different orbital pattern and consist more of icy than of rocky materials. Meteorites originate most likely from medium-sized asteroids (100–250 kilometers in diameter) that aggregated from the cold coalescence of metals, oxide grains, carbonaceous materials, and chondrules. Chondrules, a diagnostic constituent of most meteorites, are spherical structures—unknown in terrestrial rocks—that formed in the cool regions of the primitive solar nebula and quickly chilled to a glassy state. Radioactive heating subsequently warmed the asteroid and produced a molten core. Further collisions broke up the microplanets and threw them into Earth-crossing orbits. Some survive a fiery passage through the Earth's atmosphere to become meteorites. Meteorites thus vary according to their source material, and they exhibit a sequence of ages according to a well-defined chronology.

Stony meteorites (aerolites) derive from the silica crusts and mantles of the asteroid and constitute 93 percent of all specimens. Iron meteorites (siderites) represent material from the core and total only 6 percent of specimens. Stony-iron meteorites (siderolites), from the core-mantle transition zone, amount to only 1 percent of known meteorites. These categories are in turn subdivided: the most important subgroups within the stony meteorites are the chondrites and the achondrites. The chondrites are distinguished by the presence of chondrules, and they show the same approximate abundance of elements as the solar system at large, with the exception of some volatiles. Many of the chondrites are breccias, older than but similar in petrology to lunar breccias, which are aggregates of rocky materials that were crushed and recemented by impact on the surface of microplanetary bodies lacking atmospheres but bountiful with gases implanted by the solar wind. The resulting matrix is a record of the solid matter and gases and the primitive mineralogy, chemistry, and solar activity of the early solar system. The iron meteorites exhibit two distinctive marking patterns: Neumann lines, parallel slippage planes that develop from deformation, and the Widmanstatten pattern, parallel lines resulting from the segregation of plates within the crystal lattice by cooling.

The meteor's descent into the atmosphere creates a fireball, the duration and intensity of which depend on the velocity of the meteor and the angle with which it penetrates the atmosphere. In vertical falls there is a short flaring; in low-angle entries, a brilliant fireball and a sustained luminous tail. When the meteor encounters the upper atmosphere, an aura of ionized air grows and glows about its nose, then is swept behind and endures as ions recombine. Commonly, the meteor tumbles, and the ionization is spread over the entire solid surface; the impinging pressure, especially with chondrites, fractures the body, and portions of the interior melt and vaporize. The surface is coated with a fusion crust and sculptured by ionizing deflation within the atmosphere; the fragments may, in turn, break up further into a cascade of interplanetary debris. As it slows, the fireball extinguishes. The particle shower descends as a cold body, landing in a narrowly elliptical pattern. The abundance of particles is largely a measure of meteorite durability. Iron meteorites are tougher than chondrites and they weather less quickly. Impact can lead to further breakage, and the geochemistry of the surface soon alters the fragments.

The age of a meteorite is thus plural. There is a cosmogenic age, the time between nucleogenesis and the formation of the meteorite parent bodies; a solidification age, the time after the major heating and cooling; a gas-retention age, the time since the body was too hot to retain helium or argon; a cosmic-ray age, the time since it broke off from the parent body and during which it was heavily bombarded with cosmic radiation; and the terrestrial age, the time of the meteorite's residence on Earth. The average solidification age is 4.5 billion years, corresponding to the coalescence of a solid solar system. By contrast, the oldest dated rocks on Earth are 3.8 billion years. The cosmic-ray age, corresponding to the duration of an asteroid in Earth-crossing orbit, averages around 5 million years for chondrites and varies from 100 to 700 million years for irons. The terrestrial age of the meteorite fluctuates widely according to the composition of the meteorite, how badly its entry and impact broke it up, and what kind of Earth environment it landed in. An average terrestrial age for a stony meteorite is probably 100 years. Consequently, most meteorites are collected soon after the initial sighting of a descending fireball. Exceptions include the giant Cape York meteorite preserved in Greenland and, of course, the Antarctic meteorites. A soft landing in snow and firn, burial from atmospheric processes, and a cold, purified, arid environment all greatly extend the potential terrestrial age. Most Antarctic meteorites are 30,000–400,000 years old, a few are recent, and at least one dates at 700,000 years.

Their great age is one reason for the abundance of the Antarctic meteorites. But their number and variety make it extremely unlikely that they represent sequential meteorite showers at the same locale; other mechanisms must also be at work to concentrate and preserve them. The explanation apparently involves the glaciology of the east sheet. The meteorites are found on large patches of blue ice. The blue ice identifies the area as a site of high ablation, vigorous winds, slow horizontal ice movement, and (from crystal sizes) a deep source for the ice. The snowfall in these areas of ablation, which are filled with stagnant or compressing ice, is swept away by katabatic wind scour and sublimation. Both the Yamato Mountains and the Allan Hills block the outward flow of the East Antarctic ice sheet. More active ice streams carry the main discharge to the sides of the mountain dam, leaving the ice in front as a kind of eddy or placer. Thus, in addition to direct meteorite falls on the area, which are retained, the blue-ice region also concentrates meteorites that have fallen over a much larger catchment basin and are brought to the site by ice flow. Deep compressive flow as well as regular ice flow gather the meteorites at the site. Since

the emergence velocity of the ice is less than the rate of ablation, the meteorites are exposed. The concentrating power of
the ice placers and the preserving power of the ice are tremendous. In fact, the placer collects ice as well as ice-embedded
debris.

At the Allan Hills the ablation zone exposes ice perhaps
600,000 years old. Even highly conservative assumptions yield
an age of 200,000 years, indicating that the ice survived the last
interglacial—an event powerful enough to have swept away the
West Antarctic sheet. This suggests that the ice placer, and its
relationship to the east sheet, has been stable for a long time.
But the placers are not permanent features of the ice sheet.
They are dynamic systems, and their formation requires special
circumstances. A major growth of ice, a change of ice direction, mountain-building by the earth dam, or an ice recession
could dissolve the placer or cause it to be relocated, reburied, or
flushed away to the calving line.

Ice placers are a stunningly rich source of information about
The Ice and about the solar system. Antarctica has not only significantly swollen the population of collected meteorites and in
some instances added uniquely to it, but it has preserved those
specimens in a relatively unaltered state. Among the rare specimens are a diamond-bearing iron meteorite, in which the diamond resulted from impact shock waves; ureilites, achondrites
in which small diamonds have formed by collisions in space;
diogenites, achondrites in which minute inclusions contain
liquid water and water vapor; and the enigmatic shergottites
and carbonaceous chondrites. Shergottites are achondrites that
are anomalous in their petrology, complex chemistry of rare-
earth elements, and youthful age. Two from Antarctica (which
doubled the world population) indicate an origin around 1.8
billion years from lava parent rock, altered by impact, which
preserves a distinct boundary between two petrological zones
and includes trapped rare gases that intimate a Martian origin.
Other achondrites possibly have a lunar origin. The carbonaceous chondrites, rich in carbon and water, have a more ancient
lineage. Some are filled with high-temperature inclusions of
anomalous composition, suggesting an origin outside the solar
system altogether. These rocky shards date from the genesis of
the galaxy. But other carbonaceous chondrites also contain low-
temperature chondrules and inclusions of primordial gases, perhaps of presolar age; organic molecules, such as amino acids,

fatty acids, and porphyrins of nonbiological origin; and assorted matter that may represent the first 1 percent of the solids
created in the solar system.

Concentrated by a process of cold accretion in the ice sheet,
the scattered aggregations of meteorites dot the icy voids of Antarctica much as their parent bodies populate the interplanetary
voids of the solar system. The Antarctic is a cosmic no less than
an Earthly sink. But its meteorites are only the biggest of the
extraterrestrial particles caught up in the slow polar vortex,
and the sheets are only the last and largest of the terrestrial ice
particles that give identity to The Ice.

Final Veil: Aurora Australis

As the ice dome rises, its air mass becomes dominated by its two
extremes: the surface inversion and the upper atmosphere.
Through the intervening stratum of air the two boundaries are
tenuously joined. Downward into the inversion drifts the invad-
ing mass to replace air sloughed off through the inversion and
ice drained infinitesimally outward by the sheet. Upward to the
outer boundaries of the planet extends the polar vortex from
the shallow troposphere to the magnetosphere, from air to ions,
from the hydrodynamics of molecular fluids to the magneto-
hydrodynamics of plasma. To the veil of fog that introduces the
exterior of Antarctica there is now a nuclear counterpoint:
the rayed drapery and luminous sheets of the aurora australis.
The geomagnetic pole joins the pole of rotation and the pole of
cold; the polar cusp joins the polar low. Ice blink is matched by
airglow, atmospheric optics by the aurora, the polar front by the
auroral oval. The diurnal revolution of the auroral oval replaces
the reductionist rhythm of the polar day, and the beating of solar flares substitutes for the cadence of erased seasons. Electromagnetic storms and solar winds—the interplanetary weather
of the solar system—replace the lost tropospheric storms of the
polar plateau. Yet the geophysical properties and esthetics of
The Ice are not only sustained but in some cases elevated to
their highest expression.

The upper troposphere may be streaked with cirrus ice clouds.
In the lower stratosphere, cirrus may be replaced by nacreous
clouds (mother-of-pearl), windswept lenticular clouds or filmy

sheets most commonly visible in the twilight of late winter.
Still higher, near the upper boundary of the mesosphere, noctilucent clouds can be viewed from the perimeter of the Antarctic (up to latitude 70 degrees). An eerie, almost celestial spectacle at an average height of 83 kilometers, noctilucents are another twilight phenomenon, visible near the horizon, usually within a month or two of the summer solstice. They last from a few minutes up to five hours, and they are composed of minuscule, high-velocity particles organized into thick waves with lengths of 5–100 kilometers and amplitudes of 1.5–3 kilometers. Their source material consists of the particulates of the upper atmosphere—terrestrial and cosmic dust and, incredibly, water vapor transported by extraordinary vertical eddies in the atmosphere. Above the noctilucents appear the most remote of atmospheric events, phenomena visible only at night: meteorite trails, airglow, and the aurora.

Collectively, these phenomena contribute to the light of the night sky. The major light sources are celestial—the stars, planets, zodiacal light, gegenschein, and above all the Moon. Meteorite fireballs are transient, episodic events. The aurora ebbs and flows with the passage of solar fronts. But there is also a background luminosity, airglow, that contributes 25–30 percent of the total light in the night sky. Each day, solar radiation disintegrates atoms and molecules of oxygen and nitrogen, along with the hydroxyl radical in the magnetosphere (100–300 kilometers above the Earth). Each night the sundered particles recombine, and in the process they liberate photons of light, a collective emission known as airglow. During intense bombardments—magnetic storms—red arcs appear in the geomagnetic temperate regions, and a subvisual reddening occurs near the geomagnetic equator. In the polar regions these effects become the aurora.

When the solar wind strikes the Earth's magnetic field, the windward side of the field compresses into a bow shock while the lee side extenuates into a long cylinder of plasma. The shape of the field is thus asymmetrical. The solar wind contains magnetic field lines from the Sun, and this field helps direct the photons and ions of the solar wind through the Earth's magnetosphere and into the upper atmosphere. The moving magnetic lines set up a gigantic electrical current that transforms the upper atmosphere into a photoelectric system not unlike a television set. Current from the windward side passes into the polar regions at a geomagnetic vortex known as the polar cusp, then exits from the cusp to the windward tail. As the tail closes the circuit, particules return to the cusp in patterns that define the auroral oval. The oval rotates around the geomagnetic pole each day, quiet on the windward side and active on the lee side, quiescent in the center and aflare with the aurora around its perimeter.

During major eruptions of the solar wind, its interactions with the upper atmosphere develop into magnetospheric storms. It takes two days for the wind from a solar flare to reach the Earth. The windward tail becomes unstable, contracts to a downstream point at which a plasma "explosion" occurs, and the particles released by this explosion rush back to the Earth to create a series of worldwide magnetic disturbances. High-energy particles are unleashed, and magnetospheric substorms mature over the polar regions—perhaps a dozen substorms to each magnetic storm. Consequently, the auroral oval swells in size and the lee (midnight) side streaks toward the geomagnetic pole. At the lower border of the bulge, bright, rayed bands edged in red light appear. The bulge may thicken at supersonic speeds, and it advances westward with the rotation of the oval. Simultaneously, along the morning side, homogeneous arcs—the quiet forms of the oval—break up and move eastward with the advancing oval. The magnetospheric substorms have stimulated auroral storms.

Aurora formation requires only 30–60 minutes. Eventually, the bulge in the auroral oval shrinks. The entire auroral substorm—from oval expansion to oval recovery—lasts an average of three hours, but the instability of the magnetospheric tail does not end with a single contraction. Under the impress of a prolonged solar-wind surge, the tail may contract quasi-rhythmically many times. Each contraction and plasma explosion shoots beams of electrons and protons—auroral particles—back to the poles, to generate another auroral substorm. The larger auroral storm may consist of a dozen substorms and last ten hours.

The aurora australis displays a variety of structures, conditions, and colors. Some auroras are diffuse in structure—patches, veils, isolated rays of atomic glowing. Others display a more coherent banded or sheetlike pattern of luminosity. When

quiet, the aurora appears dim, visible mostly as arcs. But when
it is active, the arcs expand, intensifying into unified bands of
rays like folded drapery. The aurora as a whole may be fragmentary or multiple, or it may take on a coronal appearance, an
optical effect dependent on perspective. Its structure may be homogeneous throughout, without a strong internal arrangement
or concentrated brightness, or it may acquire a striated appearance, which is most commonly associated with patches and
high-elevation arcs. If the aurora becomes active, however, it
develops a vigorous internal texture characterized by rays—
streaks of auroral particles and the by-products of their atmospheric interactions oriented vertically according to the Earth's
magnetic field. As the display intensifies, the color, density, and
length of the rays change.

The aurora may be quiet, its normal equilibrium state, or it
may be active when solar flaring induces an auroral storm.
An active aurora can change shape and move within seconds; an
auroral substorm may mature in as little as ten minutes. If an
active aurora displays rapid, nearly rhythmic oscillations of
brightness, then it is described as pulsing. The pulses may be
characterized as pulsating, where the brightness is uniform
throughout the structure; flaming, where the sky appears to be
illuminated by surges of brightness rising toward the magnetic
zenith; flickering, where large portions of the display show
irregular flashes of luminosity, like an unsteady flame; and
streaming, where irregular patches of brightness propagate
horizontally across homogeneous structures. From these considerations it is possible to organize a natural history of auroras.

Its colors make the aurora the dawn and dusk of the polar regions. The auroral particles, a kind of magnetically directed
electron beam, imprint the aurora on the polar upper atmosphere in much the same way that a television tube projects an
image on its screen. The particular colors of the aurora result
from the interaction of the auroral particles with the molecules
and atoms of nitrogen and oxygen that comprise the upper atmosphere. Since the particles have a range of energies, they penetrate to various depths and affect the constituents of the upper
atmosphere differently. The struck molecules and atoms are
excited, dissociated, ionized. Secondary electrons of lower energy cascade downward to interact with other particles in the
atmosphere.

Oxygen dominates the composition of the outer atmosphere in the auroral realm (500–1,000 kilometers). As atoms are excited or ions recombine, light is emitted. The colors of the aurora depend on the spectral characteristics of affected atoms. Many of the emissions are outside the range of visible light—infrared and in some cases ultraviolet. The most common light of the aurora, a greenish-yellow, results from the excitation of oxygen atoms by secondary electrons and from the recombination of oxygen molecules (first dissociated by auroral particles), which then split into two oxygen atoms—one of which is excited and consequently emits the diagnostic greenish-yellow light. Once the excited oxygen atom radiates light in this spectrum, however, it must emit more light at a lower wavelength before it can be restored to a stable, unexcited state. These lower emissions account for the reddish lower border featured in intense displays and for a more diffuse reddish glow around the perimeter of the auroral oval. The ionization of nitrogen, meanwhile, generates a blue or purple tint that is sometimes dominant after or during active displays. Other fringe effects result from the cascade of high-energy protons through oxygen, a diffuse belt of luminosity known as the proton aurora. The polar cap glow, another luminous aura, develops over the polar regions several hours after an intense storm, as solar cosmic rays consisting of high-energy protons rush into the magnetosphere.

The aurora is not only a final geophysical but an esthetic border, a parting gloss on those properties that make The Ice what it is. The aurora gives color, motion, and shape to a scene that is otherwise singularly inert, empty with an awful simplicity. The contrast is almost absolute: aurora, evanescent and diverse, and polar plateau, powerful in bulk and invariant in appearance. This—the meeting of Ice and space—in some ways complements the meeting of Ice and Earth along the pack. In place of the Southern Ocean there are the fluids of the magnetosphere. Yet there is one monumental difference: unlike floes and bergs, riding restlessly in wind and water, the ice sheet does not join in the movements of the upper atmosphere but only reflects them. Its fluids contrast with The Ice without contributing to it.

Still, the aurora participates in the esthetic syndrome of the Antarctic. It adds depth to the atmospheric optics of the polar night, and like them its appearance is magnified by the absence of competing or modulating effects. It is awesome rather than beautiful, lacking the subtlety and surprise of light and air; its motion is cold and mechanical, like the shimmering of distant starlight; its colors are restricted to the limited palette of the atomic spectrum. It is so brilliant because the polar plateau is so bleak. The intensity of radiation is no greater during the polar night than during the polar day; in fact, it is less. During the austral summer Antarctica receives more radiation than anywhere else on Earth. But that radiation, including its aurora, is lost in a blinding, reflected white. During the polar night, however, direct sunlight is banished; solar radiation is received indirectly through the displays of the magnetosphere; and without competing light sources, the aurora flickers and flares around its polar oval—active along the perimeter, inert in the geomagnetic void at the core. The ice sheet, like darkness, enhances the aurora by a reductionism that obliterates competing features.

This scene, too, is ultimately passive: the sky of the polar night is an enormous screen on which are projected the particles and designs that bind Earth to Sun. The ice sheet, in turn, receives and reflects these lights. Plateau and aurora do not interact: The Ice receives from the aurora but gives nothing in return. It heightens the aurora by removing competing effects, not by adding to them. Plasma, shaped only by lines of magnetic force, contrasts with solids frozen to bedrock. The sheet endures while the aurora flares, dances, and dies. While both ice sheet and aurora express a relationship with the Sun, the aurora responds on a scale of minutes and days, while the ice sheet slows that interaction to a scale of millennia and geologic eons.

The aurora is the last of the veils surrounding The Ice. It screens Antarctica from interplanetary space as the circumpolar fogs cloak Antarctica from the remainder of the Earth. Auroral particles and secondary debris spiral downward in a geomagnetic vortex, itself superimposed over a polar vortex that governs the lower atmosphere; cosmic rays and solar wind interact with the upper atmosphere to produce the aurora, much as the polar fronts of atmosphere and ocean mix to generate sinuous bands of water, air, and cloud. The auroral oval completes the sealing of Antarctica, the final expression of its geophysical isolation, the completion of a white box. The cascade of debris stimulated by the auroral particles joins a general drizzle of microparticles—terrestrial and extraterrestrial both—that rains slowly down, like cosmic house dust, upon The Ice.

BEGINNINGS

The surface of the ice dome flexes slightly, like the bending of light around a white dwarf star or the infinitesimal curving that brings a geometric plane at infinity back upon itself.

Eventually, the height of the ice dome is reached. No longer does ice flow, however slightly, into the dome from anywhere else. Only a sprinkling of fine ice crystals descends upon the dome, grain by microscopic grain, millimeter by quiescent millimeter. At its periphery, Antarctica remains a climatically controlled ice terrane. But increasingly, as one advances toward the interior, it becomes an ice-controlled climate. Ice replaces everything that is not ice. Ice creates more ice. Ice defines ice.

Somewhere along the rising dome of the ice sheet, a threshold is crossed; a Schwarzschild singularity of Ice, at which reductionism is complete; the final terrane, at which space and time appear to vanish in an icy entropic immobility, at which everything and every thought seem trapped in a frozen vortex of self-induction and self-reflection.

The Source.

The Cold Peace
The Geopolitics of
Antarctica

*The disappointment I now met with did not
affect me much; for to judge of the bulk
[Antarctica] by the sample [South Georgia] it
would not be worth the discovery. . . . I make
bold to declare that the world will derive no
benefit from it.*

  —Capt. James Cook, *Journals* (1775)

*Dux [Mawson] jumped ashore and ran up
the valley waving a flag and looking as
pleased as punch—and so he was because at
last we were in a position to make a legal,
complete and entire observance of claiming
land, which we forthwith proceeded to do,
building a cairn, hoisting the flag, reading
the same proclamation as on the 13th, God
save the King, and cheering. In all other attempts (except, of course, at Cape Denison)
there has been some little thing wrong:—
"Proclamation" was only an island; the first
proclamation on the 13th floated out to sea
and the second on the 13th had no board or
proclamation, but this time things have been
done properly—mainland, cairn, board, proclamation, several people, lusty singing. . . .*

  —R. G. Simmers (1931)

Empire never lagged far behind exploration. The discovery of the world ocean soon spawned the great maritime empires of Western civilization; and through coastal settlements, the West laid claim to vast domains in the continental interiors. The exploration of the continents proceeded hand in glove with the settlement of sparsely populated regions, with at least the claim of imperial jurisdiction over many populated lands, and with armed conflicts among the European contestants for lands, peoples, and natural resources. The challenges discovery posed thus extended far beyond intellectual assimilation in the arts and sciences: there were serious, often deadly issues of geopolitics, economics, social theory, and international law at stake.

Because of its tumultuous expansion, Western civilization was continually compelled to develop new theories of empire and law by which to govern the acquisition of new territories and by which to determine the rights and responsibilities of conquerors and conquered. The practice of claiming lands, peoples, and resources evolved into customary law, and the Law of Nations became one of the intellectual and political consequences of the voyages of discovery. Recognized procedures emerged by which sovereignty or special spheres of influence could be asserted, by which discovery could lead to legitimate settlement or empire. The issues were less complex where uninhabited lands were discovered, more troublesome where native peoples already occupied the territory. Equally, some territories—notably the high seas—acquired a special status as an international commons.

Out of sheer momentum if nothing else, this tradition was applied to Antarctica, with results that are both incongruous and hopeful. Not surprisingly, the new epoch of exploration announced by IGY, which made accessible regions of the Earth and near-space that were previously uninhabitable, challenged the procedures and assumptions by which colonies had formerly been established, international spaces proclaimed, and natural resources appropriated. Yet the Antarctic situation was special. Unlike the deep oceans or interplanetary space, Antarctica had been visited by humans prior to IGY, and by the mid-twentieth century it had become an honored part of the history of several nations.

Unlike the other continents, however, there were no obvious natural resources to haul back to the mother country, only scientific information; no real prospect for exporting colonists for settlement; and no native peoples or in situ civilizations over which to rule. Economic resources seemed distant at best, traditional concepts of settlement appeared wildly inappropriate, and the geopolitical and military quandaries of acquired colonies—and the ethical issues that were never far distant—simply did not exist. A continent that is covered over 97 percent of its surface by ice sheets and that doubles its continental ice cover through floating ice shelves and seasonal pack ice would seem to be a cultural and economic sink, more intractable than the poorest, most rebellious colony. The Ice stripped Antarctic civilization to such simple institutions as exploration, then seemingly arrested any further social or political evolution. There were only momentum, nationalist pride, and international rivalry to justify land claims. The reductionism of The Ice had removed other considerations and imposed, by its enormous singularity, a geopolitical unity.

But the isolation of Antarctica was never total, and the value of Antarctic lands, like the significance of Antarctic information, was never intrinsic to The Ice but was something that interested cultures created. Ice and civilization are not incommensurable. Humans have successfully settled most of the ice-charged Arctic Circle, and *Homo sapiens* emerged as a species during the global ice age that dominated the Pleistocene. Arctic lands and islands little more hospitable than Antarctica have been settled, their natural resources mined and harvested, and their political sovereignty asserted with military power and might of law. To a considerable extent, resources are what people make of things, and value is what people believe something has. Even Antarctic ice has become a potentially valuable resource, and as an exporter of raw data Antarctica has become integral to a world economy of knowledge.

No one wants to be left out. Confronted with ignorance, nations will follow the lead of those who appear to know. If one person or nation is interested, others will be. Competition itself becomes a value, and rivalry becomes an end rather than a means. A territorial claim in Antarctica, moreover, may enjoy domestic or international significance quite apart from any attempt to colonize The Ice itself. No nation wants to surrender title unilaterally when it is unlikely that others will follow suit. Although the isolation, intensity, and size of Antarctica have rendered it special, industrialization has made it accessible and modern science has made it desirable. Yet the geopolitical assimilation of the continent is unobvious; Antarctica exists in metastable political equilibrium; and whether The Ice endures as a geopolitical entity or disintegrates catastrophically will depend on the climate of world opinion.

"I landed . . . and took possession of the country"

Jurisprudence and political theory responded vigorously to the expansion of Europe. In many ways, the reworking of legal texts into a universal, interrelated system of legal principles paralleled, and often prefigured, the development of modern science. In particular, as tribes evolved into nations and as the voyages of discovery rewrote geography far beyond the bounds of ancient Rome, questions of ownership and political sovereignty emerged for which there were few legal precedents. To the traditional means of acquiring land or jurisdiction—conquest, treaty, or purchase—had to be added the process of discovery. Thus, Columbus' voyage to the New World immediately embroiled Spain and Portugal in a quarrel over ownership. Papal bulls (*Inter Cetera*) were issued that sought to divide new lands between the two contestants along a line of longitude, and with the Treaty of Tordesillas (1494) Spain and Portugal agreed to a partition of the New World from pole to pole. But as more land was revealed, as more nations dispatched expeditions to explore and assert territorial claims, and as empires of American Indians fell before European arms, the legitimacy of the whole process of discovery and conquest—and its intellectual justification—came under scrutiny. Procedures had to be established by which claims could be recognized and conflicts among competing claimants resolved. Old precepts of medieval law, prior experience with the infidel Turk and Moor, and rules of intertribal behavior were all inadequate.

The great jurists of the Renaissance—from Francisco de Vitoria (1480–1546) to Hugo Grotius (1583–1645)—responded to the challenge by articulating principles that were ultimately abstracted from Roman and medieval codes. Through these principles discovery could be transformed into sovereignty, just wars of conquest could be waged, new peoples could be governed, and the high seas (upon which all of the maritime empires depended) could be kept free and open. The old Roman concept of *jus gentium*, the law among peoples, was expanded and reconstituted into a canon of international law. Yet much as discovery was ethnocentric, so was the new Law of Nations. It legitimated European exploration, and it sought to rationalize and regulate the conduct of European nations in both the Old World and the New. It subsumed other legal orders under a rapidly enlarging European jurisprudence, much as other maritime civilizations were incorporated into the larger sea-borne empires of Europe and as local lore was federated into the intellectual system of European geography. Though the *jus gentium* prescribed proper relationships (however unenforceable) between discovering and "discovered" peoples, the discovered peoples themselves had no part in formulating the law, and they could properly consider it illegitimate. Consequently, Europeans appealed to the concept of a fundamental natural law upon which other laws could be based. Later, jurists argued from positivist principles based on the unquestionable success of European states in establishing hegemony around the globe.

By the time James Cook sailed to the Antarctic pack, eighteenth-century jurists were codifying many of the customary practices relative to discovery—an intellectual counterpart to the systematics of Linnaeus and Werner, the dictionary of Johnson, and the *Encyclopédie* of Diderot. Emmerich von Vattel, a student of Grotian philosophy, published his *International Law* (1758), Johann Moser was writing his multivolume *Essay on the Newest European International Law* (1777–1780), and Jeremy Bentham was a few years away from substituting the expression *international law* for the archaic *Law of Nations*. In the canon were provisions by which discovery could be translated into legal title and a territorial claim into political sovereignty.

Initially the mere sighting of unknown lands was an adequate claim to discovery. First sight conveyed the right of first discovery. But even by the time of Grotius, right of discovery required more—a landing, the performance of symbolic acts of possession, some assertion by the discovering nation that it accepted the lands claimed on its behalf. How rigorously these provisions were followed depended on whether other nations were interested in the same lands and whether they could advance a competing claim based on fuller discovery. The completeness of discovery also depended on the character of the discovered lands. The most complete discovery occurred with an uninhabited land, a *terra nullius*. If lands were inhabited, then discovery had to be followed by some act of cession, through conquest, treaty, or purchase. But truly uninhabited lands were rare, and as exploration intensified, they became rarer. The concept of *terra nullius* was expanded to include lands occupied by "inferior" civilizations such as nomads or primitive tribes that lacked fixed residency or European concepts of land title. And it was enlarged by the concept of a hinterland, so that a coastal claim could be extended into the continental interior.

Gradually, too, the right of first discovery evolved into the right of inchoate title, under which discovery did not convey full title but only an exclusive right to occupy an area. To legitimate the claim, inchoate title had to be succeeded by effective occupation within a reasonable time. In practice, the concept of effective occupation replaced the concept of first discovery. Inchoate title was particularly useful for such lands as uninhabited islands, for which the prospects for any kind of settlement were remote. What constituted effective occupation varied according to circumstances. Barren volcanic atolls, used intermittently by sailors, did not require the same attention as inhabited lands or areas subject to active colonization.

Thus, during his first voyage Cook had secret instructions from the Admiralty that should he find any "country uninhabited," he should "take possession for His Majesty by setting up proper marks and inscriptions as first discoverers and possessors."[1] The same instructions extended to the celebrated second voyage, and although "it did not seem probable that any one would ever be benefited by the discovery," on the morning of January 17, 1775, Cook claimed South Georgia for Great Britain. "I landed at three different places, displayed our colours, and took possession of the country in his majesty's name, under a discharge of small arms."[2] South Georgia was the classic case of a *terra nullius*, a no-man's-land, unencumbered by vexatious questions about native peoples, for which Cook's actions served as an adequate basis for first discovery.

But the islands had seals, and the sealers who succeeded Cook—both British and American—laid a basis for further claims. William Smith reportedly refused to tell Americans at Montevideo about the location of his discovery (the South Shetlands) because "he had not taken possession of the land in the name of his Sovereign Lord the King" and no doubt did not wish interlopers in his lucrative sealing grounds.[3] Edward Bransfield carried "formidable" instructions that somewhat ponderously encouraged him to continue the good work of establishing

claims and to "inform the Captains or Masters" of any foreign
vessel he might encounter about the British claim. While Nathaniel Palmer, like most American sealers, searched for seals,
his British counterparts such as George Powell were eagerly
landing, leaving bottles, cairns, and notes, and claiming islands
as well as naming them.[4] In Palmer's defense, it should be said
that the British practice of claim-making had an obsessive, ritu-
alistic quality and that the official U.S. position with regard to
claims was ambivalent. As late as 1823 (and again in the Oregon
controversy with Britain), the U.S. Supreme Court ruled that
discovery was adequate to establish title; but in disputes with
Russia (1824), the U.S. argued that "real occupation and possession" were necessary.[5] For his part, the Russian Bellingshausen
was content to remain on ship and use the names of tsars (Peter
I and Alexander I) for two island discoveries, "indestructible
monuments which will commemorate the names of our Em-
perors to the remotest posterity."[6]

With the advent of formal exploring expeditions to the Antarctic, the practice intensified. Dumont d'Urville, apparently
watching his rival, hoisted the tricolor in 1840 and took possession of "these lands . . . according to an old custom, carefully
observed by Englishmen."[7] James Ross ensured Britain's claim
over the "newly-discovered lands"—later identified as the entire
continent—by planting the Union Jack on Possession Island
(Cape Adare), cheering, and drinking "to the health, long life,
and happiness of Her Majesty and His Royal Highness Prince
Albert."[8] Surveying the conflicting U.S., French, and British
claims to the first sighting of the continent, Ross urged that
"each nation therefore be contented with its due share, and lay
claim only to the discovery of those portions which they were
the first to behold."[9] He had already attacked Wilkes's claims as
erroneous. Besides there was plenty of ice to go around, and the
only apparent significance to the discovery was national pride,
not national wealth.

By the time the heroic age of Antarctic exploration got under
way, 400 years after Columbus and da Gama had dramatized the
problem of translating discovery into sovereignty, a rather complete body of international law existed to govern the whole process of claims, titles, and jurisdictions. The scramble for African colonies had heightened interest in the subject, and the
Berlin Conference (1885) had adopted principles of international law to rationalize the process and reduce the prospects

for armed conflict among the competing European states. As part of its codification, the conference adopted a definition of effective occupation, prescribed that the occupying state not only announce its intentions but actually extend its administrative control, and insisted that public announcement of the claim be made to prevent controversies and armed conflict over competing claims. Effective occupation meant that there was both possession, usually manifest by an uninterrupted and permanent settlement, and administration, by means demonstrating that the territory was in fact governed. Symbolic acts alone conveyed only fictitious sovereignty. Land discovered but not effectively occupied would revert to the status of *terra nullius*. These principles—developed by the conference to resolve claims in equatorial Africa—were cavalierly extended throughout the globe a few years later by a panel of international jurists. The legitimacy of the Berlin articles, however, was not universally recognized; the U.S., for example, did not sign the document. In 1896 the U.S. State Department clarified its position on the doctrine of effective occupation by arguing that "possession" need only be "reasonable under all the circumstances in view of the extent of the territory claimed, its nature, and the uses to which it is adapted and is put. . . ."[10]

This assertion clearly had significance for any claims made in Antarctica. But while the legal machinery for Antarctic claims was present, Antarctica was dramatically different from the Americas or Africa. However outrageous the assumptions and principles that governed European imperialism in Africa, the African experience—and the anticolonial reaction to it— was no less absurd when applied to Antarctica. The absence of native peoples vastly simplified the process of acquiring title without recourse to wars, treaties, and dubious purchases. At the same time, legal title traditionally resided in *terra firma*, not *glacies firma*. The floating ice shelves and marine-based west ice sheet might be considered, on technical grounds, parts of the high seas, not part of the continent. Antarctica, moreover, resisted the traditional mechanisms of occupation—control over native peoples, agricultural settlement by immigrants, and even meaningful economic outposts that required at least a modicum of administrative machinery. By the time effective occupation of Antarctica was possible, largely in the form of permanent scientific bases, international circumstances had profoundly changed: Western civilization was rapidly divesting

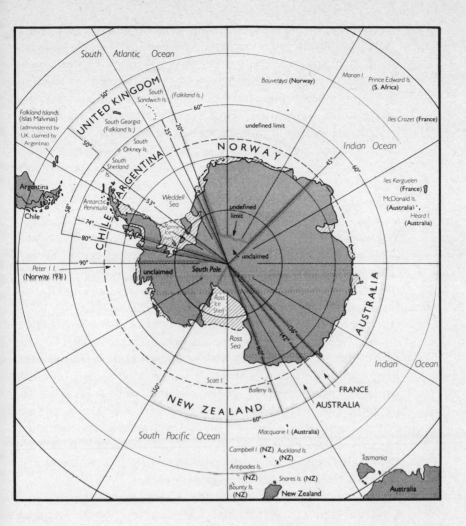

Territorial claims in Antarctica. Note the overlapping claims of Britain, Chile, and Argentina, which stem from irreconcilable differences over the Falkland Islands; the indefinite boundary of Norway's claim, which reflects Norwegian reluctance to accept concepts of the territorial sea and the sector principle that might compromise its Arctic holdings; and the unclaimed region of West Antarctica, which is widely conceded as the "American sector." Redrawn, original courtesy National Science Foundation.

itself of former colonies, the concept of sovereignty over *terra nullius* was eroding, discovery had brought the West to environments that were uninhabitable except through technological life-support systems, and the whole superstructure of Western law was challenged by alternative legal orders that desired new political and economic institutions. International law thus recapitulated the peculiar status of Antarctica within the history of exploration and the history of the earth sciences: Antarctica might be considered equally the last of the colonial land rushes by the West or the first of the new, internationalized regimes.

Whether nations progressed beyond acts of discovery and symbolic possession usually depended on political economics. What moved Antarctic claims past abstruse issues of national glory was the revival of whaling in the late nineteenth century and its relocation to the Southern Ocean. Before the development of pelagic whaling from factory ships, whalers had to tow their kills to land bases in order to process them. The control of suitable harbors meant, in effect, the control of the whaling industry. In South Georgia, Britain possessed the best land site nearest the richest whaling waters. In 1893 France annexed the Kerguelen Islands as a potentially valuable whaling site. Early in the twentieth century, as the expeditions of the heroic age explored the coast, both France and Britain began to license private companies to operate on their islands and the surrounding seas. In 1906 Britain enacted special ordinances to control the whale harvest, and two years later issued letters patent proclaiming the Falkland Islands Dependencies.

The dependencies—administered for convenience by the Governor-General of the Falklands—included South Georgia, the South Orkney Islands, the South Shetland Islands, and Graham Land (Antarctic Peninsula). Their mainland territory formed a wedge that converged along lines of longitude toward the pole; apparently Britain was mimicking the sector principle advanced a year earlier for the Canadian Arctic. Britain continued to issue leases, including some to Chile and Argentina, and seasonally dispatched a magistrate to Deception Island in the Bransfield Straits. Since the Southern Ocean, not the Antarctic continent, contained the valuable resources, British claims over the Antarctic Peninsula remained nebulous and uncontested. Within a year, however, Shackleton's *Nimrod* expedition moved claims from the shore to the interior. David, Mawson, and Mackay "hoisted the Union Jack . . . and took possession of Victoria Land for the British Empire" and later repeated the ceremony for the "area now containing the Magnetic Pole." Shackleton himself, having struggled half-starved to his farthest south ("shot our bolt"), raised the Union Jack, deposited a brass cylinder full of stamps and documents, and took possession of the polar plateau "in the name of his Majesty" before hastening on his desperate march back to Ross Island.[11] The experience apparently whetted Mawson's appetite. His Australasian Antarctic Expedition was promoted not only to further geographic discovery and science but "to raise the Union Jack and take possession of this land for the British Empire."[12] As a result, Mawson introduced enduring Australian interests to East Antarctica. Combined with Scott's *Discovery* expedition and Bruce's National Scottish Expedition, Mawson's expedition ensured that no other nation approached the British Empire in the extent of its Antarctic claims. Especially after the *Terra Nova* tragedies, Antarctica had perhaps an equal claim on Britain.

The heroic age somewhat accidentally introduced a range of new participants into the Antarctic claims controversy. An Argentine ship rescued the Nordenskjöld party in 1903, after the *Antarctic* had sunk in the pack, and a year later Argentina agreed to maintain the meteorological station that the Scottish National Expedition had established at Laurie Island (South Orkneys). A Chilean vessel rescued the Elephant Island survivors of Shackleton's *Endurance* expedition (1916). Through British licenses both Argentina and Chile operated commercial ventures in the Scotia Arc region. Shirase's *Kainan* expedition raised the Japanese flag over the Ross Ice Shelf and renamed it the Yamato snowfield,[13] and in 1912 France served notice (widely ignored) that it had inalienable rights in Adelie Land. Two German expeditions advertised a German presence, but so bad was the pack ice that both Drygalski and Filchner had their ships frozen in and neither succeeded in really reaching the continent proper. Recently independent Norway was in the forefront of Antarctic whaling, and Amundsen had planted its "beloved flag" at the South Pole and named the polar plateau after King Haakon VII.

Directly or indirectly, the coordinated assault on Antarctic exploration meant that a host of nations now had a basis in discovery for territorial claims. The continent could not be considered a single indivisible entity for which one act of discovery could serve as an adequate basis for claim over the entire uninhabited continent. Rather, from the onset, multiple, simultaneous discovery and international rivalry had characterized the history of Antarctic exploration and claim-making. World War I only partially interrupted the process. In 1917 Britain issued new letters patent that attempted to specify the exact dimensions of its claim over the Antarctic Peninsula (longitudes 20–80 degrees West) and established a Committee on Research and Development in the Falkland Islands Dependencies, which evolved into the Discovery Committee and later the British Antarctic Survey. The claim went beyond the concept of a hinterland to invoke a sector principle. The British claim itself was generally ignored.

More important than the Antarctic was the status of the Arctic. In 1907 Britain (on behalf of Canada) had unilaterally announced sovereignty over all of the lands north of Canada, up to the North Pole, according to a sector principle—a proposal that was almost universally repudiated. Two years later Robert Peary put the North Pole at the disposal of the United States, an act that President Taft, a former jurist, graciously ignored. An aggressive nationalist, Peary wanted the Monroe Doctrine extended to Greenland and regretted that the U.S. had not purchased Greenland from Denmark at the same time it had acquired the Virgin Islands. But the Arctic did figure prominently in the geopolitical realignments that occurred after World War I. The Svalbard (Spitsbergen) Treaty was open for signing in 1920; Denmark declared sovereignty over all of Greenland in 1921; Canada absorbed Ellesmere Island in 1922 and three years later applied the sector principle to all Arctic lands between the island and the North Pole; the U.S. (1924) claimed all lands north of Alaska; and the Soviet Union, now firmly under the control of the Bolsheviks, cavalierly applied the sector principle in 1926 to the Russian Arctic—to high seas as well as to any lands present but not yet discovered.

The Antarctic was not completely ignored. The Treaty of Versailles had compelled Germany to renounce any territorial rights, but it left the nominal victors to pursue their own Antarctic strategies. An important consideration was the emergence of pelagic whaling—which meant that Britain no longer exercised control over industry licensing, revenue, and any conservation effort—and Carl Larsen's relocation of Antarctic whaling to the Ross Sea. The key personality was Leopold Amery in the British Colonial Office, who decided as early as December 1919 to pursue a policy of gradual British annexation ("without undue ostentation") so that "the whole of the Antarctic should ultimately be included within the British Empire."[14] Thus, in 1923 Britain matched its claims to the Antarctic Peninsula and Weddell Sea with one over the Ross Sea and its land borders, another important whaling site. The Orders-in-Council determined that the Ross Dependency should be administered through the governor-general of New Zealand, much as claims in the peninsula were administered through the governor of the Falklands. France responded by publishing its claim to Adelie Land and various subantarctic islands; like Britain's claim, France's included conservation principles (over whaling) and placed administrative control under the nearest French magistrate, in this case on Madagascar. In part, the French annexation was intended to forestall a British-Australian claim to Wilkes Land on the basis of Shackleton's and Mawson's interior discoveries.

But Wilkes had perhaps been the first to sight Adelie Land, and the U.S. was now forced to take a position on Antarctic claims or risk the loss of any inchoate title that it possessed. Revealingly, Secretary of State Charles Evans Hughes argued the U.S. position not in reply to international politics but in response to inquiries by U.S. citizens. There could be no basis for title, Hughes insisted, without effective occupation. This meant settlement and development, and since Antarctica was widely regarded as permanently uninhabitable, the U.S. considered claims based on discovery alone to be invalid. The U.S. would not advance any claims in Antarctica, but neither would it recognize the claims of anyone else. It wanted an open-door approach, free access everywhere for everyone. In the meantime, Argentina advanced a tepid claim to the South Orkneys (1925), which it extended two years later to include South Georgia— apparently insisting that its quarrel with Britain over the Falkland Islands (Malvinas) included the entire Falkland Islands Dependencies as well.

At Australia's insistence, British policy in Antarctica was included on the agenda of the British Imperial Conference (1926). Britain had some basis for a claim that would assert title over the lands between the Falkland and Ross dependencies, a claim over all of East Antarctica except the nebulous Adelie Land. The conference's *Summary of Proceedings* catalogued those areas for which "British title already exists by virtue of discovery." The "concerned" parties, in turn, studied available information "with special reference to their possible utilization for further developing exploration and scientific research in the Antarctic regions." Amery saw to it that the conference considered that "ultimately it may be still possible to assert and maintain British control over the whole Antarctic region."[15] Antarctica was included on the agenda for the 1930 British Imperial Conference. Mawson's BANZARE expedition firmed up Australian interest and prerogative to Wilkes Land, and a British Order-in-Council in 1933 formally claimed this vast territory and placed it under Australian authority. By the time the 1937 Imperial Conference addressed Antarctica, however, other nations were seriously advancing Antarctic claims of their own.

Argentina initiated a long series of sub-rosa operations intended to compromise the British claim to sovereignty over the disputed Falkland Islands Dependencies. First a radio was erected at Laurie Island. Britain insisted that the station carry a British call sign; Argentina ignored the request, then tried to sneak an application through the International Telegraph Bureau under Argentine title. When confronted by Britain, Argentina openly claimed the South Orkneys on the grounds of effective occupation and, through the bureaucracy of the International Postal Bureau, surreptitiously claimed South Georgia as well. Britain and Argentina were thus stalemated. Meanwhile, Norway proclaimed sovereignty over Bouvet Island in 1928, reminded other states in 1929 that it still held inchoate title to the South Pole region, and empowered Lars Christensen to take possession of any *terra nullius* he might discover. In 1931 Norway formally claimed Peter I Island.

Norwegian claims were clearly intended to support an enormous whaling industry, but Norway was able to mass potentially formidable counterclaims to the claims of other nations, especially Australia. Mawson tirelessly lectured the British Commonwealth on the need to forestall the Norwegians, and his fellow Australians on the value of Antarctic possessions. In practice, Mawson met with Riiser-Larsen in 1930, while each was making claims in Enderby Land, and a rough boundary between Australian and Norwegian territory was accepted.[16] Norway, however, hesitated before officially acting on the claims of its explorers, while Australia recognized the potential strategic and economic importance of its Antarctic territories and enacted an Australian Antarctic Territory Acceptance Bill (1933) soon after the British Order-in-Council, though its provisions became effective three years later. As Lord Casey argued, "If we do not take this sector and claim sovereignty over it, some other country will, and it is undoubtedly to the benefit of Australia to be in possession of this land surface, with its unknown potentialities, so close to our shores." [17]

Though there might be some whaling revenues, competition had generated its own momentum and justification. In fact, economic considerations involving Antarctica diminished, to be replaced increasingly by nationalistic and ideological concerns. Traditionally, Antarctic revenues had come from whaling, but pelagic whaling could not be regulated through control over nearby shores. The collapse of the whaling economy in the early 1930s because of overhunting, the adoption of the International Convention for the Regulation of Whaling (1935), and the entry of nations (Japan and Germany) that were not parties to the International Whaling Convention all lessened the economic attraction of Antarctica to Norway.

The big news, however, was the reentry of the United States in 1928 with the first Byrd expedition. The airplane allowed rapid discovery and the airdropping of claims documents. It also made accessible for the first time a portion of Antarctica (Marie Byrd Land) that had been stubbornly impenetrable to ships and for that reason had been the only unclaimed sector. Gould's geologic party to the Queen Maud Mountains passed outside the range of the Ross Dependency, constructed a rock cairn, and deposited a tin can with a note that claimed "in the name of Commander Richard Evelyn Byrd . . . this as a part of Marie Byrd Land, a dependency or possession of the United States." [18] It was a grand gesture, a small part of Byrd's endless campaign to educate Americans to an Antarctic commitment. "In the immediate future," he lectured, "there is nothing—we know that—but a hundred years is a short time in the life of a nation and we should think more of the future than we do." [19]

The U.S. did not officially act on the claim and steadfastly refused to recognize any national claims to Antarctica. Byrd himself envisioned Little America as the basis for a new kind of colony. While the State Department dawdled over how to thank Britain for its offer to help Byrd "while he was in their territories" without recognizing the legitimacy of those territories, Byrd thought that "sportsmanship" counted more in Antarctica than "strict letters of the law." He willingly acknowledged the primacy of British and Norwegian explorers to the Barrier and insisted pragmatically that "men cannot fight each other in the Antarctic because the one universal enemy is cold."[20] Meanwhile, the *Eastern Greenland* case (1933) redefined the standards of effective occupation for lands that were virtually uninhabitable. Lincoln Ellsworth's flight across West Antarctica confirmed, with some official sanction, American priority of discovery over that region, and citizen Ellsworth claimed much of the land for the U.S.

Officially, the State Department remained indecisive or evasive. When citizens inquired about American territorial "rights" and senators introduced resolutions to act on inchoate title, the State Department merely reasserted the Hughes Doctrine, with the provision that the U.S. reserved the right to make claims at a future time. What was incontestable, however, was that Byrd's expeditions established a quasi-permanent American presence in Antarctica, whether or not discovery and symbolic acts of possession were translated into official titles. Eventually, American inchoate rights based on discovery would supersede in extent even those of the British Commonwealth, and Marie Byrd Land would remain an unclaimed but widely acknowledged "American sector."

Meanwhile, as the world again drifted toward global war, territorial contestants firmed up their claims. In 1937 Argentina publicly announced that its previous claims to South Orkney and South Georgia now included all of the Falkland Islands Dependencies. To support its position, Argentina advanced a potpourri of documents and legal arguments, as though sheer bulk and variety could bring conviction. Though it insisted that Argentine occupation was superior to British discovery, Argentina also based its claim on the principle of *uti possidetis juris*, that Antarctica had never been a *terra nullius*, that Argentina had always possessed an Antarctic appendage. In effect, this amounted to an assertion of squatter's rights without the bother of actually squatting. In 1938 France, Britain, and Australia concluded an agreement to allow air travel across their respective Antarctic territories, delineated the boundaries of Adelie Land, and explicitly recognized one another's claims. Also in 1938, the signatories of the International Whaling Conference agreed to enforce the provisions of the convention, the first international attempt to regulate whaling. The old argument for territorial claims—revenue from and protection of whaling—lost its force. But the claims continued. Hubert Wilkins flew reconnaissances over territory claimed by Australia and landed for a possession ceremony at an offshore island.

More ominously, some Japanese societies urged Japan to advance territorial claims based on the discoveries of Shirase, and Nazi Germany dispatched an expedition under Dr. Alfred Ritscher (1938–1939) "to secure for Germany her share in the approaching division of the Antarctic among world powers."[21] Personally endorsed by Hermann Göring, the expedition's seaplanes mapped along Queen Maud Land, dropped spearlike shafts with emblazoned swastikas to the ice sheet, and mounted shore parties to raise the flag of the Third Reich—"a German colony," exulted the expedition's geographer, that would be settled according to "the economic interests of Greater Germany." Germany named its Antarctic territory Neu-Schwabenland.[22] The German press spoke glowingly about imminent formal claims. The invasion of Poland, however, exchanged territorial claims in Antarctica for those in Europe and redirected attention from photogrammetric flights over the continent to submarine warfare around it. A German U-boat (*Pinguin*) once captured the entire Norwegian whaling fleet off the disputed coast of Queen Maud Land.

The specter of the Third Reich in Antarctica rallied responses from Norway, the U.S., and Latin America. With the German Antarctic Expedition positioned along Princess Astrid Coast, King Haakon VII of Norway—thirty years after Amundsen had named the polar plateau in his honor—proclaimed title over Queen Maud Land. Norway refused to apply the sector principle, which might have undesirable complications for its Arctic claims. Instead, Norwegian Antarctic territory included the coast and an indefinite hinterland that, ironically, did not extend to the South Pole. The Allies had encouraged the old king in his attempt to forestall a German claim, though the Soviet Union protested the inclusion of Peter I Island. Germany ignored the act, determined to proceed in Antarctica "unhindered by the rights of sovereignty of other nations."[23] It would acquire Neu-Schwabenland indirectly through the invasion of Norway a year later. Meanwhile, the U.S. State Department secretly instructed Lincoln Ellsworth to perform acts that might provide a basis for American title. Three days before the Norwegian proclamation, Ellsworth obligingly air-dropped a metal cylinder with a message claiming for the U.S.—"so far as the act allows"—the area along his line of flight, roughly the American Highlands.[24]

At the same time, at President Roosevelt's request the State Department prepared an interagency Antarctic policy study. The group recommended permanent settlements by the U.S. and Roosevelt created the U.S. Antarctic Service (USAS) in July 1939, personally insisting that Byrd "run the program."[25] Among its instructions, the USAS was reminded that "no member . . . shall take any action or make any statements" that would compromise the Hughes Doctrine, while simultaneously encouraging members to take—without public announcement—"any appropriate steps . . . which might assist in supporting a sovereignty claim by the United States Government."[26] The two bases—one at Little America (adjacent to Marie Byrd Land) and the other along the Antarctic Peninsula—were abandoned in 1941. But the U.S. was already pursuing an alternative strategy to keep Nazi Germany out of the Western Hemisphere.

At the Interamerican Conference at Lima (1938), Secretary of State Cordell Hull maneuvered a declaration that reaffirmed the sovereignty of the American states against foreign intervention. In 1940 he strengthened the military implications of Antarctica by proposing that the Monroe Doctrine be extended to the South Pole.[27] American concern, of course, was with the intentions and U-boats of Nazi Germany and the security of the Drake Passage. But Latin America was more wary of Britain than of Germany and accepted the wording of the declaration accordingly. Argentina, in particular, was friendly to the Nazi regime, and it was now locked in a legal war of attrition with Britain over the Falklands and the Falkland Islands Dependencies. In 1939, suspicious of Norway's declaration, Argentina established a permanent National Antarctic Commission to embolden claims in the Antarctic. Alarmed at Argentine maneuvers, Chile prepared a legal brief for an Antarctic claim of its own, and a year later Chilean President Cerda invoked the sector principle to proclaim sovereignty over the Antarctic Peninsula, renamed Territorio Chileno Antartico. Within a week, Argentina reaffirmed the dimensions of Antartida Argentina, which now overlapped with Chilean as well as British territorial claims. Both Argentina and Chile exploited the fact that Britain was preoccupied by its own survival.

Argentine suspicion of Britain was matched by British suspicion of Argentina. In 1942 Argentina formalized its claims; that

year and the next it expanded activities from the annual relief
of the meteorological station on Laurie Island to the establishment of ramshackle bases on South Shetland and the peninsula and the performance of symbolic acts of possession. The British responded by creating the Falkland Islands Dependencies Survey and by launching Operation Tabarin. The Tabarin military expedition removed the various emblems of Argentine sovereignty and restored British emblems—a show of force adequate to place Antarctica outside the realm of hostilities for the duration of the war.

The war ended with a lesser rather than a greater Germany, and the Treaty of San Francisco forced Japan to renounce any Antarctic claims. But the decade after World War II saw a round of enlarged, ominous international posturing. New players were introduced, and the quarrel between Britain and Argentina deteriorated. Resource issues, for which there was some precedent and mechanisms of arbitration, came to be of less significance than nationalistic and ideological concerns, for which negotiations were impossible. The Perón regime, elected in 1946, made Antartida Argentina an inextricable issue of ultranationalism for Argentine domestic politics. The Cold War threatened to carry its geopolitical rivalry to the poles, and the militarization of Antarctica appeared imminent. Never subject to colonialism in any meaningful way, Antarctica was increasingly caught up in the rhetoric and politics of postwar anti-colonialism. It became, in the words of worried observers, a "continent in search of sovereignty." More aptly, it became a continent in search of an alternative to sovereignty.

Putting the Cold War on Ice

Much of the postwar uncertainty about Antarctica revolved around the intentions of the United States. In 1946 the State Department reiterated its traditional support for the Hughes Doctrine, but between 1946 and 1948 the U.S. also mounted its massive Antarctic Developments Project (Operations Highjump and Windmill) under the direction of the U.S. Navy. In fact, the Defense Department was far more interested in the Arctic, where it now confronted the Soviets, than in the Antarctic, where Byrd convinced it to go. Highjump complemented Operation Nanook, and it was hoped that the experiments in logistics and equipment would prove useful in "interior Greenland." Byrd, in titular command, flew over the pole and ceremoniously dropped a box containing the flags of all the member nations of the U.N. But Highjump's orders included instructions to consolidate and extend "United States sovereignty over the largest practicable area of the Antarctic continent."[28] The belief was widespread that the U.S. was preparing, at last, to exercise its latent claims. Paul Siple observed that "by mapping all of the Antarctic and being the first to sight the still unseen two-thirds of the continent, the United States could be in a unique position to claim Antarctica for its own, should it so desire."[29] As tentatively formulated in August 1948, that claim would include "all Antarctic territory which has been explored and mapped by United States expeditions." Only a sector sliver between 35 degrees West and 13 degrees East would be left to the British, Chileans, and Argentines.[30]

Meanwhile, the Inter-American Treaty of Reciprocal Assistance (Rio Treaty) was signed in 1947, and the "American Security Zone" was apparently extended to the Antarctic. In formulating a program for the U.S. Antarctic Service, President Roosevelt had informally suggested that the U.S. and other American states consider some kind of Antarctic protectorate. Perhaps feeling that the U.S. would side with the Americas rather than its European allies, Chile and Argentina put aside their squabbling long enough in 1948 to proclaim a declaration of common defense of the "South American Antarctic continent" against Britain. Argentina had in fact sent naval squadrons to defend Argentine "domestic territory" in the Antarctic Peninsula, Britain dispatched warships to defend the Falkland Islands Dependencies; and only a makeshift agreement not to send arms south of 60 degrees prevented an outbreak of general hostilities. Britain proposed to Chile and Argentina that they submit their dispute to the International Court at The Hague.

Both Chile and Argentina refused, preposterously insisting that the contested lands were a "domestic" issue. To bolster their shaky legal case, they mustered endless briefs based on ideas like the sector principle, geological affinity, and Pan-American primacy—none of which had any precedent or found a receptive audience. The facts are that the two Latin American countries had decided that Antarctic territory was essential to their strategic and domestic interests and that they were willing to invest substantially in Antarctica to establish at least squat-

ters rights. Instead of a legal drama, the world witnessed the
annual spectacle of British operatives tearing down Argentine
plaques and erecting British plaques, only to have the Argentines subsequently visit the same site, remove British symbols
and replace them with Argentine symbols, and so on. To some
Britons, Antarctic duty became known as the "silly season"; to
others, the situation was a needless bluster that might escalate
into armed conflict. In 1952 the Argentine navy actually fired
over the heads of a British meteorological party, and a year later
British officials arrested two Argentines for trespass and dismantled Argentine and Chilean huts. In the meantime, Britain
continued to propose the International Court as a solution, and
in 1954 unilaterally submitted the dispute to the court; the
court vacated the case when Argentina and Chile refused to ac-
knowledge the court's jurisdiction. Beginning in 1947, the U.S.
was embroiled in a similar round of posturing, as the British
"Magistrate, Marguerite Bay" formally protested the raising of
an American flag by the Ronne expedition—a private venture—as it reoccupied the old American USAS base at Stonington Island.

The prospect that Antarctica might follow the example of Africa was repugnant to many. Even during the heroic age, scientists had argued for some kind of international rule. Alarmed
over territorial bellicosity, Rudmose Brown pleaded that "the
imperial partition of the continent is a fantastic conception,"
that "it would be a gesture of international friendship if all
states abrogated the valueless political claims in Antarctica and
regarded the continent as a neutral territory in perpetuity." The
Times lectured that "Antarctica is not a fit subject for national
rivalries or political bargaining. Its future, if in doubt, should
be declared by law in the interests of science."[31] But to many
observers it appeared inevitable that Antarctica would be drawn
into the geopolitics of the Cold War, even as its northern conjugate, Greenland, was.

The U.S., in particular, was of mixed opinion. The Defense
Department saw little strategic value to Antarctica other than
to deny a Soviet presence; the value of the breathtakingly vast
American claim was that it would leave no undiscovered regions for a potential Russian counterclaim. That belief and
President Truman (then embroiled in a political fight with Admiral Byrd's brother, Senator Harry Byrd) abruptly canceled a
third installment on the Antarctic Developments Project. With

respect to the Arctic, in 1926 the Soviets had denounced the doctrine that discovery alone was a legitimate basis for territorial title, and they had no basis other than Bellingshausen's shipborne sightings for Antarctic claims. The State Department apparently hoped that an enormous claim by the U.S. would lead to some sort of condominium that could control the saber-rattling among the claimant states and forestall a Soviet intrusion. Besides, if the U.S. advanced territorial claims, the act would compel the U.S. to take side in the competing claims over the Antarctic Peninsula. This would be a classic no-win situation, and it might deny something the U.S. had always insisted on—open access for American nationals to all of the continent.

Accordingly, the State Department circulated invitations among the claimant nations to meet and discuss possible regimes. If not through a condominium, perhaps Antarctica could be administered under a multiple U.N. trusteeship.[32] Although pelagic whaling revived after World War II, it involved other jurisdictions, and the International Whaling Convention (1946) offered a solution outside the vexing territorial issue. In 1948, while it sent out invitations for a political conference, the State Department requested the National Academy of Sciences to outline a future scientific program for the U.S. in Antarctica.

But questions of national pride and domestic politics could not be easily resolved. The Argentine-British controversy festered hopelessly, and the Soviet regime suddenly announced that it would not accept any Antarctic regime to which it was not a party. Eventually, Argentina and Chile proposed scientific cooperation and a five-year moratorium on territorial claims (the Escudero proposal). But all the furor—and the prospects for some sort of American declaration—had brought Antarctica to Soviet attention. The Soviet Geographical Society staged a special conference on Russia and Antarctica, asserted Russian priority to discovery, resolved "the indisputable right of the Soviet Union to participate in the solution of problems of the Antarctic," and declared "Antarctic Day." In June 1950, the Soviet Union restated these propositions as its official position on the Antarctic question. Territorial squatting and diplomatic squabbling had led to the one outcome that all the claimants least wanted: Soviet intervention. The Cold War had come to The Ice.

All the claimants moved to shore up their Antarctic territories. Argentina continued its opéra bouffe guerrilla war with Britain, created an Instituto Antartico Argentino to oversee its activities and placed the institute under the Ministry of the Army (1951), purchased an icebreaker, erected seven stations on the disputed territory, and "reestablished" its "National Territory of Tierra del Fuego, the Antarctic and the Islands of the South Atlantic" (1957). Australia, proud of its Antarctic explorers and alarmed about Soviet intervention, established the Australian National Antarctic Research Expeditions (ANARE) in 1947, and in 1953–1954 created a permanent base on the continent, Mawson Station, and enacted legislation that would extend the laws of the Australian Capital Territory to its Antarctic claims. Chile had established an Antarctic Commission in 1942, but reorganized it, transferred operations to the armed forces, erected a base in 1947, and in 1955 and 1956 passed the Statute of the Chilean Antarctic Territory, which provided for administration through the Magallanes Province. To demonstrate national conviction, the Chilean president personally inaugurated O'Higgins Station in 1948 and with due pomp denounced the "bad habits of antiquated European imperialism," blithely dismissing Latin American imperialism with the assertion that Latin America's Antarctic rights were "unquestionable."[33] Under the inspiration of Paul-Emile Victor, France reaffirmed its interest by creating the Expéditions Polaires Françaises (1947), which sent scientific parties to Greenland and Adelie Land. A station was operated off the Adelie Coast, beginning in 1950. In 1955 France removed the administration of Adelie Land from the governor-general of Madagascar, rechristened its territories Terres Australes et Antarctiques Françaises (TAAF), and placed it directly under the colonial ministry. New Zealand was hampered not only by long-standing indifference but by uncertainty over the nature of its claim: Britain had never technically transferred the Ross Dependency to New Zealand as it had for Australia. But popular attention turned to Antarctica as a result of American activities, the Trans-Antarctic Expedition, and IGY. In 1955 New Zealand announced for the first time that it had intrinsic interests in Antarctica because of geographic proximity and moved to assert its sovereignty by means of various symbolic acts and the establishment of scientific stations. Though its whaling interests subsided, Norway maintained a vigorous presence in the Antarctic through the Norsk Polarinstitutt and through a leading role in the Norwegian-British-Swedish Antarctic Expedition (1949–1952), which operated on lands within the Norwegian claim.

None of the claimant nations had a longer presence in Antarctica than Britain, and none had so complicated a political
presence. Britain's former empire was rapidly crumbling, but
while Britain was prepared to share its Antarctic claims through
a condominium or an international regime, it was not ready to
abandon them completely to bellicose interlopers or to Cold
War antagonists. Consequently, Britain sought to protect its interests in the Falkland Islands Dependencies against Chile and
Argentina, with arms if necessary, but through international
adjudication or some international regime if possible. At the
same time, Britain reinforced its political claims through an invigorated science program. It participated in the Norwegian-
British-Swedish Antarctic Expedition, and the establishment of
the British National Institute on Oceanography (1950) sought
to revive the Discovery Committee exploration of the Southern Ocean.

As a potential claimant of huge proportions, the U.S. was determined to see its interests advanced, but it repeatedly floundered on the determination of just what those interests were. Its
American allies quarreled with its European allies over Antarctica. The U.S. was uncertain whether asserting a claim would
improve or worsen tensions in the region and was unclear how
to refuse recognition to one claim without indirectly recognizing another. Above all, the U.S. desired to keep the Soviets out
of Antarctica. So isolated was The Ice from strategic considerations, however, that neither the State Department nor the
Defense Department could say why the Soviets should be excluded, other than that their appearance would open yet another region to potential discord. In 1948, the U.S. attempt
to break the deadlock among Britain, Argentina, and Chile
through some sort of international regime or condominium
only aroused Soviet suspicions. And once the Soviets expressed
official interest, the U.S. had to respond. The 1948 proposals
were rejected all around.

The new Soviet interest in Antarctica, however, elicited policy memoranda from the National Security Council in 1954 and
1955 that outlined U.S. objectives: freedom of exploration and
scientific research, access to natural resources, and "orderly
progress" toward a resolution of the territorial questions, all
with "control" by the U.S. and "friendly parties." President
Eisenhower meanwhile rejected the latest recommendation
from an interdepartmental study group that the U.S. advance

territorial claims, at least in West Antarctica, while he agreed
with the National Security Council that the U.S. presence in
Antarctica should be second to none.[34] The U.S. continued to
equivocate: it deposited claims and reserved the right to act on
them at a later time, declined to recognize any claims so far advanced, and insisted on open access.

It was within this deepening maelstrom—the same year
(1952) that the Argentine navy fired over a British party—that
the International Council of Scientific Unions appointed its
Special Committee for the International Geophysical Year. IGY
became one of those imponderable, chance events that unex-
pectedly intervene to change the course of human affairs. The
African misadventure would become almost a travesty of Western expansionism. The Arctic would become the scene for
laissez-faire geopolitics, of ever-intensifying military and political maneuvers. But because of the IGY experience, Antarctica would be different. The West would look not through a
glass darkly, as with Africa, but into a brilliant ice mirror. The
death of Stalin brought the Soviets into IGY; IGY introduced
them to Antarctica in a peaceful, face-saving way; and the U.S.
and U.S.S.R. would impose a de facto condominium of scientific
enterprise that would temporarily shelve the territorial claims
that neither recognized. Both superpowers, in fact, publicly ad-
vocated essentially the same position: they recognized no claims
and reserved the right to advance claims of their own. In Antarctica would evolve, in the words of Dag Hammarskjöld, a
"balance of prudence." On The Ice the Cold War would be simplified into a Cold Peace.

IGY defined the contemporary circle of players interested in
Antarctica. In addition to claimant states, Belgium, Japan, the
Union of South Africa, the Soviet Union, and the United States
all mounted national scientific expeditions. The size of a nation's investment was taken as a measure of its seriousness with
regard to Antarctic politics. Moreover, IGY extracted, however
reluctantly, agreement on the principle that scientific parties
should have free movement around the continent, and it provided a quasi-governmental infrastructure by which these activities could be coordinated. When IGY was extended for an
additional year (International Geophysical Cooperation), the
Antarctic participants stayed. It became apparent that those
with the greatest investments had no intention of leaving. As
long as the Russians stayed, so would the Americans. Since only

claimant nations—and not even all of them—recognized the legitimacy of their Antarctic claims, there was no solid basis in international law for driving off the new stations. Apart from considerations of scientific cooperation, a number of nations now enjoyed squatters rights to Antarctic territory. The old regime of squabbling territorial claimants—however politically volatile—became increasingly meaningless before international law. The rousing success of Antarctica under IGY, however, promised an alternative: in 1957 the ICSU organized a Special Committee for Antarctic Research (later, Scientific Committee for Antarctic Research, SCAR) to assist with the coordination of national research programs. The U.S. reevaluated its post-IGY presence with a conference on the organization of polar research, held at Dartmouth (1958–1959). Led by the U.S., the new participants prepared to negotiate a treaty by which Antarctica could be governed.

World opinion as well as practical considerations argued for some sort of new Antarctic regime. After the failure of the International Court, New Zealand pressed ahead for a United Nations trusteeship over Antarctica, and India issued the first of several pleas that the General Assembly take up the question of Antarctica. The U.S.-based Commission to Study the Organization of the Peace detailed its prospectus for an internationalization of Antarctica under U.N. auspices. President Eisenhower addressed the U.N. to urge for a peaceful resolution, placed the U.S. Antarctic program under the civilian National Science Foundation, and arranged for informal consultations among the Antarctic players that led in the following year to formal negotiations in Washington, D.C. The Antarctic Conference progressed rapidly to the Antarctic Treaty (1959), which entered into force in 1961. Thus began the Pax Antarctica.

The success of the treaty is perhaps attributable more to what it did not do than to what it did. In essence the treaty confirmed the status that Antarctica had enjoyed under IGY: the continent would be open for scientific research, demilitarized, and spared nuclear weapons testing (and nuclear waste dumping); national stations would be open to inspection; and Antarctica would be administered—"in the interests of all humanity"—by the Antarctic Treaty nations. The treaty distinguished between signatory nations, which signed and agreed to the treaty, and consultative nations, which actively engaged in Antarctic research. Amendments to the treaty were the prerogative of the consultative nations. But the treaty did not establish a permanent secretariat. It gave every consultative nation a veto by insisting that all decisions or recommendations be unanimous. It made no real provisions for enforcement of the treaty, relying instead upon mutual pressures to conform and upon the participants' realization that a regime of chaos would aid no one. It consisted of self-denying statements, the acceptance of obligations without the conferring of special rights.

Above all, the treaty dealt with the sovereignty issue by a calculated ambiguity. It neither recognized nor denied existing claims: signing the treaty would neither advance nor prejudice future claims to territory, but no new claims could be made while the treaty was in force. The treaty provisions constituted an injection of modernist philosophy into positivistic law, a kind of principle of complementarity applied to the concept of sovereignty. The Antarctic Treaty was, in fact, a limited-purpose agreement that resolved the most pressing issues and deferred, perhaps indefinitely, a resolution on others. Its main value as a precedent was that it was the first limited nuclear test ban treaty. But the Antarctic Treaty had the capacity to evolve. Any nation could sign the treaty, and nations that demonstrated a significant commitment to Antarctic research could be granted consultative status. The provision for regular meetings among the consultative nations established a de facto legislative body, though recommendations adopted at the meetings had to be ratified by national legislatures before they had jurisdiction over their nationals in Antarctica. SCAR was made an advisory body, and special institutions, particularly conventions to govern the conservation of Antarctic organisms, have expanded the range of the treaty's authority.

The Antarctic Treaty successfully established a Pax Antarctica, a recognizable Antarctic Community, and a functional Antarctic System. Strains within the treaty framework are abundant. The most divisive issue—sovereignty—persists. The community remains segregated into the claimants and nonclaimants, signatory and consultative nations. Since the treaty entered into force, however, there have been numerous adjustments in national programs for Antarctic research to accommodate the new regime. South Africa, for example, built a permanent station in Queen Maud Land. Britain transferred its claims from a dependency of the Falklands to a separate British Antarctic Territory, supported by the British Antarctic Survey (1962).

Twenty years later, Argentina invaded the Falklands and claimed
all of the old dependency before being repulsed by Great Britain. Still, hostilities did not extend south of 60 degrees. The
prospect of mineral resources promises to further strain the internal balances within the Antarctic System. At the same time,
the Antarctic Community as a whole faces collective challenges to its legitimacy from nontreaty nations. The United Nations offers an alternative political order, and Antarctica was
only part of the new environments that IGY had advertised.
The deep oceans and outer space pose regimes outside traditional concepts of territorial sovereignty. These external
stresses balance somewhat the internal strains of the system.
Posturing and rhetoric aside, it is universally acknowledged
that the Antarctic System is far superior to what it superseded
and that, once dissolved, it will not be easily reassembled.

It had not all been grim *realpolitik*. Amid the solemn legalisms and punctilious pretensions, there had occurred plenty of
comic interludes: Bransfield's proclamation party, in the midst
of pious declarations, nearly overwhelmed by a "most intolerable stench" emanating from a penguin rookery upwind; the indomitable James Ross wading through mounds of guano and
throngs of outraged, pecking penguins to drink the king's health;
d'Urville, rushing ashore to confirm French priority of discovery while aping British ceremonials; an overly zealous Nazi
from the German Antarctic Expedition saluting a nonplussed
emperor penguin with chants of "Heil Hitler"; the American
Ronne and the British magistrate of Marguerite Bay tromping
through the winter snow with formal notes of protest over
whether the Americans should fly their flag; American dele-
gates to IGY planning sessions impulsively volunteering the
U.S. to build a South Pole station, first noncommittally, then to
forestall a Russian station; Britain, Chile, and Argentina printing competing postage stamps and arranging rival coroners for
their territorial claims; Argentina and Chile solemnly declaring
that their titles descended from fifteenth-century papal decrees;
Argentina sending its entire cabinet to the Antarctic Peninsula
to demonstrate solidarity with Antartida Argentina, dispatch-
ing commando-type raids to skulk around British bases and tear
down notices of British sovereignty, flying an Argentine woman
in the late stages of pregnancy to a base so that the baby could
be born on its inalienable "domestic" territory.

There had been signs of humanity and good judgment as well:
the Chilean and Argentinean rescues of British explorers, Byrd's
assertion that sportsmanship counted as much as legal language, the merger of American airpower and British dogpower
by the Ronne Antarctic Research Expedition and the Falkland
Islands Dependencies Survey for exploration and rescue, the
Commonwealth of Science that evolved out of IGY, and the un-
commonly good sense of the Antarctic Treaty itself. "You know,
there's nothing personal about all this flag nonsense," Major
K. S. Pierce Butler informed a member of the Ronne party. "I'm
just trying to carry out orders. As far as I'm concerned you can
fly it all you like. Like Ronne, I came out here because I wanted
to."[35] Time and again, Byrd's pragmatic observation that in Antarctica everyone had to unite against the cold has proved more
durable than visions of national glory. But Byrd's remark had
been premised on an Antarctica in which simple survival was a
success and for which there were no terrestrial resources other
than the ice that was melted down for drinking water.

Inferior Mirage: Antarctica's Natural Resources

If sovereignty is the potential destabilizer of Antarctic politics,
then natural resources are the potential destabilizers of sovereignty. The extent of those natural resources is largely speculative. In general, they conform to the same concentric patterns
that characterize the Antarctic environment: they are most
abundant and best recognized around the perimeter and become progressively rarer and more speculative toward the interior. While valuable resources exist locally, overall The Ice is
not a source or a cornucopia of biotic and mineral resources but
a sink that will absorb vast quantities of money, labor, and information before it will yield returns. The development of adequate technology, economic markets, and political institutions
will require enormous investments of intellectual and financial
capital.

The biological riches of the Southern Ocean have been known
and, in the case of seals and whales, exploited for nearly two
centuries. Regulation of the whaling industry was a principal
objective in the declaration of early territorial claims. Only in
recent years has attention turned to other marine organisms
such as fish and squid. The critical concern, however, is with

krill, the crucial link in the phenomenally productive trophic chain. The first attempt to harvest krill was made in 1964 by a Soviet trawler. Through the late 1960s the total catch remained negligible. Then, if only for experimental purposes or to forestall a Soviet krill hegemony, fishing vessels were dispatched by other nations—Bulgaria, Chile, West Germany, Japan, Poland, South Korea, and Taiwan. In 1973–1974 the total krill harvest amounted to 22,000 metric tons; by 1976–1977, largely because of Soviet and Japanese fishing, the harvest had risen to 135,000 tons; and by 1979–1980, to some 477,000 tons. The great swarms of krill—a huge quantity of biomass—and the rich proportion of protein they contain (15 percent) led enthusiasts to boast that krill might double, perhaps triple the world food harvest from the ocean.

That is not likely to happen. Krill rapidly decomposes when removed from the frigid Southern Ocean; it has little texture and less taste; and its general unpalatability—whether it is whole or homogenized into a paste—may condemn it to serve as a cheap source of animal food or as a camouflaged supplement to traditional foodstuffs. Should the value of marine protein increase dramatically, however, the technological problems can be overcome. More difficult are problems of politics and conservation. Krill's critical position within the regional food chain argues for care lest the human harvest ripple catastrophically through the entire system. This recognition has led to the adoption by SCAR nations (and others) of an elaborate research program, Biological Investigations of Marine Antarctic Systems and Stocks (BIOMASS), and the adoption by the treaty nations of a Convention on the Conservation of Antarctic Marine Living Resources, an extension of the traditional concern over the regulation of whaling and sealing to encompass the entire spectrum of Southern Ocean species. It is hoped that the BIOMASS research program will allow the harvest to proceed according to ecosystem principles. It is likely that human consumption will by and large replace the consumption of krill and fish formerly exercised by large marine mammals, principally whales.

More politically volatile is the question of mineral resources. In 1983 the U.S. Geological Survey summarized the situation by observing that "no known petroleum or mineral resources occur in Antarctica."[36] But the evidence is overwhelming that major deposits do occur on the continent or its shelf. With 97 percent of the land covered by land ice and the shelf seasonally blanketed by sea ice and patrolled by marauding icebergs, however, the "question is not whether [minerals] exist but whether they will be found," or if discovered whether they can be economically mined.[37] Theoretical interest in Antarctic minerals stems from the consolidation of plate-tectonics theory: sedimentary basins around Antarctica appear to match up with others of Gondwanaland that are, or have the potential to be, oil reservoirs; the Amery Ice Shelf occupies a probable failed rift, similar to the petroleum-rich Benue Trough in West Africa; the Dufek Massif in the Pensacola Mountains is comparable in size and character to the fabulously mineralized Bushvelt Complex in South Africa; the Antarctic Peninsula, though different in some significant ways from the Andes, is similar enough geologically to suggest that it, too, might contain important metallogenic provinces.

Practical interest in Antarctic minerals, however, derives from the successful example of mining in the Arctic and Siberia and the 1973–1974 Arab oil embargo, which demonstrated to the industrial nations how vulnerable their supplies of strategic minerals might be. What seemed technologically remote now seems plausible, and what appeared to be hopelessly expensive and unnecessary now appears potentially valuable and perhaps essential to national interests. At a minimum, no nation wishes to be left out of discoveries. And as more countries covet potential Antarctic mineral wealth, the more insistent will the claimant nations become about their prior, "inalienable" rights.

Geophysical research has identified the major sedimentary basins of Antarctica. Most are in West Antarctica and along the continental shelf. The interior basins are generally inaccessible because moving ice sheets will prevent drilling. But drilling may be possible on the continental shelves. Two of the largest basins are in the Weddell and Ross seas. In 1972 and 1973 the *Glomar Challenger* of the Deep Sea Drilling Project encountered traces of methane, ethane, and ethylene—evidence of hydrocarbon diagenesis—in three of four holes drilled in the Ross Sea. The decision was made to cease drilling before the operation led to a blowout. Hastily, projections were advanced about the potential size of offshore Antarctic oil and gas fields; the U.S. Geological Survey estimated deposits of 45 billion barrels of oil and 115 trillion cubic feet of natural gas, though it considered only a third of this quantity recoverable. In 1978 a study by the Rand

Corporation speculated that four to ten supergiant fields (30–100 billion tons of oil) remained to be discovered on Earth. Obviously, Antarctica—comprising nearly 10 percent of the Earth's surface, most of which has been explored with far less sophistication than the remainder of the Earth—was a likely candidate for the still-undiscovered fields. Though actual exploratory drilling was placed under a moratorium until the treaty nations could evolve some sort of regime for the management of Antarctic minerals, preparatory geophysical studies are intensifying. Twice the U.S. State Department has refused requests by American oil companies to explore the shelf. Yet the fact remains that no oil or gas has actually been discovered, nor is any likely to be found until systematic exploration begins.

Antarctica presents formidable barriers to offshore drilling. Its climate is much harsher than that in the Arctic, its mixture of sea ice and land ice (bergs) is more dangerous, there are no suitable ports or transportation infrastructure, weather forecasting is poor, the Antarctic shelf is half as wide and twice as deep as average continental shelves, and the environmental consequences of a blowout and oil spill are possibly more disastrous. Vast sums of money and research will be required to develop the technology necessary to extract oil and gas—and the technological issues are far simpler than the political ones. The waxing and waning of current oil supplies suggests that the economics of Antarctic oil is not yet favorable. For countries like Japan, however, which are completely dependent on imported oil, price considerations may be secondary, and it is worth recalling that in the early 1960s common wisdom held that Arctic minerals would never be economically extracted. As the world's existing oil reservoirs shrink, those in the Antarctic will be tapped.

The same may be true of other Antarctic minerals. Trace concentrations are found nearly everywhere, but no definable ore body has been discovered. Still, every national research program has included a geologic component; the U.S. was slower than most to specify that the "prediction and assessment of resources" should be a consideration of its Antarctic research program (1970); and to date, serious ore exploration has not been widely attempted.[38] In most areas of the world, prospecting has historically begun with the location of accessible surface deposits, which streams have usually transported into placers. The elements are then traced back to a mother lode. The only analogous process in Antarctica is the ice-placer mechanism that collects meteorites. But geologic analogies and plate reconstructions suggest likely sources for mineral deposits. The only significant discoveries so far are iron (Prince Charles Mountains) and coal (Transantarctics). They have been found, in part, because they are so abundant everywhere and therefore of little commercial value. The most promising location for a major deposit of strategic minerals is the Dufek Massif, which is very similar in size, composition, and history to the Bushvelt Complex. But while the heaviest mineralization in the Bushvelt occurs along the lower strata, in the Dufek Massif the heaviest mineralization is submerged beneath glacial ice. Even here a major deposit would cost perhaps three times as much to develop as equally rich deposits almost anywhere else in the world.

Some manganese nodules and metalliferous muds are present on the ocean floor, but they are of low metallic value compared with more accessible deposits elsewhere in the world ocean. Their status, moreover, is doubly complicated by the murky sovereignty question. The claimant nations insist that they enjoy territorial waters and an exclusive economic zone in accordance with the new Law of the Sea, an assertion that only the meager, quarrelsome cadre of fellow claimants recognizes. But the Antarctic Treaty defines its own jurisdiction as latitude 60 degrees, and it places the high seas, shelves, and deep oceans of Antarctica outside the provisions of the Law of the Sea.

The principal Antarctic mineral, of course, is glacial ice, which may prove to be a usefully packaged source of fresh water. The idea of transporting Antarctic bergs to desert lands has long been around. At the end of the nineteenth century a few small bergs had even been towed up the coast of Chile in the cold Humboldt current, and in 1973 two U.S. researchers suggested that icebergs might be a source of fresh water for arid lands in the Southern Hemisphere. The idea quickly escalated into wilder speculations that the bergs could be transported to deserts and metropoli in the Northern Hemisphere as well. Then in 1977 Prince Muhammad al-Faisal of Saudi Arabia formed Iceberg Transport International, hired Paul-Emile Victor and Cicero (a French engineering consortium), and announced his intention to haul Antarctic bergs to Deserta Arabia for considerably less than the price of desalination plants. An international symposium debated the question, largely from a technical standpoint. A number of patents and ingenious inventions had been proposed concerning transport and processing of the bergs, but as calculations improved, the likelihood that bergs could be successfully hauled across the tropics became vanishingly small. Though Saudi Arabia ended its funding, scientific interest in icebergs continues, and it is probable that bergs will be transported to the deserts of Australia or South America at least on an experimental basis. The greatest impediments are political: ice is a mineral, and no claimant nation will allow ice to be removed without recognition of sovereignty, while no nonclaimant nation is likely to submit to extortion on the basis of territorial claims that it has never recognized as legitimate.

Similar considerations have plagued Antarctic tourism, another constantly promoted activity that has floundered amid geopolitical uncertainty and the rigor of the Antarctic landscape. In 1980 it was estimated that 31,000 people had visited Antarctica as paying tourists, adventurers, or guests of national scientific expeditions, about a third of them on daytime overflights and many of the rest on cruise ships.[39] Tourism is concentrated along the coastline, where there exist spectacular mountain scenery, broken glacier fields, marine life (especially the universally delightful penguin), and, not surprisingly, other humans. Nearly three-fourths of all the visits occur at nine scientific stations. Travel, of course, is expensive. Chile sponsored the first tourist flight (1956), and Argentina conducted the first Antarctic cruise (1958). West Germany, Italy, Spain, Chile, Britain, Australia, and New Zealand have arranged cruises, but two U.S. companies—Lindblad Travel and Society Expeditions—are responsible for the most tourists and the most frequent tours. The cruises concentrate heavily on the Antarctic Peninsula, though a longer circumnavigation of the continent is available. Ironically, since tour ships cannot navigate through heavy pack ice, the areas they visit are those least representative of Antarctica—sites where there is considerable variety of mountain scenery and marine life and a relatively mild maritime climate. Even so, the *Lindblad Explorer* has twice run aground and been damaged. Perhaps the scientists' chief complaint has been the disruption of scientific projects as small bases grapple with throngs of curious tourists.

Overflights, which began in a serious way in 1977 with Air New Zealand and Qantas, have been more troubled. In November 1979—as the U.S. prepared to commemorate the fiftieth anniversary of Byrd's flight to the South Pole—an Air New Zea-

land DC-10 slammed into Mt. Erebus. All 275 people on board
died instantly. The tragedy, however, highlighted more than the usual risks of air travel: it illustrated the peculiar political and environmental circumstances of Antarctica. The plane had no provisions for emergency survival on ice; there was no mechanism for rescue or evacuation; and had it not crashed in the vicinity of the American and New Zealand bases, the wreckage might never have been located at all. The tragedy created a national scandal in New Zealand and an international embarrassment. The search for scapegoats (and compensatory money) even extended to the U.S. Navy, as families of crew members pressed lawsuits amounting to $17 million on the contention that the airfield maintained by the navy on the ice shelf at McMurdo had been negligent in failing to warn the New Zealand pilot adequately about weather conditions and about his flight path into the lower levels of Mt. Erebus. "This bit of gall," as Philip Quigg observes, "overlooks the facts that the plane crashed in territory claimed by New Zealand, that the overflights were not approved by the Antarctic Treaty powers, and that the United States Navy never assumed any responsibility for the safety of the tourist planes."[40]

But of course the U.S. did assume responsibility on humanitarian grounds for search and rescue operations. The cost was considerable, but the commercial operators offered no compensation. Earlier, in 1967, the U.S. had presciently formulated a policy on tourism that sought to affirm the principle of open access to the continent without surrendering practical control over its Antarctic operations or effectively subsidizing the costs of unofficial Antarctic visitation. There is no simple solution. Access is difficult except through national programs, yet national programs are dedicated to scientific research, a neutral activity, rather than to tourism, which generates revenues, involves commercial companies, and suspiciously resembles a species of "settlement." Among other troubling considerations are the self-styled adventurers who travel over, around, or above Antarctica at no explicit expense to national programs but who would likewise command emergency search and rescue operations in the event of trouble and who implicity challenge the delicate balance of courtesies that keeps the sovereignty issue in check. They are, in effect, free riders.

How to exploit natural resources without encouraging free riders, or allowing an open-use program to degrade an international commons, or inflaming nationalistic sentiments on the sovereignty conundrum is not obvious. Part of the problem is a profound ignorance. Not only are Antarctic mineral resources wholly speculative, but the only means to muster the science to inquire into them and to master the technology demanded for their extraction is to assume that they do exist and attempt to mine them. In part, too, there is widespread concern that the environment not be grossly disrupted. The nineteenth-century experience with seals and the twentieth-century debacle with whaling in the Southern Ocean are obvious negative exemplars, and the success of the environmental movement in the industrial nations has rallied considerable public sentiment behind rigorous conservation guidelines. The U.S. State Department has accordingly prepared environmental impact statements for various scenarios of resource exploitation. The legitimacy of the Antarctic Treaty before world opinion—acquiescence to the belief that the consultative nations are indeed administering Antarctica on behalf of world interest—depends in part on the perception that the treaty nations are not simply plundering Antarctica for their own enrichment.

Antarctica's outstanding resource is, of course, its information content, the natural laboratory it offers science. It may be that information extraction, as practiced by modern industrial science, will serve as a model for economic exploitation, much as the example of international cooperative science during IGY inspired a political solution to the Antarctic question. After all, there are many similarities between mineral extraction and the collection and processing of information in Antarctica and the larger geopolitical economy under which specimens and data are removed and integrated into a world market of ideas. Not the least of these is that the amount of information available is not something inherent—immutable and self-evident—in the landscape but something dependent on the will, the technological capabilities, and the intellectual infrastructure of a civilization. Equally, the amount of investment in Antarctic mining, as in Antarctic science, will depend not so much on the specific economic (or intellectual) value of Antarctic mining as on its political significance. It is likely that the claimant nations will engage in resource development to support assertions of title, that the consultative nations will participate to sustain a competitive political presence, and that the first natural resources exploited will go to the maintenance of scientific bases.

So long as the Antarctic Treaty remains in force, the principal expression of political ambition will continue to be science or resource exploitation in the support of science. The Commonwealth of Science will endure in Antarctica not because it is the purest of human activities but because circumstances in Antarctica have made it the most neutral. Yet no less than oil or platinum, knowledge is power. Science is an instrument of Antarctic politics, but it also legitimates that politics and strengthens the information infrastructure of the nations who engage in it. The character of the Antarctic System makes this knowledge available to all—there is no free-rider problem—but use does require acceptance of Western science. At a time, however, when non-Western nations have added to demands for a new international economic order more demands for a new international information order, the legitimating role of Western science in the governance of Antarctica may be questioned. Like other natural resources, information intensifies the sovereignty quandary and leaves unresolved the ultimate choice of an appropriate political regime.

Northern Conjugates: The Arctic Analogy

Antarctica was the last of the continents to be explored by Western civilization and the first of the new environments to be explored by IGY. It could, accordingly, follow one of two analogies: the Arctic, to which traditional concepts of sovereignty, with modification, have been applied, or the international domains of the deep oceans and outer space, for which new governing principles have been developed. Or its unique environment and the historical timing of its discovery could propel Antarctica to a unique political solution, one distinct from analogies to other regimes and not itself a precedent for the administration of other lands. Thus, Antarctica could be as unusual geopolitically as it is geophysically.

Antarctica is unusually harsh and isolated, but its political development cannot be explained solely through environmental circumstances. The history of its Arctic conjugates demonstrates this fact well. The Southern Ocean is more accessible than the permanently frozen Arctic Ocean; the ice-free areas feature climates no worse than the inhabited regions of the north polar region; and the high cost of Arctic operations has been no impediment to development when the resource has been sufficiently valuable or the political needs suitably high. Mines operate on Greenland, the Kola Peninsula, Arctic Canada and Alaska, Spitsbergen, and polar Scandinavia (warmed by the Gulf Stream). Offshore oil is drilled along the North Slope of Alaska and in the storm-prone North Sea. Gold and diamonds are mined at Oymyakon, Siberia, near the cold pole of the Northern Hemisphere. Major military bases ring the Arctic Circle from Murmansk to Thule. With enormous icebreakers, the Soviet Union has developed a Northern Sea Route through the Arctic pack. Severe cold, pressure-pack ice, permafrost, seasonal muck, and isolation are all impediments to polar mining or militarization that have found a technical solution through the elaboration of traditional technology. Habitability is a relative concept, and *Homo sapiens*, after all, is an Ice Age species. The new residents of the Arctic do not live off the land but off the larger society that they serve.

Traditional concepts of sovereignty have proven adequate to resolve political controversies in the Arctic. In fact, only after sovereignty in some form was extended to a *terra nullius* did the area become politically stable. One advantage of the Arctic over the Antarctic is that most Arctic lands are contiguous with national territories; even the Canadian archipelago is so close to mainland Canada that there were few difficulties in extending traditional sovereignty over them. There have, however, been important innovations. The development of Arctic lands came late enough and slowly enough that special political and economic concessions have been extended to native peoples in Alaska, Greenland, and Canada. Concepts of territorial sovereignty have been refined: from Svalbard (Spitsbergen) came a concept of limited sovereignty, from Arctic Canada emerged the disputed sector principle, from floating ice stations developed issues of jurisdiction for criminal acts and civil liabilities, and from Greenland came new international standards for the concept of effective occupation. None of these issues derived solely from environmental circumstances; rather, they expressed historical and cultural circumstances. The environmental conditions were influential primarily in deciding just when these cultural factors would enter into force for a particular area. Still, the Arctic lands have figured in the evolution of Western civilization for centuries, and Arctic-based precedents are only incompletely applicable to the Antarctic. The closest analogies

to the Antarctic situation are the histories of Svalbard and
Greenland.

The Svalbard archipelago (latitude 74–81 degrees North) was discovered by Norse adventurers in 1194, and along with Greenland it was made a tributary to Norway in 1261. Dutch explorers rediscovered it in 1596, during the search for a Northeast Passage, and its wealth of marine life soon inspired a major whaling and sealing industry, international rivalry for control over the islands, and a boisterous Dutch settlement of 1,000–2,000 people. In 1614 England annexed the islands, but the Danish-Norwegian king declared the archipelago to be still a part of Greenland, and the Dutch disputed the commercial concessions given to the Muscovy Company. In 1618 a Dutch-English commission divided the coast into separate spheres of influence. During the Thirty Years' War national encampments were armed, and the Danish-Norwegian monarchy accepted British and Dutch rights to hunt on Spitsbergen. Over the next century French and German ships also competed for fish, whales, and furs; and in the eighteenth century, Russian hunters joined them. Meanwhile, overkilling of whales, bans on the use of whale oil for soap (1632), and political problems with the renewal of chartered monopolies led to the collapse of the whaling industry. The sovereignty questions evaporated. Svalbard relapsed into the status of a *terra nullius*. Seasonal hunting and fishing (and occasionally sealing) persisted, however, and in 1784 Norway tried to reestablish an annual presence on the islands. By the early nineteenth century, Norway could claim a preeminence of interest in Svalbard and sporadically mounted scientific expeditions. By the end of the century, Svalbard had become an important point of departure for Arctic exploration, rivaled only by Greenland.

In 1870–1871 the Swedish-Norwegian government approached the other European nations that had, from time to time, engaged in Svalbard activities to see if they would accept Swedish-Norwegian sovereignty over the archipelago. Russia balked and the idea subsided except for a few observers, such as Nordenskjöld, who pleaded for the establishment of a permanent settlement that would provide the effective occupation demanded for the recognition of sovereignty. But it was mineral resources that finally revived interest in the area. It had long been known that Svalbard possessed abundant, accessible coal seams. In 1899 a supply of Spitsbergen coal was shipped to Norway, and the next year a Norwegian coal company was founded to mine it in a systematic way. The need for capital brought in British, German, and American companies. Squabbles over competing mine claims, squatting by companies and individuals, concern over environmental problems, and alarm that Svalbard would become an uncontrolled omnium-gatherum like Alaska all led the Norwegian government in 1907 to revive the question of administration without, apparently, invoking the testy issue of sovereignty. Negotiations proceeded sluggishly on the "Spitsbergen problem." By 1910, and again in 1912, Norwegian, Swedish, and Russian delegations agreed, in effect, to a condominium solution—a joint rule by the three nations over the archipelago. But a 1914 international conference on Svalbard rejected the arrangement; the major powers, several of which could advance claims of discovery or previous occupation, refused to be left out of any Svalbard condominium.

The conclusion to World War I led to a resolution. The Treaty of Brest Litovsk between Russia and Germany stated that both countries would work for an international regime in Spitsbergen that would guarantee them equal status. Norway, however, insisted on its prerogative, convinced at last that there was no alternative to a declaration of sovereignty. Svalbard could not be administered endlessly as an international commons. Norway brought the issue before the Versailles Peace Conference. On an American suggestion a commission was appointed to survey the situation, and in 1920 a Treaty of Svalbard (Spitsbergen) was prepared. It had been suggested that Svalbard be truly internationalized through a League of Nations mandate administered by Norway, but there seemed to be no real alternative to sovereignty.

Instead, the concept of sovereignty was modified so that Norway was acceded sovereignty but other signatory nations were permitted equal access to resources, and in practice their nationals remained subject to the jurisdiction of their own governments. At least needed reforms were now possible: a mining code was enacted to regulate the coal industry, land titles were straightened out, and provisions were included to demilitarize the region. The Svalbard Treaty entered into force in 1925. The Soviet Union agreed to the treaty only on the understanding that Norway recognize the Soviet government as de jure. Even so, the Soviet Union still hesitated until 1935 to sign the treaty,

in the belief that Svalbard was of strategic interest to its ports
and military bases around the Barents Sea.

Not surprisingly, Svalbard did become involved in World War
II. After Germany invaded the Soviet Union, Svalbard—along
with Iceland and Greenland—was declared vital to the sea
route by which the U.S. supplied Britain and Russia. It was an
important meteorological base, and it was occupied by both Allied and Axis guard units. German bombers and naval forces
successfully attacked the Allied bases several times. In 1944 the
Soviet Union informed Norway that it wanted the Treaty of
Svalbard declared invalid and that it wished one island in the
archipelago given to Russia and the remainder to be administered under a Soviet-Norwegian condominium. Temporarily,
Norway agreed to joint defense responsibilities. When the war
ended, the Soviets wanted to make the emergency provisions
permanent, but Norway rejected the idea in 1947 and joined
NATO in 1949. This act put Svalbard under NATO protection,
though Norway insisted that no military bases would be established within the archipelago. The Soviet Union, for its part,
continued to maintain a large coal-mining operation, which
effectively ensured a vigorous Soviet political presence.

The history of Greenland is even more instructive. It was discovered earlier (982) than Svalbard and settled in traditional
ways from Iceland (985). The largest settlement, Godthåb, was
located on fjords in the southwest portion of Greenland; Juliane-
håb was sited at Cape Farewell on the southern tip. These settlements, in turn, supported voyages of discovery and settlements
to the New World. At its peak (ca. 1100), the colony flourished
with perhaps 6,000 people. In 1261 Norwegian sovereignty was
extended over Greenland in return for guaranteed trade. Then
the climate cooled and ice threatened sea lanes and settlements, Norse hegemony waned, and the Greenland colony disappeared. By 1342 the western settlement was abandoned; by
the end of the fifteenth century the eastern followed. Whether
the Norse colonists died off slowly, perished before the eastward
migrations of the Eskimo, or were assimilated into Eskimo society is unknown. But the idea of the Greenland colony was
never completely lost. Icelandic and Norse sagas established
a written historical record. Within a few decades of the final
demise of the eastern settlement, Europeans rediscovered the
New World. By the late sixteenth century Martin Frobisher and

John Davis had visited Greenland. Practically every voyage in search of the Northwest Passage would at least pass through the Davis Strait, which separates Greenland from the Canadian archipelago.

In 1721 a second group attempted colonization, under the inspired Danish missionary Hans Egede. At least part of the motivation was to search for the legendary Greenlanders, segregated from Christendom like the Coptics in India or the blue-eyed "Welsh Indians" whose melancholy fate had presumably abandoned them in the Upper Missouri River. No residual population was ever discovered, but the search animated a host of travels around Greenland, and the religious character of the appeal (and absence of significant populations) meant that the Danish monarchy exercised a paternalistic, relatively mild dominion over the distant island. The island was effectively quarantined, sparing Greenlanders from the worst scourges of exotic disease. The economy was closed, regulated by monopoly (Royal Greenland Trading Company), and profits were to be reinvested in Greenland. Natives were expected to be self-supporting on native foods, though gradually they were introduced to a money economy. Likewise, the policy evolved that Greenland would be self-sustaining, involving neither profit nor loss to Denmark.

The search for a Northwest Passage and then for Sir John Franklin, general interest in continental exploration, the journeys of Nordenskjöld across the Greenland ice sheet, the first International Polar Year, the expeditions of Drygalski, and the obsessive marches of Robert Peary across the northern ice sheet and the polar pack all rallied scientific interest in Greenland. By the early twentieth century German, American, British, and Danish expeditions traveled almost annually to Greenland. Especially in the early years Greenlanders, notably the remarkable Knud Rasmussen, figured prominently in the exploration of the interior. No longer simply a departure point for assaults on the North Pole, Greenland offered a relatively accessible ice sheet for glaciological inquiries, a critical test for the theory of continental drift, an important source of ethnographic data, and a vital component of the second International Polar Year. Since it was inextricably bound with European weather and forecasting, Greenland became important for air traffic. It also came to be seen as a potential source of such strategic minerals like cryolite, which is used in aluminum production.

All this vigorous international attention caused Denmark to shore up the legal status of its enormous but thinly populated colony. In particular, Peary's extensive travels, his offer to claim the North Pole for the U.S., and his invocation of the Monroe Doctrine, with its implication that Danish colonization was unwelcome, were cause for concern. Only in 1916 did the U.S. formally express satisfaction with Danish sovereignty over Greenland. In 1921, as the Svalbard problem reached an amicable solution and as Denmark prepared for the bicentennial of its re-established colony, Denmark reaffirmed sovereignty over all of Greenland—not only the western fjords, where settlements had always congregated, but over the northern dry valleys, the eastern shore, and the interior ice sheet. Most nations acquiesced. Then in 1931 Norway decreed that Denmark did not effectively occupy eastern Greenland, that the land was a *terra nullius*, and that Norway would settle and assume sovereignty over it. This was the same period when Norwegian whalers were actively establishing the basis for territorial claims in Antarctica.

By mutual consent, the *Eastern Greenland* case was brought before the International Court at The Hague. In 1933 the court decided for Denmark. It declared, in effect, that Greenland was a coherent geographic unit and that Danish administration had been adequate for a generally uninhabitable land. Observing that minimal governance had traditionally been acceptable for nations to establish title, it argued that Denmark had shown an adequate spirit of possession (*animus possessionis*) regarding the whole of Greenland and a suitable presence (*corpus possessionis*) in the principal locales. A more oblique but serious challenge, however, resulted from World War II. When Germany overran Denmark in 1940, the governors of West Greenland established a "Greenland Administration"—which meant, in practice, a temporary state of independence. One governor remained in Greenland, another in the United States. Soon afterward, an American-Greenland Commission was created to advise the new Greenland Administration, along with a Greenland Delegation to oversee exports and imports. Increasingly, the United States became a surrogate for Denmark. In April 1941 Greenland officially became a protectorate of the U.S. "until it is agreed that the present dangers to the peace and security of the American continent have passed."[41] The U.S. was granted the right to construct military bases, to move American supplies freely, and to enjoy full jurisdiction, though Danish sovereignty remained technically in force and local authorities dealt directly with Greenlanders. Meanwhile, Iceland was also declared strategically a part of the Western Hemisphere.

Unlike Svalbard, Greenland would not be demilitarized after the war. Large-scale military exercises continued in the Arctic (Operations Frostbite, Nanook); the U.S. Army created a Snow, Ice, and Permafrost Research Establishment, with strong connections to Greenland and Alaska; and the Antarctic Developments Projects had, as an objective, the testing of equipment and operations for possible use in Greenland. In 1946–1948 Admiral Byrd prepared a Greenland study that became a blueprint for an array of defensive facilities. In 1951 Denmark and the U.S. signed joint defense agreements intended to maintain the U.S. military presence in Greenland. The air base at Søndre Strømfjord was joined by a larger facility at Thule (1951–1952), huge Distant Early Warning (DEW) radar stations were constructed on the interior ice sheet (1954), and military needs for information—conveyed in a five-year plan for research—were merged with a revival of civilian, international scientific expeditions to Greenland, culminating in the glaciological investigations of IGY. The Arctic Ocean became a polar Mediterranean, a sea integral to postwar geopolitical strategies; and the Arctic Circle became an armed perimeter of the Cold War.

But the war had also brought a heady spirit of independence to Greenlanders. However benevolent Danish administration, Greenlanders increasingly saw themselves as colonials in a world that mocked Western European imperialism and witnessed the breakup of formerly far-flung empires. A Greenland Commission established in 1948 recommended political and economic reforms, and in 1953 Greenland elected members to the Danish parliament, effectively replacing colonial status with a more equal political integration. Yet the de facto American protectorate remained. Questions about ownership of offshore shelves, the pack ice, and the abyssal plains of the Arctic Ocean were resolved by the Law of the Sea Treaty.

The Svalbard and Greenland examples both have some relevance to Antarctica. The *Eastern Greenland* case established precedent in international law for a minimal standard of occupation in polar environments. The Svalbard Treaty suggested the applicability of the limited sovereignty concept. Neither case, however, offers a complete analogy for Antarctica. Antarctica was discovered much later, it lacked even feeble connections with civilizations, and it is not near geopolitical battlegrounds. However rabid the Argentines are about the Falklands, they were not willing to extend their 1982 war with Britain beyond South Georgia to Antarctica proper, and Antarctica is not as likely an ignition point for East-West conflicts as the Arctic or the Middle East. None of the Great Powers is a claimant to Antarctic territory. While Antarctica may become a hostage to the rhetoric of North-South controversies, there are no Antarctic natives or colonists. There will be no Antarctic declaration of independence or revolt for self-rule; the rhetoric of colonialism is as suitable to Antarctica as the Richtner expedition's salutes to penguins. The scale of Antarctica is significant. Even Greenland is defined—geophysically and geopolitically—by its surroundings. Within the greater Arctic, its ice sheet is an enclave. Antarctica, however, is defined from and by its ice sheet, which is an exclusive and informing presence.

Antarctica is neither a true *terra nullius* nor an international commons. The Arctic demanded sovereignty in someone, somewhere, and Arctic history gave ample antecedents for contestants. In both the Svalbard and Greenland cases sovereignty was sustained and invested in a single country, though legal and political limitations were imposed. An investiture of sovereignty would resolve some Antarctic problems. There are, for example, many practical legal issues that assume either sovereignty or nonsovereignty, that require a citizen or a corporation to be either on national territory or on foreign territory: civil and criminal codes, tax laws, civil rights, environmental protection legislation, and of course access to natural resources. Some collective decision-making procedure, some institutional capacity to collect information and enforce controls, and some rationale for legitimizing its operations are essential. Moreover, when resource exploitation occurs outside a system of explicit territorial sovereignty, there is uncertainty about responsibilities as well as rights, the potential tragedy of the Antarctic commons. Even within a collective regime, such as the Antarctic Treaty system, there is potentially a free-rider problem. Nontreaty nations have right of access to Antarctica and its resources without being bound by the provisions of the treaty. Unless exclusive rights are granted for commercial enterprises, free riders can similarly move in to reap benefits without costs and without conforming to conservation guidelines.

For this reason, as well as nationalist sentiment on the part of the claimant nations, there is interest in bringing Antarctica into a legal order based on traditional concepts of sovereignty. Like the Arctic, Antarctica would be declared a *terra nullius* and would be partitioned according to precedent. For Argentina and Chile, in particular, anything less than a full assertion of sovereignty would probably mean the downfall of the existing domestic regime. Political variations on this theme include the prospect of condominium or consortium rules over portions of the continent or a Svalbard-like regime based on limited sovereignty. A U.S.–New Zealand condominium over the Ross Dependency and the unclaimed ("American") sector in Marie Byrd Land is often mentioned as a likely candidate. Any such moves would restore Antarctica to the *status ante quo* the Antarctica Treaty.

But the disadvantages to the application of traditional concepts of sovereignty are formidable. There are conflicting territorial claims for which arbitration is unacceptable. The two largest nations with Antarctic investments, the U.S. and the U.S.S.R., have no present claims but would advance some in a territorial scramble. Other nations would submit claims on the basis of discovery, the sector principle, or an assertion of *uti posseditis juris*. Guidelines for environmental protection would be difficult to enforce. Since condominium rule has been proposed and rejected in the past, there is no reason to believe that titles would be universally recognized as legitimate. And sovereignty would almost certainly mean militarization. If the Arctic has become a polar Mediterranean, Antarctica would become a polar Balkans.

It is more likely that investment of sovereignty will not resolve the Antarctic question, even conditionally. Rather, as Keith Brennan has argued, "sovereignty will have to find an alias."[42] The appearance of sovereignty must be kept without its substance. In brief, the Arctic is a study in cultural and political pluralism, a palimpsest of histories and a mosaic of competitive jurisdictions. But Antarctica captured its visitors in its own cold vortex; the Western regime was slowed rather than accelerated. Over its brief human history The Ice has imposed a unity of interest not unlike the unity that the ice field has imposed over its various ice terranes. The stability of both fields, ice and politics, is speculative. Sovereignty controls the politics of Antarctica as sea level controls the shelves and sheet of West Antarctica. A rising tide of nationalism—among claimant

nations or Third World aspirants—could unpin the Antarctic
Treaty, and the geopolitical unity of Antarctica could disintegrate catastrophically.

Pax Antarctica

An alternative to the concept of Antarctica as a *terra nullius* is
that of Antarctica as a *terra communis*—not a land of no one,
subject to traditional concepts of title and sovereignty, but a
land of everyone, a common heritage of mankind to be man-
aged for the collective good. The *terra communis* concept substitutes for the Arctic analogy an analogy to the fate of those
other IGY-exposed lands, the deep ocean and outer space. The
modern debate over the legal status of all three regions was
broached at the same time. In 1958, as the U.S. circulated invitations for an Antarctic conference, the United Nations arranged for a Committee on the Peaceful Uses of Outer Space
and convened the first of the Geneva Conventions on the Law of
the Sea. There was a symmetry to these discussions. The Outer
Space Committee debated the upper limits of national airspace,
the Law of the Sea convention discussed the outer limits of the
territorial sea, and the Antarctic Conference established limits
on extraterritorial sovereignty. IGY had not only demonstrated
the access to all these areas that technology had made possible:
it dramatized (for example, with Sputnik) the potentially strategic interests that each region held, and it suggested by example that a cooperative international solution was possible.

The Antarctic Treaty was politically the simplest of the three
domains because it involved the fewest parties. The success of
the negotiations, in fact, forestalled a move by the U.N. to place
on its agenda a discussion about a suitable international regime
for Antarctica. The Antarctic Treaty was concluded in 1959 and
entered into force in 1961. The Outer Space Committee reports
concluded in 1961 with a Resolution on the Peaceful Uses of
Outer Space, declaring that international laws (including the
U.N. Charter) applied in space and on celestial bodies and that
such areas were open for exploration and use by all states. In
1966 the U.S., in heated rivalry with the Soviet Union's space
program, announced that it would seek a U.N. agreement to prevent any state from claiming title to any celestial bodies, including the Moon. An Outer Space Treaty was signed in 1967.

Two years later, Americans landed on the Moon and declared innocuously that they had come in peace for all humanity. Another Moon Treaty, upgraded ideologically to incorporate principles from the Law of the Sea negotiations, was approved by the U.N. in 1979, though important nations, including the United States, have declined to ratify it.

The controversy revolved around the concept that celestial bodies were the "common heritage of all mankind." This seemingly innocent, if romantic, phrase had been introduced in 1970 into the sluggish Law of the Sea conferences. Initially, the conferences sought to codify the Law of the Sea, update the concept of high seas, define the limits of the territorial seas, oversee the use of the continental shelves, and provide some conservation measures. Between the 1958 and the 1960 Geneva Conferences on the Law of the Sea, four conventions had been developed. But the early conferences failed to resolve some key issues, and by 1974, when a new round of negotiations began (Caracas Conference), the Law of the Sea had become inextricably entangled with Third World politics, the Group of 77, the North-South conflict, and calls for a new international economic order. The Law of the Sea—especially its provisions for expanding the territorial sea and for creating exclusive economic zones over 200 miles of the continental shelf—directly affected many nations for which programs in outer space and Antarctica were hopelessly remote.

The critical geographic problem was the newly explored and mapped deep ocean, which, apart from its contributions to the theory of plate tectonics, contained mineral deposits in the form of manganese nodules. The idea gained force that the deep ocean should be a *terra communis*, that its resources should be exploited under the direction of special international agencies for the good of nations otherwise incapable of exploiting them. There were important if subtle differences between the new common-heritage concept, favored by the Group of 77, and the more traditional concept of open use, favored by the industrial nations. The distinction is roughly analogous to that between the concepts of affirmative action and equal opportunity. In practice, rather than endowing "disadvantaged" nations with an economic windfall, the program might very well discourage any mining at all. Amid many doubts on the part of the industrialized nations, an International Seabed Authority was established to oversee deep-sea mining, and the new Law of the Sea convention was opened for signature in 1982. The U.S., in particular, has hesitated to sign. The common-heritage principle, however, was extended to the new Moon Treaty, and almost certainly it will be argued for Antarctica.

The consequences of the Law of the Sea convention for Antarctica are not yet known. Among practical effects is that long-range fishing fleets will probably move to the Southern Ocean to replace traditional fisheries lost to the newly established exclusive economic zones. For claimant states, the need to assert title to Antarctic territory now extends to the territorial sea and exclusive economic zones. This means that offshore drilling for oil and gas cannot avoid the sovereignty question. It is also unclear whether the International Seabed Authority has jurisdiction within the Antarctic Treaty zone or whether the Antarctic Treaty has installed an alternate regime for everything south of 60 degrees latitude. But the challenge posed by the Law of the Sea convention may be even more fundamental: the common-heritage concept implicitly questions the legitimacy of the Antarctic Treaty and the Antarctic System which, in practice, govern the region "on behalf of mankind." Only the successful negotiation of the treaty kept the U.N. General Assembly from addressing the status of Antarctica. The possibility that natural resources might actually be mined, the doctrine that Antarctica should also be considered a priori a common heritage of mankind, and the prospect that nations otherwise distant from Antarctica and its abstruse sciences might claim a portion of its riches have all revived interest by the Group of 77, the U.N., and propagandists for a new international economic order. During the 1970s, various U.N. committees addressed selected topics which were relevant to Antarctica.

Meanwhile, environmental groups advanced another version of the *terra communis* concept: that Antarctica should be set aside as a nature preserve. At the 1972 Second World Conference on National Parks, supported by the U.N. Environment Program, it was suggested that Antarctica be declared a world park. At a minimum, resolutions have been passed urging an indefinite moratorium on resource exploitation. Arctic nations have established often vast preserves in Alaska, Canada, Greenland, Svalbard, and Siberia. At the Third World Conference on National Parks (Nairobi) the proposal to establish a world park was repeated with recommendations that the subject be brought before the Antarctic Treaty nations and the U.N. General Assembly.

In the meantime, an Antarctic and Southern Ocean Coalition—modeled on the alliance that had successfully campaigned for Alaskan wilderness—was organized among eighty-three environmental groups; and the tactics that had been developed over the past thirty years were applied to Antarctica, including the inevitable picture book (*Let's Save Antarctica!*). The Antarctic Community was not indifferent to conservation principles, which had since the days of British licensing constituted one of their claims to legitimacy. But to expect preservationist sentiment to prevail over the entire region was chimerical. In particular, culturally bound concepts like the American idea of wilderness would have a difficult time gaining global acceptance, and virtually no environmental concepts have much applicability to the vast bulk of the continent, the polar plateau. In this frozen sink, there is not much wild; the plateau is at once the least and most humanized of all Earthly landscapes; by normal standards, in the interior there is nothing that could pass for scenery, wildlife, or ecosystems, only ideas and ice. The Ice preserves everything and excludes everything.

There is nothing intrinsically destabilizing about U.N. interest in Antarctica or oversight of the Antarctic Treaty. Since the founding of the League of Nations, several Antarctic nations, even claimant states, had advanced the idea of a trusteeship or multiple trusteeships. But the common-heritage concept, if pursued rigorously, went beyond notions of stewardship. It pronounced as a "common heritage" what had been a fundamental experience for a select group of nations and questioned their collective legitimacy as an administering body under the treaty. It is an important fact that the Antarctic Treaty does not have universal status; it applies only to those nations that elect to sign it, though a limited number of nations have the capability to involve themselves in Antarctica other than through political maneuverings. Behind the common-heritage concept, too, is the suggestion that the Antarctic nations constitute an exclusive gentleman's club that has unjustly appropriated a global prerogative. In its more ideological versions, the common-heritage concept demands, in effect, that the historically active Antarctic nations renounce national heritages of which they are properly proud. It brings to Antarctic discussions an anticolonial rhetoric as inappropriate as the colonial cant that was applied to Africa a century earlier.

Paradoxically, this challenge to the Antarctic System has

helped reinforce the sense among the historically active Antarctic nations that they constitute a special community and
that they have shared interests which distinguish them from
other nations. They could rightly argue that they already freely
distribute to the world their principal Antarctic product, information. No less than the fear of chaos, concern over the intentions of nontreaty nations has become a rallying point for treaty
nations. They have proposed a third possibility for the political
administration of Antarctica—that Antarctica be treated not as
terra nullius or as *terra communis* but as *terra Antarctica*: it
should be recognized as a unique historical and geographic entity for which the Antarctic Treaty is a suitable point of departure. The self-referential character of The Ice would be reflected
in its political regime.

The Antarctic Treaty formally established what Steven Burton has aptly termed the Antarctic Community.[43] The community consists of two related societies: any party that agrees to
the treaty qualifies as a signatory nation, while those parties
that also demonstrate a substantial commitment to scientific research in Antarctica may become consultative nations. The
consultative nations constitute, in practice, the legislative organ
of the Antarctic System and meet every two years at a different
member country. SCAR serves as an advisory staff, the host
country provides the secretariat, and consultative meetings are,
from time to time, supplemented by gatherings on special topics. Originally, twelve nations—six claimants and six nonclaimants—comprised the consultative body. Two additional
nations, West Germany and Poland, have since been added; and
Belgium, despite the fact that it has not participated in active
Antarctic research since IGY, has been retained. Resolutions
require unanimity, but the shared fear of chaos, the inability
for any member to act unilaterally, and the need by the entire
community to protect its interest against challenges by non-
Antarctic nations all encourage consensus. Most importantly,
the Antarctic Treaty was designed not as a comprehensive agreement but as one that addresses specific needs and that has the
capacity to evolve to meet new needs. It can be amended and it
can incorporate new instruments, such as legal conventions, by
which to expand its authority.

Through its resolutions the Antarctic Community has enacted a code of conduct for Antarctic expeditions and station
activities, granted special protection to sites singled out as

having unique scientific and historic interest, and prepared legal instruments by which to conserve Antarctic living resources. The latter process began in 1964, with the creation of Agreed Measures for the Conservation of Antarctic Seals. This led to the London Convention (1972) on the Conservation of Antarctic Seals. In addition to its greater comprehensiveness, the London Convention enjoys a different legal status. The Agreed Measures are wholly in-house; they apply only to signatory nations of the Antarctic Community. But any nation can accede to the London Convention. While a nation has to agree to the general provisions of the Antarctic Treaty as a condition of signing the London Convention, it does not have to become a signatory nation. The scope and legitimacy of the London Convention have thus been greatly enhanced. The London Convention was, in turn, expanded into the comprehensive Canberra Convention (1980) for the Conservation of Antarctic Marine Living Resources. Sealing is no longer a commercial activity in the Southern Ocean, but whaling, fishing, and krill trawling are. The Canberra Convention encompasses all these activities, has adopted a general ecosystem-management principle (rather than a species-specific approach), and in 1982 established a commission to oversee the provisions. Accordingly, other international organizations, such as the Food and Agriculture Organization (FAO), have recognized the legal authority of the consultative nations to protect the Antarctic marine ecosystem.

Its success with marine resources has emboldened the Antarctic Community to proceed with an analogous convention by which to regulate a mineral regime. At the 1972 Consultative Meeting the question was remanded for study. At a special meeting on minerals held in 1975, the Antarctic Community agreed to a moratorium on exploratory drilling so long as progress was being made on negotiations toward a convention. Political problems are both internal and external: claimant nations refuse any concessions that might compromise their titles, and nontreaty nations have begun to clamor for some principle of "global sharing" according to the common-heritage concept. In 1976 the consultative nations haltingly moved toward the enunciation of four general principles: an affirmation of the legitimacy of the Antarctic Community, insistence on support for the treaty in its entirety, a commitment to environmental protection, and an expressed lack of "prejudice" concerning "the interest of all mankind."[44] Agreement on the moratorium fol-

lowed, and SCAR (along with the U.S. Department of State)
commissioned environmental impact statements. Formal discussions began in 1982.

The Antarctic Treaty was designed to continue indefinitely. It included a provision, however, that would allow for a review after thirty years if any of the consultative nations so requested. Thus 1991 is an informal deadline for the resolution of major controversies. For the most part, resolution means agreement on a convention for Antarctic minerals. If a mechanism is devised, there is little incentive for any consultative nation to ask for a review. In fact, there is considerable hazard in proposing one, because the larger problems the Antarctic System faces involve not only accommodation within the Antarctic Community but a collective external accommodation between the community and the rest of the world. The historically active Antarctic nations will not allow Antarctica to exist in complete isolation, and other countries will not allow the continent to exist as a special preserve of the Antarctic Community. The community must not only work out its internal dissensions but establish its legitimacy before the uninvolved nations and reconcile the Antarctic Treaty and its conventions with other instruments of international law, such as the Law of the Sea. It is not as a club or a cartel that the Antarctic System will succeed but as a special, though nonexclusive, community.

The Antarctic Treaty provides for such accommodations by allowing free access to the continent and to membership. No state is excluded, and only a demonstrable commitment to Antarctic research is needed to acquire consultative status. This commitment is expensive, but it assures that nations involved in decisions about Antarctica have first-hand knowledge about the region and tangible interests in the outcome, and it allows for the transnational character of science to reinforce the sense of global stewardship implied in the treaty. There is no reason that a consortium of nations could not establish a research station and acquire a single collective seat among the consultative nations. Already the admission of two new members to consultative status has put the claimant states into a minority at consultative meetings. Faction, as James Madison observed, is not universally disruptive; it can be a powerful force for checking political ambition. That Argentina and Chile, so uncompromising in their territorial assertions, are also members of the Group of 77 further complicates the composition of Antarctic politics. As an old engineering adage puts it, the solution to pollution is dilution.

But for nations eager to promote a new international economic order, access is not sufficient: only an aggressive process of global sharing will be acceptable. Moreover, it is entirely possible for a nation to participate in resource exploration or to establish research stations without signing the Antarctic Treaty. Free riders are thus a political as well as an economic issue. The accession of China and India to the treaty, however, is an encouraging sign that the Antarctic Community will expand from within the parameters of the treaty and that it will be legitimized in world opinion. In 1984 the number of signatory nations increased from twelve in 1961 to thirty-four. In 1983 the U.N. General Assembly requested the Political Committee to "prepare a comprehensive factual and objective study on all aspects of Antarctica, taking fully into account the Antarctic Treaty system and other relevant factors."[45] The recognition that the Antarctic System has so far worked is a strong argument for its survival and a check on those nations that see Antarctica as only an instrument for the redistribution of wealth.

The Antarctic Treaty came early enough in Antarctic history to be an integral, organic presence, not a legal afterthought. By 1991 the Antarctic Treaty (and its IGY antecedents) will have existed for thirty-four of the ninety-two years that the Antarctic mainland has had a human presence, and the treaty will have governed Antarctica for virtually all of the epoch of continuous settlement. The treaty came too late to avoid territorial claims but perhaps early enough to render those claims into symbolic expressions for which sovereignty is, in practice, an antiquated term honoring the historic experience of a nation in Antarctica and a badge of membership in the collective stewardship of the continent.

Although the treaty period officially marks a hiatus in claim-making, the claimant states and those states that have reserved the right to make claims in the future have exploited the Pax Antarctica to bolster their positions. All have some sort of national institute for Antarctic studies, some governmental organ that assesses Antarctic policy, and bases in Antarctica from which they would have to be forcibly evicted. The Soviet Union, for example, has established permanent coastal bases in every claimant sector and a chain of stations leading to the East Ant-

arctic plateau, and it coordinates policy and research through
its Arctic and Antarctic Scientific Research Institute. By contrast, the United States occupies the symbolically important
South Pole (Amundsen-Scott Station), a marine biology station
on the Antarctic Peninsula (Palmer), a major entrepôt at the
historically and scientifically important Ross Island (Mc-
Murdo), and other, temporary bases throughout the continent
as the need appears. From the start of the treaty, the U.S. has
assumed the role of inspector general, arranging for inspection
tours of all Antarctic stations every three or four years.

The Antarctic System has at least guaranteed that those who
have practical experience in Antarctica will be responsible for
drafting a convention. That knowledge base has always been
the most important of Antarctic resources. For a political economy based on information, modern science has provided an
international infrastructure without a free-rider problem or a
potential tragedy of the Antarctic commons. But science is a
Western institution. It conveys certain Western values and assumptions, and it most benefits those societies that are best
able to absorb scientific data. The universality of the Antarctic
System will depend, in good measure, on the perceived universality of Western science. This is not a given. Paralleling demands for a new international economic order, there have arisen
cries for a new international information order. The legitimacy
of scientific inquiry and the neutrality of scientific knowledge
could be challenged, and with it the foundations of the Antarctic System. "Just as Antarctica's unique environment must
be protected from exploiters," argues Philip Quigg, "so must its
political and economic future be protected from ideologues."[46]

The Antarctic was the last, imperfect expression of Western
territorial imperialism. Now it is metastably poised amid a
change in intellectual and political climate, like a residual ice
mass in an interglacial. Yet all of the arguments about incorporating Antarctica within outside political structures, either
within a concept of national sovereignty or within the common-heritage ideology, have an air of fantasy about them. The
outstanding traits of The Ice are its power as a sink and its extraordinary albedo. It is not the character of The Ice to give but
to take: it is self-absorptive and self-referential. The greatest of
its natural resources may be its preternatural emptiness; it is
less a *terra nova* than a *tabula rasa*. Not the act of taking from

the Antarctic but the act of bringing to the Antarctic generates information. Though *terra Antarctica* seems to possess what people and nations believe it to have, its greatest asset is not any resource it possesses but the stripped and reradiated revelations it makes about those who stare into it.

Epilogue.
The Source

When you return from the country of Refusal,
What will you think of us? Down there, No
was final.

    —Katha Pollitt, "To an Antarctic Traveller"
      (1982)

This is the period between life and death. This
is the way the world will look to the last man
when he dies.

    —Richard Byrd, *Alone* (1938)

Increment by infinitesimal increment the ice dome flexes upward, then reaches its summit: its shape like a gigantic convex
mirror, an all-sky lens, pointing dumbly to space.

The source region for the ice field forms a narrow ellipse, an
elongated ice divide, along the summit of the East Antarctic ice
sheet. The ice is at its highest here (3735 meters), at Dome Summit atop the subglacial Gamburtsev Mountains, and its deepest (4760 meters), at Dome C overlying the Wilkes subglacial
trench. Here resides the cold pole of the Earth: the minima of
terrestrial processes and information, the cold quiescent eye of
the polar vortex. No other ice terrane flows into this one. The
flat apex of the ice dome is sustained only by the peculiar precipitation of the high, arid interior. The many-domed ice divide
is not the sole source of ice; local accumulation along the perimeter is several times greater. But this terrane contributes to
every other, while no other region contributes to this one. It is
self-referential, autistic: the fixed core of the crystalline spheres
that surround Antarctica, the Unmoved Mover.

It has reduced everything to ice, and the ice is distilled into
its most elemental forms. The geography of the source region is
that of a slightly curved ice mound of enormous dimensions
and unrivaled simplicity, a dome deeper than the tallest peak in
America and broader than the continents of Europe or Australia. The ice dome mantles an ancient continental shield of
unparalleled stability; 150 million years from now, Africa and
Europe will have crumpled into a lithic weld; Australia, India,
North America, and East Asia will amalgamate into a new
supercontinent; South America will slide to destruction in a
mid-Atlantic trench; but Antarctica will remain torpid and progressively isolated at the pole. The geology of the upper crust is
reduced to the geology of a single mineral.

The ice originates from the simplest of crystals and is organized into the simplest of ice masses. Accumulation is meager;
ablation is trivial and melting is unheard of; shear stress and deformation are negligible. The purity of the ice is equivalent to
that of triply distilled water. The structure of the ice is comparable to the most quiescent of abyssal plains, silently accepting
a fine drizzle of organic microparticles. The weather of the ice
dome is that of a sheath of unrelievedly cold air. Precipitation
occurs by the spontaneous nucleation of water vapor into ice.
Clouds, when they exist, are the simplest imaginable. The ice
apex is inaccessible to tropospheric storms. Winds are feeble,

the katabatics originating here from the slow sloughing of the source-region air outward. Topographic relief is, at best, a geomorphology of sastrugi. Seasons consist of night, day, and twilight; the multiple planetary rotations of year and day merge into a single cycle. Space, time, contrast, motion, events—all seem to dissipate or be frozen into immobility. Depth, texture, and complexity are reduced to surface. For all of this The Ice is the cause and consequence.

Yet here, too, the reductionism ends. The microparticulate lattices of ice crystals, even those lacking a nuclear core, provide a quantum unit of information out of which the ice field will be constructed. The distant contrast of Ice to Earth is replaced by a comparison of Antarctica to other ices of the solar system—the interstellar ice dusts, the nuclei of comets, the ice rings of Saturn and Uranus, the Oort cloud, the dry-ice caps of Mars, the icy moons of Jupiter, Saturn, Uranus, and Pluto, and the ice planet, Pluto. The ice does not approximate an antimatter, intent on vaporizing substance, but a state of absolute zero, where matter dissociates from energy.

Paradoxically, the source is in fact a sink, a profoundly inert receptacle for matter, energy, and information. It is known not for what it generates but for what it receives and reflects. Its influence is passive. Perhaps its defining attribute—physical and intellectual—is its albedo. Like its radiation budget, which is always negative, its information budget is poor. The source absorbs enormous quantities of energy before it emits parcels of data. Only a civilization rich in energy and intellectual activity can enter the site and emerge with a residue of information. The Ice is a great, distorted mirror. The properties of the mirror may be studied, but the outcome is ultimately a better understanding of the civilization that gazes into it.

DIAMOND DUST

Nature has many tricks wherewith she convinces man of his finity . . . but the most tremendous, the most stupefying of all, is the passive phase of the White Silence. All movement ceases, the sky clears, the heavens are as brass . . . [man] trembles at his audacity, realizes that his is a maggot's life, nothing more. Strange thoughts arise unsummoned, and the mystery of all things strives for utterance.

And the fear of death, of God, of the universe, comes over him . . . it is then, if ever, man walks alone with God.

—Jack London, "The White Silence"

The summer solstice: polar noon. The Sun shines with a cold whitish glare. The turquoise sky is washed out with iceblink. The horizon is everywhere unbounded by a plane of ice. The Sun spirals around the horizon in a ghostly minuet with a quarter Moon. A thin veneer of cirrus clouds slowly creeps across the sky. Almost imperceptibly, there is a flash of prismatic light in the air, then another, and another yet, until the air is dancing with a fine sparkling of color, the interaction of sunlight on an otherwise invisible spray of ice crystals. Around the Sun a halo forms, then much farther away a second; the sky becomes inscribed with an optical geometry of haloes, arcs, streaks, and mock Suns. Then the clouds thicken slightly, spreading like a white film. The optical effects fade. The horizon shrinks, then vanishes. All distinctions, colors, and shapes disappear in the diffuse, smothering light of a whiteout.

It is among the cleanest of Earth environments. Its height, aridity, remoteness, almost perfect lack of any substance but ice, and barrier of storms that scrub out most transported debris make Antarctica a remarkably purified place. Yet even the ice crystals that filter down upon the source region contain microparticulates, some of which are incorporated into ice as nuclei for condensation and freezing; others simply rain down as a dry dust. These miniature impurities derive from ocean spray, terrestrial debris, extraterrestrial matter, and industrial pollutants. Not much comes from local sources. A few special areas are laced with locally derived dust, and the normally dormant Antarctic volcanoes occasionally erupt. Most of the insoluble particles are fine, well sorted, and smooth and are deposited at the final global sink. Most anthropogenic pollutants are screened out by distance, by the equatorial barrier to advective flow from the Northern Hemisphere to the Southern, and by the filtering storm belts around Antarctica. The desert regions of Australia and South America contribute some debris; major volcanic emissions contribute others. Nitrates apparently originate from auroral fixation—the interaction of solar particles with the upper atmosphere—and are the end product of a chain of ionization reactions. The majority of particulates derive from ocean-surface aerosols transported in the warm air that slides inland over the inversion layer. Yet these, too, quickly dissipate in heavier precipitation along the coast. By the time air reaches the source region it is purged of most particulates, deficient in the requisite nuclei for condensation. Precipitation is correspondingly dry. Particulates descend independently of ice crystals, and ice crystals often form without nuclei or with particulates randomly included in a crystalline matrix.

Even the source ice crystals out of which the unfathomable ice domes are constructed have been ruthlessly simplified. They can precipitate without storms and they consist of the most unsophisticated particles. Water exhibits more solid phases than any other known substance. Hexagonal ice, cubic ice, high-pressure polymorphs, vitreous or amorphous ice, clathrate hydrates: ice formed by the freezing of water, ice from the deposition of water vapor at very low temperatures, ice from the freezing of water under pressure, ice from water at temperatures so low (-140 degrees C.) that no crystalline lattice can develop, ice from the concatenation of water solids. As a form of atmospheric precipitation, ice can fall as graupel, sleet, hail, or snow. Snow, in turn, is an aggregate of smaller ice crystals: plates, stellars, columns, needles, spatial dendrites, capped columns, and irregular crystals, each of which may show structures that are hexagonally symmetric, hollow, or filigree. Below -40 degrees C., ice crystals form around microparticulates, ice nuclei. The crystal shape, or habit, varies with temperature and water-vapor pressure. The greatest variety of crystals forms between 0 and -20 degrees C., and the most elaborate snowflakes form from the compounding of ice crystals at temperatures near freezing. As the cold intensifies, the amount of water contained in the air diminishes, the variety of ice crystals simplifies, and the complex process of heterogeneous nucleation—which requires that appropriate ice nuclei be present—is reduced to a process of homogeneous nucleation, the spontaneous solidification of water vapor to ice. The transition occurs at -40 degrees C.

The water vapor is brought inland in the warm isothermal layer of air that advances over the inversion. As the air advects inward, it cools by radiation loss at 2 degrees C. per day. Its temperature averages between -35 and -40 degrees C. The low temperatures are related to vapor pressures. At -2 degrees C. the vapor pressure is fifty times greater than at -42 degrees C. In most environments condensation occurs when the water-vapor pressure reaches saturation; there is ample moisture and enough condensation nuclei and cloud condensation nuclei around which water vapor will collect. Of the total mass of air, less than 1 percent may be supersaturated with respect to water. In the interior of Antarctica, however, there is neither sufficient water nor abundant nuclei. Supersaturation is possible only because it is relative to ice, not water, and the required vapor pressure is lower for ice than for water. Accordingly, supersaturation with respect to ice can be much higher, up to 20 percent or more. This is in fact the normal state. During most of the year—certainly through the 9–10 months of winter, when temperature gradients are most pronounced and the warm air advection is strongest—the air above the inversion and below 5 kilometers is saturated or supersaturated with respect to ice. This thick, supersaturated layer of air is necessary for ice precipitation.

The supersaturated air interacts with the underlying sheath of cold, dry, stable air that constitutes the inversion. Some mixing will occur. Ice clouds may form, high cirrus or middle-level altostratus, and ice crystals will precipitate. The crystals fall through the inversion like an icy pollen, gently stirred by sunlight. Of the clouds at Dome Summit, some high cirrus varieties occur 53 percent of the time, and altostratus clouds occur 9 percent of the time; 38 percent of the time the sky is clear. The mechanisms of ice precipitation and the characteristic shapes vary accordingly. High clouds tend to form bullet crystals (1 millimeter long), and middle clouds preferentially create combination forms of side planes, bullets, and columns (also 1 millimeter). In both cases, the ice crystals form in the clouds, then descend to the ground. Depending on the vapor pressure of the entered air mass, they may reshape or recombine, but even in clear air ice precipitation—diamond dust—is common.

How this occurs is not certain. Some ice precipitation apparently results from spontaneous nucleation at temperatures below −40 degrees C., with the simplest crystals in the shape of thin hexagonal plates and columns (needles) about 0.2 millimeter long. Columnar shapes predominate. During major diamond-dust "storms," however, as many as half of the total crystals may be plate crystals—hexagonal, scalene hexagonal, pentagonal, rhombic, trapezoidal, and triangular. Other episodes may result from a kind of cloud seeding, in which crystals precipitated from high clouds pass through supersaturated air. The crystals fragment, the ice shards act as nuclei, and vapor pressure deposits water directly onto them. In rare cases, very low clouds develop, and the freezing of water droplets produces stepped-column crystals.

At Dome Summit, simple but aggregate ice crystals—hence, snow—fall perhaps 28 days out of the year. Differential vapor pressures between the air and newly fallen ice abstract more water from the air—hoarfrost—about 225 days a year. But ice-crystal deposition, from clouds or clear air, occurs 247 days a year, and it constitutes perhaps 87 percent of the annual accumulation. Elsewhere in the source region, diamond dust is present perhaps 317 days a year, although most is deposited during short episodes—what passes for storms—when significant masses of supersaturated, warm air are brought to the interior. The total quantities involved, however, are meager. Most of the deposition occurs during the winter, when warm-air advection is best developed. During the summer, sublimation and wind deflation redistribute the flimsy 10–20 millimeters of ice crystals.

Diamond dust is the typical precipitation of the source region, but it is not unique to Antarctica. It occurs widely in cold regions of the Earth, and it is ubiquitous in the upper troposphere, forming a kind of background microparticulate drizzle. Nearly everywhere it is quickly overwhelmed by other, more complex, and quantitatively important processes of precipitation. In Antarctica, those higher-order processes have been eliminated. Diamond dust becomes prominent by virtue of the relentless reductionism—the erasure of alternative processes— that is the essence of The Ice.

ICE ON ICE:
THE ESTHETICS OF THE SHEET

Suddenly I saw the cold and rook-delighting heaven
That seemed as though ice burned and was but more ice,
And thereupon imagination and heart were driven
So wild that every casual thought of that and this
Vanished.

—William Butler Yeats, "The Cold Heaven"

The autumnal equinox: polar twilight. The Sun spirals low over the ice field, slowly ebbing into a widening vortex. For half a day it rises above the horizon, and for half a day it passes below it. At the pole the Sun maneuvers exactly at the line of the horizon, but the source regions are skewed to latitudes 80 to 70 degrees South. A twilight wedge of prismatic color rises and subsides with the rotation of the Sun. At its highest point, the cold Sun casts long sheets of reds and lavenders across the ice and under the filmy strata of clouds. The ice glows a deep cobalt blue. Below the horizon only the red glimmer of the twilight wedge endures. The night sky deepens into blues, purple, and near-black. Celestial lights suppressed by the omnipotent sunlight of the austral summer shine through clear skies, diffract through high clouds into coronas, reflect and refract through diamond dust into muted haloes, arcs, and streaks. Moonlight, starlight, and airglow burnish the ice crust like platinum. Diffuse patches and rayed sheets of the aurora dance eerily across the sky, reflected—ever reradiated—by The Ice.

The effects are stunning, impressive by virtue of their size rather than their subtlety. The colors are those of white light as segregated by a prism, the atomic spectra as emitted by excited ions. The only structure is that provided by the microrelief of the ice surface, shadowy marks like thick brush strokes. The only motion is the measured spiral of the Sun. The power of the scene is largely attributable to its immense simplicity. The reductionism of The Ice has removed the intermediary processes that would modulate and reshape effects or that would allow the intrusion of chance events or unique, surprising combinations. Paradoxically, the distillation does not clarify but disorients. There is no east or west, except by arbitrary designation. There is no normal chronometer, since the pole and the Sun compress all of the Earth's time zones together. At the source regions representational art is, of necessity, abstract art. Perspective vanishes into an unbounded surface. Figures, shapes, colors—all are reduced to an absolute, mechanical minimum. No need here to search through abundance and complexity for an essence: all that one sees is all that there is.

This is a geography of encroaching nihilism. Ice covers Earth and saturates the sky. Everything The Ice touches it reduces. The Source becomes the sum of its negations. There is no shape, no perspective, no color, no movement, no objects, no inherent contrast. The scene is meaningful only by comparison to other scenes, comparisons that always seem to end in negation: The Ice absorbs, it does not emanate. It challenges not only visual arts but literature. Language is pared to monosyllables, stripped of descriptive complexity . . . ice . . . dust . . . sky . . . cloud . . . sun . . . blue . . . white . . . moon . . . cold. Sensation without ideas. Sounds without sentences. Only by importing, and in vast abundance, ideas and words created elsewhere are there a vocabulary and a syntax sufficiently complex to survive the journey to the Source. But the reductionism is not total; for humans there is always the contrast between known and unknown.

Amid this vortex of ions and ice, there is a smaller but vastly more important rotation. Drills bore into The Ice, twisted ultimately by the turning of the mind. The terrible inertia will be resisted, the surface penetrated. There is information to be created. The mirror is not to be simply peered at but polished and pondered. Languages, sciences, and images will be devised to take from The Ice something more than is brought to it. Ice crystal will be connected to iceberg. For the Source is at last revealed: not ice but idea. Humans are not drawn into The Ice by a mechanical gravity: they go deliberately, in defiance of information gradients, obeying a mental inertia of motion that contests The Ice's fatal inertia of rest. The power of the ice receptor to reflect depends upon the capacity of the mental source to emanate.

ENDS OF THE EARTH

And there, there overhead, there, there, hung over
Those thousands of white faces, those dazed eyes,
There in the starless dark, the poise, the hover,
There with vast wings cross the canceled skies,
There in the sudden blackness the black pall
Of nothing, nothing, nothing—nothing at all.

—Archibald MacLeish, "The End of the World"

The winter solstice: polar midnight. The Sun has long since spiraled into a darkness that announces a great implosion. Airglow and starlight fail to illuminate the surface. Above and around the ice dome flicker patches of yellow-green light, the atomic luminosity of the aurora. Quickly the patches grow, structure themselves into deeply corrugated sheets; a reddish radiance lines the lower hems, and the sheets ripple into great folded drapes. The auroral substorm falters, and another takes its place, then another. The all-sky lens of the ice dome reflects everything in alien silver light. The storm subsides. The aurora blinks off. The cosmic curtain opens.

Stars mix with tenuous stringers of diamond dust, as if in imitation of the vast thin clouds of interstellar gas, ice, and dust that constitute the bulk—the undifferentiated and unformed mass—of the universe. Crystal by crystal the diamond dust falls on The Ice, a primordial powder settling in the silent cold.

Slowly a thin film of cirrus clouds spreads across the sky, like an oil slick, until only the surface sheath of ice and air remains in a darkness absolute. No light enters and none escapes. Ice clouds seal off the sky and ice sheets seal off the earth. The scene dereifies into infinitesimal specks of Ice, a cloying mist of diamond dust suspended formlessly within a black box. For an instant—here at the height of the solstice, at the dead center of the vortex—space becomes vanishingly small, time pauses in frozen hesitation, and mind disconnects from referents.

The Ice dissolves into a black veil. Beyond it there is nothing more.

Afterword

So, floating on the margin of the ensuing scene, and in full sight of it, when the half-spent suction of the sunk ship reached me, I was then, but slowly, drawn towards the closing vortex. . . . Till, gaining that vital center, the black bubble upward burst; and now . . . the coffin life-buoy shot lengthwise from the sea, fell over, and floated by my side.

—Ishmael, in Herman Melville, *Moby-Dick* (1851)

Writing, like politics, is the art of the possible. *The Ice* is not the book I thought I was going to write when I began this project, and it is not the book I believed I would do when I returned from Antarctica. It is the book I was able to write with the talent, experiences, and time available. The apologia is an old genre of Antarctic writing: here is mine.

Originally, I expected to write a brief history of the earth sciences in the United States; Antarctica would comprise a small component of that story. That was the gist of my proposal for the Antarctic Fellowship sponsored by the National Endowment for the Humanities. The fellowship requires that the recipient spend one to three months in Antarctica with the U.S. Antarctic Research Program. I elected to stay all three months, traveling widely on a space-available basis. It was a spectacular introduction to the Antarctic, and while still on The Ice I decided to write a book specifically about Antarctica. By the time I returned I discovered that I didn't have the time available, within the span of a year's fellowship, to complete such a work. The Grand Canyon Natural History Association, meanwhile, contacted me about the possibility of reworking some old ideas into an intellectual history of the Grand Canyon for its monograph series. The overall project thus evolved into a new stage. I decided to do two complementary studies.

One would be a long interpretive essay on the Grand Canyon, an earth emblem of importance for the nineteenth century. Its focus would be that intriguing blend of science and esthetics, organized around a journey, that Clarence Dutton published as the *Tertiary History of the Grand Canyon District* (1882). The second study would examine an earth emblem of comparable power for the twentieth century, and it would attempt to achieve for Antarctica, within the confines of contemporary philosophies, what Dutton had for the Grand Canyon in the context of nineteenth-century thought. My fellowship tenure would coincide with the centennial of Dutton's monograph. This design severely limited the amount of pages I could devote to particular themes, although I tried to retain at least in synoptic form those ideas about exploration and the history of the earth sciences with which I had begun the project and for which I felt an obligation to NEH to complete. This design also demanded considerable research into a dizzying array of subjects for which I had little preparation. During the remaining tenure of the fellowship, I was able to complete the Grand Canyon project and accomplish a good deal of my retooling; but it was apparent that, with teaching and other projects, I could not complete the manuscript for many years unless I had large blocks of time in which to work. After several rejections, I realized that I would not capture another fellowship so soon after my first. I requested a leave of absence from the University of Iowa, which the history department graciously granted—not the least of its many generosities toward me. Within the time and resources available I completed the book.

The Ice, then, is the product of two class organizations: the National Endowment for the Humanities and the National Science Foundation (USARP). Without them the book would never have been conceived. I would like to thank my principal contacts in both organizations: David Coder of NEH and Guy Guthridge of NSF. But many others assisted in one form or another with the financing, encouraging, and educating that the book demanded. Donald Weinstein, chairman of the history department at the University of Arizona, offered a visiting appointment for a semester that put me in contact with a major Antarctic library and brought in enough money to see the writing through. Duncan Patten of the Center for Environmental Studies granted me adjunct status, with access to the library at Arizona State University. Others who helped on The Ice, and afterward, include James Collinson, David Elliott, Ian Whillans, Noel Kemp, Christian Schluchter, Edmund Stump, George Denton, Russ Kinne, Garry McKenzie, Dave Bresnahan, Paul Carter, the officers and crew of the U.S.C.G.C. *Glacier*. Special acknowledgments go to Holly Carver and Gregory Gullickson, who may be credited for much that is good in the manuscript and none that is flabby or erroneous. To all of them I give my thanks.

The principal collaborators, however, have been my family. Without their insight and support there would be no book. Time and again, lifebuoys appeared out of the vortex through the generosity of our extended family. Sincere thanks to them all: Mrs. Barbara Pyne, James Pyne, Gwen and Woody Sandberg, Kyle and Sandra Tebbs, Irvin and Alice Allen, Jessie Werner. Within our nuclear family, Lydia and Molly made real sacrifices necessary to give me the time to write, and Sonja— from her insistence that I apply for the fellowship and leave her and the kids for three months of winter, to her uncomplaining sacrifices when we didn't know where our next month's rent was coming from—is the real originator and producer of the book. To her, in inadequate payment for her efforts, I dedicate this book.

Chandler, Arizona

Notes

PROLOGUE

1. James Eights, "On the Icebergs of the Ant-Arctic Sea," in Louis O. Quam, ed., *Research in the Antarctic*, AAAS Publication 93 (American Association for the Advancement of Science, 1971), p. 5.
2. Frank Debenham, *In the Antarctic* (London, 1952), p. 98.

1. THE PACK

1. See W. Schwerdtfeger, *Weather and Climate of the Antarctic*. Developments in Atmospheric Science 15 (Elsevier Science Publishing Co., 1984), p. 41.

2. NO MIDDLE WAY

1. J. Tuzo Wilson, *IGY: The Year of the New Moons* (Alfred A. Knopf, 1961), p. 288.
2. Daniel J. Boorstin, *The Discoverers* (Random House, 1983), pp. 278–289.
3. Quoted in F. M. Auburn, *The Ross Dependency* (Martinus Nijhoff, 1972), p. 31.
4. J. C. Beaglehole, ed., *The Journals of Captain James Cook on His Voyages of Discovery*, vol. 2, *The Voyage of the Resolution and Adventure, 1772–1775* (Cambridge University Press, Hakluyt Society, 1961), pp. clxvii–clxix.
5. J. H. Parry, *The Discovery of the Sea* (University of California Press, 1981), pp. xi–xii.
6. Beaglehole, *Journals of Captain Cook*, p. 643.
7. Boorstin, *The Discoverers*, pp. 278–289; Katha Pollitt, *Antarctic Traveller* (Alfred A. Knopf, 1982), p. 58. Quotations from the latter, copyright © 1982 by Alfred A. Knopf, Inc., are reprinted by permission of Alfred A. Knopf.
8. Beaglehole, *Journals of Captain Cook*, pp. 637–638.
9. Ibid., p. 693.
10. Frank Debenham, ed., *The Voyage of Captain Bellingshausen to the Antarctic Seas, 1819–1821* (Hakluyt Society, 1945), p. 14.

11. Ibid., p. 417.

12. William Stanton, *The Great United States Exploring Expedition* (University of California Press, 1975), p. 363.

13. Mark Twain, *Autobiography* (Gabriel Wells, 1925), vol. 2, p. 120.

14. Quoted in Kenneth J. Bertrand, *Americans in Antarctica, 1775–1948*, American Geographical Society Special Publication 39 (American Geographical Society, 1971), p. 203.

15. William H. Goetzmann, "Paradigm Lost," in Nathan Reingold, ed., *The Sciences in the American Context: New Perspectives* (Smithsonian Press, 1979), pp. 21–34.

16. Parry, *Discovery of the Sea*, p. xiii.

17. Douglas Botting, *Humboldt and the Cosmos* (Harper and Row, 1973), p. 76.

18. L. P. Kirwan, *A History of Polar Exploration* (Norton, 1959), p. 224.

19. Garry D. McKenzie, "Geopolitical and Scientific Roles of the United States in Antarctica" (unpublished report, Mershon Center, National Security Awards Seminar, 1983), p. 24; C. Stewart Gillmore, "The Early History of Upper Atmospheric Physics Research in Antarctica," in L. J. Lanzerotti and C. G. Park, eds., *Upper Atmospheric Research in Antarctica*, Antarctic Research, vol. 29 (American Geophysical Union, 1978), pp. 236–262.

20. Robert E. Peary, *The Secrets of Polar Travel* (Century, 1917), p. 86.

21. Leslie Fiedler, *Love and Death in the American Novel* (Stein and Day, 1966), p. 26.

22. Quoted in Rachel Weiss, "Antarctica and Concepts of Order: Two Installations," *Leonardo* 17 (1984): 97.

23. Apsley Cherry-Garrard, *The Worst Journey in the World: Antarctic 1910–1913*, 2nd ed. (Dial Press, 1930), p. 547.

24. Peary, *Secrets*, pp. 312–313.

25. Herman Melville, *Moby-Dick* (Norton, 1967), p. 465.

26. Richard E. Byrd, *Little America* (G. P. Putnam's Sons, 1930), pp. 193, 192.

27. Richard E. Byrd, *Discovery* (G. P. Putnam's Sons, 1935), p. 5.

28. Personal communication with Peter Anderson.

29. Quoted in H. Wexler, "Antarctic Research during the International Geophysical Year," in U.S. National Committee for the IGY, *Antarctica in the International Geophysical Year*, Geophysical Monograph No. 1 (American Geophysical Union, 1956), p. 7.

30. Byrd, *Discovery*, pp. 4, 6.

31. Quoted in Richard S. Lewis, *A Continent for Science* (Viking Press, 1965), p. 97.

32. Byrd, *Little America*, p. 392.

33. Sir Harold Spencer Jones, "The Inception and Development of the
    International Geophysical Year," in Special Committee for the
    International Geophysical Year, *Annals of the International
    Geophysical Year* (Pergamon Press, 1959), vol. 1, pp. 401–402.
34. Paul Siple, *90° South* (G. P. Putnam's Sons, 1959), p. 244.
35. Ernst Stuhlinger, "Antarctic Research: A Prelude to Space Re-
    search," *Antarctic Journal of the U.S.* 4 (1969): 2.
36. Henry Menard, "Very Like a Spear," in Cecil J. Schneer, ed., *Two
    Hundred Years of Geology in America* (University Press of New
    England, 1979), pp. 19–30.
37. Sydney Chapman, closing presidential address at IGY Congress,
    Moscow, 1958.
38. Quoted in H. G. R. King, *Antarctica* (Blandford Press, 1969),
    p. 234.
39. Paul Carter, *Little America* (Columbia University Press, 1979),
    p. 237.
40. Pollitt, *Antarctic Traveller*, p. 60.
41. Lloyd V. Berkner, "International Geophysical Year," Industrial
    College of the Armed Forces, Publication L59–97 (1959), p. 4.

3. THE SHELF

 1. Robert Scott, *Scott's Last Expedition* (Dodd, Mead, and Co.,
    1913), vol. 2, p. xv.
 2. Ann Savours, ed., *Edward Wilson: Diary of the Discovery Expedi-
    tion to the Antarctic Regions 1901–1904* (Blandford Press, 1966),
    p. 229.
 3. Apsley Cherry-Garrard, *The Worst Journey in the World: Antarctic
    1910–1913*, 2nd ed. (Dial Press, 1930), p. 332.
 4. Richard E. Byrd, *Little America* (G. P. Putnam's Sons, 1930),
    pp. 279–280.
 5. Byrd, *Little America*, p. 123.
 6. Ibid., p. 366.
 7. Laurence Gould, *Cold* (Brewer, Warren, and Putnam, 1931),
    p. 102.
 8. Frederick A. Cook, *Through the First Antarctic Night 1898–1899*
    (William Heinemann, 1900), pp. 290, 365.
 9. Byrd, *Little America*, p. 237.
10. Robert E. Peary, *The Secrets of Polar Travel* (Century, 1917),
    pp. 51–52.
11. K. K. Markov et al., *The Geography of Antarctica* (Israel Program
    for Scientific Translation, 1970), p. 352.
12. Ibid., p. 356.

13. E. H. Shackleton, *The Heart of the Antarctic* (J. B. Lippincott Co., 1909), p. 1.

14. Paul Siple, *90° South* (G. P. Putnam's Sons, 1959), pp. 18–19.

15. Byrd, *Little America*, p. 198.

16. Richard E. Byrd, *Alone* (G. P. Putnam's Sons, 1938), pp. 7, 106, 8.

17. James Ross, *A Voyage of Discovery and Research in the Southern and Antarctic Regions during the Years 1839–1843* (David and Charles Reprints, 1969), vol. 1, pp. 218, 228.

18. Shackleton, *Heart of the Antarctic*, vol. 1, pp. 284–285.

19. Roald Amundsen, *The South Pole* (John Murray, 1912), vol. 2, p. 26; vol. 1, pp. 208, 178; vol. 2, p. 164.

20. Quoted in Cherry-Garrard, *Worst Journey*, p. 551.

21. Gould, *Cold*, pp. 229–230.

22. Byrd, *Little America*, pp. 97, 90; *Alone*, p. 36.

23. Gould, *Cold*, p. 104.

24. Quoted in Amundsen, *South Pole*, vol. 2, p. 232.

25. Byrd, *Alone*, p. 172.

4. HEART OF WHITENESS

1. Apsley Cherry-Garrard, *The Worst Journey in the World: Antarctic 1910–1913*, 2nd ed. (Dial Press, 1930), pp. viii, 577.

2. Richard E. Byrd, *Alone* (G. P. Putnam's Sons, 1938), p. 179.

3. James Eights, reprinted works, in Joel W. Hedgpeth, "James Eights of the Antarctic (1798–1882)," in Louis O. Quam, ed., *Research in the Antarctic*, AAAS Publication 93 (American Association for the Advancement of Science, 1971), pp. 30, 6.

4. Thomas Kenneally, "Origin of a Novel," *Hemisphere* 13 (1969): 12.

5. J. C. Beaglehole, ed., *The Journals of Captain James Cook on His Voyages of Discovery*, vol. 2, *The Voyage of the Resolution and Adventure, 1772–1775* (Cambridge University Press, Hakluyt Society, 1961), p. xlvi.

6. Ibid., p. 638.

7. Andrew Kippis, *The Life of Captain James Cook* (London, 1788), p. 510.

8. Edgar Allan Poe, *Selected Tales* (Oxford University Press, 1967), p. 11.

9. Charles F. Horne, ed., *Works of Jules Verne* (Vincent Parke, 1911), vol. 14, pp. 285, 359, 391.

10. Quoted in Warren S. Walker, introduction to James Fenimore Cooper, *The Sea Lions* (reprint: University of Nebraska Press, 1965), p. xiii.

11. Thomas Philbrick, quoted in Paul Carter, *Little America* (Columbia University Press, 1979), p. 15.

12. Frederick Cook, *Through the First Antarctic Night* (reprint: C. Hurst, 1980), p. xv.

13. Frank Hurley, *Argonauts of the South* (G. P. Putnam's Sons, 1925), p. 41.

14. Alistair Mackay, in E. H. Shackleton, *The Heart of the Antarctic* (J. P. Lippincott, 1909), vol. 2, p. 143.

15. Capt. R. F. Scott, *Scott's Last Expedition* (Dodd, Mead, and Co., 1913), vol. 1, pp. 417, 408.

16. Apsley Cherry-Garrard, introduction to George Seaver, *Edward Wilson of the Antarctic* (John Murray, 1933), p. xxxi.

17. Joseph Conrad, *Heart of Darkness and The Secret Sharer* (Signet Classics, 1950), pp. 147, 157.

18. Apsley Cherry-Garrard, *The Worst Journey in the World: Antarctic 1910–1913*, 2nd ed. (Dial Press, 1930), pp. v, 228.

19. Ibid., pp. 565, 549. Not everyone wanted the saga of the *Terra Nova* expedition left with Cherry-Garrard's assessment, however. Most of the principals of the expedition published their own accounts, and Frank Debenham, later director of the Scott Polar Research Institute, and Griffith Taylor wrote more lighthearted reminiscences about the expedition: *In the Antarctic* (John Murray, 1952) and *With Scott: The Silver Lining* (Dodd, Mead, and Co., 1916), respectively. But the story of the Polar Party was never far behind the narrative: its peculiar tragedy gave the *Terra Nova* expedition a dimension no other could attain. And the participants shared a common intellectual syndrome. Debenham, for example, brought the argument from Design down to The Ice (p. 11): "One cannot live for a while amidst the vast, lonely and yet magnificent scenery of the Antarctic without feeling dwarfed . . . and in the hands of a Providence or a Power." No one in such circumstances could accept chance as an explanation, or "if he does he really means that there is something behind the Chance."

20. Herbert Ponting, *The Great White South* (Robert McBride, 1923), p. 192.

21. Hurley, *Argonauts*, pp. 289–290.

22. Ibid., p. 122.

23. Scott, *Scott's Last Expedition*, p. 162; H. J. P. Arnold, *Herbert Ponting: Another World* (Sidgwick and Jackson, 1975), p. 28.

24. Arnold, *Ponting*, p. 29.

25. Ponting, *Great White South*, p. 136.

26. Debenham, *In the Antarctic*, p. 121.

27. Shackleton, *Heart of the Antarctic*, vol. 2, p. 380.

28. Ponting, *Great White South*, pp. 184–185.

29. George Seaver, *Edward Wilson of the Antarctic* (John Murray, 1933), p. 77.

30. H. G. R. King, "Heroic Painter of the Antarctic," *Geographical Magazine* 48 (1976): 214.

31. Scott, *Scott's Last Expedition*, vol. 1, pp. 203–204.

32. Robert Scott, *The Voyage of the Discovery* (Charles Scribner's Sons, 1905), vol. 2, p. 53.

33. Cherry-Garrard, *Worst Journey*, pp. 205–206.

34. King, "Heroic Painter," p. 214.

35. Seaver, *Edward Wilson*, p. 247.

36. Ibid., p. 294.

37. Edward Wilson, *Diary of the "Discovery" Expedition to the Antarctic Regions 1901–1904* (Blandford Press, 1966), p. 279.

38. Quoted in Konstantin Bazarov, *Landscape Painting* (Octopus Books, 1981), p. 100.

39. Ibid., p. 155.

40. Barbara Rose, *American Art Since 1900*, rev. ed. (Praeger Publishers, 1975), p. 130.

41. David Mountfield, *A History of Polar Exploration* (Dial Press, 1974), p. 189.

42. Don L. Stuart, "Who Goes There?" in Raymond J. Healy and J. Francis McComas, eds., *Famous Science-Fiction Stories* (Modern Library, 1957), p. 531.

43. Quoted in Paul Carter, *Little America* (Columbia University Press, 1979), p. 107.

44. H. P. Lovecraft, *At the Mountains of Madness* (Ballantine Books, 1964), pp. 1, 36–37.

45. Emil Schulthess, *Antarctica* (E. P. Dutton, 1960), no pagination.

46. Ibid.; again, the book is not paginated.

47. Roger Tory Peterson, *Penguins* (Houghton Mifflin, 1979), p. 31.

48. Eliot Porter, *Antarctica* (E. P. Dutton, 1978), acknowledgements.

49. Ibid., p. 105.

50. Ibid., p. 114.

51. Ibid., p. 110.

52. Eliot Porter, *Intimate Landscapes* (E. P. Dutton, 1979), p. 11.

53. Ibid., p. 11.

54. Porter, *Antarctica*, pp. 15–16.

55. Rose, *American Art*, pp. 202, 130.

56. See Rachel Weiss, "Antarctica and Concepts of Order: Two Installments," *Leonardo* 17 (1984): 95–99. Weiss has begun a campaign, in the form of an exhibit titled "Imagining Antarctica," to promote modern art about Antarctica.

57. Letter to author from Guy Guthridge, Office of Information, Division of Polar Programs, National Science Foundation, 17 December 1984.

58. Calvin Tomkins, *The Bride and the Bachelors* (Viking Press, 1965), p. 204.

1. Walter Sullivan, *Continents in Motion* (McGraw-Hill, 1974), p. 340.

6. EARTH AND ICE

1. Frank Dawson Adams, *The Birth and Development of the Geological Sciences* (reprint: Dover Books, 1954), p. 216.
2. Arthur Holmes, *The Age of the Earth* (Harper, 1927), p. 56.
3. Frank Debenham in Capt. R. F. Scott, *Scott's Last Expedition*, (Dodd, Mead, and Co., 1913), vol. 2, p. 302.
4. Griffith Taylor, *With Scott: The Silver Lining* (Dodd, Mead, and Co., 1916), p. 3.
5. Chamberlin, in W. A. J. M. van Waterschoot van der Gracht et al., *Theory of Continental Drift* (American Association of Petroleum Geologists, 1928), pp. 87, 83.
6. Taylor, *With Scott*, p. v.
7. Ibid., pp. v, 11.
8. R. E. Priestley and C. E. Tilley, "Geological Problems in Antarctica," in W. L. G. Joerg, ed., *Problems in Polar Geography* (American Geographical Society, 1928), p. 324.
9. Ibid., p. 253.
10. Ibid., p. 328.
11. Richard E. Byrd, *Discovery* (G. P. Putnam's Sons, 1935), p. 5.
12. Henry Menard, *Science: Growth and Change* (Harvard University Press, 1971), p. 44.
13. Ibid., p. 144.
14. Byrd, *Discovery*, p. 5.
15. H. P. Lovecraft, *At the Mountains of Madness* (Ballantine Books, 1964), p. 68.
16. Henry Menard, "Very Like a Spear," in Cecil J. Schneer, ed., *Two Hundred Years of Geology in America* (University Press of New England, 1979), p. 30.
17. J. Tuzo Wilson, *IGY: The Year of the New Moons* (Alfred A. Knopf, 1960), p. 190.
18. J. Tuzo Wilson, ed., *Continents Adrift* (W. H. Freeman, 1971), preface.
19. Wilson, *IGY*, p. 274.
20. Rhodes Fairbridge, "The Geology of the Antarctic," in Frank A. Simpson, ed., *The Antarctic Today* (Wellington, 1952), p. 95.
21. Arthur Ford, "Review of Antarctic Geology," *International Geophysics Bulletin* 82 (April 1964): 1, 17.
22. Raymond Adie, "Geological History," in Raymond Priestley et al., eds., *Antarctic Research* (Butterworths, 1964), p. 160.

23. Campbell Craddock, "Antarctica and Gondwanaland," in Mary A. McWhinnie, ed., *Polar Research: To the Present, and the Future*, AAAS Selected Symposium 7 (Westview Press, 1978), p. 63.

24. J. Tuzo Wilson, "Continental Drift," in Wilson, *Continents Adrift*, pp. 45–46.

25. A. P. Crary, "Presidential Address," in A. J. Gow et al., eds., *International Symposium on Antarctic Glaciological Exploration (ISAGE)*, Publication 86, International Association of Scientific Hydrology (W. Heffer and Sons, 1970), p. x.

26. Raymond Priestley and C. S. Wright, "Some Ice Problems of Antarctica," in W. L. G. Joerg, ed., *Problems of Polar Research* (American Geographical Society, 1928), pp. 335, 336, 332, 337.

27. Byrd, *Discovery*, p. 6.

28. Robert P. Sharp, "Objectives of Antarctic Glaciological Research," in A. P. Crary et al., eds., *Antarctica in the International Geophysical Year*, Geophysical Monograph No. 1, Publication 462 (American Geophysical Union, 1956), p. 34.

29. Quoted in Paul Siple, *90° South* (G. P. Putnam and Sons, 1959), p. 89.

30. Quoted in Crary, "Presidential Address," p. xvi.

31. International Union of Geodesy and Geophysics, *Antarctic Symposium*, Buenos Aires, 1959, Monograph No. 5 (Imprimé par L'Institut Géographique National, 1960), p. 14.

32. Crary, "Presidential Address," p. x.

33. J. Weertman, "Glaciology's Grand Unsolved Problem," *Nature* 160 (1976): 284.

8. THE COLD PEACE

1. Quoted in F. M. Auburn, *The Ross Dependency* (Martinus Nijhoff, 1972), p. 17.

2. Quoted in E. W. Hunter Christie, *The Antarctic Problem* (Hazell Watson and Viney, 1951), p. 56.

3. Ibid., p. 72.

4. Ibid., pp. 76, 97.

5. Gerhard von Glahn, *Law among Nations*, 3rd ed. (Macmillan, 1976), p. 274.

6. Christie, *Antarctic Problem*, p. 106.

7. Jacek Machowski, *The Status of Antarctica in the Light of International Law* (Warsaw, 1968; English translation, National Technical Information Service, 1977), p. 55.

8. James Ross, *A Voyage of Discovery and Research in the Southern and Antarctic Regions during the Years 1839–1843* (David and Charles Reprints, 1970), vol. 1, p. 189.

9. Ibid., p. 275.
10. Richard Olney, quoted in Philip Quigg, *A Pole Apart* (Free Press, 1983), p. 122.
11. E. H. Shackleton, *The Heart of the Antarctic* (J. B. Lippincott, 1909), vol. 2, pp. 94, 181; vol. 1, p. 393.
12. R. A. Swan, *Australia in the Antarctic* (Melbourne University Press, 1961), p. 132.
13. Ibid., p. 126.
14. See P. J. Beck, "British Antarctic Policy in the Early Twentieth Century," *Polar Record* 21 (1983): 475–483; and Garry D. McKenzie, "Geopolitical and Scientific Roles of the United States in Antarctica" (unpublished report, Mershon Center, National Security Awards Seminar, 1983).
15. C. Hartley Grattan, *The Southwest Pacific since 1900* (University of Michigan Press, 1963), p. 616; and Beck, "British Antarctic Policy," p. 481.
16. Swan, *Australia in the Antarctic*, pp. 193–194.
17. Ibid., p. 208.
18. Laurence Gould, *Cold* (Brewer, Warren, and Putnam, 1931), pp. 207–209.
19. Walter Sullivan, *Quest for a Continent* (McGraw-Hill, 1957), p. 356.
20. Paul Carter, *Little America* (Columbia University Press, 1979), pp. 136, 203.
21. Ibid., p. 205.
22. Sullivan, *Quest for a Continent*, p. 126.
23. Carter, *Little America*, p. 205.
24. Ibid., p. 206.
25. Ibid., p. 208.
26. Kenneth Bertrand, *Americans in Antarctica, 1775–1948*, American Geographical Society, Special Publication 39 (American Geographical Society, 1971), p. 473.
27. Carter, *Little America*, p. 217.
28. Sullivan, *Quest for a Continent*, p. 174.
29. Paul Siple, *90° South* (G. P. Putnam's Sons, 1959), p. 81.
30. Quigg, *A Pole Apart*, p. 134.
31. Swan, *Australia in the Antarctic*, p. 358.
32. Quigg, *A Pole Apart*, pp. 137–138.
33. Sullivan, *Quest for a Continent*, p. 283.
34. Quigg, *A Pole Apart*, pp. 137, 49.
35. Carter, *Little America*, pp. 230–231.
36. John C. Behrendt, ed., *Petroleum and Mineral Resources of Antarctica*, Geological Survey Circular 909 (Government Printing Office, 1983), p. 1.

37. William B. Hall, "Polar Mining," *Mining Congress Journal* 61 (July 1975): 46–51.

38. Quigg, *A Pole Apart*, p. 88.

39. Rosamunde J. Reich, "The Development of Antarctic Tourism," *Polar Record* 20 (1980): 213.

40. Quigg, *A Pole Apart*, p. 101.

41. Vilhjalmur Stefansson, *Greenland* (Doubleday, 1947), p. 282.

42. Keith Brennan, "Criteria for Access to the Resources of Antarctica: Alternatives, Procedure and Experience Applicable," in Francisco Vicuña Orrego, ed., *Antarctic Resources Policy* (Cambridge University Press, 1983), p. 226.

43. See Steven J. Burton, "New Stresses on the Antarctic Treaty: Toward International Legal Institutions Governing Antarctic Resources," *Virginia Law Review Association* 65 (1979): 421–512.

44. Quigg, *A Pole Apart*, p. 194.

45. Quoted in *Antarctic Journal of the United States* 19 (June 1984): 9.

46. Quigg, *A Pole Apart*, p. 218.

Sources

Since my purpose is to create a context for evoking and understanding Antarctica, I have made no attempt to summarize comprehensively either its natural or human history. Fortunately, the self-contained character of Antarctica is recapitulated in the published literature that pertains to the continent: virtually all of that literature is summarized within a few sources and is consolidated by a master bibliography. Initially, I intended to include within a listed bibliography not only all these works but all the articles I consulted, especially those pertaining to technical matters. When it became apparent, however, that the length of the original manuscript would have to be reduced significantly, the easiest way to eliminate pages was to substitute a bibliographic essay for the vastly longer listing of sources that the original draft included. Consequently, this essay will provide an introduction to those materials and to a handful of others, not recognized in the notes, that I have found helpful. I believe that this new purpose merges well with the old.

Antarctic research is blessed with an extraordinary reference tool, the *Antarctic Bibliography*, published by the Library of Congress under the sponsorship of the National Science Foundation. An international reference, the bibliography includes English abstracts for all entries and masterful cross-referencing. As of 1984, thirteen volumes and two cumulative indices for over 35,000 original entries have been published, beginning with references for 1962. Ongoing referencing is available in *Current Antarctic Literature* and its *Indexes*, which are published under the same program. For the literature prior to 1962, see Library of Congress, *Antarctic Bibliography, 1951–1961*, and U.S. Naval Photographic Interpretation Center, *Antarctic Bibliography* (reprint: Greenwood Press, 1968), which provides an annotated reference to the international literature up to 1951. Also valuable is the Library of Congress, *United States IGY Bibliography, 1953–1960* (National Academy of Science, 1960). Another annotated guide, which includes Arctic as well as Antarctic references, is the Scott Polar Research Institute's *Recent Polar Literature*.

Several periodicals cover the Antarctic scene with some comprehensiveness: the *Polar Record* (1931–), published by the Scott Polar Research Institute; and the *Antarctic Journal of the United States* (1965–), published by the U.S. Antarctic Research Program. Especially helpful are the annual review volumes of the *Antarctic Journal*, which begin in 1978. Most national programs, however, have some kind of house organ by which to report their activities. Publications resulting from the Soviet Antarctic Expeditions are routinely translated into English by the National Science Foundation. A complete listing of available works is given in "Translations of Polar Literature in English," *Antarctic Journal of the United States* 16 (March 1981): 8–12. To these periodicals should be added, for ice-specific references, the *Journal of Glaciology* (1948–).

Most of the scientific research conducted since IGY has been consolidated into several publication series, atlases, and symposia. The *Antarctic Research Series* (1963–), published through the American Geophysical Union, consists of monographs and lengthy articles. Titles are divided into two broad groups: Biological Sciences (List B) and Physical Sciences (List P). The *Antarctic Map Folio Series* (1964–1975), published through the American Geographical Society, gives somewhat more synthetic and geographic treatment to major Antarctic topics by means of nineteen folios. Both the research and folio series cover virtually all aspects of Antarctic science, from snow to human adaptations. In addition, two of the folios are specifically directed to historians: Folio 3, "Antarctic Maps and Surveys, 1900–1964," by George D. Whitmore, and Folio 19, "History of Antarctic Exploration and Scientific Investigation," by Henry M. Dater.

Antarctica has been the subject of numerous international symposia, another legacy of IGY. Symposia publications that I consulted are listed below, along with other books relevant to particular disciplines. For the earth sciences these include: International Union of Geodesy and Geophysics, *Antarctic Symposium*, Buenos Aires, 1959, Monograph No. 5 (Imprimé par L'Institut Géographique National, 1960); Raymond Adie, ed., *Antarctic Geology*, Proceedings of the First International Symposium on Antarctic Geology (North-Holland Publishing Co., 1964); Raymond Adie, ed., *Antarctic Geology and Geophysics* (Universitetsforlaget, 1972); Campbell Craddock, ed., *Antarctic Geoscience* (University of Wisconsin Press, 1982); and R. L. Oliver et al., eds., *Antarctic Earth Science* (Australian Academy of Science, 1983). Also valuable is the compendium edited by Raymond Priestley et al., *Antarctic Research* (Butterworth, 1964), which summarizes British science, and the one edited by Trevor Hatherton, *Antarctica* (Frederick A. Praeger, 1965), which has a New Zealand bias. Also useful for historical insights is *Antarctic Research: The Matthew Fontaine Maury Memorial Symposium*, American Geophysical Union Monograph 7 (1962).

Similar references for glaciology include A. A. Husseiny, ed., *Iceberg Utilization*, Proceedings of the First International Conference (Pergamon Press, 1978); International Glaciological Society, "Proceedings of the Conference on the Use of Icebergs: Scientific and Practical Feasibility," *Annals of Glaciology*, vol. 1 (International Glaciological Society, 1980); International Glaciological Society, "Proceedings of the Third International Symposium on Antarctic Glaciology," *Annals of*

Glaciology, vol. 3 (International Glaciological Society, 1982); International Union of Geodesy and Geophysics, *Symposium on Antarctic Glaciology*, International Association of Scientific Hydrology, Publ. 55 (UNESCO, 1961); A. J. Gow et al., eds., *International Symposium on Antarctic Glaciological Exploration (ISAGE)*, International Association of Scientific Hydrology, Publ. 86 (W. Heffer and Sons, 1970); and the *Journal of Glaciology* 24 (1979), "Symposium on Dynamics of Large Ice Masses." Among general works on glaciology, I found that T. Armstrong et al., *Illustrated Glossary of Snow and Ice* (Scott Polar Research Institute, 1966), was indispensable; W. S. B. Paterson, *The Physics of Glaciers*, 2nd ed. (Pergamon, 1983), was helpful as an introduction to ice mechanics; George H. Denton and Terence J. Hughes, eds., *The Last Great Ice Sheets* (Wiley-Interscience, 1981), while nearly indigestible, was an encyclopedia of ideas, data, and references; Brian John, *The Winters of the World* (David and Charles, 1979), gave ready access to the concept and history of ice ages; Clifford Embleton and Cuchlaine A. M. King, *Glacial Geomorphology* and *Periglacial Geomorphology*, 2nd ed. (Halsted Press, 1975), were solid and constant references; and Fred Hoyle, *Ice: The Ultimate Human Catastrophe* (Continuum, 1981), although eccentric, was fun and informative. While space prohibits complete acknowledgments for articles I consulted that were not published in the books above, I should mention T. J. Hughes, "West Antarctic Ice Streams," *Reviews of Geophysics and Space Physics* 15 (1977): 1−46, as an enlightening summary.

Biology is ably represented through SCAR symposia, of which I consulted principally George Llano, ed., *Adaptations within Antarctic Ecosystems*, Proceedings of the Third SCAR Symposium on Antarctic Biology (Smithsonian Institution, 1977). About a third of all Antarctic science deals with biology, but since biology is a minor interest of mine, I did not pursue it further. The BIOMASS program has stimulated a tremendous outpouring of comprehensive anthologies of Antarctic biology, several of which appeared (but were not consulted) during my writing.

My interest in oceanography, meteorology, meteorites, and the upper atmosphere was likewise restricted. For the most part I relied on Southern Ocean material contained in the above folios and symposia, in general descriptions of Antarctica, and on M. J. Dunbar, ed., *Polar Oceans*, Proceedings of the Polar Oceans Conference (Arctic Institute of North America, 1977). Since the manuscript was completed, a new synthesis has appeared: George Deacon, *The Antarctic Circumpolar Ocean* (Cambridge University Press, 1985). For meteorology, I referred to Werner Schwerdtfeger, *Weather and Climate of the Antarctic*, Developments in Atmospheric Science 15 (Elsevier, 1984), and P. D. Astapenko, *Atmospheric Processes in the High Latitudes of the Southern Hemisphere*, Section II of IGY Program (Meteorology), No. 3 (Israel Program for Scientific Translations, 1964). For the aurora I used Robert H. Eather's interesting *Majestic Lights: The Aurora in Science, History, and the Arts* (American Geophysical Union, 1980), and the International Union of Geodesy and Geophysics, *International Auroral Atlas* (University of Edinburgh, 1963). For atmospheric optics, I found Robert Greenler, *Rainbows, Halos, and Glories* (Cambridge University Press, 1980), to be delightful. It should be read in conjunction with Douglas Mawson, "Meteorological Optics," in E. H. Shackleton, *Heart of the Antarctic*, vol. 2, pp. 367–381. And, finally, on the question of Antarctic meteorites, perhaps the most synthetic volume is Colin Bull and Michael E. Pipschutz, eds., *Workshop on Antarctic Glaciology and Meteorites*, LPI Technical Report 82–03 (Lunar and Planetary Institute, 1982); a useful introduction can be found in Ursula Marvin, "Meteorite Placer Deposits of Antarctica," *Episodes* 3 (1982): 10–15.

General or popular books on the Antarctic seem to be overwhelmed by the explosive growth of the scientific literature. Most popular treatments focus on the explorations of the heroic age, on penguins, or on questions of politics and resource exploitation. Probably the best all-around introduction remains H. G. R. King, *The Antarctic* (Arco, 1969). Entree into Antarctic science may profitably begin with Mary A. McWhinnie, ed., *Polar Research: To the Present, And the Future*, AAAS Selected Symposium 7 (Westview Press, 1978), which does not completely supersede Louis Quam, ed., *Research in the Antarctic*, AAAS Publ. 93 (American Association for the Advancement of Science, 1971). Perhaps the most contemporary summary of natural history is contained in the Institute for Polar Studies, "A Framework for Assessing Environmental Impacts of Possible Antarctic Mineral Development," 2 parts (U.S. Department of State, 1977). An attempt to describe Antarctic geography and history by systematic contrast with the Arctic, but one that I found somewhat labored and disappointing, is David Sugden, *Arctic and Antarctic* (Basil Blackwell, 1982).

Among other works concerned with natural resources and politics should be mentioned Francisco Vicuña Orrego, ed., *Antarctic Resources Policy* (Cambridge University Press, 1983); John C. Behrendt, ed., *Petroleum and Mineral Resources of Antarctica*, Geological Survey Circular 909 (Government Printing Office, 1983); and John Splettstoesser et al., eds., *Mineral Resource Potential of Antarctica* (University of Texas Press, 1984). More popular treatments include Barbara Mitchell and Jon Tinker, *Antarctica and Its Resources* (Earthscan, 1980); J. F. Lovering and J. R. V. Prescott, *Last of Lands . . . Antarctica* (Melbourne University Press, 1979); and William E. Westermeyer, *The Politics of Mineral Resource Development in Antarctica* (Westview Press, 1984). Strongly recommended are Philip W. Quigg, *A Pole Apart: The Emerging Issue of Antarctica* (New Press, 1983), and, in spite of its legalisms,

Steven J. Burton, "New Stresses on the Antarctic Treaty: Toward International Legal Institutions Governing Antarctic Resources," *Virginia Law Review* 65 (1979): 421–512. Also helpful is the scholarly F. M. Auburn, *Antarctic Law and Politics* (Indiana University Press, 1982). A handy, if bulky, reference for specialists is W. M. Bush, *Antarctica and International Law: A Collection of Inter-State and National Documents*, 2 vols. (Oceana Publications, 1982, 1984). For an introduction to international law, I relied on Gerhard Von Glahn, *Law Among Nations*, 3rd ed. (Macmillan, 1976), which contained a useful treatment of sovereignty and claim-making. In addition to Sugden, *Arctic and Antarctic*, I found Borge Fristrup, *The Greenland Ice Cap* (University of Washington Press, 1966), to be a fascinating blend of historical and glaciological information, and both the popular book by Tim Greve, *Svalbard: Norway in the Arctic Ocean* (Grøndahl, 1975), and the more scholarly Willy Østreng, *Politics in the High Latitudes—Svalbard* (McGill-Queen's University Press, 1978), to be helpful.

More vexing is the problem of Antarctic history, the history of earth science, and the history of exploration. Even if restricted to books, the literature is large. As a partial compromise, I have selectively listed the most important published primary accounts at the conclusion to this essay. I owe a special debt to William Goetzmann, whose idea that epochs of exploration coincide with general intellectual syndromes is one of those simple yet fundamental insights that make history intelligible. While we do not agree over many particulars about the Second Great Age of Discovery, I have tried to apply this concept to the history of Antarctic discovery. For over ten years, however, I have argued that, if we can accept the rationale for segregating a Second Age from a First, we ought to discriminate a Third Age from the Second—an age announced by IGY and associated with a modernist syndrome. The arguments for a Third Age I can, I believe, claim as my own. Nonetheless, I have found a few books so consistently helpful that they are worth identifying. Among popular accounts I should mention David Mountfield, *A History of Polar Exploration* (Dial Press, 1974); L. P. Kirwan, *A History of Polar Exploration* (Norton, 1960); and, especially good for integrating exploration with whaling and politics, C. Hartley Grattan, *The Southwest Pacific to 1900* and *The Southwest Pacific Since 1900* (University of Michigan Press, 1963). J. H. Parry, *The Discovery of the Sea* (University of California Press, 1981), was indispensable. Although popular and now somewhat dated, Walter Sullivan's two volumes—one on Antarctica, the other on IGY—are highly recommended: *Quest for a Continent* (McGraw-Hill, 1957), and *Assault on the Unknown* (McGraw-Hill, 1961). J. Tuzo Wilson, *IGY: The Year of the New Moons* (Alfred A. Knopf, 1961), makes a readable, insightful counterpoint to the endless *Annals of the IGY* (Pergamon Press, 1959–), the first volume of which, *The Histories of the International Polar Years and the Inception and Development of the International Geophysical Year*, is full of information.

Most of the countries active in Antarctic research have produced histories of national involvement. For specifically American histories, there are the comprehensive Kenneth J. Bertrand, *Americans in Antarctica, 1775–1948*, Special Publication 39 (American Geographical Society, 1971); William Stanton, *The Great United States Exploring Expedition* (University of California Press, 1975), which describes the Wilkes Expedition; Lisle Rose, *Assault on Eternity: Richard E. Byrd and the Exploration of Antarctica, 1946–1947* (Naval Institute Press, 1980), which carries the story through the Antarctic Developments Projects; and the consistently charming Paul Carter, *Little America: Town at the Edge of the World* (Columbia University Press, 1979), which in spite of its title provides a general, accessible overview of American activity in Antarctica. I examined British, Australian, and New Zealand histories largely within the context of geopolitics.

For the most part, I have tried to interpret earth-science history lightly and within the context of my previous efforts: *Grove Karl Gilbert: A Great Engine of Research* (University of Texas Press, 1980), and *Dutton's Point: An Intellectual History of the Grand Canyon*, Monograph 5 (Grand Canyon Natural History Association, 1983). Among newer books that I found helpful, I should mention Mott T. Greene, *Geology in the Nineteenth Century* (Cornell University Press, 1982); Roy Porter, *The Making of Geology: Earth Science in Britain, 1660–1815* (Cambridge University Press, 1977); and Joe D. Burchfield, *Lord Kelvin and the Age of the Earth* (Science History Publications, 1975). Although not intended as a history per se, Henry W. Menard, *Science: Growth and Change* (Harvard University Press, 1971), deserves special notice. Menard's study may be complemented by Susan E. Cozzens and Henry Small, "Citation Analysis of Antarctic Research" (unpublished report to National Science Foundation, 1982). While the best way to observe the evolution of the earth sciences in Antarctica is to consult the progression of symposia, two shorter articles are worth citing: Rhodes W. Fairbridge, "The Geology of the Antarctic," in Frank A. Simpson, ed., *The Antarctic Today* (A. H. and A. W. Reed, 1952), and R. J. Tingey, "Heroic Age Geology in Victoria Land," *Polar Record* 21 (1983): 451–458.

To my knowledge, no one has systematically examined Antarctic literature and art. Artists who ventured to Antarctica seem to be completely overshadowed by the explorers, and Antarctic fiction seems to evolve out of prior literature rather than personal experience on The Ice. A nice collection of heroic-age photos is contained in Jeannie Boddington, *1910–1916 Antarctic Photographs: Herbert Ponting and Frank Hurley* (St. Martin's Press, 1979). Paul Carter's *The Creation of Tomor-*

row: *Fifty Years of Magazine Science Fiction* (Columbia University
Press, 1977) helped to place one tradition of Antarctic literature into
perspective. For an introduction to Edward Wilson as an artist, see
H. G. R. King, "Heroic Painter of the Antarctic," *Geographical Magazine* 48 (1976): 212–217. Many of Wilson's Antarctic works, some in
color, have been reproduced with his journals: Ann Savours, ed., *Edward Wilson: Diary of the Discovery Expedition to the Antarctic Regions
1901–1904* (Blandford Press, 1966), and H. G. R. King, *Edward Wilson:
Diary of the Terra Nova Expedition to the Antarctic 1910–1912* (Blandford Press, 1972). For the other photographers, in their own words, see
Herbert Ponting, *The Great White South* (R. M. McBride and Co.,
1922); Frank Hurley, *Argonauts of the South* (G. P. Putnam's Sons,
1925); Emil Schulthess, *Antarctica* (Simon and Schuster, 1960); Roger
Tory Peterson, *Penguins* (Houghton Mifflin, 1979); and Eliot Porter,
Antarctica (E. P. Dutton, 1978). Other artists are represented in the
general reports of the expeditions.

The most comprehensive sets of Antarctic maps are contained within
the *Antarctic Map Folio Series*, but each national program has published maps of at least its own sphere of influence. Topographical maps
of the continent are available through the American Geographical Society (1965) at a scale of 1:5,000,000; the National Geographic Society
(1975) at a scale of 1:8,841,000; and the U.S. Geological Survey, which
offers an abundance of topographical, geological, and satellite-image
maps at scales of 1:250,000 and 1:500,000. A guide, "Maps Published of
Antarctica by the U.S. Geological Survey" (1977), is available on request. The USGS has assembled a valuable collection of satellite images (LANDSAT) of Antarctica through the international "Satellite
Image Atlas of Glaciers"; on behalf of SCAR, the USGS houses all Antarctic cartographic materials produced by the U.S. and SCAR nations,
and it holds the aerial photographs of Antarctica taken by the U.S.
Navy since 1946 (approximately 250,000 images). The U.S. Board of
Geographic Names publishes a gazetteer, *Antarctica: Official Standard
Names*, 3rd ed. (Government Printing Office, 1969). Though somewhat
dated, the *Atlas of Antarctica* (1967), written by Soviet scientists, is
also useful; an English translation of captions is given in *Soviet Geography* 8 (1975): 262–507. A handy distillation of regional geographic
information is contained in the *Polar Regions Atlas* (1978), published
by the Central Intelligence Agency. And no discussion of Antarctic
maps is complete without mentioning the magnificent *Antarctica:
Geophysical and Glaciological Folio* (1982), produced by the Scott Polar
Research Institute; it includes, among various geophysical topics, a
complete subglacial map of the continent as well as a map of glacial
flowlines.

My project did not require much archival work, but I examined the
major depositories in the U.S. Many of the official documents were

consolidated into a Center for Polar Archives (1967) within the National Archives; the center has since been formally dissolved, but the records remain in a compact unit within the Science, Technology, and Natural Resources Division. Guides are available for most of the material, and the published proceedings of a conference held to inaugurate the center offer a helpful introduction to the holdings: Herman R. Friis and Shelby G. Bale, Jr., eds., *United States Polar Exploration* (University of Ohio Press, 1970). Major record groups include RG 401, Gift Collection of Materials Relating to Polar Regions; RG 313, Records of Naval Operating Forces; Records of the United States Antarctic Service; and the Cartographic and Photographic (still and motion picture) Divisions. The Naval Support Force, Antarctica, has maintained files and a historian; the National Academy of Sciences has an excellent archive, helpful for IGY materials and the Committee on Polar Research; and the National Science Foundation (USARP) has its own files and photos. Most U.S. Navy photos have been accessioned into the Defense Audiovisual Agency (Navy Photographic Center), but guides are poor.

My decision to emphasize books over articles reflects, of course, my training in the humanities; to Antarcticans, nearly all of whom are scientists, it may appear questionable. I can only appeal to my purposes, which are not those of a scientist, and to the demands of space: putting the material into the notes reduces the size of the bibliography but not the size of the manuscript. If anyone would like to know the specific works consulted for any portion of *The Ice*, he or she is welcome to write. To those who feel that their special contributions have been slighted, I offer apologies.

SELECTED PRIMARY ACCOUNTS OF ANTARCTIC EXPLORATION

Amundsen, Roald. *The South Pole*. 2 vols. John Murray, 1912.

Beaglehole, J. C., ed. *The Journals of Captain James Cook on His Voyages of Discovery*. Vol. 2, *The Voyage of the Resolution and Adventure 1771–1775*. Hakluyt Society, Extra Series 35. Cambridge University Press, 1961.

Borchgrevink, C. E. *First on the Antarctic Continent*. C. Hurst, 1901.

Byrd, Richard E. *Alone*. G. P. Putnam's Sons, 1938.

———. *Discovery*. G. P. Putnam's Sons, 1935.

———. *Little America*. Columbia University Press, 1979.

Cherry-Garrard, Apsley. *The Worst Journey in the World: Antarctic 1910–1913*. 2nd ed. Dial Press, 1930.

Cook, Frederick A. *Through the First Antarctic Night 1898–1899*. William Heinemann, 1900.

Cook, James. *A Voyage to the South Pole and Round the World* (1777). 2 vols. Reprint: Libraries Board of South Australia, 1970.

Debenham, Frank, ed. *The Voyage of Captain Bellingshausen to the Antarctic Seas 1819–1821*. Hakluyt Society, 1945.

Dufek, George J. *Operation Deepfreeze*. Harcourt, Brace, and World, 1957.

Ellsworth, Lincoln. *Beyond Horizons*. Book League of America, 1938.

———. "My Four Antarctic Expeditions," *National Geographic Magazine* 76 (1939): 129–138.

Fuchs, Sir Vivian, and Sir Edmund Hillary. *The Crossing of Antarctica*. Cassell, 1958.

Giaever, John. *The White Desert: The Official Account of the Norwegian-British-Swedish Antarctic Expedition*. Trans. E. M. Huggard. Chatto and Windus, 1954.

Gould, Laurence. *Cold*. Brewer, Warren and Putnam, 1931.

Hurley, Frank. *Argonauts of the South*. G. P. Putnam's Sons, 1925.

Huxley, Leonard, ed. *Scott's Last Expedition*. 2 vols. Dodd, Mead, 1913.

King, H. G. R. *Edward Wilson: Diary of the Terra Nova Expedition to the Antarctic 1910–1912*. Blandford Press, 1972.

Mawson, Douglas. *The Home of the Blizzard*. 2 vols. J. P. Lippincott, 1915.

Nordenskjöld, Otto, and J. G. Andersson. *Antarctica; or Two Years amongst the Ice of the South Pole*. Hurst and Blackett, 1905.

Ponting, H. G. *The Great White South*. McBride, 1922.

Priestley, Raymond. *Antarctic Adventure: Scott's Northern Party*. E. P. Dutton, 1915.

Ronne, Finn. *Antarctica, My Destiny*. Hastings House, 1979.

Ross, James. *A Voyage of Discovery and Research in the Southern and Antarctic Regions during the Years 1839–1843*. 2 vols. David and Charles Reprints, 1969.

Rymill, J. R. *Southern Lights: The Official Account of the British Graham Land Expedition, 1934–1937*. Chatto and Windus, 1938.

Savours, Ann, ed. *Edward Wilson: Diary of the Discovery Expedition to the Antarctic Regions 1901–1904*. Blandford Press, 1966.

Scott, Robert. *The Voyage of the Discovery*. 2 vols. Charles Scribner's Sons, 1905.

Shackleton, E. H. *The Heart of the Antarctic*. 2 vols. J. P. Lippincott, 1909.

———. *South*. Macmillan, 1920.

Siple, Paul. *90° South*. G. P. Putnam's Sons, 1959.

Weddell, James. *A Voyage Towards the South Pole Performed in the Years 1822–24*. Reprint: U.S. Naval Institute Press, 1970.

Wilkins, Hubert. "The Wilkins-Hearst Antarctic Expedition, 1928–1929." *Geographic Review* 19 (1919): 353–376.

Index

Abbot Ice Shelf, 122

Accumulation zone. *See* Source regions

Adelie Land, 48

Adie, Raymond, 275

Adventure (ship). *See* Cook, Capt. James

Aerial photography, 100, 101, 200

Africa (contrast to Antarctica), 88, 171–172, 329–330, 347, 372

Agassiz, Louis, 279

The Age of the Earth, 261

Ages of the Earth, 248–259, 267, 271–273, 284

Agreed Measures for the Conservation of Antarctic Seals, 374

Airglow, 317

Airplanes (impact on exploration), 98–100

Alhmann, Hans, 281

Allan Hills, 312, 314–315

Alone (1938), 170, 191

American Association of Petroleum Geologists, 105, 260–261, 263

American Geographical Society, 105, 274, 282

American school of geology, 105–106, 260–262. *See also* Earth sciences

Amery Ice Shelf, 101, 122, 123, 124, 293, 353

Amundsen, Roald, 86, 87, 89, 90–92, 94, 100, 144

Amundsen Sea, 33, 74, 293, 304

Anchor ice, 3, 30, 62, 124

Anderson, Peter, 102

Annals of the IGY, 112

Antarcandes, 44, 48, 218, 222, 257, 265

Antarctic and Southern Ocean Coalition, 372

Antarctic Andes. *See* Antarcandes

Antarctic art (history of), 149–205

Antarctic atmosphere (summary of), 40–50. *See also* Inversion; Winds

Antarctic Bibliography (1962), 113, 274

Antarctic bottom water, 36–38

Antarctic circumpolar current (ACC), 14–15, 33–40

Antarctic circumpolar vortex, 3, 43, 44

Antarctic coastal current, 33–40

Antarctic Commission (Chile), 345

Antarctic Community, 349, 350, 373–378. *See also* Antarctic System; Antarctic Treaty

Antarctic Conference, 348

Antarctic convergence, 15, 32, 33–40 passim, 44, 52, 81

Antarctic Developments Project, 99, 107, 341, 343

Antarctic divergence, 36–40 passim, 52

Antarctic earth science symposia, 272, 274

Antarctic front (atmospheric), 43, 44

Antarctic front (oceanographic), 36

Antarctic intermediate water, 36–37

414
Index

Antarctic lakes, 230–231
Antarctic literature, 149–205
Antarctic Peninsula, 33, 48, 54, 76, 77, 81, 86, 88, 220, 222, 237
Antarctic plate, 216–226
Antarctic System, 349, 350, 372–378
Antarctic Treaty, 348–350, 372–378. *See also* Antarctic Community; Antarctic System
Antarctica
  analogy to Mars, 69, 225
  biology of, 50–56
  contrast to Africa, 88, 171–172, 329–330, 347, 372
  contrast to Arctic, 31–32, 39–40, 52–53, 54, 67–68, 80, 89–92, 334, 354, 359–369
  contrast to Grand Canyon, 6, 152, 253–255
  contrast to other continents, 19–20, 88–89, 258, 330
  esthetics of, 17–20, 56–60, 132–137, 144–147, 185–201, 235–240, 320–321, 385–387
  exploration of, 65–115
  geology of, 214–226
  geopolitics of, 40, 323–378
  literature and art of, 149–205
  maps, 4–5, 34, 41, 46, 83, 215, 331
  natural resources of, 351–359
  relationship to deep oceans, 324, 369–371
  relationship to earth sciences, 241–288
  relationship to IGY, 268–278, 324
  relationship to outer space, 110–111, 324, 369–370
  as world park, 371–372
  See also Esthetics; Glaciology; Ice terranes; The Ice
Antarctica (1960), 194–197, 281

Antarctica expedition, 87
Anthropology, 91, 267
Anvers Island, 237
Arctic
  contrast to Antarctic, 31–32, 39–40, 52–53, 54, 67–68, 80, 89–92, 334, 354, 359–369
  exploration of, 39–40, 67, 80, 85, 89–92, 359–369
  geopolitics of, 359–369
Arctowski, Henryk, 87, 256–257
Argentina
  claims by, 335–336, 338, 340–350, 375–376
  quarrel with Britain, 106, 335–336, 338, 340–350, 367
Art
  history of, in Antarctica, 149–205
  as information, 72, 201–205
  modernism and Antarctica, 185–201
  relationship to science, 153
  See also Antarctic art; Esthetics; The Ice
At the Mountains of Madness (1939), 192–194
Atmosphere. *See* Antarctic atmosphere; Inversion; Winds
Atmospheric ices (summary of), 3
Atmospheric optics, 56–60, 132–137, 146, 316–322
Aurora australis, 316–322
Aurora expedition, 87, 177, 257
Auroral oval, 316–322
Australasian Antarctic Expedition, 87, 257, 333
Australia, 306
  claims by, 332–333, 335–337, 345
  exploration by, 50, 74, 77, 88, 107
Australian Antarctic Territory Acceptance Bill, 336–337

Australian National Antarctic
Research Expeditions, 107,
345
Austro-Hungarian Arctic expedition, 109

Balleny, Capt. John, 77
Banks, Joseph, 158
BANZARE. *See* British–Aus-
tralian–New Zealand Ant-
arctic Research Expedition
Barrell, Joseph, 267
Barrier. *See* Ross Ice Shelf
Bartram, William, 161
Basal ice, 3, 300–301
Bay of Whales, 98, 101
Beardmore Glacier, 182, 276, 278
Belgica expedition, 86–87, 139,
257
Belgium, 86, 347
Bellingshausen, Fabian Gottlieb
von, 76, 77–78, 159, 329
Bellingshausen Sea, 33, 44, 86
Bergs. *See* Icebergs
Bergy bits, 3, 30
Berkner, Lloyd, 109, 265
Berlin Conference (Africa),
329–330
Berlin Conference (geographic),
86, 95
Big Eye, 141, 143
Biological Investigations of Ma-
rine Antarctic Systems and
Stocks, 352–353
Blizzards. *See* Katabatics; Winds
Blue ice, 3, 8–9, 314
Boas, Franz, 69, 91
Bolling Advance Base, 102
Bonpland, Aimé, 84
Boorstin, Daniel, 66
Borchgrevink, Carsten, 86–87,
89, 92, 256
Bowen, Norman L., 260, 262
Bransfield, Capt. Edward, 76,
328–329

Bransfield Strait, 76, 166
Brash ice, 3, 30, 53
Brennan, Keith, 368
Briscoe, Capt. John, 77
British Antarctic Expedition, 87,
281
British Antarctic Survey, 106,
334, 349
British Antarctic Territory, 266,
349
British–Australian–New Zealand
Antarctic Research Expedi-
tion (BANZARE), 98–99
British Commonwealth Trans-
Antarctic Expedition, 114–
115
British Graham Land Expedition,
101
British Imperial Conferences, 336
British Imperial Trans-Antarctic
Expedition, 87
Brown, Rudmose, 343
Bruce, William S., 87, 257
Brückner, Eduard, 280
Bull, Henrik, 85
Burdick, Capt. Christopher, 76
Burton, Steven, 373
Butler, K. S. Pierce, 351
Byrd, Richard E., 89, 97–108,
135, 142, 144, 150, 265, 337–
338
Byrd borehole, 298–300
Byrd expeditions, 98, 100–101,
104, 106, 189–191. *See also*
Byrd, Richard E.
Byrd Glacier, 223, 234–235
Byrd Station. *See* Byrd borehole
Byrd (subglacial) trough, 294

Calving, 125–129
Campbell, John Wood, 191–192
Canada, 332
Canberra Convention for the
Conservation of Antarctic
Marine Living Resources, 374

Cape Adare, 85, 86, 87, 93
Cape Crozier, 173, 181. *See also*
    The Worst Journey in the
    World
Cape Royds, 179
Carter, Paul, 113
Challenger expedition, 81, 85
Chamberlin, Rollin T., 261
Chamberlin, Thomas, 255, 260,
    262
Chapman, Sydney, 109, 112
Charcot, J.-B., 87, 257
Charpentier, Johann von, 279
Cherry-Garrard, Apsley, 92, 135,
    150, 172–175, 183, 258
Chile (claims by), 340–348, 350,
    375–376
Christiansen, Lars, 97
Chronometers, 127, 245–249,
    250, 255, 262, 269, 271–274,
    276
Church, Frederick, 115, 152, 155
Circumpolar deep water, 36–37,
    38, 39, 52, 54
Circumpolar vortex, 2–3, 21, 26,
    33, 42, 368
Claims. *See* Geopolitics; Territo-
    rial claims
Clarence Island, 76
Climate. *See* Antarctic atmo-
    sphere
Coastal ices (summary of), 3.
    See also Fast ice; Ice shelf;
    Ice tongues
Colbert, Edwin, 277–278
Cold War
    claims during, 341–351
    impact on Antarctica, 107,
        341–344, 346–347
    impact on glaciology, 283–285
    impact on Greenland, 366
Coleridge, Samuel T., 162–163,
    192
Colonization, 137–143, 330, 332.

See also Geopolitics; Territo-
    rial claims
Committee on Research and De-
    velopment in the Falkland
    Islands Dependencies, 334
Committee on the Peaceful Uses
    of Outer Space, 369
Common heritage (concept
    of), 369–377. *See also* Terra
    communis
Comparative planetology, 269
Congelation ice, 3, 27–32, 53, 63
Conrad, Joseph, 2, 171
Conservation, 357–359, 371–372.
    See also Natural resources;
    Whales
Constable, John, 187
Consultative nations, 375–376
Continental drift (history
    of), 105, 256, 268–278. *See*
    also Earth sciences; Plate
    tectonics
Continental shelf, 38
Contractional hypothesis, 254
Convention on the Conservation
    of Antarctic Marine Living
    Resources, 352–353
Cook, Frederick A., 86, 89, 139
Cook, Capt. James
    as Enlightenment explorer, 75,
        155–162, 244–245, 328
    explorations of, 69–70, 74–75,
        81
    impact of, 75, 77, 82
Cooper, James Fenimore, 153, 166
Cosmogony. *See* Theories of the
    Earth
Cosmology. *See* Theories of the
    Earth
Craddock, Campbell, 275–276
Crary, A. P., 276–277, 285
Crary ice rise, 130
Crevasses (types of), 212–213
Croll, James, 280

CSAGI. *See* Special Committee
for the International Geophysical Year
Cuvier, Georges, 250

Dallman, Capt. Eduard, 81
Dansgaard, Willi, 284
Dante, 3, 6, 163
Dartmouth Conference, 348
Davis, Capt. John, 76
Davis, William Morris, 260
Debenham, Frank, 18, 179, 257
Deception Island, 106
Deep Sea Drilling Project, 353
Denmark, 334, 365–366
De Saussure, H. B., 279
Design (concept of), 154, 161,
162, 186, 246, 287–288
Deutschland expedition, 87
Diamond dust, 381–385
and optical displays, 133–135
See also Ice crystals
Dietz, Robert, 270, 276
Discovery Committee, 98, 334,
346
Discovery expedition, 87–88,
181, 182, 257, 333
Disintegration theory, 286–287,
302–304. *See also* Ice sheets;
Ice shelf
Dome C, 297–298, 299
Dome Summit, 380
Don Juan Pond, 230
Doré, Gustave, 152, 163, 182–183
Drake Passage, 39, 49, 74, 218–
219, 306
Dry Valleys, 198, 290
esthetics of, 235–240
geology and geomorphology
of, 226–235
Drygalski, Erich von, 87, 89, 90,
281
Dufek, George, 194–195, 285
Dufek Massif, 222, 353, 355

D'Urville, Dumont, 77–79, 329
D'Urville expedition, 77–79, 159
Du Toit, Alexander, 266
Dutton, Clarence, 253–255

Earth (as ice planet), 3, 6
Earth sciences
ages of the Earth, 248–259,
271–273, 284
and Antarctica, 241–243,
266–267
and exploration, 105–106, 108,
242, 256–258, 262–267,
268–278
glaciology (history of), 278–
288
in heroic age, 256–259
history of, 241–288
and IGY, 108, 268–278
theories of the Earth, 243–248
East Antarctica, 33, 35, 44, 48,
79, 99, 101, 119, 122, 216,
219–220, 292–294
East sheet, 292–312 passim
East wind drift. *See* Antarctic
coastal current
Eastern Greenland case, 338,
365–366
Effective occupation (concept
of), 328
Egede, Hans, 364
Eights, James, 17–18, 76, 151
Elephant Island, 76, 94
Ellsworth, Lincoln, 101, 338,
339–340
Ellsworth Land, 220, 293–294
Ellsworth Mountains, 294, 309
Enderby, Charles, 77, 85
Endolithic cyanobacteria, 225
Endurance expedition, 87, 94,
177–178
Enlightenment, 75, 81, 84, 157–
162, 245–251. *See also* Cook,
Capt. James

Equilibrium line altitude (ELA), 210, 211–213. *See also* Glaciology, of glacier
Eskimos, 40, 67–68, 69, 89, 90–91
Esthetics
  and atmospheric optics, 132–137, 320–321
  of glaciers, 235–240
  history of literature and art (Antarctica), 149–205
  of ice sheet, 289–292, 385–387
  of ice shelf, 132, 144–147
  of icebergs, 17–20
  modernism and Antarctica, 185–210
  of pack ice, 56–60
  of source regions, 385–387
  of The Ice, 201–205
Evans ice stream, 124
Evans Névé, 237–239
Evolution. *See* Earth sciences; Historicism
Ewing, Maurice, 269–270, 285
Exobiology, 225
Expéditions Polaires Françaises, 345
Exploration, 65–115
  contrast, Arctic to Antarctic, 67–68, 89–92
  and earth sciences, 105–106, 108, 242, 256–258, 262–267
  heroic age of, 86–97
  impact of airplane on, 98–100
  impact of IGY, 108–115, 268–278
  and modernism, 114–115
  problems of assimilation, 73–74
  relationship to art and literature, 155–205 passim
  relationship to civilization, 137–143
  relationship to science, 82, 84–85, 256–258, 262–267
  and Romanticism, 81–82
  Second Great Age of Discovery, 82–97
  special problems of Antarctica, 66–67, 84–85, 88–89, 324–325
  Third Great Age of Discovery, 108–115
  as Western institution, 69–74

The Face of the Earth, 264
Fairbridge, Rhodes, 275
Falkland Islands Dependencies, 98, 332, 335, 346
Fanning, Edmund, 76, 163
Fast ice, 3, 62–63, 126. *See also* Pack ice
Ferrar, H. T., 257, 258–262
Fiedler, Leslie, 91
Filchner, Wilhelm, 87
Filchner Ice Shelf, 123, 130, 132, 293–304
Finsterwald, S., 279
Fisher, Rev. Osmond, 254
Floe (properties of), 30–32
Foehn winds, 45, 48
Forbes, John, 279
Ford, Arthur, 275
Forster, E. M., 173–174
Forster, Georg, 82, 158, 160–162
Forster, John Reinhold, 158
Fossil-equivalents, 251
Fossils, 250–251, 276–278, 281
Foster, Capt. Henry, 77
Foundation ice stream, 123–124
Fractures, 126–130. *See also* Calving; Crevasses
Fram expedition, 87, 90
France
  claims by, 329, 335, 338, 345, 350
  exploration by, 77–79, 87, 107, 345
Franklin, Sir John, 80, 88, 364
Frazil ice, 3, 27–32, 53, 62
Free-rider problem, 357–358, 376
French Antarctic Expedition, 87
Freud, Sigmund, 95, 191

Friedrich, Caspar David, 152, 181
Fuchs, Vivian, 114–115

Gamburtsev Mountains, 216, 220,
     309
Gauss, Carl Friedrich, 78
Gauss expedition, 87, 257
Geneva Conventions on the Law
     of the Sea, 369
Geochronology. *See* Chronome-
     ters; Geologic time
Geognosy, 244, 248
Geologic time, 244–259, 271–
     273, 284
   chronology, 248–255, 260–262,
     266–268, 271–274, 284
   chronometers, 127, 245–249,
     250, 255, 262, 269, 271–274,
     276
Geology
   of Antarctica, 214–226
   of Dry Valleys, 226–235
   history of, 241–288
   See also Earth sciences
Geology (1905), 255
Geomorphology
   of Antarctica, 220–232
   eolian, 228–230
   fluvial, 223–224, 228, 230
   periglacial, 223–225, 228
Geophysics. *See* Earth sciences
Geopolitics
   Arctic analogy, 40, 359–369
   deep oceans (Law of the Sea),
     369–372
   and exploration, 40, 323–341
   history of (Antarctica), 323–
     378
   impact of natural resources,
     351–359
   outer space (and Moon), 369–
     370
   United Nations, 369–370, 371,
     376
   See also IGY; International law

Geoscience. *See* Earth sciences
Gerlache, Lt. Adrien de, 86
German Antarctic Expedition,
     87, 101, 257, 339
Germany
   claims by, 334, 339–340
   exploration by, 81, 87, 97, 101
Getz Ice Shelf, 122
Gilbert, G. K., 260
Glacial epochs, 287, 304–312
Glacial history
   of Antarctica, 216–220, 304–
     312
   of Dry Valleys, 231–233
Glacial ice. *See* Ice; Ice terranes
Glacials. *See* Glacial epochs;
     Ice Age
Glaciers
   alpine, 210–214, 232–235,
     278–279
   Byrd Glacier, 223, 234–235
   esthetics of, 235–240
   glaciology of, 209–214
   outlet, 10, 223, 234
Glaciology
   of glacier, 209–214
   glaciological conferences,
     285–286
   history of, 278–288
   of ice crystals, 381–385, 386
   of ice sheet, 279–280, 292–304
   of ice shelf, 117–148
   of icebergs, 7–17
   of pack ice, 27–33
   of source regions, 380–385
Glaciology of the Antarctic Pen-
     insula (program), 286
Glen, J. W., 283
Glossopteris, 257
Goddard, Robert, 112
Goetzmann, William, 82
Gondwana. *See* Continental
     drift; Gondwanaland
Gondwanaland, 105, 214–226,
     276, 305–306

Gould, Laurence, 89, 103, 113, 144, 260, 337
Graham Land, 99
Grand Canyon, 6, 152, 253–255
Grand Chasm, 130
Grand Manner, 154, 160
Grand Tour, 160, 161
Grease ice, 3, 28, 30
Great Britain
    claims by, 76, 326–350 passim
    exploration by, 66–81, 82–101, 106–114, 170–175, 262
    quarrel with Argentina, 106, 335–336, 338, 340–350, 367
Great Chain of Being, 160, 245–246, 250
Great Ice Barrier. See Ross Ice Shelf
Greeley Expedition, 88
Green ice, 3, 9, 20
Greenland, 39–40, 67, 88, 226, 280, 307–308, 343, 360, 363–368
Grotius, Hugo, 326–327
Ground ices (summary of), 3, 224–225
Grounding line, 121–132 passim
Group of 77, 370, 371
Growlers, 3

Hackmann, Robert, 272
Hall, Charles Francis, 88
Halos, 134–135. See also Atmospheric optics
Heart of the Antarctic, 155
Heat death, 255
Heezen, Bruce, 269–270
Heim, Albert, 279
Herbert, Wally, 67
Hero, 76
Heroic age
    art and literature of, 168–175
    exploration during, 86–97
    geologists of, 256–259

glaciology by, 281
territorial claims during, 330–335
Hess, Harry, 270
Hillary, Edmund, 115
Hinterland (concept of), 328
Historicism, 267, 287–288
    as cultural phenomenon, 159–162, 251–252
    in earth sciences, 248–263, 267
Hodge, William, 158–159, 162
Holmes, Arthur, 255, 261, 267
Hughes, Charles Evans, 335
Hughes, Terrence, 287
Humans
    as Antarctic organisms, 55–56, 67, 137–143
    as explorers, 65–115, 120
    See also Art; Earth sciences; Geopolitics; Life; Literature of Antarctica
Humboldt, Alexander von, 78, 82, 84–86, 89, 161, 262
Humboldt current, 16
Hurley, Frank, 169, 177–178
Hutton, James, 244, 262, 279

Ice
    as geologic agent, 220–232
    as natural resource, 355–356
    types of (summary), 3, 8–9
    See also Glaciology; Ice terranes; names of particular ices; The Ice
Ice Age, 278–280. See also Glacial epochs
Ice biota, 30, 53
Ice crystals
    atmospheric, 3, 380–385, 388
    oceanic, 27–30
    and optical displays, 133–135
    See also Glaciology
Ice flowers, 3, 30
Ice fronts, 3, 121–132 passim

Ice paddies, 3, 30
Ice placers, 314–315
Ice sheets, 44, 210, 212
  esthetics of, 289–292, 385–387
  glaciology of, 279–280, 292–
    304
  as ice terrane, 289–322
  See also East sheet; Ice shelf;
    Peninsular sheet; West sheet
Ice shelf, 12, 38, 210
  esthetics of, 132, 144–147
  glaciology of, 121–132
  as ice terrane, 117–148
  meteorology of, 132–134
  stability of, 129–130
Ice stalactites, 3, 30, 31, 63, 131
Ice streams, 3, 122–124, 300–
    302
Ice terranes
  glacier, 207–214, 235–240
  ice sheet, 289–322
  ice shelf, 117–148
  iceberg, 2–21
  pack ice, 25–63
  source regions, 379–385
Ice tongues, 12, 122–123, 210
Iceberg Transport International,
    355–356
Icebergs, 69, 125
  esthetics of, 17–21
  glaciology of, 7–17
  as ice terrane, 2–21
  political economics of, 355–
    356
Iceblink, 58, 316
Iceland, 366
Icescape. See Esthetics; The Ice
IGY, 66, 69
  history of, 108–115
  impact of, 268–278, 324, 347,
    350, 369–378
  relationship to Antarctica,
    66–69, 108–115, 268–278
Inchoate title, 328

India, 348, 376
Infiltration ice, 3, 30, 63
Information
  and art, 19–20, 201–205
  and exploration, 66–68, 72
  as natural resource, 358
  and The Ice, 66, 68, 201–205,
    242–243, 278, 291–292, 316,
    358, 378
  See also Earth sciences; Es-
    thetics; Exploration; The Ice
Instituto Antarctico Argentino,
    344–345
Interamerican Conference at
    Lima, 340
International Antarctic Glacio-
    logical Project, 286
International commons. See
    Common heritage; Terra
    communis
International Council of Scien-
    tific Unions, 109, 347
International Court, 342–343
International Geographical Con-
    gresses, 86–87
International Geophysical Coop-
    eration, 113, 347
International Geophysical Year.
    See IGY
International Glaciological So-
    ciety, 284, 286
International law (development
    of), 324–328. See also Geo-
    politics
International Polar Years, 88, 109
International Seabed Authority,
    371
International Union for Geodesy
    and Geophysics, 109
International Whaling Conven-
    tion, 337, 338, 344
Inversion, 45–50, 132–135, 294,
    296, 316, 383–384. See also
    Antarctic atmosphere; Winds

Japan, 87, 339, 341, 347, 354

Kainan Maru expedition, 87
Kane, Elisha, 80, 88
Katabatics, 10, 47–49, 61, 225, 296, 297. See also Inversion; Winds
Kemp, Capt. Peter, 77
Kenneally, Thomas, 153, 170
Kerguelen Island, 81, 109
King George Island, 76
Kipling, Rudyard, 86, 89
Kippis, Andrew, 161
Krill, 52, 54–55, 351–352
Kuhn, Thomas, 270, 273
Kurtz, 171, 172, 175

Lakes (Antarctic), 230–231
Lambert Glacier, 122, 123, 213, 293
Land ice (summary of), 3. See also Glaciers; Ice; Ice sheets; Ice shelf; Ice terranes; Source regions
Larsen, Capt. Carl, 85
Larsen Ice Shelf, 48, 122
Las Malvinas. See Falkland Islands Dependencies
Laurasia, 216–226 passim
Law of Nations. See Geopolitics; International law
Law of the Sea, 355, 369–372
Le Français expedition, 87
Lichens, 50, 225, 231
Life
    human adaptations to Antarctic, 137–143
    summary of (Antarctica), 50–56, 137
Literature of Antarctica, 149–205
Little America, 101–102, 106, 142
London, Jack, 93, 167–168
London Convention on the Conservation of Antarctic Seals, 374

Long Eye, 141, 143
Lovecraft, H. P., 192–194
Lystrosaurus, 114, 276–278

Marie Byrd Land, 294, 338
Markham, Clements, 85, 87, 182
Marlowe, 171
Mars, 51, 69, 225, 288
Marston, George, 184
Maury, Matthew Fontaine, 80, 87
Mawson, Douglas, 87, 93, 98–99, 177, 180, 209, 312, 333, 336
McMurdo Sound, 29, 179, 220–221
Melchior Island, 106
Meltwater, 9–10, 13, 31, 57, 62, 230, 231, 300
Melville, Herman, 164, 167
Menard, Henry, 263, 264, 270
Meserve Glacier, 233–235
Meteor expedition, 97–98
Meteorites, 312–316
Meteorology, 40–50, 132–135, 281, 296–297. See also Atmospheric optics
Mirages, 135–136. See also Atmospheric optics
Moby-Dick, 96, 164
Modernism, 89
    and Antarctica, 114–115, 152, 154–155, 185–201
    as art, 154–155
    relationship to exploration, 114–115
Monroe Doctrine, 334, 340
Moon, 40, 114, 272, 277–278, 317, 370
Morrell, Capt. Benjamin, 76, 163
Motherwell, Robert, 188
Mountain ices (summary of), 3. See also Glaciers
Mountains (Antarctic), 216–226. See also Antarcandes; Geology; Glaciers; Transantarctic Mountains

"MS. Found in a Bottle," 164
Multi-year ice, 2–3, 31
Murray, John, 85, 256
Museum of Modern Art, 104, 189

Nacreous clouds, 316–317
Nansen, Fritjof, 67, 89
Narrative of A. Gordon Pym
    (1838), 164–166
A Narrative of Four Voyages
    (1832), 163
National Academy of Sciences
    (U.S.), 107, 344
National Antarctic Expedition, 87
National Science Foundation
    (U.S.), 201, 348
National Security Council
    (U.S.), 346–347
Natural history, 72, 82, 156–159,
    161, 242
Natural law, 327
Natural philosophy, 72, 82, 157–
    158, 242
Natural resources (Antarctica),
    324–325, 351–359, 373–375
Nautilus, 99
New international economic
    order, 359
New international information
    order, 359
New Schwabenland, 101, 339
New Zealand (claims by), 335,
    345, 348, 356–357, 368
Newman, Barnett, 201
Nimrod expedition, 87, 94, 169,
    257
Nordenskjöld, Otto, 87, 93, 257,
    262, 281
Norsk Polarinstitutt, 345
North Pole, 85, 86, 88
Northern Party, 93
Norway
    Antarctic explorations by, 86–
    87, 89–92, 93–94, 97, 99,
    107, 284, 345

claims by, 333–337, 339, 345–
    346
and Greenland, 338, 363, 366
and Svalbard, 361–363
Norwegian-British-Swedish Ant-
    arctic Expedition, 107, 269,
    345, 346
Nussbaum Riegel, 235–236
Nye, J. F., 283

Oasis (rock), 226–227. *See also*
    Dry Valleys
Oceanography. *See* Southern
    Ocean
Odishaw, Hugh, 112
Oil (Antarctic), 353–354
Onyx River, 228, 230
Operation Highjump, 107, 200,
    341–342
Operation Tabarin, 106, 341
Operation Windmill, 107, 341
Orogens (Antarctic), 216–226
Orowan, E., 283
Outlet glaciers, 223. *See also*
    Byrd Glacier
Owen, Russell, 190, 193

Pack ice
    esthetics of, 56–60
    glaciology of, 27–33
    as ice terrane, 25–63
    role in exploration, 67, 69, 74,
    90, 162
Paleontology, 250–251
Pallas, Peter, 81
Palmer, Capt. Nathaniel, 76, 329
Palmer Land. *See* Antarctic
    Peninsula
Pancake ice, 3, 30
Pangaea, 216–226 passim, 261,
    276
Paraselenae, 134–135
Parhelia, 134–135
Parry, J. H., 72, 82
Patterned ground, 228

Patterson, Claire, 261
Peale, Titian, 80
Peary, Robert, 67, 86–92, 140, 334
Peary system, 92–94
Penck, Albrecht, 280
Pendleton, Capt. Benjamin, 76, 78
Penguins, 52–53, 55, 197, 258–259
Peninsular sheet, 292–304 passim
Periglacial processes, 220–232
Permafrost, 3, 224–225
Peterson, Roger Tory, 197
Pine Island Glacier, 293, 303–304
Planetesimal hypothesis, 256, 260, 279
Plate tectonics
  in Antarctica, 216–226
  history of, 268–278, 286
  See also Continental drift;
    Earth sciences
Poe, Edgar Allan, 153, 163, 164–168, 192, 194
Polar easterlies, 45
Polar front (atmospheric), 43, 44
Polar front (oceanographic), 36
Polar Party, 93, 97, 170–175. See also Scott, Capt. Robert;
  Terra Nova expedition; The Worst Journey in the World
Polar plateau ices (summary of), 3. See also Ice sheets; Source regions
Polar vortex, 2–3, 316–318, 321–322
Polar year. See International Polar Years
Pollitt, Katha, 75, 115
Polynyas, 28–29, 58, 62
Ponting, Herbert, 171, 176, 177, 178–181
Porter, Eliot, 197–200
Portolan charts, 73
Pourquoi Pas? expedition, 87
Powell, Capt. George, 76, 329

Priestley, Raymond, 93, 257, 262–263, 281, 282
Prince Charles Mountains, 222, 355
Problems of Polar Research (1928), 105, 282
Project Mohole, 112

Queen Maud Land, 15, 77, 216
Queen Maud Mountains, 103
Quest expedition, 95–96
Quigg, Philip, 357, 377

Rasmussen, Knud, 364
Rauschenberg, Robert, 204
Reid, H. F., 279
Remote sensing, 98, 112, 268
Rennick Glacier, 213, 237
Resolution (ship). See Cook, Capt. James
Reynolds, Josiah, 78, 163–164
Right of discovery, 327–336
Riiser-Larsen, Capt. Hjalmar, 89, 97, 336
"The Rime of the Ancient Mariner," 162
Rio Treaty, 342
Ritscher, Alfred. See German Antarctic Expedition
Roberts, Henry, 158
Rock glaciers, 224
Romanticism (characteristics of), 81–82, 84, 89, 152–155, 161, 166, 176–177, 252
Ronne, Finn, 107
Ronne Antarctic Research Expedition, 107
Ronne Ice Shelf, 120, 122, 132, 222, 292–304
Roosevelt, Franklin, 88, 106
Roosevelt, Theodore, 93
Ross, Capt. James Clark, 77–79, 144, 329
Ross Dependency, 335, 368
Ross expedition, 78, 159. See also Ross, Capt. James Clark

Ross Ice Shelf, 79, 87, 93, 117–148
    passim, 222–223, 234, 293–
    304
Ross Ice Shelf Geophysical and
    Glaciological Study, 286
Ross Ice Shelf Project, 286
Ross Island, 79, 93, 227
Ross Sea, 29, 33, 37, 44, 49, 79,
    99, 120, 232
Royal Geographic Society, 77, 85
Royal Society Range, 179
Runcorn, S. K., 270
Russia. See Soviet Union
Rymill, John, 89, 101

Saline ice, 3, 8–9
Salisbury, Rollin, 255
Samuel Enderby and Sons, 77, 85
Sastrugi, 131, 296–297
Saudi Arabia, 355–356
Schulthess, Emil, 194–197
Science
    history of earth sciences,
        241–288
    relationship to Antarctica,
        242–243, 376–378
    relationship to art, 153, 156–157
    relationship to exploration,
        63–115, 241–288
    See also Earth sciences
Science fiction, 152, 192–194,
    264–265. See also Campbell,
    John Wood; Coleridge, Sam-
    uel; Literature of Antarctica;
    Lovecraft, H. P.; Poe, Edgar
    Allan
Scientific Committee on Ant-
    arctic Research (SCAR),
    113, 348, 373, 375
Scotia expedition, 87
Scotia Sea, 33, 36, 54
Scott, Capt. Robert, 87, 88, 93,
    94, 144, 170–175, 183
Scott Polar Research Institute,
    99, 266

Scottish National Antarctic Ex-
    pedition, 87, 257
Sea fog, 43
Sea ices (summary of), 3. See
    also Ice; Pack ice
The Sea Lions (1849), 166–167
Sea smoke, 43
Sealers, 75–76, 78, 80, 163, 329,
    374
Sea-floor spreading, 276
Seals (biology of), 52, 55
Second French Antarctic Expedi-
    tion, 87
Second Great Age of Discovery,
    82–97
Sector principle, 332–334
Service, Robert, 88, 93, 168
Shackleton, Lt. Ernest, 87, 92,
    94, 95–96, 140, 144, 332–333
Sheffield, Capt. James, 76
Shirase, Lt. Choku, 87
Shoemaker, Eugene, 272
Shore ice, 3, 61–63. See also
    Glaciology; Ice shelf
Signatory nations, 376
Siple, Paul, 111, 140, 342
Skeletal ice, 3, 29–30
Smith, William, 76, 250, 328
Smithsonian Institution, 79, 80
Snow. See Ice crystals
Snow, Ice, and Permafrost Re-
    search Establishment, 366
Solar system ice, 6, 290–292, 381
Solar wind, 316–319
Source regions, 210,' 322
    esthetics of, 385–387
    glaciology of, 380–383
    as ice terrane, 380–388
South Orkney Islands, 76
South Pole, 66, 86–88, 134
South Sandwich Islands, 77, 160
South Shetland Islands, 75–76,
    77
Southern Cross expedition, 87,
    256

Southern Ocean, 2, 10, 16, 20, 27, 32, 33, 35, 36, 37, 38, 39, 42, 44, 50, 52, 53, 55, 69, 74, 75, 77, 85, 97, 98, 291
Sovereignty (concept of), 327–328, 329–332, 348–350, 360, 364–369, 375–376. See also Geopolitics; Terra nullius; Territorial claims
Soviet Union (Russia), 274
  claims by, 110, 334, 339, 344, 346–347, 376–377
  exploration by, 76–78, 81, 88, 110, 346–348, 376–377
Sparrman, Anders, 158
Special Committee for the International Geophysical Year, 110, 113, 347
Spencer, Herbert, 254
Sphinx of Ice; or Antarctic Mystery (1897), 165–166
Spitsbergen. See Svalbard
Sputnik, 111
Stability
  geopolitical, 324–325, 368, 377
  glaciological, 301–304
Stanton, William, 80
Stefansson, Vilhjalmur, 67, 69, 91
Stella, Frank, 187–188
Stokes, F. W., 184
Stonington Island, 106
Stuart, Don L. See Campbell, John Wood
Suess, Eduard, 255, 256, 264, 267
Surge theory, 287
Svalbard, 226, 360–363
Svalbard (Spitsbergen) Treaty, 334, 362–363
Sverdrup, Harald, 281
Swedish Antarctic Expedition, 87, 257
Symmes, William, 78

Tally, Ted, 170
Taylor, F. B., 255
Taylor, Geoffrey, 257
Tennyson, Alfred, Lord, 96–97, 164
Terra australis, 66, 73–74, 163
Terra communis (concept of), 324, 369–378
Terra Nova expedition, 87, 93, 96–97, 170, 257
Terra nullius (concept of), 327–328, 330, 332, 360
Terre Adelie, 79
Territorial claims, 106
  Arctic, 359–369
  by Argentina, 335–336, 338, 340–350, 375–376
  by Australia, 332–333, 335–337, 345
  by Chile, 340–348, 350, 375–376
  by France, 329, 335, 338, 345, 350
  by Germany, 334, 339–340
  by Great Britain, 76, 326–350 passim
  history of, in Antarctica, 324–351, 369–378
  by New Zealand, 335, 345, 348, 368
  by Norway, 333–337, 339, 345–346
  by Soviet Union, 110, 334, 339, 344, 346–347, 376–377
  See also Antarctic Treaty; Terra communis; Terra nullius
The Ice
  as desert, 10
  esthetics of, 56–60, 201–205, 385–387
  as information, 66, 68, 201–205, 242–243, 278, 291–292, 316, 358, 378
  as mirror, 67, 91, 377, 381

as modernist, 19, 152, 172, 386–387
as reducer, 66–67, 152, 202–205, 236, 290, 321, 325, 377, 385, 386
as scene for exploration, 66–69, 94–95, 120
as self-referential, 373, 377, 380
as sink, 7, 66–68, 141, 150, 202–205, 243, 282, 291, 316, 325, 351, 377, 381
as underworld, 175
as vortex, 2–3, 20–21, 26, 368, 387
See also Esthetics; Glaciology; Ice terranes
The Portal, 235, 239–240
Theories of the Earth, 243–248. See also Continental drift; Earth sciences; Plate tectonics
Theory of Continental Drift, 105, 260
Third Great Age of Discovery, 82, 84–85, 108–115. See also IGY
Through the First Antarctic Night, 139
Thwaites ice stream, 303–304
Tilley, C. E., 262–263
Tourism (Antarctica), 356–357
Transantarctic Mountains, 44, 114, 219, 222–223, 257, 294, 306, 309, 355
Transit of Venus, 81, 109
Travelogue, 92, 161–162
Trolltunga berg, 11, 15
Twain, Mark, 80
Tyndall, John, 279

"Ulysses," 96, 164
Union of South Africa, 347
United Nations, 348–350, 369–370, 371, 372, 376

United States
exploration by, 77–80, 88, 93, 97–115
policy toward Antarctica, 106, 112–113, 337–350, 368–369
research program of, 274, 337
U.S. Antarctic Research Program (USARP), 274
U.S. Antarctic Service, 99, 106
U.S. Exploring Expedition. See Wilkes expedition
U.S. Geological Survey, 263–264, 352, 353
U.S. Navy. See Antarctic Developments Project; Wilkes expedition
U.S. State Department, 330
Ussher, Bishop James, 246
Uti possidetis juris, 338

Van der Gracht, Van Waterschool, 184
Verne, Jules, 165–166
Victor, Paul-Emile, 345
Victoria Land, 179, 235, 237, 238, 239
Vostok, 213
A Voyage around the World (1777), 158
A Voyage towards the South Pole and Round the World (1777), 74, 158
Voyages Round the World (1833), 163
Voyages to the South Seas . . . (1838), 163

Weddell, Capt. James, 77
Weddell gyre, 15, 29–40 passim, 48, 62, 79
Weddell Sea, 15, 29–40 passim, 48, 54, 62, 76, 78, 94, 115, 120
Weertman, Johannes, 285

Wegener, Alfred, 255, 256, 260–261, 266
Werner, Abraham Gottlob, 244, 248–249, 252, 262
West Antarctic Ice Sheet Project, 286
West Antarctica, 33, 35, 44, 48, 119, 122, 216, 219–220, 292–294
West sheet, 44, 292–312 passim. See also Ice sheets
West wind drift, 15, 33–40 passim. See also Antarctic circumpolar current
Weyprecht, Lt. Carl, 109
Whales
  biology of, 52–56 passim
  and conservation, 98, 337, 338–339, 351–352
  and exploration, 77, 78, 80, 85, 97–98
White ice, 3, 9
Whiteout, 43, 56–57, 136–137, 382. See also Atmospheric optics
"Who Goes There?" (1938), 191–192
Wild, Frank, 95
Wilkes, Lt. Charles, 77–80, 97
Wilkes expedition, 78–80, 159. See also Wilkes, Lt. Charles

Wilkes Glacier, 213
Wilkes Land, 77, 88
Wilkins, Hubert, 89. See also Wilkins-Hearst expedition
Wilkins-Hearst expedition, 98–100, 101
Williams, Ralph Vaughan, 170
Wilson, A. T., 287
Wilson, Edward, 93, 135, 181–185
Wilson, J. Tuzo, 66, 270–271, 274, 276–277
Winds, 15–16, 45–50, 132–133, 170, 230, 296–297. See also Antarctic atmosphere; Katabatics; Inversion
Winter Journey (Crozier Party), 93, 172–175, 258
World War II
  and Antarctica, 111, 341
  and glaciology, 283–285
  and Greenland, 366
  and Svalbard, 363
The Worst Journey in the World (1922), 172–175, 191
Wright, C. S., 281, 282
Wright Valley, 228, 230, 233

Yamato Mountains, 312, 314